Charles Schmidt

The Social Results of early Christianity

Charles Schmidt

The Social Results of early Christianity

ISBN/EAN: 9783743305809

Manufactured in Europe, USA, Canada, Australia, Japa

Cover: Foto ©ninafisch / pixelio.de

Manufactured and distributed by brebook publishing software (www.brebook.com)

Charles Schmidt

The Social Results of early Christianity

THE SOCIAL RESULTS OF EARLY CHRISTIANITY

BY

C. SCHMIDT

Professor of Theology in Strasburg

Translated by Mrs. THORPE

WITH PRELIMINARY ESSAY BY

R. W. DALE, LL.D.
Birmingham

LONDON
W<small>m</small>. ISBISTER L<small>imited</small>
56 LUDGATE HILL
1885

Butler & Tanner,
The Selwood Printing Works,
Frome, and London.

THIS TRANSLATION

IS DEDICATED TO

SIR ANDREW CLARK, BART.,

IN RESPECTFUL ADMIRATION OF THE SYMPATHY AND SACRIFICE, WHICH, BY THE CONSECRATION OF SCIENCE, PHILOSOPHY, AND SKILL, GIVE A LIVING TRANSCRIPT OF THE EARLY TEACHING OF THE CHURCH, AND FORM A BRIGHT LINK IN THE CHAIN OF THE HISTORICAL CONTINUITY OF THE RESULTS OF CHRISTIANITY.

CONTENTS.

	PAGE
Translator's Preface	ix
Preliminary Essay	xi
Introductory Letter from the Author	xxvii
Preface	xxix

BOOK I.—PAGAN SOCIETY.

Introduction 3

CHAPTER I.—THE PRINCIPLE AND AIM OF ANCIENT SOCIAL MORALITY.

§ 1. Happiness 5
§ 2. The State 10
§ 3. Citizens. Foreigners. Riches 15
§ 4. Friendship. Vengeance 19

CHAPTER II.—THE FAMILY.

§ 1. Women. Marriage 26
§ 2. Love. Hetæræ and Concubines 38
§ 3. Adultery and Divorce 44
§ 4. Children. Paternal Authority 49
§ 5. Education 55

CHAPTER III.—THE LABOURING CLASSES.

§ 1. Work 63
§ 2. Poverty. The Poor 67
§ 3. Slaves. Slavery in General 75
§ 4. Treatment of Slaves 82
§ 5. Occupations of Slaves. Actors. Gladiators . . 87

CHAPTER IV.—CONSEQUENCES AND EXCEPTIONS.

§ 1. Decline of Ancient Society 107
§ 2. Purer Opinions 111

CONTENTS.

CHAPTER V.—RELATIONS OF ANCIENT MORALITY TO PAGANISM.

§ 1. Moral Impotence of Paganism 119
§ 2. Weakening of Religious Beliefs 123
Conclusion 130

BOOK II.—CHRISTIAN SOCIETY.

CHAPTER I.—FUNDAMENTAL PRINCIPLES OF CHRISTIAN MORALITY.

§ 1. The Kingdom of God, and its Founder 137
§ 2. The Apostles and the Apostolic Church 152

CHAPTER II.—CHRISTIAN SOCIETY IN GENERAL, AND ITS RELATIONS WITH THE STATE.

§ 1. Equality. Brotherly Love 176
§ 2. Relations of Christian Society to the Ancient State . . 181

CHAPTER III.—THE FAMILY.

§ 1. Women. Marriage 188
§ 2. Children 203

CHAPTER IV.—THE LABOURING CLASSES.

§ 1. Work. The Free Workman 212
§ 2. Slaves 215
§ 3. Gladiators and Actors 227

CHAPTER V.—THE POOR AND UNFORTUNATE.

§ 1. Riches and Poverty 237
§ 2. Christian Beneficence towards the Poor in General . . 245
§ 3. Widows and Orphans 257
§ 4. The Oppressed and Captives 259
§ 5. The Sick 264

CHAPTER VI.—ENEMIES.

§ 1. Personal Enemies. Criminals 276
§ 2. Foreigners. War 280
Conclusion 285

BOOK III.—TRANSFORMATION OF CIVIL SOCIETY THROUGH THE INFLUENCE OF THE CHRISTIAN SPIRIT.

CHAPTER I.—STRIFE BETWEEN THE CHRISTIAN AND PAGAN SPIRIT.

§ 1. General Character of Christian Influence on Pagan Society 293
§ 2. Obstacles to Christian Influence 295

CONTENTS.

CHAPTER II.—THE CHANNELS OF CHRISTIAN INFLUENCE.

	PAGE
§ 1. Apologies and Sermons	305
§ 2. Christian Example	320
§ 3. The Charity of Christians towards Pagans	323
§ 4. The Part of Stoicism in the Influence of Charity	329

CHAPTER III.—INCREASING HUMANITY IN PAGAN PHILOSOPHERS.

§ 1. Seneca	337
§ 2. Pliny and Plutarch	353
§ 3. Epictetus	362
§ 4. Marcus Aurelius	370

CHAPTER IV.—INCREASING HUMANITY OF LEGISLATION DURING THE PAGAN PERIOD OF THE EMPIRE.

§ 1. Influence of the Christian Spirit on the Emperors and Jurisconsults	380
§ 2. Women and Marriage	387
§ 3. Children in general. Poor Children	390
§ 4. Slaves	397

CHAPTER V.—PROGRESS OF IMPROVEMENT IN THE LAWS DURING THE CHRISTIAN PERIOD OF THE EMPIRE.

§ 1. The Emperors to Theodosius	409
§ 2. Women. Marriage	417
§ 3. Children	425
§ 4. Slaves	428
§ 5. The Poor and Unhappy	436

CHAPTER VI.—REACTION OF THE PAGAN SPIRIT ON THE CUSTOMS OF CHRISTIAN SOCIETY.

Conclusion	447
Notes	463
List of Authors Quoted	465
Index	469

TRANSLATOR'S PREFACE.

I have to thank M. Schmidt for permission to translate his book into English, Dr. Dale for his Preliminary Essay, and J. L. Paton, Esq., for assistance with the classical notes.

The completeness with which M. Schmidt gives the authorities upon which his statements rest, adds greatly to the value of his book.

Born into a world in which the institutions are at least coloured by Christianity, we can hardly realize either what they have been without it, or to what they may yet rise with a fuller appreciation of its principles and spirit.

It is an intelligent knowledge of what Christianity has accomplished for humanity, its realized results leading to a study of its aims and central motives, that is likely to bring about the vivid belief in its life-giving mysteries; the intelligent, new application of its principles, which will be the greatest means for the transformation of the Social Order to a true ideal.

Man,

"the heir of all the ages, in the foremost files of time,"

should not throw aside his lesson-book of History

unread; lengthening ages add to its value, increasing intelligence deepens its meaning.

"Men, my brothers, men the workers, ever reaping something new:
That which they have done but earnest of the things that they shall do."

MARY THORPE.

Lenton House, Lenton,
 July, 1885.

PRELIMINARY ESSAY.

THE admirable Essay by M. Schmidt, of Strasburg, on "*La Société Civile dans le Monde Romain et sa Transformation par le Christianisme*" has long been known and valued by students of Church history.

By translating it into English, I trust that my friend Mrs. Thorpe will secure for it a still larger number of readers in this country. For it illustrates a subject which is creating a deep and even a painful interest among all classes of the English people—the relations of the Christian Faith to the improvement of the material condition of mankind and the reformation of the Social Order. At a time when many of us are regarding almost with despair the miseries of large masses of mankind, it may renew our courage to recall the brilliant story of what was accomplished by the Christian Gospel for the regeneration of human society in the early Christian centuries.

But the evils which now require redress are not precisely the same as those which existed in the Roman world; and the economical and social conditions of modern nations are very unlike those which environed the Christian Church during the first four or five hundred years of its history. The splendid achievements illustrated in this Essay would do us more harm than good if they so mastered our imagination as to prevent us from discovering the new and unfamiliar ways in which the Christian revelation should exert its force in correcting the inequalities of our own Social Order, and redeeming our own countrymen, our contemporaries, our neighbours, from their hereditary poverty and suffering.

We may do honour to the courage and administrative power of famous bishops, who organised relief and found employment for cities and provinces suffering from famine; we may recall with admiration the times when a great hospital for the aged, the poor, the sick was a part of the organization of every great Church; we may honour the memory of saintly men who were ready to sell the silver and golden vessels used in the celebration of the most sacred service of the Church in order to redeem men from slavery; and yet regard with indifference, with distrust, or even with positive hostility those new methods in which Christian Charity is attempting to remedy the new forms of social injustice and the new forms of suffering incident to modern civilization. We may build the tombs of the prophets and yet crucify their successors.

It is not only in theological belief that tradition may be too strong for us. Both in practical life and in speculation originality is the characteristic of a real and vigorous faith. If we are to do our own work in our own age, we must derive our chief inspiration and guidance—

not from the services which the Church rendered to countries, to centuries, to populations very unlike our own—but from the Christian revelation itself, which is not a tradition, but a fresh and living word from God, our Father in Heaven, to His children in every age.

I.

At the root of all our theories concerning the ideal Social Order lies our conception of the nature of man. Before we can determine what are the obligations of Society to individual men and to classes of men—before we can discover the obligations of individual men and of classes of men to Society—we have to arrive at some conclusion concerning the powers and capacities, the real contents and possibilities of human life. How does man differ—if he differs at all—from those inferior races which we enslave—which we compel to live for *us*, not for themselves—which we train to do our work—which we kill for food? Our whole theory of the political, economical, and social organization of society will depend upon the answer which is given to this question.

The Christian revelation answers it in a very surprising manner. The answer is not worn out. It is of a kind that must make it full of inspiration to the latest ages of human history. It contains an immense reserve of unexhausted energy. It has never yet been adequately expressed, either in the institutions of Society or in the organisation of Churches. Indeed it has not received its true place in any of the Confessions, the

Creeds, the Articles of the great Councils and Synods of Christendom. Theologians have never adequately defined it. About the Christian idea of *God* there have been prolonged controversies which have left their memorials and monuments in famous creeds; but the controversies about the Christian idea of man have been much less thorough. They have rarely passed beyond the narrow limits of the questions which were at issue more than fourteen hundred years ago between Augustine and Pelagius. They have approached the subject on only one side, and have left large provinces of truth wholly unexplored. They have issued in no definite conclusion that has been confirmed by the acceptance of the Church through successive generations. Notwithstanding the conflict between the East and the West on the procession of the Spirit, the doctrine of the Nicene Creed has substantially represented for fifteen centuries the belief of the overwhelming majority of those who bear the Christian name in relation to some of the deepest questions concerning the nature and life of God. There has been no such approach to unanimity in relation to the deepest questions concerning the nature and life of man. Even in Western Christendom, where Augustine has always been honoured as the great doctor of the ancient Church, Augustine's theory of human nature has never secured any real control of Christian thought. Its authority has been partial and intermittent.

But though the Christian doctrine of man has been so imperfectly elaborated by scientific theology, about the substance of it there can be no doubt; and it has exerted an immense influence on Christian life and conduct. For the Christian doctrine of man is really a part of the Christian doctrine of God. The two are not only inseparable; the one is largely included in the other.

I suppose that to most men in these days, and perhaps to many orthodox Christians, the controversies which occasioned the convening of the Council of Nicæa and the doctrinal definitions of the creed inaccurately attributed to Athanasius, lie far remote from Christian conduct. The doctrine of the Trinity is regarded as a strain on the resources of faith rather than an inspiration and law of practical righteousness. That there is any real and direct relation between that great mystery and Christian morals or the Christian ideal of the Social Order, never occurs to them. And this is one reason why Christian morality is wanting in originality, vigour, courage, and grace; and why the Christian ideal of society has not become infinitely nobler. But the Christian doctrine of man is implicated in the Christian doctrine of God; or, to speak more exactly, in the Christian doctrine of the Trinity; and the Christian doctrine of man determines the Christian theory of morals and the Christian theory of society.

The faith of Christendom, its theology, its worship, and its ethics rest on the revelation in the Lord Jesus Christ of the eternal life of God. That it should be possible for God to be manifested under the conditions of a human history, implies a kinship between man and God. And this alliance between God and Humanity in the person of the Lord Jesus Christ was not transient. In Him the eternal Son of God *became* man; in Him the eternal Son of God *remains* man. The human nature of the Lord Jesus Christ, exalted and transfigured, its powers enlarged beyond the limits of our thought, is the permanent manifestation and organ of the life of God. The awful personal supremacy over all worlds and all ages which we attribute to God belongs to Christ. We never knew the immeasurable possibilities of expansion and development belonging to human nature, its possibilities of power, of wisdom, of moral and spiritual perfection, until we received the revelation of the august greatness of the Son of Man who is also the Son of God, and who is enthroned "far above all rule and authority and power and dominion, and every name that is named, not only in this world, but also in that which is to come," all things being put "in subjection under His feet."

Nor is the Incarnation of our Lord Jesus Christ, and His permanent union with our race an isolated and abnormal fact. It is God's witness to the ideal relation of all men to Himself. Man, according to the earliest representation of him in the books which preserve and illustrate in various forms—in history and in song, in prophecy, proverb, prayer, and myth—the successive movements of the revelation of God to the Jewish people and to prophets that heard His voice and saw His glory before He called Abraham to be the head of the elect nation—man, belongs on the one hand to the material universe; he sprang from the dust; he shares the physical life of inferior races: but he belongs, on the other hand, to an invisible and eternal order; he was made in the image of God, and received the inspiration of the divine life. According to the fuller and clearer discoveries of a later age, his higher life has its fountains in the eternal life of the Son of God.[1] Men were created in Christ, the eternal Son of God, the eternal Word of God, and were created to share His eternal relations to the Father. We are branches of Christ, the eternal Vine; branches which began to grow out of the eternal roots but yesterday, but destined, if we are loyal to the idea of our life, to remain in Christ for ever. The Vine is necessary to the branches; the branches are also necessary to the Vine; and, without relying on the precarious argument from analogy, it may be said that the human race and its relations to Christ and to the Father through Him are, in a very true sense, necessary to the fulfilment of the ideal of Christ's own life and of Christ's own relations to the Father.

Christian theology finds its ultimate conception of man, the transcendent ideal of the life of man, the prophecy and assurance of his perfection, in the eternal life of God and in the august mystery of the Trinity. In union with the Son of God we share His relations to the Father and His eternal perfection and blessedness.

For this every man was created. To those, therefore, who have received the Christian revelation there is in every man—no matter how mean and wretched his external condition, how feeble and neglected his intellectual

[1] A divine word, said some of the ancient Stoics, is at the root of the life of every man—a noble conception carrying the inference that every man's history, according to the law of his being, should be a translation into character and conduct, not of any ideal of perfection arbitrarily constructed or chosen by himself, but of a divine thought and purpose.

b

powers, how coarse his habits, how gross his vices—the possibility of realizing this wonderful glory. They discover in every man indications of the greatness to which God has destined him. In his perceptions, however obscure, of the authority of duty, and of the infinite contrast between right and wrong, they recognise his actual and present relations to Christ, " the Light that lighteth every man "; in his capacity for religious faith and worship, however corrupt may be his creed, and however superstitious the rites by which he attempts to propitiate the unseen powers which he supposes are able to desolate or to defend and augment his happiness, they recognise his actual and present relations, not merely to an invisible and eternal world, but to the invisible and eternal God.

The moral freedom which he possesses is necessary to the fulfilment of the Divine idea of his perfection; but in the power of that same moral freedom the Divine idea may be defeated. The will of God is not always done. It is God's purpose that all men should be temperate, industrious, kindly; many men are profligate, indolent, malicious. Man was created for virtue; he may live in vice. And as God's purpose may be defeated in man's moral relations to his fellow-men, it may also be defeated in man's moral and spiritual relations to God Himself. But it remains true that he was created that he might share the Divine life in Christ, and be eternally one with God in Him.

This conception of man lies at the root of Christian morals, and determines the Christian ideal of the Social Order. All our duties to other men—in the family, in business, in general society, in public life, as members of the same municipality, as citizens of the same commonwealth—are governed by it; and the only Social Order which can satisfy the Christian conscience is one that rests on the assumption, that all men were created to be brethren in Christ, and for eternal union with God in Him.

II.

It may be objected that the Christian conception of the grandeur of man's relations to God and to eternity, if it were ever to take possession of the faith and the imagination of those who bear the Christian name, would paralyse their hostility to social injustice and their pity for all the miseries of the race. What is there, it may be asked, in the most cruel sufferings of this transient earthly life to touch the compassion of those who seriously believe that man was created for eternal righteousness and glory?

(1) The objection, however plausible it may look, and whatever strength it may derive from abnormal and fanatical growths of the Christian life, finds no support in the general *history* of the Christian Church. The fresh enthusiasm of the first converts to the Christian faith led to what a cool criticism may pronounce to have been a reckless and pernicious provision for the poor. The early Church, the Church of the first few chapters of the Acts of the Apostles, took the form of a philanthropic organization. Those who received the Christian gospel

became suddenly indifferent to wealth; lands and houses were sold, and the proceeds of the sale were put into the treasury of the Church,—not to maintain a splendid ritual, or to support missions, but to feed the hungry and to clothe the naked. They ceased to care about comfort and luxury for themselves, but they cared a great deal for the relief of the wants of other men. Throughout the history of the Church, whenever Christian faith in the glories by which we are surrounded has been most vigorous, there has been the most compassionate pity for the temporal miseries of mankind.

(2) The objection finds no support in the *teaching* of the Lord Jesus Christ. Nothing is more characteristic of that teaching than its perfect sanity. He did not, like the Stoics, attempt to convince men that hunger and thirst and nakedness are not real evils. He told them, indeed, to seek first God's kingdom and God's righteousness, and not to be anxious about what they should eat and what they should drink, and wherewithal they should be clothed; but He added: "Your Heavenly Father knoweth that ye have need of these things." God recognises the reality of the physical wants of the race: Christian men—if they wish to recover the image of God—must recognise them too.

(3) The objection finds no support in the *history and example* of the Lord Jesus Christ. He who came to reveal to men that they are akin to God, that they are destined by the Divine purpose to union with God and to immortal blessedness in Him, was "moved with compassion" by every form of physical suffering. His miracles, which to

the men of His own time were among the signs that He came from Heaven, have perhaps their chief value in our own age as striking, startling, and most impressive illustrations of the characteristic aim of the Christian redemption—the recovery of the race from misery as well as from sin. They teach us that it is the permanent duty of those who find the law of perfection in the life of Christ, to feed the starving—not merely by acts of charity, but by promoting a national policy which will increase the productive power of industry, and secure a more equitable distribution of the wealth which industry creates; to lessen pain and suppress disease—not merely by care for the sick, but by sanitary legislation which will prevent sickness; to conquer death itself—not by restoring the dead to life, which is beyond our power, but by social and economical reforms which will augment the vigour of human life and prolong its duration.

(4) The objection finds no support in the *Christian conception of human nature.* According to that conception, man is not a spiritual being with an accidental and transient connection with a physical organization; body and soul are equally necessary to the integrity of human life. Manicheeism, which attributes the visible world to the devil, and regards the flesh with hatred and contempt, was one of the heresies which the Church had to fight in early centuries, and which it condemned as fatal to the revelation of God in Christ, and fatal to Christian morality. The life of man is a unity, though it touches the earth on one side and God on the other.

To increase the health and vigour of man's physical nature is a work worth doing for its own sake. The discovery of man's relations to the eternal Son of God creates new motives for doing it. The physical condition of large masses of the people, even in the wealthiest and most highly civilised countries, is unfriendly to common morality. When we give them better health by giving them purer air, better water, more wholesome food, we are contributing aids to their moral improvement; and every advance in the moral condition of the race contributes to the fulfilment of the Divine idea of human perfection.

The intellect of all descriptions of men is worth cultivating for its own sake; and we honour God by cultivating it, for "it is the inspiration of the Almighty that giveth them understanding." But by a wise cultivation of the intellect we make men capable of surer and more delicate moral judgments; and, other things being equal, of a wider and exacter knowledge of the contents of the Christian revelation; for the functions of the intellect are not suspended by the light which falls direct from Heaven on those who are taught of God. There have been times when ecclesiastical authorities have regarded with hostility and with dread the quickening of the popular mind, the audacious spirit of a robust and independent scholarship, and the splendid discoveries of science; but these have not been the times when spiritual faith was most active. And whatever crimes against the human intellect have been committed by the rulers of the Christian Church, it is to the Christian Church that Europe owes its popular schools and its universities.

If, therefore, the Church has become indifferent to the material and intellectual interests of mankind, it has forgotten both the teaching and the example of Christ, it has misapprehended the Christian conception of human nature, it has broken with its own best traditions.

III.

But the question recurs—and some recent discussions give it exceptional urgency—whether the fires of Christian enthusiasm for the relief of the present miseries of the race may not, as a matter of fact, be subdued by the supreme interest which has been claimed for the invisible and eternal objects of religious faith, and whether the development of Christian morality may not suffer from the devotion of a large measure of Christian thought and energy to speculation on the nature of God and on His relations to mankind. It is supposed that we should do more for morals if we cared less for theology, and that the Nicene Creed has made the Church indifferent to the Sermon on the Mount. It appears incredible that those mysteries of the Divine life which cannot be completely explored by the boldest, hardiest, and most adventurous thought, and which may seem to be inaccessible to the common mind, can have any real relation to the Morals and Social Order of Christian nations.

But there is nothing surprising in the assumption that

truths which lie far beyond the reach of the great masses of mankind may have the most powerful influence on their lives and fortunes. Scientific discoveries, which are intelligible only to experts, change the organization of great industries and impoverish or enrich millions of men to whom the first principles of science are unknown. Philosophical speculations, which in their principles and methods are beyond the comprehension of the undisciplined intellect, have been the origin of political and social revolutions. If the Christian revelation concerning the life of God were really above the reach of the intellectual commonalty of the race, it might still be true that this revelation has the power to produce the most beneficial changes in the morality of nations and the most stupendous revolutions in their Social Order.

But, however intricate, perplexing and difficult may be the speculations of theologians on this great mystery, the substance of the revelation is received by millions of untaught men for whom the commonest technical terms necessary to define it have no meaning. The mystery is verified in their personal experience. They know that their life is a life in the eternal Son of God, and therefore a life in union with the Father. They know, too, that it was for this life that all men were created.

It may be answered that this immediate and spiritual knowledge of the great mysteries of Faith is enough, and that as soon as any attempt is made to define them there is peril that the glory of the vision will be quenched. But the intellect has its rights in every province of human life, and the attempt to suppress them will always be mischievous. These rights will be won by violent revolt if they are not frankly conceded and surrounded with honourable guarantees. If there is a divorce between faith and reasoned thought, faith will become superstitious and the intellect will become atheistic.

It is only by a return to those transcendent facts which have given to the Christian Gospel in past ages its power over the social life of Christendom that its power will be renewed and enlarged in our own times. Here lies the secret of that freshness and originality of moral thought which is necessary to the Christian Church if it is to retain—or recover—the moral leadership of Europe. Here are the fountains of that inspiration and vigour which alone can enable the Church to translate its new and loftier moral ideals into practice. For the elevation of the Social Order we need a deeper reverence for man—for every man; and it is to be found in the relations of every man to the Eternal Son of God. These give sanctity to the outcast and confer an awful dignity on the meanest and most miserable of the human race.

It is no metaphor that Christ uses in His dramatic representation of the judgment of the nations—"I was an hungred, and ye gave Me meat; I was thirsty, and ye gave Me drink; I was a stranger, and ye took Me in; naked, and ye clothed Me; I was sick, and ye visited Me; I was in prison, and ye came unto Me"—for between Christ and the hungry, the starving, the naked, the desolate, the sick, the oppressed, there are relations so close that the service which we render to them is rendered to Him. They were created to share His eternal life and righteousness, to be one with Him as He is one with the Father. "Inasmuch as ye did it to one of these least, ye did it unto Me."

"Thou shalt love the Lord thy God with all thy heart, and with all thy soul, and with all thy mind. This is the great and first commandment. And a second like unto it is this, Thou shalt love thy neighbour as thyself." *Like*—because the relations between man and God are so vital, that to love God perfectly is impossible without loving man. "He that honoureth the Son," Christ said, "honoureth the Father"; and in honouring men who were created in the Son, we also honour the Father. Moralists have nothing to gain from quarrelling with theologians; social reformers may find inspiration and strength in the central mysteries of the Christian Faith.

R. W. DALE.

BIRMINGHAM.

INTRODUCTORY LETTER FROM THE AUTHOR TO THE TRANSLATOR.

Madam,

I am pleasantly surprised to learn that this book, first printed thirty years ago, should seem to you sufficiently valuable to be translated for the use of your countrymen.

Well received on its first appearance, translated into German and Dutch, it nevertheless contains some chapters that need revision, either to complete them by the result of more recent publications, or to strengthen them by new arguments.

Various circumstances, of slight interest to the public, prevent me from undertaking that task. This I ought not to conceal whilst thanking you for approving the book as it is.

In our day, when the world is so full of sin and misery, and the remedies proposed are often more dangerous than the evils they are intended to cure, I remain convinced that the Christian faith and the love it inspires are the only efficacious means of raising the moral and material condition of the masses of the people. On right-hearted men a pictorial representation of this truth, such as I have attempted to sketch, may perhaps make more impression than abstract discussion.

It is for the sake of this practical aim that you have wished to make use of my work.

May it serve the cause you hope to help by its translation.

   I am, Madam,
     Yours with deep respect,
         C. SCHMIDT.

STRASBURG,
 November, 1884.

PREFACE.

In A.D. 1849 the French Academy proposed the following theme for a prize essay: "To trace the influence of Charity on the Roman World during the first centuries of the Christian era; to prove how, while showing all respect for law and property, it wrought a change by persuasion, through the power of Religion; and to show in the constitutions which were thus established the new spirit with which it had imbued civil society." After an attentive examination of the scheme, I thought it necessary to commence by indicating the character of the ancient spirit, the doctrines and social morality of antiquity, in order to show more clearly what was new in the spirit with which Christian charity had imbued civil society. I thought, too, that it was not the intention of the Academy to restrict attention solely to the bearing of charity on the poor. That would give only one side of a subject, which, embracing the whole round of civil society, necessarily includes, besides the relations of rich and poor, those of man and woman, father and children, master and servants. I have therefore divided my work into three parts.

In the first I shall give a brief sketch of ancient social morality, which I shall trace to its sources; viz. the egoism of the citizen and the despotism of the State.

In the second I sum up Christian social morality, which is only an application of charity to the various relations of life; and with this I combine a picture of Christian life and institutions during the earlier periods of our era.

The third part is intended to show how the ancient maxims and Roman laws, which affected civil society, were transformed by charity; or, to speak according to the programme, how this society was imbued with a new spirit. It will be apparent, therefore, that I have not taken the word charity in the restricted sense of alms-giving or benevolence. The Gospel, in freeing the soul and proclaiming the equality of all men, restored to their personal dignity, has replaced the despotic and exclusive spirit of the ancient world by a new social principle—that of love.

This love, which is inseparable from the respect due to all men, whatever their external status, is charity in its highest sense; it is the fundamental virtue of Christianity, the central motive of all the feelings we ought to entertain one towards another.

From this point of view I have taken for motto a saying of St. Augustine, "Where charity is not, justice cannot be."

In a treatise published under trying conditions, one of the most distinguished men of our age has said, "Justice is the bridle of humanity, charity is the spur."[1] Antiquity, which wished to use the bridle only, and which employed it in the sole interest of the few, was compelled to end by relaxing it, after being deceived as to its nature and strength. To Christianity the glory belongs of having applied to souls the spur which impels them to abnegation and sacrifice, and which makes it possible to

[1] M. Cousin, *Justice et Charité*. Paris, 1848.

manage the bridle in the interest of all. This is the true condition of social life. Without the free sacrifice of man for man, society is only a violence or a chimera. Justice itself, *i.e.* respect for individual rights, needs to be enlightened and vivified by charity.

When I pictured to myself the present state of society (which is not without resemblance to the early times of the rise and progress of the Gospel), where we have so vast a field for the activity and self-sacrifice inspired by charity in all the relations of life, it seemed to me that the Academy required no erudite work, but one easily understood by all, which would give an historical apology for Christianity, based on its moral effects and social influence. This idea of writing a book for the public in general has guided me in the choice and arrangement of materials. Had I written solely for the learned, I would have developed several points more slightly, while various questions of criticism would have been more fully discussed. I can say with truth that I have cited no fact which is not supported by positive and authentic testimony. It would have been easy to add many interesting details, but, in dealing with a subject so vast, I have kept strictly to what seemed to me the essential characteristics of the centuries and epoch with which I was occupied.

Several points, which belong to the general question, have been treated elsewhere with superior ability and scientific method in special works, such as those of MM. Villemain, Troplong, Naudet, Wallon, Moreau-Christophe, Martin, etc. To me was left the task of making such a picture of the whole as might draw attention to the social transformations effected by the influence of Christianity.

I have refrained from making applications to the present day, only because I am convinced they are useless to the readers of an historical work, who are quite able to compare for themselves the past with the times in which they live.

I attribute the success of my work with the French Academy rather to my desire to do good than to its inherent merits. This eminent body, after hearing the report—only too kind to me—presented by the illustrious secretary, M. Villemain, awarded an equal prize to the work of my honourable colleague, M. Chastel, of Geneva, and to mine. I should fail in my duty if I did not take this opportunity of expressing my warm thanks to the Academy for the distinction it has accorded to my book. I do not imagine that this will wholly shield me from criticism; but I hope that the public also will bear in mind my intention to aid in spreading the ideas and sentiments inspired by Christian charity, and with which many of our contemporaries are not yet sufficiently imbued.

March, 1853.

BOOK I.

PAGAN SOCIETY.

INTRODUCTION.

At the epoch when Christianity appeared Rome was at the summit of her power and glory. The greatest part of the then known world obeyed her laws; her civilization, with its benefits and its vices, was established in Europe, Asia, and Northern Africa; her legions had planted their victorious eagles everywhere; her institutions, her customs, even her language had followed them, and the world had become Roman, not in name only, but in thought and deed.

The social and moral state of the Empire was alike in both East and West: it was the result of a fusion of Grecian civilization with that of Republican Rome. This fusion was easily accomplished, for notwithstanding the difference between the Roman and the Greek genius, the two civilizations rested on the same fundamental principle.

It will not be needful to go back to the heroic traditions of primitive ages in order to recognise this principle, and to characterise generally the spirit of Roman society in the ages with which we are engaged. We need not seek these germs, half hidden in the shadow of the myths, but we must follow their historical development, both in the institutions which gave a legal sanction to the customs, and in the opinions of the philosophers, who justified both law and customs by their theories.

From this double source we shall draw the materials

for composing the following picture of the life and spirit of Roman society. We shall show the generally received ideas about men and their mutual relations in civil life, and thus unite the principal characteristics of ancient social morality.

Historical facts will confirm the results of this study: all the internal history of pagan society will be shown to be the inevitable fruit, the fatal consequences, of the spirit and social principles of antiquity. The ethical principles of the ancients do not differ from their practical morals; or to speak more exactly, we shall find in their ethical principles the expression of their practical morals reduced to a system or formulated in laws.

CHAPTER I.

THE PRINCIPLE AND AIM OF ANCIENT SOCIAL MORALITY.

§ 1. *Happiness.*

In ancient times man sought, as he does now and always, to make himself happy. That the end and aim of life is happiness was the moral principle by which individuals guided their whole conduct.

The pagan, knowing little of the deep and eternal realm of the soul, generally sought this happiness in external things, in the more material enjoyment of the senses. Material enjoyment is in its own nature egoistical. Everything is referred to personal desire; the "I" reigns supreme, the centre and spring of all activity; it has an exclusive reign; it hates those who resist it, and despises those whom it uses, unless they are sufficiently strong to make themselves feared. We shall soon see that in this is summed up the social morality of antiquity, whose sole principle is egoism.

The philosophers Democritus, Aristippus, and the Sophists have unvaryingly declared that the sole aim of human activity is to seek happiness in enjoyment. They were faithful interpreters of those who had the means of making themselves happy in the sense of pagan antiquity. Other less materialistic philosophers have tried to moderate the principle of ancient morality by less vulgar definitions of supreme good; but they also have been unable to rise above the demands of egoism. If they speak of the possibility of a less sensuous happiness, they not the less allow external enjoyment to exist by its side; they refer man to virtue, but their virtue is neither deep, nor clear from impure alliance. Their morality, founded on self-love, knows nothing of duty towards all men; it consecrates contempt for the weak and hatred of enemies, and does not tend to the realization of true justice. It is a morality governed by existing facts and intended to help them by philosophic sanction and support; it is not a doctrine *superior* to these facts, intended to correct and transform them.

It will not be necessary for us to give here detailed developments of the moral systems of antiquity; it will be enough to recall their fundamental principles, reserving for the end of this work the ideas of philosophers about social relationship and different classes of men. We content ourselves with saying here that these practical ideas, far from being the results of the purer speculations to which several amongst the ancient sages attained, are only the theoretical justification of the customs and institutions of antiquity.

Socrates places happiness in wisdom, in the knowledge of the supreme good, of God. For him this knowledge of good is inseparable from the practice of good; wisdom is one with virtue; but we question him in vain as to what is good and just in life. He leaves his disciples in doubt in this respect, or rather the doubt has not even arisen in their soul, for Socrates did not inquire with them whether the customs and laws were in accordance with virtue and wisdom or not.

It is true that Plato combats the opinion that enjoyment is the supreme good. He, in his turn, says that virtue is the only happiness of the soul, and that God is the supreme good. He has beautiful aspirations towards God, in which he recognises His infinite perfections; but though he attains a certain elevation in his speculations, he falls back into pagan egoism when he touches practical and social questions. We find him affected by this egoism even in the midst of his Utopia of the ideal society.

As to Aristotle, he is no utopian. Taught by experience, he states that men perform all their actions with a view to happiness, and he believes happiness to exist simply in this practical activity. But he wishes our actions to be in accordance with our reasonable nature. The more this rational activity is developed, the happier man will be, and the nearer he will approach to pure virtue. It would seem from this that the practice of virtue must be the source of happiness. But this virtue itself is only external; its principle resides in the desires and interests of man, in his egoism. This lies beneath the opinion of Aristotle, that utility is the standard of right, and that it is only through the observation and judgment of men that we can find the medium between extremes, and discern between bad and good. Thus, in the last analysis, the moral principle is founded only on personal interest enlightened by experience.

Stoicism appears to rise above the calculations of an interested prudence. It lays down as a law for the man who aspires to the happiness to be obtained from virtue, that he shall live in conformity with the intelligent nature of the soul. The perfection of this nature is supreme virtue, and in its practice consists supreme happiness; for the perfection of intelligent nature is to be inaccessible to all impressions produced by external things and chances. Virtue and happiness reside, consequently, in calm of the soul, in imperturbability of spirit, which resists the passions whatever may be their cause or object, and dwells unshaken amidst the affections. To preserve this precious calm, the Stoic will harm no one, in order that no one may have an excuse for troubling him with offences or complaints. It is therefore still personal interest which inspires the Stoic; his system, no less than the others, is founded on egoism.

It is the same with the new academy, who, attaching themselves partly to Stoicism and partly to the doctrines of the Peripatetics, sought to reconcile duty and interest, justice and utility. It was the school of men of the world who were anxious to have in everything an irreproachable external appearance. Cicero is its chief representative. The morality of this philosopher is summed up in the precept to live honourably, that is to say, in conformity with the intelligent nature. Honourable is that which is to be praised in itself, without reference to material utility. We know it by consulting the common judgment of men. What they generally agree to blame or despise is bad, and what they praise or honour is good. Cicero believes that he has proved that the terms good and honourable are synonyms, as well as the terms disgraceful and bad. Returning to utility, whose exigencies could not be conquered by ancient morality, he declares that what is good is useful; the good being what is honourable, he definitely concludes that all that is honourable is also useful.

We should have little to say against this principle of the Roman philosopher had he given us any other standard of what is honourable than the judgment of men, which is generally so misleading and contradictory. If there is no motive superior to love of self, each one is led to consider that to be honourable and good which favours his wishes. He therefore limits himself to the avoidance of external conduct which would shock the crowd; he is contented with this decorum, for which Cicero, as a moralist and man of the world, reserves all his enthusiasm. Any one who has the conscience to observe decorum may even set himself above public judgment. It is in this sense that Cicero gives the assurance that, to live happily, it suffices to have the tranquil content given by virtue itself when practised freely; that is, without seeking it either in external benefits or even in a deeper satisfaction.[1] We see what becomes of the union of honour and utility, of duty and interest in this system of morality, which is as egoistic as all those of antiquity. It is evident that after this reconciliation duty is infallibly sacrificed to personal interest. Duty only begins when it is not opposed by personal interest, and actions may be unfettered provided that decorum is observed. Thus, according to Cicero, morality is measured by the approval of men, or at least by freedom from their blame. It is principally a rule of conduct for the man of the world, who, occupying a high position in society, is more exposed than others to the view and criticism of the multitude.

In the rapid examination we have just made we have recalled only the most eminent representatives of ancient thought. If the moral principle of men so learned and so wise was unable to free itself from egoism, from the desire of enjoying undisturbed happiness, the rule of conduct of those who knew nothing of philosophy was sure to be neither more strict nor more certain.

§ 2. *The State.*

In considering the character of ancient morality, we might be tempted to believe that it was a morality intended only for individuals, which imposed upon them neither social duties nor reciprocal obligation. But there was an egoism greater than that of the individual, the egoism of the State. We shall be convinced of this when we have seen the way in which the philosophers, representatives in this respect of the general spirit of antiquity, looked at the means of realizing individual happiness. This means, according to them, was the State. To live in a well-organized State was the highest condition of the well-being of man.[2] This idea, which is true in a certain sense, ceases to be so when it justifies the supremacy of the State at the expense of the rights of individuals.

Aristotle is the first who expresses philosophically the political thought which was the basis of Greek social order. The State, he says, exists rationally before the individuals who compose it, as the whole exists before being divided into parts; it is in its nature superior to its members, who give themselves to it because they only have being through it; it is the condition of their existence, growth, and prosperity.[3] The whole organization of ancient States rested on this idea: as the part is nothing without the whole, so they believed man to be nothing apart from his relations as citizen,—his existence depended entirely on that of the State. The State was anterior and superior to all individual personality, and absorbed it entirely.

Plato, in his speculations on the model republic, was unable to free himself from this conception of a State which stifled the individuality of its members. His ideal is the ideal of public egoism, or more properly speaking, the ideal of the united egoisms of a certain number of privileged men. Such was the ancient State. To Plato, seeking the conditions of a perfect republic, the State is everything. It is the sole aim of the activities of its members; there is nothing that ought not to be sacrificed to it. Those who cannot serve it have no reason for existence; policy permits them to be despised, if it does not command them to be destroyed. As the State *is* all, it also *possesses* all. It is not a natural right to have private property, it is not even a privilege; it is a mark of inferiority, for only those who are excluded from the community of the State—those who work, labourers, the industrial classes—can possess anything of their own. The true members of the State do not work; they have no private property; they have everything in common, even the women. The family is destroyed for them; their children belong to the State, they are the wealth of all. Supreme happiness consists in directing such a State; and it is the philosopher who is the most capable of this direction—of being the perfect king. This perfect king need think of nothing but the prosperity of the State. It matters little to him if the individual is happy, so long as the State prospers, though it should be at the expense of whole classes of its members. The State is composed only of a small number of men, of an aristocracy divided into castes, from which those who belong to them can never separate themselves.

—Human individuality is thus completely overlooked and sacrificed to a chimerical community, in which the only real thing is the egoism of those who profit by it and the misery of the others. All the errors of the social morality of this great philosopher proceed from this mistake. We shall see proofs of this farther on. We do not know how far Plato desired the realization of his utopia, whose whole principle was entirely in accordance with the ancient spirit. What we do know is that he taught that when the progress of things in the State no longer suited the sage, who was unable to alter it, he should withdraw from public life and attend solely to his own affairs, abandoning the State, that could be no longer useful to him, to its ruin.[4] Plato himself followed this ungenerous advice in respect to his native town.[5] By his theories and example he gave political philosophy, and perhaps Greek civilization itself, a tendency which removed it further from ancient and more patriotic habits. This school was suitable only for the aristocracy, who learned there to rise above the growing corruption of the people, through disdain; and who alone would have benefited could the Platonic Republic have been realized. It was not a school in which a man could learn the energy and devotion necessary to save his fellow-citizens. The ancients themselves asked whether the philosophy of Plato had not inspired more tyrants than enemies of tyranny. Plutarch collected the names of some friends of liberty who came from the Platonic ranks, to which Athenæus opposed a long list of oppressors formed in the same school.[6]

The counsel given to the sage to leave the State to its ruin when he could not save it, was not the general opinion. Plato himself expresses the latter when he says that human activity should have no other aim than the good of the State, and that the highest purpose of life is to serve one's country.[7] Aristotle gives still more formal expression to this. No one should think that he is anything in himself, that he has an individual value and right; each is something only so far as he is a part of the whole. He ought not therefore to seek what is for his personal benefit, but to consecrate himself wholly to the common good.[8] This last is the only true standard of justice; it is this which should rule all social duties and relations. Socrates had already been contented to refer those who wished to know what was practically good and just to the laws of the State.[9] Cicero reproduces the same ideas. He acknowledges the natural need of sociability, common to all men, as the origin of the State; but like the philosophers of Greece who, when speaking of the State, saw only the Republics of Athens or Sparta, he also confounds the ideal of the State with the Roman Republic, and declares that to serve Rome is the noblest aim for man's activities.[10]

In antiquity everything appears thus in the State, whhic claims and absorbs the vital forces of its members. The individual himself is nothing; it is only as a citizen that he is of value. He is a person only in the community of the State; outside that community he is overlooked, despised, trodden under foot by the State as well as by those who have the privilege of making part of it.

It follows from this that ancient morality recognises no other social duties than duties towards the State, and no other virtues than political ones. Man being essentially a *political animal*,[11] what other duties and virtues can there be that he ought to practise? Plato, Aristotle, the Stoics, Cicero, recognise no virtues but those of the citizen. Wisdom, courage, moderation, justice are the only necessary ones for him who wishes to share the direction of public affairs. The man who possesses these and adds to them decorum, the ornament of life, is the model man, the perfect citizen.[12] The whole history of the golden age of Greece and Rome bears witness that the virtues which were most highly developed were the political ones. The principle of the greatness of the ancient republics was precisely this indissoluble union of the personality of the citizen with the State. The individual was great only when he accepted this position with all its consequences, and learned to live and die for the State to which he belonged and which alone had the right to dispose of him. Also antiquity only recognised as services to the country those which were rendered to the government or in defence of the soil. The tomb of Æschylus called to mind that he fought at Marathon, but ignored his glory as a poet. On the other hand, the ancient State did not permit individual virtue to rise above the common level: it banished Aristides, and condemned Socrates to death.

We must not be astonished that we do not find love of country numbered amongst political virtues. The possibility of citizens without patriotism never occurred to Aristotle and Cicero. Man, being absorbed by the State and identified with it, could not help feeling attached to the community to which he owed his existence and whose glory he shared. But at a later time, when these bonds were loosened through the corruption of the citizens and the decay of the State, Tacitus reminds his age that love of public affairs, piety towards the country, was the highest of all duties. To reproduce once more the character of ancient Rome, he wished that individual advantage and honour should be unreservedly subordinated to the honour and benefit of the State. Virtue was for him only a free sacrifice of all private interests to the interests of Rome.

These were noble efforts of the great historian to rekindle a patriotism which grew less from day to day; but his efforts were ineffectual, for if the Romans of the time of Tacitus had no longer the virtues of past ages, Rome also was no longer ancient Rome. It would have needed a purer and more sublime devotion than ancient patriotism to inspire self-sacrifice for the welfare of degraded men who idly yielded to vile despots. Cicero had already foreseen this insufficiency of political virtue, and wished to strengthen it by the support of religion. He added to motives drawn from the requirements of the State one that was deeper in its nature, the fear of the gods. This should be joined to love of country to lead men to respect social transactions and to refrain from public crimes.[13]

§ 3. *Citizens. Foreigners. Riches.*

We have seen that the happiness of the individual through virtue is linked with the public welfare, which is the result of some social virtues practised by all those who compose the State. But of whom is this State composed? Can it of its own nature gather all men to its bosom? In other words, are all men capable of virtue, and can they consequently hope to be happy?

Ancient civilization, through the mouth of its wisest men, answers No. Happiness is only for the Greek or Roman, because the commonwealth of the State, as egoistic as individuals, is reserved only for the citizen of these countries. Other peoples are barbarians, beneath the dignity of enemies, below the human race; the Greek and Roman alone are men. The barbarian, that is the foreigner, is through his own nature in the same rank as the slave; he is not capable of commanding, he is made to serve. It is perfectly just to rule over foreigners or to sell them for slaves; those are wrong who refuse to do so, for this is the destiny appointed to them by nature.

That is the opinion of Socrates and Aristotle,[14] to

which Plato adds his own. If, according to him, the Greeks ought not to bring one another to slavery because they are all equally men, yet they only act in conformity with justice when they turn their arms against the barbarians to enslave them.[15] The contempt for foreigners, of which Grecian history shows so many examples, was held to the same extent in Rome. It was the cause of all the unjust wars, of all the violations of the right of the people, the remembrance of which tarnishes the Roman name. Cicero approved, as just and natural, the submission of other nations to Rome. Foreigner and enemy are synonyms to him. He does not wish that he who is not a citizen should be treated as such.[16]

The ancient nations have been often praised for their hospitality. If it was offered, it was only in rare and exceptional cases; for how could he who despised the barbarian as in an inferior condition, and who saw in him only a natural enemy, feel desirous of doing him good? When the ancients speak of hospitality, they mean only the duty of giving a splendid reception to illustrious guests, especially rich and powerful citizens, that the honour may be reflected on the Republic.[17] The guest is welcomed through national ambition, not benevolence; the house is open to him, not because he is a man, but because he is illustrious. Hospitality therefore is not a duty for every one: it is possible only for the rich, and for him it is an accidental duty depending on the rank of the guest.

The foreigner is thus excluded from the Greek and Roman State, and consequently from happiness, of which, according to Greek and Roman wisdom, the State was the supreme condition.

But at least every Greek, every Roman will have his place in the State, his share of happiness?

We are so accustomed to speak of the liberty of these ancient republics, that we are almost led to believe that every man there was a happy and free citizen. But it never was so. From the time when in society personality is ignored, when the State is represented as superior and anterior to the individual, it may be safely said beforehand that there will be no true liberty for all. In antiquity the worth of man was determined by external and accidental circumstances; it was not respected on account of the dignity of human nature, but only in proportion to the position filled in the State. Man as man was nothing; he was something only as a citizen, but this qualification did not belong to every one.

We must not forget that the aim of the State being the welfare of the citizen, the best State would be that where he would find the most advantage in return for his political virtues. But, according to the ancients, the exercise of these virtues requires leisure. Therefore only he who has leisure can be a citizen; that is to say, he must have no pre-occupation, no care on the subject of a livelihood. "The title of citizen," said Aristotle, "belongs only to those who need not work to live."[18] To live without work it is needful to have a fortune. Hence comes the principle that property makes a citizen; and as man is only respectable according to his position in the State, he who has enough wealth to have no need to work is the only man worthy of esteem.

Plato does not conceal this. Although he demands community of wealth in his ideal Republic, he declares that in the established order the rich man only can be considered a good citizen. It is he alone whose life has an aim; that of the man who works has none.[19] We find the same principles in Rome also. Personal consideration is given there only to property, riches, and numerous slaves. Fortune takes precedence of virtue and probity, and a man is only esteemed for his possessions.[20] Consequently nothing is more natural than the eagerness with which all methods of amassing riches were seized upon in Greece and Rome. According to Cicero, wisdom commands a man to increase his fortune, provided that he can do it without injustice.[21]

The pride of the citizen in the ancient States was the inevitable consequence of this method of measuring a man's civic capacity and worth by his fortune. The citizen alone was truly man, he only could practise virtue. The State guaranteed protection to him alone, and as we said before, the State was only the union of those who had the qualifications of citizens. All the other inhabitants of the country were outside the State, which repelled them in its political egoism, as the citizen in his individual egoism despised them whilst employing them in his service. The citizen, finding himself placed so high in the State, thought only of the greatness of his country because that greatness was also his. In the externals of life he avoided everything low, *servile, barbarous*, in order to seek for what would add to the lustre of his name.

This pride was the virtue recommended by philosophers under the name of greatness of soul. Their magnanimity was very different from what we call so in modern languages that have been transformed by Christianity. It was only the contentment of the citizen proud of serving his country by his aristocratic virtues, carefully observing outward decorum, and regarding with supreme disdain all those who were not rich enough to share the advantages of his title. Humility, that is inferiority of position, was a subject of contempt for the philosophers of paganism.[22] Lowliness of mind was with them inseparable from inferiority of condition. From their purely outward point of view, they never dreamt that the name of humility would be given one day to one of the purest virtues.

§ 4. *Friendship. Vengeance.*

We will indicate the principles by which citizens were guided in their relations between themselves, before we examine the attitude of the proud and egoistic morality of antiquity towards the humble classes; that is, those who were not citizens, and were considered unworthy to be so. We do not refer to official or business relationships, ordered and protected by the laws, and in which men could associate without any abatement of their complete mutual indifference; we will speak only of the relations founded upon reciprocal sentiments, either of goodwill or hatred.

The motive of all the acts of the citizen was egoism. This individual egoism was subject only to the despotic power of the State. Still, notwithstanding its power in all circumstances where the State was not concerned, it could not completely stifle the need of sympathy which draws the hearts of men together, however it repressed this need within narrow limits. The natural sentiment of kindliness showed itself in the form of friendship, but was unable to break the bonds of political pride. Even the wisest of the ancients thought friendship could only be possible between equals.[23]

They did not believe that men of different social conditions could feel drawn towards each other, or that it was possible for a rich and powerful citizen to feel a close affection for one weaker and poorer than himself. It was well said that virtue and accord of soul were the conditions of true friendship; but the beautiful writings of the philosophers about this matter produce just the same effect because they recall the aristocratic character of ancient virtue. Besides, in searching to the roots of things, we are compelled to acknowledge that even those who speak the most warmly of the happiness of friendship reduce it to an egoistic principle, to utility. Socrates and Aristotle regard it as supremely useful, both in happiness and in misfortune.[24] Pythagoras, who has been called the legislator of friendship, though he restricted its sphere more than the other ancient sages, desired a community of wealth,[25] besides one of sentiment. Zeno defined it as a community of all that is necessary for life.[26] The general opinion clearly was, that friends were required rather as helpers in time of need,[27] than for the satisfaction of reciprocal good feeling.

Cicero, who often gives us glimpses of a less egoistic spirit, goes one step farther. According to him, friendship is, after wisdom, the greatest good, not on account of any considerations of utility, but for itself, because it responds to the natural need for affection. He says its true fruit is love itself.[28] We find in antiquity some beautiful instances of such disinterested and nobly devoted affection.[29] The great admiration with which historians mention these examples proves, however, that these strong and durable friendships were rare. It was seldom that they could bear the supreme test of misfortune. The poets call it a gift, almost beyond hoping for, to possess a friend who is the same in bad as in good fortune; they think a friend who is faithful amidst calamity is a more delightful sight than a sea without a storm to the navigator.[30]

This disappearance of friendship before unexpected reverses was in conformity with the principle of common life, which reduced the union of friends to one of reciprocal utility. What was the good of retaining affection for a friend who could be of no more use? It was an interested traffic: services were exchanged. When one of the parties was no longer in a position to help the other, he felt bound no longer, and remorselessly deserted him in his time of greatest need. Ovid expresses in some verses his sorrow for the universal egoism of antiquity.[31]

It was to avoid these easily broken bonds that philosophers insisted so much on prudence in the choice of friends, and the necessity of avoiding flatterers; they recommended only a small number of friends, whose services could be depended upon.[32] Some even carried egoism so far as to demand that men should be attached to no one, each being sufficiently occupied with his own affairs, and nothing being more inconvenient than to be mixed up with those of others.[33]

This was the principle of Roman society in the time of the decadence of the Empire. It had become incapable of all noble sentiments, worn out, debauched, and egoistic to the last degree. "If," says Martial, "thou wishest to spare thyself a reason for regret, do not attach thyself too strongly to any one; thou wilt have less joy, but in return thou wilt also prepare for thyself less sorrow."[34] According to the testimony of Plutarch, friendship no longer existed, even in families between the children of the same parents; they believed that brotherly love had been possible in heroic times, but examples of this fabulous union were no longer to be seen, except at the theatre.[35]

If friendship, reduced to interested requirements, was neither close nor sure, the same egoism profoundly deepened hatred, and increased the difficulties of surmounting its abysses. The general maxim of antiquity, approved by philosophers and sanctioned by legislators, was *talion*. "We must outrage those who outrage us," said Æschylus.[36] The common opinion in the time of Socrates, as in the time of Quintilian, was, that to return evil for evil was not to commit injustice.[37] The sages proved by the pleasure which naturally accompanies vengeance, that it is in conformity with human nature.[38] They strove especially to prove that it was demanded by the dignity of the citizen; to suffer evil without indignantly returning it was a mark of servile lowness,[39] whilst the anger roused by injury was the sign of a strong soul, a cause of heroic actions.[40] It was a manly virtue, a duty, to harm the enemy, as it was to render service to the friend.[41]

Cicero thinks he is the truly good man who injures no one so long as he is not provoked by receiving injury.[42] Thus virtue consists in not beginning the strife. A man should refrain from harming others, that he may not be exposed to their anger;[43] but when once offended, all consideration ceases, and if interest advises the use of the law of *talion*, it is perfectly justifiable; provided it be used with prudence, in order not to harm one's self.[44] Aristotle, whilst praising anger as a stimulant to virtue, will not allow excess in vengeance, in accordance with his principle that virtue resides in the medium between extremes.[45] The Stoics also forbid the mastery of passion, for fear of disturbing the calm of the soul. One must revenge one's self, but without anger. It is then, in their opinion, not vengeance, but a just chastisement. Evil ought necessarily to entail punishment. It is cowardly weakness to tolerate it, and makes one an accomplice of the crime to leave it unpunished.

It is in this sense that Cicero addresses the magistrates, saying that they would act contrary to their duty if they allowed themselves to be influenced by the entreaties of the accused, even when they were perhaps more unfortunate than guilty; and that they ought to punish great crimes and slight offences with equal severity.[46] In strict law the Roman philosopher might be right, but from the ground of humanity he was wrong. There, as in a thousand other cases, the "*summum jus*" might become the "*summa injuria.*"

It is true that antiquity has left some recommendations to pardon and indulgence, but they were inspired by the same pride which authorized anger and hatred. Nothing was in more complete accordance with the ancient spirit than the direction to the citizen to show his strength to the enemy who injured him, that he might not be dishonoured and conquered by him; but he could show his greatness of soul in two ways, either by revenging the offence or despising it. He could suppress all signs of hatred, or have recourse to *talion*, according to the circumstances and social position of the offender. Men revenged themselves if to refrain would appear cowardly, and remained impassive when it was in the interest of manly dignity to look down on the injury with superb disdain. To take revenge always was considered contrary to Greek civilization and Roman gravity. It was to act like a barbarian, a foreigner;[47] it was to show a weak and small soul.[48] Nothing was more worthy of a great and illustrious man than clemency and the forgetfulness of injuries.[49] The higher the place of the citizen in the Republic, the less can he be injured by offence. It is the less able to harm his own opinion of his merit, or weaken the esteem with which his fellow-citizens surround him.

It was to these men, who thought themselves stronger the more they were filled with pride, that the counsels of the philosophers were addressed. They were to remain masters of themselves in anger, to return injuries with silence, and to rise above low things unworthy to occupy a sage. They may be satisfied with the repentance of the offender,[50] or even go so far as to be reconciled with him; they may perhaps take the first steps, yielding something of right and returning injuries with redoubled benefits, but this must only be when they find it will be useful for themselves.[51] This is not the pardon inspired by love, it is only a new sign of egoism, another way of satisfying personal interest.

The ancient authors are full of examples which confirm all we have said in this respect. If in antiquity facts were oftener in accord with the principles of the theory than since the introduction of Christianity, it is because ancient moralists limited themselves to the generalization of the daily phenomena of common life and thus formulated the data of experience into philosophical precepts; whilst Christian morality, which has no earthly origin, is superior to deeds, and rules them from her heavenly height in order to sanctify them.

Ancient morality was entirely outward, and instead of combating anger, hatred, and vengeance, approved them. She gave the strength of her syllogisms to the most violent passions; and instead of aiding to unite men, she multiplied and justified the causes of divisions. We are therefore right in repeating that she cannot detach men from earth, and that egoism is her fundamental principle. The end of this work will prove this still further.

(1) *Acad. Quæst.*, IV. 46, vol. x. p. 131. *Tusc. Quæst.*, V. vol. x. p. 531 ff. (2) Plat., *De Rep.*, VI. p. 342 ff. (3) *Polit.*, I. 1, § 11, p. 6. (4) *De Repub.*, VI. p. 344. (5) Niebuhr accuses Plato severely of having been a bad citizen. *Kleine hist. und philolog. Schriften.* Bonn, 1828, 8th, vol. i. p. 470 ff. (6) *Athen.*, XI. 119, vol. iv. p. 389. Plutarch, *Adv. Colotem*, c. 32, vol. xiv. p. 194. (7) *De Repub.*, VI. p. 342; VII. p. 424. (8) *Polit.* VIII. i. p. 244. (9) Xenoph. *Memor.*, IV. 4, § 12, vol. iv. p. 238. (10) See his works *De Legibus* and *De*

CHAP. I.] PRINCIPLE AND AIM OF ANCIENT SOCIAL MORALITY. 25

Republica. (11) *Polit.* I. 1, § 9, p. 5. (12) Cicero, *De Off.*, I. 6 ff., i. 27, vol. xii. p. 11 ff., p. 42. (13) Cicero, *De Legibus*, II. 7, vol. xi. p. 370. (14) Socrates, ap. Xenophon, *Mem.*, II. 2, § 2, vol. iv. p. 83. Arist., *Polit.*, I. 1, § 5, p. 4. (15) *De Rep.*, V. p. 294. (16) *De Off.*, I. 12; III. 11. vol. xii. pp. 19, 130. (17) Cicero, *De Off.*, II. 18, vol. xii. p. 99. (18) *Polit.*, III. 3, § 2, p. 75. (19) *De Repub.*, III. p. 168. (20) Horace, *Sat.*, I, and vv. 61, 62. One of the old poets had already said: "Ubique tanti quisque, quantum habuit" (Seneca, Ep. 115, vol. iv. p. 96). (21) Cicero, *De Repub.*, III. 9, ed. Lemaire, p. 303. (22) For example, Cicero, *Tusc. Disp.*, V. 10, vol. x. p. 543. (23) Arist., *Ethic. Nicom.*, VIII. 13, p. 364. (24) Xenoph. *Memor.*, II. 4-80, vol. iv. p. 96 ff. Arist., *Ethic Nicom.*, VIII., 1, 6, pp. 355, 356. (25) Jamblich., *Vita Pythag.*, c. 16 *Franeker*, 1598, qto., p. 73 ff. (26) *Diog. Laert.*, VII. 1, no. 64, vol. ii. p. 786. (27) See too Plutarch's *Works*, vol. vii. pp. 157, 287; *Maximus of Tyre*, dissert. 5 and 20, in his Dissert. (ed. Reiske, 1774, 8°), vol. i. p. 82 ff. and p. 378 ff., and orat. 32 of Themistius in his *Orat.*, p. 322 ff. The general idea was that "friendships were desirable not so much from kindly feeling and affection, but rather for the sake of protection and assistance" (Ap. Cicero, *De Amic.*, c. 13, vol. xii. p. 224). (28) *De Amic.*, c. 9; ib., p. 219; *Epp. ad diversos*, III. ep. 13, vol. vii. p. 98. (29) Valer. Max., IV. 7, p. 223 ff. (30) Eurip., *Electra*, v. 558-560. vol. ii. p. 734; *Orestes*, v. 708, 9, vol. i. p. 87. (31) *Tristia*, I. eleg. 9, v. 5, 6, vol. iii. p. 206; *Epp. ex Ponto*, II. ep. 3, v. 7 ff., *ib.*, p. 353. (32) See the works quoted p. 18, note 5. (33) "Excessive friendships," said certain philosophers, "should be eschewed, in order that one person may not have to be anxious for several. Each man had enough and more than enough of his own troubles; it was burdensome to get mixed up too much with those of other people" (Cicero, *De Amic.*, c. 13, vol. xii. p. 224). (34) Lib. XIII. epigr. 34, vol. ii. p. 190. (35) Plutarch, *De fraterno amore*, vol. x. p. 36. (36) *Prometh. Vinctus*, 1006, ed. Blomfield. Leipz., 1822, p. 66. (37) Socrates, ap. Plat., *Crito*, vol. viii. p. 178. Quintil., *Instit. orat.* VII. 4, vol. ii, p. 37. (38) Aristot., *Rhet.*, II. 2-4, Strasb., 1570, fo. 157 ff. (39) Plato, *Gorgias*, vol. i. p. 354. Aristot., *Eth. Nicom.*, IV. 5, p. 75. (40) Aristot., *ib.*, IV. 2, p. 67. (41) Isocr., *Areopagiticus*, § 42, vol. ii. p. 166. (42) Cicer., *De Offic.*, III. 19, vol. xii. p. 141. (43) Cicero, *De Repub.*, III. 10, ed. Lemaire, p. 305. (44) *Gnomici*, p. 230. (45) *Ethic. Nicom.*, IV. 2, p. 67. (46) *Pro Murena*, § 30, vol. v. p. 36. (47) Eurip., *Hecuba*, v. 1069, vol. i. p. 49. (48) Juvenal, *Sat.* XIII. v. 189 ff., p. 142. (49) Cicer., *De Off.*, I. 25, vol. xii. p. 40. (50) *Ib.*, I. 11, p. 18. (51) *Ib.*, II. 18, p. 99. Cf. Valer. Max., IV. 2, p. 198.

CHAPTER II.

THE FAMILY.

§ 1. *Women. Marriage.*

WE have already found that antiquity, taking no account of individual character, had no true standard for the dignity of man. The individual being absorbed in the State, his worth depended only on accidental externals. To fulfil his mission of citizen, a man needed to be capable of assisting in the government, as well as the defence, of the Republic. Now this demands virtues that require for their exercise complete power over one's person, time, and action, as well as bodily strength. Those who are gifted neither with physical strength nor the riches which give liberty, are without the means of being virtuous. They are incapable of rendering direct service to the State, which consequently excludes them from the prosperity which it ensures for its citizens; they have no legitimate place in the public community, nor in the systems of philosophers. Ancient morality refuses to recognise them, or acknowledges them only to despise them, and to justify the right of the strong to use them for any selfish personal requirement. Thus the population of the State was divided into two classes: those who were strong and free, and those who were not. The first only are citizens; in the second class may be placed women, children, men who are obliged to work for their living, the poor and weak, and the slaves. These despised classes included the majority of the population. Notwithstanding this, posterity has too often praised the liberty of the Greeks and Romans, and proposed it as a pattern for modern society. This liberty was only the exclusive privilege of a small number of rich and powerful citizens. The ancient republics were in reality the most oppressive aristocracies.

Let us now examine the position given by ancient civilization to the classes whom we have just called the despised classes. We will begin with *women*.

The pagan, who, in his barbarous state, valued nothing but physical strength, and when civilized recognised nothing beyond political life, necessarily considered woman as belonging to a lower rank in the social order.[1] Himself strong and free, he threw upon woman the work which he despised as unworthy. He treated her with disdain or indifference; though considering her worthy to serve his own pleasure or perpetuate the duration of the State. In support of this we will quote passages from some poets who cannot be accused of exaggeration, and we shall also refer to the testimony of philosophers and legislators. They tell us that if in the time of the Homeric heroes woman was surrounded with the esteem which her ways deserved, it was no longer so in the time of the highest civilization in Greece. On account of her natural weakness she was judged unsuitable for the struggles of political life. In this Christianity agrees with the wisdom of the ancients, but it does not therefore refuse to acknowledge her dignity of soul, and it assigns to her a more peaceful and hidden domain than to man. The ancients, on the contrary, considered that woman, being unable to fill a place in the State, was on that account naturally inferior to the sex which has the privilege of strength.

Aristotle admitted a natural difference between the woman and the slave. He praised many of his countrymen for not imitating the Orientals, who reduced woman to the most disgraceful servitude; but he himself held the opinion that if she has a will, it is a powerless one; that if she is capable of virtue, it is a virtue which is very little different from that of the slave.[2] In Athens woman was treated all her life as a minor. If she married, her tutor or master, as the law called him, was her husband; if she remained unmarried, her father or some other relation exercised the rights of guardian over her; she could only inherit property in default of male heirs, and the number of these was increased to make her succession more unlikely.[3] In Rome, both in the customs and laws, manly majesty was contrasted with the physical and intellectual weakness of women, who, humble and subordinate, were not allowed to forget to offer due homage to that majesty.[4]

This degrading inferiority necessarily developed vices in woman rather than her higher qualities. It was thought that these vices had their roots in her very nature. She was said to incline to evil more than did man, whose faculties she did not possess. Only her faults were looked at, whilst no one dreamt that the burdens and isolation from which she suffered, both at home and in society, prevented her virtues from showing themselves. This way of regarding woman was not adopted only by the vexed and weary spirits whose verses[5] have been preserved by Stobæus, it was also the opinion of Greek philosophers and Roman statesmen.[6] "If nature had allowed us to be without women, we should have been relieved of very troublesome companions," said the censor Metellus Numidius before the assembled people.[7]

When in Rome, through the progress of an artificial civilization, women endeavoured to emancipate themselves, wasting their fortune by foolish expenses, and claiming some of the honours reserved for men, the public authorities interfered to stop the evil; but not having a higher opinion of the nature of woman, they went beyond their aim. A law was passed, based on contempt for an inferior sex, to exclude daughters, even an only daughter, from the paternal inheritance.[8]

We should be unfaithful to history if we denied that, even in the most degenerate times of Greece and Rome, we meet with some women who compelled men to respect them; but this exceptional respect does not weaken our opinion as to the general condition of women in ancient times.

This condition remained the same in marriage; the legal union with a husband, instead of raising woman enslaved her still further. We are not exaggerating, for in the opinion of philosophers and lawgivers, marriage was not a union of soul, but only a union formed in the interest of the State, to perpetuate it. It had no moral importance for the individuals who contracted it, but was only a political institution intended to increase the number of citizens. He who married fulfilled a duty to the State; therefore the advantages, which were purely material, were received by him and not by the woman.

According to Plato, it was necessary in marriage to think more of usefulness to the State than of personal taste.[9] It is true that besides the political aim of marriage, there is the higher one of bringing into the world servants for the gods, and passing on the name of father to a grateful posterity,[10] but he never quitted the political standpoint. He wished the first laws in a well constituted State to be intended for the regulation of marriages.[11] He himself proposed a similar law, which shows how much importance can be attached to what he says about the higher aim of the union between man and woman. He desired that in the perfect Republic the warriors should have the women in common. A sort of community of this kind was carried out in Sparta. Girls lived in freer intercourse with men there than elsewhere. It was intended to give them in this way a manly education, but it only produced a boldness which shocked the ancients themselves. When women married, this freedom ceased, to give way to that of men. Nowhere was human individuality more coldly and completely sacrificed to the interest of the State than in Sparta. Lycurgus, in a famous law, ordered that the old man who had a young and beautiful wife should give her up to younger and stronger men.[12]

Such laws inevitably produced licentiousness and immodesty in women. Euripides pointed out this fatal result, and Plato himself blamed it. Aristotle finds in it the cause of the decay of Sparta.[13] This philosopher, with his clear reason, saw how the community of women and wealth proposed by Plato was contrary to the aim of the whole of human society. "Man," he says, "only attaches himself strongly to what is his own. He takes trouble only for those he loves. If, then, all was in common, there would be no longer any family ties.[14] That confusion would be established which Aristophanes has wittily pictured in his 'Comedy of the Assembly of Women.'"[15]

Though Aristotle reproved the Platonic community in Sparta, because he gave the family an importance incompatible with these immoral chimeras, he retained none the less the idea of a purely civil aim in marriage: the family must be organised because it is the base of the commune, which is the base of the Republic. Marriage still remains only a political union, a duty towards the State.[16] Ocellus Lucanus, the Pythagorean, taught the same principles; he also holds that marriage was not instituted for individual happiness, but to preserve and perpetuate the society of which husband and wife form a part. They ought to live in peace between themselves, in order to set a useful example to their children, and thus to make them better citizens.[17]

These political considerations ought to direct the choice of a wife. It was suited to the aristocratic character of Greece that each should seek a wife only in rank equal to his own. In Plato's Republic no one desires a wife outside his own class, and the community itself was restricted to the higher classes.[18] The choice amongst women of equal rank was decided by physical reasons.[19] To this was added the consideration of fortune, as the advantages of the union were always for the husband in his position of citizen, and for his family. Most frequently the father chose for the son, from which followed a marriage without inclination or mutual affection. If there was passion, it only arose from sensuality. Philosophers themselves recognised no other love between man and woman than that of the senses; frequently it was not even the wife to whom it was given.

The relations between man and woman in a union contracted after such principles could not be intimate. In the golden age of Greece and Rome there had been marriages founded on true affection and reciprocal esteem. Woman took her natural place, managing the interior of the household. She was not mixed up with the noisy business of men, but presided, calm and respected, as matron and mother of the family, over the domestic economy. She superintended the education of her daughters, and often even that of her sons.[20] But in proportion as the view of marriage as a political institution prevailed, these marriages became increasingly rare. Woman retained her household domain, but no longer received the veneration of her husband and the respect of her servants. She was bound to consider herself naturally inferior to her lord and master; she was shut up in a special part of the house, from which she could not honourably escape, and where she lived isolated amid her slaves, occupying herself with work that men considered servile.[21]

It is true that Aristotle had said that it was not in accordance with the customs of the Greeks to look upon a wife as on the same level with the slaves;[22] but he energetically enforces her submission to the absolute authority of her husband. He is the soul, to which dominion belongs; the wife is only the body, which must obey.[23] In the house the husband reigned supreme; the advice of the wife was not considered in his resolves. Legally, any action taken on her suggestion counted for nothing and was of no value.[24] He sought on all occasions to maintain in her sight his dignity as a citizen and freeman, and to impress her with his manly majesty.[25] He hardly condescended to speak to her. "Is there any one," asks Socrates of Critobulus, " with whom thou talkest less than with thy wife?" "No one," answered the disciple, " or at least very few people."[26] If he was intimate with any woman, it was with his mistress, for the fidelity which with jealous vigilance he exacted from his wife, he did not consider himself bound to observe.[27]

In Rome we find the same spirit and the same customs. If possible, the pagan ideas about marriage were even harsher than in Greece, and more coldly formulated in civil legislation. There also the supreme interest in marriage was the interest of the State. There also the liberty of the citizen was bound by the aristocratic constitution of the Republic, which forbade him to marry beneath his rank, or to disgrace a free family by introducing a member of servile origin.[28]

Augustus permitted free men to marry into a lower rank, and all but senators might marry those who were enfranchised.[29] At a later time this concession was extended to senators, with the restriction that the wife was only held legitimate by special favour of the emperor, or after the husband had given up his senatorial dignity.[30] The daughters of senators were still forbidden to marry freedmen, and such marriages were held void.[31] The equality of rank between husband and wife required by Roman law did not prevent the same complete subordination of the woman as in the Grecian Republics.

In antiquity, particularly in Rome, the child was so far the property of the father that he could dispose of him as he liked. He might kill him; how much more then might he sell him. In Rome the primitive method of concluding a marriage seems to have been to buy the daughter from the father. In ancient Roman law one of the chief kinds of marriage was that by purchase, *per coemptionem*, a custom which in later times only existed symbolically. This sale invested the husband with marital authority. Having bought his wife, he became her master and owner, as of any other object so acquired. Besides this form of marriage, there was a more solemn one, accompanied with certain religious ceremonies; this was the marriage by *confarreation*. A third form, simpler and briefer, was when a woman, with the consent of her father, agreed to be married for a year, for the sake of a child: this was marriage *per usum*.

These different kinds of marriage, particularly the two first, entailed evil results on women, which are only new proofs of what we said of the jealous pride of the citizen of the ancient States. In marriage woman passed from the power of her father to that of her husband; the law said she passed *under his hand*. Also this hand weighed on the wife with inflexible harshness. Woman was saluted with the titles of mistress, *domina*, and mother of the family, but these titles were derisive; the husband alone governed the household, and the wife saw in him her master and judge. When she left her father's house for that of her husband, she passed, so to speak, from one father to another; she became the adopted daughter of her husband.[32] Remaining a minor as before, her state continued to be a kind of servitude. Being in a manner the daughter of her husband, she was entirely in his power. He could dispose of her as of his other children, or anything whatever that belonged to him. The Roman, like the Spartan, husband might lend his wife to another.[33] At a later time examples of this disgraceful traffic are still found, reflecting more shame on the traders than on the unfortunate sufferers.[34]

By the *manus*, that is the transmission of authority over the woman, the father gave to the husband the right of possessing the wealth which was her dowry; and he remained in possession of this even after a divorce.[35] There were also cases where the ownership of the woman's wealth remained with the father. This was when she was not emancipated before marriage. In that case she did not pass under the *hand* of her husband, but remained still under her father's power. He retained the right of reclaiming her from his son-in-law.[36] It is probable that these marriages, where the wife was, so to speak, lent, were less common than those in which she passed with body and wealth under the husband's authority; for after the consideration of the State, the fortune was most considered in arranging a marriage, and there even came a time when this motive prevailed over political interest. The young man who served his country by marrying, expected to profit from it himself by increasing his riches, and the father especially, whose consent was indispensable, considered the dowry the most suitable motive to guide his choice. It was the dowry which made the wife legitimate. Married women without fortune were looked upon almost as concubines.[37]

The wife, placed under the husband's *hand*, considered as his daughter, inherited his fortune if he died without children or a will. If he had children, she shared equally with them in the inheritance. The death of her husband did not allow her to return to her own family; she was bound to his by an indissoluble tie. Although a widow, she remained a minor without rights, and was placed under the guardianship of *agnates*, that is relations on the male side, as she had been under her husband's guardianship during his life. This guardianship was a political measure in the husband's interest, to strengthen his authority over what belonged to him; and in the interest of his family, to retain the fortune in it by ensuring the succession of male relatives. It was far from being a wise and benevolent precaution in the woman's interest, to protect her rights and aid her weakness.

These humiliating results of Roman marriage to the woman who submitted to the yoke strongly helped to relax the ties of the conjugal bond, and to take away even the importance of its civil and political character. From the fall of the Republic, the growing indifference to religious rites caused marriage by confarreation to be disused;[38] and marriage by co-emption became equally rare. Men and women inclined to shake off the legal formalities and practices of worship. The most frequent form of marriage at this time was that in which two people agreed to live together for the sake of a family. This was a simple mutual agreement, without either civil or religious consecration, and by which neither felt seriously bound. Tutelage itself lost its power through this weakening of the conjugal tie. Successive concessions and the increase of corruption took away much of its legal strictness. A law in the time of Claudius released free women from the oversight of the *agnates*.[39] They had only guardians chosen by the magistrates, the husband, or the father. Released from the care of the *agnates*, who were more severe as they were more interested, rich Romans yielded to luxury and debauchery of all kinds. The law gave them a juster liberty than they had before enjoyed, but they only profited by it to give freer scope to their vices.

Marriage, regarded simply as a political institution, produced, besides the degradation of woman, laws against celibacy and contempt for widowhood. It appears that amongst the Greeks, except in very early times, a woman rarely remained a widow. It was a melancholy and desolate state, and the woman who was compelled to endure it was more despised than pitied. There were special temples where the women went to beseech Diana to send them second husbands.[40] The husband, owner and master of his wife, might preserve her from widowhood by leaving her by will to a friend who would receive her as a legacy.[41] Antiquity took no care of widows who were poor. In the early times of the Roman Republic they were freed from some taxes; but at a later time, when penalties were inflicted for celibacy, this exemption was discontinued. On the one hand they were in the charge of interested *agnates*, whilst on the other they were liable to the penalties of celibates if they did not re-marry within a certain time.

The penalties against celibacy are amongst the strangest laws of antiquity. In these Republics, where personal liberty is said to have been surrounded with so many guarantees, how could this liberty have been so tyrannously shackled as to compel a man and woman to marry contrary to their wishes? But there is nothing here to surprise us; after the individual is absorbed by the State, there can be no true liberty, because there is no respect for personal rights. If the conjugal union has only a civil and political aim, if the family is only formed in the interest of the State, naturally the State will attach the greatest importance to the conclusion of marriages. It favours them by the advantages that it accords to husbands, as well as by the penalties which it inflicts on celibates. It enforces these penalties, because to refuse to marry was to omit a duty towards the Republic; it is to put personal taste before the needs of the country, and is thus an act of independence quite contrary to the spirit of antiquity.

In several States of Greece, especially Sparta, there were laws against celibates. It was the same in Rome, where, after the most ancient times, they expiated by fines the crime of wishing to remain unmarried.[42] But these coercive measures did not stop the evil they were intended to remedy. In Rome, after the time of the Republic, the number of celibates became very considerable. Individual egoism progressed in proportion as political virtues grew weaker. Therefore, as marriage had a purely external aim, with no profound and close union of soul, it follows that no one any longer took a wife through pure patriotism.

The censor Metellus told the people that marriage was the sacrifice of private pleasure to a public duty.[43] Let us bear this in mind, for very soon public duty was sacrificed to private pleasure, and men preferred celibacy to union with a troublesome companion. Those who married in the higher classes were influenced generally by their wish to gain a fortune or to perpetuate an illustrious race; whilst the others, witnessing the foolish extravagance of Roman ladies, and seeing nothing in women beyond the pleasures of the senses, were little inclined to enter the bonds of legal marriage.

Things had reached this point after the civil wars which depopulated Italy. Augustus enacted laws which have become celebrated, to encourage the Romans to marry; privileges and exemptions were granted to married men who had children, and penalties imposed on celibates and on those married people who at a certain age had no children, either adopted or real.[44]

These laws, which are contrary to the nature of man, and which slight his liberty, had no power to improve society. Customs were stronger than the laws, more efficacious remedies were needed; but the morality of antiquity could not rise to the restoration of woman, and a pure and spiritual aim in marriage. This is a height inaccessible to the egoism of man.

§ 2. *Love. Hetæræ and Concubines.*

We have been considering the consequences of marriage, in its ancient form, upon woman. We must now see how she was regarded in Greece and Rome in respect to her relations with man outside the legal marriage tie.

In consequence of the purely political and external character of marriage, the law and the moralists made few objections to extra-matrimonial relationships. Man had supreme authority. To him belonged the liberty and strength which woman lacked. He could abuse her unrestrainedly. He regarded her as intended to furnish the State with citizens or minister to his pleasures. The ancients often spoke of love; it was sung by poets and discussed by philosophers, but they did not mean that spiritual and holy feeling which arises in the depths of our being and establishes a sweet calm and disinterested sympathy between two souls, which endures through all changes, and survives death itself. Ancient egoism could know nothing of such love, or at best could but feebly foreshadow it. What they called love was only the passion and desire of the senses. The ancients more frequently spoke of its fury than of its sweeter charms. They sang of the transports which bewildered the mind and conquered the will. They professed it was caused by a god in delirium, who exerted his irresistible power over gods and men, and even over the animals which people both land and water.[45] This last characteristic shows, more than all the rest, that sensuality was the only principle of ancient love. It is on this account that the most serious philosophers desire that love shall be avoided. The sage cannot yield to it, because it makes him the slave of his body and troubles the calm of his soul.[46] It is unworthy of a free man to put himself in the power of a woman; according to Cicero there is no servitude more miserable.[47]

Perhaps platonic love, which has been so much praised from the middle ages until our time, may be brought up in contradiction to this statement. This love has been represented as the ideal union of the purest souls. One can hardly say to how much poetic and contemplative mysticism it has given rise. Unfortunately, all this differs from Plato. The invention of platonic love has doubtless arisen from a tale in "The Symposium" about two halves, who seek each other, and feel themselves mysteriously attracted towards one another. But on a close view this tale seems to be rather ironical than sentimental. The love spoken of in "The Symposium" in language worthy of the poets is a purely philosophical love, which is only attained by parting with earthly love, which is in some respects an inferior degree of it. This last is only the love of the senses. Plato recognised no other between man and woman. The character of Eros is only the desire to reproduce. The whole of Plato's theory of love rests on this idea, which was suited to a civilisation which deified physical forces and was absorbed in external nature. There are, according to Plato, two kinds of love, according to what one desires to produce: sensual love, and the nobler desire of creation in the sphere of the mental powers. This is true love, the love of the beautiful and good; fruitful in sublime creations, it is the possession of the philosopher only, and does not exclude the other love, which is even necessary, as the first degree and point of departure.

Ancient authors relate that Plato did not always remain on the heights of philosophical love, nor disdain the less abstract delights of the inferior degree. If we need further proof how little Plato was under the power of sentiment, we may recall his theory of the community of women in the perfect Republic. In the last analysis, he and all antiquity, with one common accord, admit no other than a physical cause for the union of man and woman in marriage. The aim is raised by its political significance, but the feelings of the heart count for nothing. If a man has desires, it is only those of the senses; if he feels a passion, no moral principle hinders him from gratifying it. In this respect nature reigns in all her plenitude and power, and philosophy and paganism rather justify and encourage than restrain.

There was a class of women who took advantage of these inclinations to withdraw from conjugal servitude, and to gain a power and influence over men not possessed by the rightful wife. It was the emancipation of woman in the sense of pagan antiquity; even in our day there are reformers of society who ask no less. In Greece, after the time when arts and letters were cultivated with an ardour fruitful in immortal works, the most eminent men of the nation, philosophers, poets, magistrates, and statesmen, sought the *hetæræ*, and yielded to the dangerous ascendency of their charms. Free in their behaviour, these women, who were not condemned to the melancholy isolation of the *gynæceum*, mixed with men, followed the lessons of the philosophers, and formed their taste by interviews with artists and poets, who, in their turn, were inspired by their graces. They thus gave themselves an education which custom prohibited to the pure young girl and the faithful wife. The husband, who could find nothing to say to his wife, who knew so little and held an inferior position, solaced himself for his domestic wearinesses by the lively and witty conversation of the courtesan. It is true the *hetæræ* were held in contempt, but that did not prevent austere philosophers and illustrious statesmen from passing their time at the feet of a Phryne or an Aspasia.[48]

The *hetæræ* were nowhere more numerous than in Corinth, where they served the temple of Aphrodite, which in the second century still justified the title of Corinth to be the most licentious city of Greece.[49] There, the married man, who cared little for his wife, was allowed to take the slaves of his own household as concubines. The only concession which the law made to morality was to deprive any children who might be born of their civil rights; but the father was allowed to adopt them, and they often shared even the love of the mother, along with her rightful children.

Things were just the same in Rome. After the last century before Christ, ancient severity of manners was relaxed in all ranks of society. It was not the people alone who frequented the *lupanar*. The rich man, the senator, the patrician, lost themselves in these places, where they found women like the *hetæræ* of Greece, a little above the lowest rank. There were dancers, mimes, players on the flute or lyre, living sometimes on their own account, and sometimes sharing the orgies of young Romans of high family, whom they ruined by their luxury. These were the Lesbias, Delias, and Cynthias of the libertine poets of the Augustan age, who were in turn sung for their wanton caresses or disdainfully deserted, according to the caprices of these impure and fleeting loves. Grave men, whose dignified position or illustrious name kept them from descending so low, saw no disgrace in living with concubines. Sallust already remarked with regret the decay of the ancient morality of the Republic.[50]

In the Augustan age these irregularities were so great that concubinage was publicly tolerated, and acknowledged and regulated by the laws; instead of being repressed, it was made almost legal. The name of *nuces injustæ* was given to habitual intimacy with a female of inferior rank, with whom marriage was prohibited by law. Concubinage became a legal union; differing from lawful marriage in that it assigned no duties to the husband, who was also free from the law against adultery.[51] This concession to the license of the age took away all force from the laws of Augustus against celibacy, and from those which forbade marriage with a woman of inferior rank. Although concubinage was no longer considered a disgrace, those whom the ancients had called concubines now took the more decent name of friends.[52] Tombs were raised to their memory, on which their description was inscribed without any shock to morality; it even happened that the name of the wife and the concubine who followed after her death were engraved upon the same marble.[53] The law went no farther than to forbid the Romans to have more than one concubine, or to have one along with a legal wife. Throughout the whole duration of the Empire the greatest men, and the emperors who were the most renowned for their virtues, such as Vespasian and Marcus Aurelius, lived openly in unions of this kind.

The public prostitutes were the only persons branded with infamy.[54] Domitian, with the hope of diminishing their numbers, degraded them still further; he deprived them of the right of inheriting or of receiving a legacy.[55] But this measure was ineffectual against an evil so firmly rooted. The State, finding itself too weak to stop this disgraceful profession, which was then, as it is still, only the result of pagan ideas about the inferiority of a weak and despised sex, had long tolerated it and even sought to profit by it. Solon had already established houses of public debauchery in Athens, and had levied a tax on the women who inhabited them, the revenue from which had sufficed to build a temple to the vagabond Venus;[56] after his time the Athenian Government annually let this revenue to private persons.[57] In Rome, after the time of Caligula, a like tax was raised by the fiscal.[58] Alexander Severus, one of the most moral of the emperors, unable to suppress this tribute raised from the vilest corruption, at least refused to receive it in the public treasury, but employed it solely for the support of the circuses and amphitheatres.[59] It is melancholy to be compelled to say that this infamous tax continued to be levied during the Christian period of the empire, and still is in our own times. When will the power of Christianity be strong enough to abolish it, along with the profession at which it is aimed, and which in striking it authorizes?

Besides this tribute, the depth of the corruption of Roman morality and the contempt of the laws and magistrates for women are still further proved by the sentences of the judges, who, in the persecutions of the Church, condemned Christians to the *lupanar*, or gave them up to the savage brutality of the executioners or of the gladiators. The "Acts of the Martyrs" give many examples of these decisions, as barbarous as they were cowardly, which compelled Christian maidens to become prostitutes or to renounce Christ.[60] The pagans understood the great respect paid to chastity by the Christians,[61] and therefore these sentences were the more odious, and showed more completely their contempt both for Christianity and for human dignity in women. "Thou hast been a prostitute," said the judge to Saint Afra; "go then and sacrifice to the gods; thou art unworthy of the God of the Christians, who knows thee not." [62] Christian virgins would a thousand times rather have given their bodies to wild beasts in the Coliseum, but in sacrificing a treasure more precious than life for their faith their heroism was still more sublime.

§ 3. *Adultery and Divorce.*

It is easy to foresee, as the result of these ideas about woman and marriage, that adultery committed by a man would not be severely punished by the ancients. The moral character of marriage was absorbed in its civil and political aspects. Adultery, then, was regarded as an infringement of the rights of the husband; as an attack on his property, which brought trouble within his threshold, where he alone reigned supreme. In both Greece and Rome immediate revenge was permitted, the husband was allowed to kill his guilty wife as well as the man with whom the crime was committed.[63] If he did not wish himself to avenge his outraged honour, he had the power of accusing his wife. This was a masculine right, and was not possessed by the woman; she could not make a complaint against her husband if he violated conjugal fidelity.[64]

The pride of the husbands wished the adulterous wife to be severely punished, but it would have been an attack on manly majesty if they had been punished in their turn. "We are men," they said; "how will the dignity of our sex bear the insult, if we submit to the same penalties as women if we are not satisfied with our wives?"[65] These accepted their humiliating position unmurmuringly. They learned absolute submission; they persuaded themselves that the husband's dignity was above attack and authorized all transgressions. If a woman was sorrowful on this account, she was told for her consolation that the virtue of woman does not consist in superintending her husband, but in conforming herself to his wishes. This derisive comfort was given by a woman, Theano, the wife of Pythagoras.[66]

Violation and rape were punished as lightly as adultery. It was hardly a disgrace for a young girl to allow herself to be seduced.[67] Violation was perfectly repaired by marriage, and was only an infringement of the laws protecting her father's property. In Athens, rape was punished as a slight offence, with mild penalties. In

Rome, where in the times of the decadence, rape, committed even by married men, was very frequent, the young girl might demand the death of the ravisher, or reparation by marriage with him.[68] To leave the decision to her, who was as often an accomplice as a victim, could hardly be to punish the crime.

The final result of all these principles and legal dispositions as to the position of women and their relationship to men was the weakening of the moral sense in a sex in whose destiny the welfare of society is more intimately bound up than was ever imagined by pagan society. The vices of men, tolerated by the law, and rather justified than energetically condemned by the morality of philosophers, were made into excuses for the vices of women.[69] After the time in Greece and Rome when ancient austerity was relaxed, and political virtues gave place to individual egoism, married women themselves broke free from the ties to which they submitted in the interest of the Republic, and hastened in the path of unruly emancipation, where they followed the *hetæræ* and courtesans. They acquainted themselves with the art and literature of Greece, which instead of forming their taste only familiarized them with vice. The time had gone by when the Romans, less corrupted than now, forbade their wives and daughters to read the poets and philosophers of Greece, in the fear that instead of learning wisdom they would find only lessons in libertinism.[70] Henceforth they eagerly read the works of the Greeks. Besides the poets, the Republic of Plato attracted and charmed them. Whilst the men took advantage of the chimeras of the great philosopher about women, to justify their numerous and changing loves,[71] the women seized this argument in favour of the unbounded licentiousness of their lives.[72] They were not attached to their family by any sentiment of duty. Giving up the care of the house and children to slaves, who were as depraved as themselves, they occupied themselves with nothing but dress and luxury, lovers and parrots, games in the circus or adventures at the *lupanar*. There was nothing in which they did not indulge or which they thought a disgrace.[73] Very few marriages remained pure;[74] a chaste wife was considered as a phenomenon astonishing by its rarity.[75] Free women who belonged to noble families asked to have their names entered amongst the public prostitutes, in order that they might not be punished for adultery. They claimed the privileges of infamy, that they might more safely continue their scandalous life. This was forbidden under Tiberius by a *senatusconsultum*, but only to ladies of the equestrian order.[76]

Even in the time of Augustus it was difficult to find young girls belonging to free families willing to devote themselves to the vestal priesthood, so eagerly sought before that time; their number had to be recruited from the enfranchised. Tiberius increased their salary and created new honorary distinctions, to attract the required number.[77] They behaved in the same disorderly manner as other women; neither the character of their office nor the punishments inflicted by Domitian restrained them from the downward paths of vice.[78] Augustus had tried to arrest the demoralization of women by some new laws.[79] He was obliged to enforce them rigorously against his own daughter Julia, who was addicted to the most scandalous excesses.[80] But these measures produced no effect on the mass of the people, contradicted as they were by the life of the emperor himself.

Licentiousness was so general in Rome that the professors of rhetoric who instructed the young Romans in judicial eloquence, chose for their special study questions relating to rape or adultery. The young advocates in their declamations endeavoured to strengthen or elude the law according to the position and wishes of the accuser or accused.[81] Justice, debased by despotism, lost its severity, and allowed the immodesty of women to be exhibited with unspeakable boldness in the highest ranks of Roman society, as completely as in its lowest depths.[82]

The facility of divorce increased instead of lessening this corruption. Divorce was in complete accord with the spirit of ancient society. Marriage, deprived of all moral character, was no longer a sacred bond, an alliance of souls, although a Roman jurisconsult had defined it as a community of things human and divine.[83] After the time when political considerations prevailed, it became only a union formed solely through personal interest. It established external relationships which imposed no duty of reciprocal fidelity, and which demanded neither concession nor sacrifice, because they did not lead to union of soul, and consequently might be broken, provided the rupture was made with the accustomed formalities. According to some writers, divorce had been unknown in Rome during several centuries.[84] The great simplicity of manners and the preponderance of the influence of the State had guarded the indissoluble duration of marriage.

Divorce was introduced as a consequence of the decline of morality, as a convenient method of gaining freedom, to pursue all the caprices of libertinism with a certain regard to the law. Throughout the whole period of the pagan empire, from the later republican times, divorce played an important part in the internal history of Roman society. Sometimes the man asked for it, sometimes the woman; it was sought without real motive and for the slightest reasons.[85] A Roman questioned by his friends why he had put away his wife, who was young, rich, and beautiful, showed them his shoe, saying, "You see this is new and beautiful; no one knows however where it pinches me."[86]

Mæcenas, the celebrated patron of artists and men of letters, passed his life in elegant and effeminate debauchery, and made himself famous by his thousand marriages and daily divorces.[87] He had so many imitators, that Augustus, after availing himself of divorce in a way that was a public scandal, was compelled to limit the ease with which marriage might be dissolved.[88] He enforced some formalities which were not enough to stop the evil.[89] Women asked for it as often as men.[90] Tertullian says that they only married that they might obtain liberty through divorce.[91] This license, which powerless laws and corrupt morality allowed to women, along with the disuse of the ancient more solemn forms of marriage, ended in complete annihilation of the husband's power, which existed only in name under the Empire.[92] Marriage thus lost the last remnant of its importance in public opinion. The depravity of woman and of all society increased at a rate to which no human law could oppose a sufficiently strong barrier. Woman in freeing herself from the tyranny of ancient institutions, had also emancipated herself from the external laws of morality; she had freed herself only to increase her burden of vice, for which the civilization of the pagan world provided no remedy.

§ 4. *Children. Paternal Authority.*

The same contempt for individual worth, the same submission of man's dignity to the State's interest, and consequently the same exercise of the right of the strongest, was found in the relation of father to children, before their emancipation.

The family, in the opinion of antiquity, was instituted only in the interest of the Republic. We shall even see it completely destroyed to allow the State to remain alone in its despotism. The father was the chief of the family, the master of the children. They owed him unlimited respect and obedience; they belonged to him; they were his property, to be disposed of according to his own will. In his relations in regard to them he might not take the counsels of natural affection, he must consult only public interest. Rome and Greece were unanimous in this respect. "The son," said Aristotle, "before attaining manhood himself belongs entirely to the father. Although superior to a slave, he has only an imperfect reason and will; therefore he is in absolute dependence upon his father, who, it is true, ought to use his power only for his son's good, but we know that his good was swallowed up in that of the State, which was the only condition of good fortune." [93] In Rome authority over children was one of the special rights of a citizen.[94] Paternity, which was rather strained than strengthened by the institutions of the ancient world, was a true magistracy in the interior of the family, and this magistracy was despotic even to cruelty. It gave the father the extravagant right of ridding himself of those children whom he considered unlikely ever to be serviceable to the State. The ancient Republics, where strength ruled and where the virtues of citizens required not only a trained intelligence but a robust body, required vigorous generations for their defence and continuance. Why then should those puny beings be reared who gave no promise of help for the State? Further, as one could only be a citizen through owning a fortune, and the poor had an aimless existence, why should that man keep his children whom he would be unable to feed, and who would be of no use to society? Therefore the right of the exposure of new-born children was given to the father by the most civilized nations of antiquity.

This right was modified in Thebes by a law which tended to save the children from death. Parents who were too poor to bring up their children presented them to the magistrates, who sold them to the first citizen who offered a price, however small it might be. The buyer kept them as slaves, and by the services they rendered to him they were expected to testify to their gratitude that he had saved their life.[95] In ancient Italy, Romulus forbade the custom of killing useless children, which he found already established; but he allowed the exposure of those who were weak or deformed, on condition that the neighbours verified their miserable condition.[96] The law of the twelve tables returned to the older and more expeditious practice; it ordered that the child born deformed should be killed without delay.[97] Directly after birth the child was presented to the father, who accepted or refused it. In accepting it he engaged to bring it up, otherwise it was exposed.[98] This formality of presentation and acceptance remained long in Rome, even to a period when in rich families habits were in this respect improved.[99]

We should certainly expect to find the philosophers, wholly dependent though they were on the egoistic spirit of antiquity, at least protest against a custom so contrary to the deepest feelings of the human heart; but, instead of blaming it, they find sophisms in its justification. Plato not only requires that deformed and ailing children shall be exposed in secret places; he also finds that it is not advisable to bring up the children of parents belonging to the lower classes of the Republic.[100] Aristotle agreed with him. He desired a law to prohibit the preservation in life of puny children.[101] Still further, these geniuses, so great in other respects, but whose natural feelings had been stifled by pagan politics, saw a danger if the population should increase beyond a certain limit. According to them, the egoistic interest of their aristocratic State required that the poor should not have too many children; especially as the poor themselves did not know what to do with them. They were willing to allow the conjugal union, but with the coldest indifference they counselled abortion. They gave the same advice to all who feared the care of a large family.[102]

These counsels of sages and permissions of legislators were followed only too often. They spread even beyond the limits intended by their authors. The citizen who had no pretext of poverty exposed other than feeble children. Sometimes a father who did not wish to divide his fortune in too many portions, or to give dowries to too many daughters, freed himself thus from the children who embarrassed his plans.[103]

This custom of exposure was continued in the Christian period of the Empire. Even in the fourth century there were parents who, notwithstanding the prohibitions of the emperor, strangled or exposed their new-born children.[104]

The fate of these unhappy exposed ones is easy to divine. Often, doubtless, they served as food for wild beasts. From time to time a married woman rescued one, to please her husband who desired an heir;[105] but generally those who were saved were destined for slavery or the *lupanar*. Whoever took charge of them possessed them as things deserted on the high road; he was their master, and could either sell them or abuse them.[106]

The child was subject to paternal authority until the day of his emancipation. If he married or obtained public office before this time, he still remained, as did also his own children, under the absolute authority of his father. The personality of children disappeared, so to speak, in that of the father. In Rome an apparently strange law did not recognise the right of the latter to accuse his son before the tribunals. *Natural* right was appealed to, to explain this refusal; as a man cannot bring an action against himself, so neither can he bring one against the child who is in his own power.[107] All that the son possessed belonged to the father; all that he gained before emancipation went to swell the paternal property. The father alone had a will in the family. He decided the marriages of the children. The daughter especially was compelled to take the husband whom her father chose. She was his chattel; he could send her away without her own consent.[108]

The sole master of his fortune, he was under no bonds to his children. The power of disposing of his wealth was without limit or condition; he could leave it to whom he would, and disinherit his children without any cause.[109] If he died without a will, the succession went to the son who, married or unmarried, was under his power at the time of his death. The emancipated sons who had left the family were excluded, as also were the daughters, whom the Voconian law had deprived of the right of inheritance. The emancipated son succeeded only in default of direct heirs in the Roman sense. If there was no son at all, the *agnates* were sought in order that the patrimony, which symbolised the race of the father, might never pass to strangers.[110]

Paternal authority was not restricted to the enormous rights that we have just mentioned; there were others equally exorbitant and founded on the same principle. In both Athens and Rome the father could sell his children, even adults; ancient Roman law bestowed upon him the right of life or death, even over those whom he had accepted at the time of their birth.[111] He filled the office of judge in the family; the right, or rather the natural duty of correction was carried to the barbarous length of bestowing the power to inflict capital punishment on the child who disobeyed paternal authority. Armed with the executioner's axe, the father compelled from his family a respect which was only fear inspired by the fiercest tyranny.

Famous examples of the enforcement of this right are well known. We will leave others the privilege of admiring the republican virtue of a Cassius or a Manlius Torquatus in condemning his son to death. We see in these facts only a proof of Roman harshness, which proudly sacrificed rightful affection to the State, if this affection yet existed in the hearts of men. Even in the time of Augustus there were fathers who availed themselves of this right. The Chevalier Erixon beat two of his sons to death. The people, it is true, rose in tumult and stabbed him.[112] Custom no longer agreed with the ancient law; but it had not been formally annulled.

We know very little of the condition in ancient society of those children who lost their parents before they were old enough to take care of themselves. In Athens the orphans of citizens were under the protection of the archons. Those whose father had died for the State were brought up at the expense of the State, through gratitude, and because they formed part of the community of the State of which the father himself was a member. In Rome there was a legal guardianship for those who had wealth to administer; but neither the State nor the more wealthy citizens cared for those who had none.

Doubtless in most cases they were reduced to seek their means of existence in servitude or infamy.

§ 5. *Education.*

The need of education was recognised by philosophers and written in the laws. Socrates said nothing was more worthy of the meditations of the sage than the methods of education for himself and those belonging to him.[113] But the external direction of ancient civilization imprinted a fatal tendency on these meditations, from which the greatest spirits were unable to free themselves.

The highest aim of education was not to develop the individuality whilst correcting its vices, but to form the child for civil life, to teach him political virtues, to excite rather than rebuke the pride of the citizen. If the child ought to be brought up only for the good of the State, it is natural that the State alone should take charge of him. The family must be sacrificed, its influence on education must be nothing, or it must be greatly restricted; for even here, in the stronghold of paternal power, the child belongs first to the Republic. Therefore Plato desired that the children of well-to-do people, that is of the aristocratic classes of society, should be entrusted to public nurses in such a way that no mother should be able to distinguish which was her own child.[114] From his earliest days the child should learn only to know the State, to which he would be devoted at a later time. Torn from the natural tenderness of the mother whom he must ignore for ever, he must be given to the cold and despotic care of the Republic, jealous of all affection of which it was not the sole object. Aristotle, notwithstanding his warmer feeling of the lawful demands of nature, also asked that the education of children should not be left entirely to the parents. He considered it to be contrary to the public interest to allow each father to educate his children himself; the State ought to take charge of education, which should be the first duty of every legislator.

This public education, in which the State was substituted for the family, was only completely realised in Sparta. This Republic was a body organized in its smallest details. Individual liberty did not exist there. Each citizen was a member whose part was decided beforehand, and who was nothing outside his assigned position. It was necessary to begin early to prepare children to take their place in this mechanism. Their education was then solely an affair of State. They were taken from their earliest years and educated away from the paternal home, in order to cultivate their strength and capabilities with a sole view to political interests. As warriors were specially needed to defend an existence brought about by conquest, the education given consisted principally of gymnastic and military exercises. Even the young girls were trained in a manner to develop their mental courage and bodily strength.[115] Such a system could only have been carried out by a legislation as contrary to human nature, as was that of Lycurgus. There was a vice inherent in it, which was bound to ruin both itself and Sparta.

Everywhere else, both in Greece and Rome, paternal education was not absolutely prohibited, though it was founded on the same definite principles. They never tried to bring up the man, before training the citizen. The man being mixed with the citizen, all their efforts tended to give the child the virtues which would assure his position in the State. The laws were the general rules of education; parents had only to point out their application in the different circumstances of life.[116]

In this education, intended chiefly to promote physical and intellectual development, little care was taken to encourage feeling and affection. It was useless to arouse the depths of conscience, as morality consisted in keeping the laws. The mother's mission was consequently reduced to the needful physical cares during the earliest years. We never hear amongst the ancients of maternal rights or duties. Antiquity neglected to place the mother's tenderness by the side of the father's formidable authority. Ancient wisdom ignored the importance of this necessary and natural tenderness in the work of education. They allowed that the mother loved her children, often even more than the father, but a Greek poet could find no better explanation of her love than one utterly discreditable to the spirit of the times.[117]

It is true that woman was permitted to watch over and guide her children in their earliest infancy; but this was not a prerogative but an almost servile charge that the father, engaged in external occupation, left to her care. If she interfered in the education of her sons, she also thought only of the virtues of the citizen. The wife of Pythagoras, writing to a friend, advised her to avoid all gentleness in educating her son, but by harsh treatment to prepare him for the practice of temperance and courage.[118] Cornelia was celebrated for the vigorous and patriotic education which she gave her sons.[119]

We shall be asked perhaps by what principles the education of girls was regulated. We understand why moralists thought so little about how they should be brought up when we remember the inferior position given to them by ancient society. Their chief virtue was submission, which was taught them by the strict authority of the father. The handiwork which helped to charm the long weariness of the wife, shut up in the *gynæceum*, was taught to the young girl either by her mother or by slaves. This imperfect education was bound to have, in the long run, results equally unfortunate for the women, as the purely political education had for the men. Both lacked a basis in the soul itself; directed solely to externals, they had no root in the moral conscience. The ancient spirit, in neglecting to combat the egoism in a child's heart, in order to develop in him only pride and civic virtues, could not give to these virtues either their true motive or their most solid support. A time was bound to come when political education would become powerless against the force of individual egoism.

In the times of the decadence, education for public life disappeared, without being replaced by that for family life, which was foreign to the temper of ancient society. The father, rushing after pleasure or lost in intrigue, no longer occupied himself with his sons; the mother, wholly given to luxury and adventures, not only wasted her children's fortune, but abandoned them to the care of impure nurses or ignorant slaves. Provided that they learned to speak Greek early, she remained perfectly indifferent to the pernicious influences to which they were exposed.[120] Others sent their children to one of the public schools, where boys and girls were mixed together, and which, without moral oversight or strict control, were only schools of precocious depravity.[121] When the children had reached the age at which their education ought to be completed by literary instruction, they were trusted to lettered slaves; and these teachers were often chosen from amongst the least capable servants. He who was good for nothing as husbandman, steward, or boatman, was thought good enough to complete the education of the sons of patricians.[122]

The development of public instruction amongst the

ancients is beyond the subject of our work. It must suffice us to have characterized the spirit of the education which was given to youth. We have seen it claimed originally by the State as one of its most important duties, yet left at last to fall into the hands of the most incapable slaves. We know that there were always consoling exceptions; but a society must be rapidly nearing its fall when the noble mission of training the mind and soul of children can be regarded as a servile occupation unworthy of a freeman. Antiquity had never required any but civic virtues. To these virtues she had owed her greatness. But they could not be taught by slaves; when they had disappeared, they were judged unnecessary. Pagan civilization had no others with which to replace them; and henceforth the descendants of the proudest republicans were educated by slaves, to be governed by despots.

(1) We do not share the opinion of Fr. Jacobs, who, in his " Beiträge zur Geschichte des weiblichen Geschlechts " (*Vermischte Schriften, Leben und Kunst der Alten.* Leipz., vol. iii. p. 159 ff.), maintains that in ancient times the condition of woman was far better than is commonly supposed. (2) *Polit.*, I. 1, 5, pp. 4, 25. (3) Cf. Van Stegeren, *De conditione civili feminarum Atheniensium.* Zwoll, 1839, p. 139 ff. (4) Majestas virorum, . imbecillitas mulicrum et levitas animi, etc.; *e.g.*, Val. Max., II. 1, § 6, p. 84. Caius, I. § 144, p. 74. (5) Stobœus, t. LXXII. Uxorem ducere non esse bonum, and tit. LXXII. Vituperatio mulierum, pp. 277, 307. (6.) Plato, *De Leg.*, VI. p. 386. Tacit., *Ann.* III. 33, vol. i. p. 152. (7) Aul. Gell., I. 6, vol. i. p. 50. (8) The Voconian Law, Cicer., *De Rep.*, III. 7 ed. Lemaire, p. 301. (9) *De Leg.*, VI. p. 368. (10) Ib., IV. p. 254; VI. p. 370. (11) Ib., IV. p. 254. (12) Xenoph., *De Rep. Laced.*, c. 1, vol. vi. p. 15. (13) Eurip., *Androm.*, 575 ff., vol. i. p. 461. Arist., *Polit.* II. 8, p. 61. (14) Arist., *Polit.* II. 2., p. 33. (15) T. II. p. 515. (16) *Polit.*, II. 2 ff., p. 33 ff. (17) De verum natura. Leipz. 1801, p. 39 ff. (18) *De Rep.*, V. pp. 272, 276; *De Leg.*, V. p. 294. (19) Xenoph., *Memorab.*, II. 2, vol. iv. p. 84. (20) Columella, *De Re Rust.*, XII. præf. in *Script. Rei Rust.*, vol. ii. p. 467. (21) Corn. Nepos, præf. p. 4. *Menandri Fragm.* p. 90. (22) *Polit.* I. 1. p. 4. (23) Ib., c. 5, p. 24. (24) Isæus, *De Aristarchi Næredebros.* 610; in *Oratt. Att.*, vol. iii. p. 121. (25) *e.g.*, Demosth., in *Androtiona*, § 53; in *O. c.*, vol. iv. p. 547. (26) Xenoph., *Œcon.* c. 3, § 12, vol. v. p. 19. (27) *e.g.*, Plautus, *Mercator*, Act IV. Sc. 6, v. 1 ff., vol. ii. p.

154. (28) *Dig.*, XXIII. tit. 2, 1. 49. (29) Ib., 1. 23. (30) Ib., ll. 27 and 31. (31) Ib., l. 42. (32) " Uxor quoque quæ in manu est . . . filiæ loco est." Caius, III. § 3, p. 207. (33) Tacit., *Annal.*, I. 10, V. 1; vol. i. p. 12, 250. (34) Tertull., *Apolog.*, c. 39, p. 122. (35) *Dig.*, XVIII. tit. 3, ll. 1 and 7. (36) Cf. the law "De liberis exhibendis."—*Dig.*, XVII. tit. 30. (37) Plautus, *Trinummus*, Act II. Sc. 2, vv. 93, 94, vol. ii. p. 161. (38) Tacit., *Annal.*, IV., c. 16, vol. 1, p. 199. (39) Caius, I. § 157, p. 78. (40) *Pausan.*, X. 38, § 6, vol. iii. p. 694. (41) Demosth., *Pro Phormione*, § 8, in *Oratt. Att.*, vol. v. p. 212. (42) Valer. Max., II. 9, p. 122. Cf. Osann, *De cælibum apud veteres populos conditione*, Giessen, 1844, qto. (43) Aul. Gell., I. vol. i. p. 50. (44) The Lex Julia and Pappia Poppæa. Dio Cassius, LIV. 16, vol. ii. p. 63. (45) See, for example, Ovid's *Amores*, and the selections from the poets Ap. Stobæus, tit. 63, 64, p. 238 ff. The love tales of the first centuries A.D. Appian, *Halieut.*, IV. vv. 37, 38, p. 41, in *Opp. Ven.*, Ald. 1517, 8°. (46) Cicer., *Tusc. Disp.*, IV. 32 ff., vol. x. p. 523 ff. (47) *Parad.* V. vol. xii. p. 252. (48) Cf. Athenæus, 1. XII. vol. v. Socrates to Theodotes, Xenoph., *Memorab.*, III. 11, vol. iv. p. 187 ff.; Pseudo Demosth., *In Neæram.*, § 45 ff, *Oratt. Att.*,vol. v. p, 556. (49) Dio Chrysos says to the Corinthians, " Ye inhabit a city more licentious than any city either of the past or present time."—*Cr.* 37, vol. ii. p. 119. (50) Sallust., *De Bello Catil.*, c. 13, vol. i. p. 23. Seneca, *De Ira*, II. 8, vol. i. p. 36. (51) *Dig.*, XXV., tit. 7, l. 3; also XLVIII. Act 5. (52) " . . . Nunc vero nomine amicam, paulo honestiore, concubinam appellari," Paulus *ap. Dig.*, L. tit. 16, 1. 144. (53) " Concubina mei amantissima." Gruber, vol. i. p. 640, No. 8; p. 631, No. 5, etc. (54) Quintil., *Insit. Orat.*, VI. 3, vol. i. p. 375. (55) Sueton., *Domit.*, c. 8, p. 381. *Dig.*, XXII. tit. 5. 1. 3, § 5. (56) Athenæus, XIII. 25, vol. v. p. 56. (57) " Πορνικὸν τέλος." Æschin., *Contra Timarchum*, in *Oratt. Att.* vol. iii. p. 289. (58) Sueton., *Caligula*, c. 40–41, p. 204. (59) Lamprid., *Al. Sev.*,c. 24, in *Scriptt. Hist. Aug.*, vol. i. p. 274. (60) Euseb., *Hist. Eccl.*, VI. 5, p. 207 ; *De Martyr. Palæst.*, cpp. 5, 8, p. 326, 331. Palladius, *Hist. Laus.*, c. 3, p. 18. In 304 A.D. St. Irene was condemned : " I direct that the apparitors and public executioner make her to stand naked in the *lupanar*; that she draw one loaf per day from the palace, the apparitors themselves taking care that she does not get away."—*Acta Mart.*, Ruinart, p. 395. See also *Acta S. Theodoræ*, Ib., p. 397, etc. Prudentius says of St. Agnes :

"This maiden to the public brothel they consign,
Unless she bow before the heathen shrine."

(*Peristeph*. hymn 14, v. 25, 26, p. 256). "They order the maiden either to sacrifice or to be taken to the *lupanar*."—Ambros., *De Virgin.*, II. 4, § 23, vol. ii. p. 168. (61) " For recently too, by condemning the Christian maiden to the brothel (*ad lenonem*) instead of to the lions (*ad leonem*), you acknowledge that to us the violation of chastity is more dreadful than any other form of punishment or death."—Tertull., *Apolog.*, 50, p. 163. Ruinart, *Acta Mart.*, p. 455. (62) " Behold our maidens meet death calmly, with their honour intact, not dreading the threats and corruptions and *lupanars* of the coming Antichrist."—Cypr., *De Mortal.* p. 233. (63) Xenoph., *Hiero*, c. 3, vol. v. p. 239 ; *Pausan.*, IX. 36, § 4, vol. iii. p. 424 ; Quintil., *Speeches*, 347, vol. iii. p. 335. (64) Lex Julia, *Corp. Jur.*, IX. tit. 9, 1. 1 ff. "With pagan men a free rein is given to all lasciviousness. Only adultery is condemned by the law, while in the *lupanar* with inferior persons there are no restrictions imposed on lust; as though, forsooth! the wrongness of the act lay in the rank of the person, not in the intention."—Hieron., *Ep.* 77, vol. i. p. 459. "But some one will say, She is not a prostitute whom I keep; she is my concubine. Most holy Bishop, thou makest my concubine into an harlot. . . . Thou sayest my handmaiden is my concubine. Do I go in to another man's wife? Do I go to the public harlot? Can I do what I like in my own house?" —August., *Sermo* 224, § 3, vol. v. p. 674–5. (65) "Sed nos viri sumus; an vero sexus nostri dignitas hanc sustinebit injuriam, ut cum aliis feminis præter uxores nostras si quid admittimus, in luendis poenis mulieribus comparemur?"—Ap. August., *De Conjugiis Adult.*, II. 8, vol. vi. p. 299. (66) "Ταμετῆς γὰρ ἀρετή ἐστιν οὐχ ἡ παρατήρησις τοῦ ἀνδὼς ἀλλ' ἡ συμπεριφορά."—Theano *ad Nicostratam*; in *Mulierum Græc. Fragm.*, p. 228. (67) Plutarch, *Quæst. Sympos.*, VII., quæst. 8, c. 3, vol. xi. p. 326. (68) Id., *Vita Solonis*, c. 23, vol. 1. p. 227; Quintil., *Speeches*, 262, vol. iii. p. 69. (69) "And this wickedness has produced, in the first instance, adultery, since the women are not content to keep good faith themselves to husbands who do not reciprocate their affection. In a word, there is no adulteress, however dead to all sense of shame, who may not plead this excuse for her sin, that she is not doing her husband a wrong, but only repaying a wrong he has done her."—Lactant., *Div. Insit.*, VI. 23, vol. i. p. 501. (70) Seneca, *Consol. ad Helviam*, c. 16, vol. i., p. 139. (71) Cf. Hieron., *Ep.* 69, vol. i. p. 415. (72) Epict., *Fragm.* 53, vol. iii. p. 84. (73) See Juvenal's sixth satire, which is summed up in these words: "Nil non permittit mulier sibi, turpe putat nil," v. 457, p. 72. (74) Tacit., *Ann.*, III. 34, vol. i. p. 154. (75) "Rara avis in terris," etc.—Juvenal, *Sat.* VI. 161, p. 69. (76) Tacit., *Ann.*, II. 85, vol. i. p. 125; Sueton., *Tiber.*, c. 35, p. 149; *Dig.*, XLVIII. tit. 5, l. 13, § 2. (77) Suet., *Octav.*, c. 31, p. 75; Tacit., *Ann.*, IV. 16, vol. i. p. 200. (78) Suet., *Domit.*, c. 8, p. 381. (79) Id., *Octav.*, c. 34, p. 78; Dio Cassius, LIV. 16, vol. ii. p. 63. (80) Seneca, *De Benef.*, VI. 32, vol. ii. p. 297. (81) Amongst the speeches ascribed to Quintilian, forty are taken up with questions of adultery, and thirty with questions of rape, vol. iii. (82) *Vide* Tacitus, Juvenal, Martial; also the picture drawn by Clem. Alex., *Pædag.*, III. 2 ff., vol. i. p. 253 ff. (83) Modestinus, *Ap. Dig.* XXIII., t. ii. l. 1. (84) Aul. Gell., IV. 3, vol. i. p. 180; Tertull., *Apolog.*, c. 6, p. 27. (85) Cœlius to Cicero, *Epp. ad Div.*, VIII., ep. 7, vol. vii. p. 256. Seneca, *De Benef.*, III. 16, vol. ii. p. 185. "Collige sarcinulas, dicet libertus (to the wife who is to be sent off) et exi; jam gravis es nobis, et sæpe emungeris, exi Ocius; et propera; sicco venit altera naso."—*Juven.*, VI. v. 146 ff. p. 69. (86) Plutarch, *Conjugialia Præcepta*, vol vii. p. 417. (87) "Qui uxorem millies duxit . . ." "Quotidiana repudia," Seneca, *Ep.* 114, vol. iv. p. 86; *De Provid.*, c. 3. vol. i. p. 227. (88) Suet., *Octav.*, c. 34, p. 78. (89) The Lex Julia. *Dig.*, XXXVIII. tit. 11, l. 1. (90) Juvenal, VI. 229, 230, p. 72. (91) "Repudium vero jam et votum est, quasi matrimonii fructus."— Tertull., *Apol.*, c. 6, p. 27. (92) Cf. M. Troplong, *De l'Influence du Christianisme sur le droit civil des Romains*, Par. 1843, p. 316 ff. (93) *Politico*, I. 5, p. 23. (94) *Dig.*, I. tit. 6, l. 3, 4. (95) Ælian, II. 7, vol. i. p. 69. (96) Dion Halic., II. 15, vol. i. p. 85. (97) "Pater filium monstrosum, et contra formam generis humani, recens sibi natum, cito necato."—Tab. 4 in Cicer., *Opp.*, vol. xi. p. 430. (98) Cf. Terence, *Audria*, Act II. Sc. 3, vv. 26, 27, vol. i. p. 36. (99) In Cicero's Orations, he often speaks of fathers who "suscipiunt" (*i.e.*, take up) their children.—*In Verr.*, II. 1. 111. c. 69, vol. iii. p. 477; *Philipp*. III. § 6, vol. vi. p. 279. (100) "It follows that the best of both sexes ought to be brought together as often as possible, and the worst as seldom as possible; and that the issue of the former unions ought to be reared, and that of the latter to be abandoned." "The issue of inferior parents, and all imperfect children that are born to the others, will be concealed, as is fitting, in some mysterious and unknown place."—*De Rep.*, V. p. 272-274. (101) "And concerning the abandonment or rearing of newborn children, let it be law that no deformed child be reared."—*Polit.*,VII. 14, p. 239. (102) Plato, *De Rep.*, V. p. 276; Arist., *Polit.*, l. c. (103) Terence, *Adelphi*, Act V. Sc. 1, vv. 23-4, vol. ii. p. 98. (104) Lactant., *Div. Inst.*, V. 9; VI. 20, vol. i. p. 388 491. Constantine's Laws A.D. 315 and 321, *Cod. Theod.*, XI. tit. 27, ll. 1, 2. (105) Cf. Juvenal, VI. 602 sq., p. 84. (106) Just. Mart., *Apol.* 1, c. 27, p. 60; Lactant., *Div. Instit.*, VI., c. 20, vol. i. p. 491. (107) *Dig.*, XLIII. tit. 2, l. 16. (108) Ib., XXIII. tit. 1. (109) Ib., XXXV. tit. 1. 1; XXVII. tit. 2, l. 11. (110) *Instit.*, III. tit. 1, § 9. (111) Plutarch, *Vital Sol.*, c. 13, vol. i. p. 212; "Law of the XII. Tables," Table IV., in *Cicer. Opp.*, vol. xi. p. 430. (112) Seneca, *De Clem.*, I, 14. vol. ii. p. 22. (113) Plato, *Theages*, in *Opp.*, vol. vii. p. 386 ff. (114) *De Rep.*, V. p. 274. (115) Xenoph., *De Rep. Laced.*, II. vol. vi. p. 16 ff.; Arist., *Polit.*, VIII. p. i. 245. (116) Plato, *De Leg.*, II. p. 76 ff. Aristot., *Eth. Nicom.*, X, 9, p. 207. (117) "Ἔστιν δὲ μήτηρ φιλότεκνος μᾶλλον πατρὸς, ἡ μὲν γὰρ αὑτῆς οἶδεν υἱοῦ, ὃ δ'οἴετκι"—Menander, Ap. Stob., tit. 76, p. 329. (118) Theona ad enbulam, in Mul. *Græc. Fragm.*, p. 224 ff. (119) See too what Plutarch says of Cato and his wife, *Vita. Cat. Mag.*, c. 20, vol. ii., p. 415. (120) *De Oratoribus Dialogus*, c. 29, in *Opp.* Taciti, vol. iv. p. 180. (121) Cf. M. Naudet's treatise, *Sur l'Instruction Publique chez les Anciens et particulièrement chez les Romains.*—*Mém. de l'Acad. des Inscriptions*, vol. ix. (1831) p. 411 ff. (122) Plutarch, *De Liberis Educandis*, c. 7. vol. vii. p. 13.

CHAPTER III.

THE LABOURING CLASSES.

§ 1. *Work.*

WE have previously shown that the citizen must occupy himself only with affairs of State. To do this he must have leisure. Only he who had no need to work for his living possessed the real qualification for citizen; he could only be truly a freeman when he could leave this work to others who were not. Work, regarded as a hindrance to public life, was despised as servile,[1] degrading to man, making him incapable of virtue, and blunting his intelligence.[2] It was the lot of the slave; only politics and war were worthy of the freeman. In ancient times agriculture had shared this honour. Socrates thought it the noblest occupation for the citizen in time of peace,[3] but it quickly fell into the contempt which was poured upon all work necessary for life.

It is easy therefore to understand what must have been the condition of those who, though not slaves, were not rich enough to devote themselves to unpaid professional work. It is true that in all the ancient republics they had a certain share of the citizen's rights; we know also that they sometimes used these rights in a manner as noisy as it was dangerous for order; but in reality they enjoyed only a very imperfect equality.

In Athens the laws of Solon excluded men of business

from public office, which was reserved solely for the leisure of the rich. In some more warlike states citizens were forbidden to follow a profession.[4] In Rome, only the patricians could attain the high dignities of the magistracy and priesthood.

In this respect, as in many others, the philosophers, instead of rising above the errors of their age, helped to support them by the empiricism of their systems.

Plato claimed for those who ranked as statesmen or warriors the privilege of living at the cost of husbandmen and artizans, for whom he could hardly find a place in his Republic.[5] He assigned the merchants to a still lower rank. Men of feeble constitution, unsuitable for other work, were the only ones whom he permitted to employ themselves in commerce, to sell in the markets of the towns the products of agriculture and skill.[6] The citizens, who were engaged with public business, and who were the guardians of the laws, alone needed virtue; it was no great evil for the artizans to become corrupt. The only danger for the city was in the degeneration of the aristocracy.[7] It is a mistake to think that these proud ideas were only platonic chimeras. Socrates thought it perfectly just to despise people whose occupations did not allow them to devote themselves either to their friends or to the Republic.[8]

Aristotle raised contempt for work and workers to the height of a philosophic theory of social morality. "There are labours," he said, "with which a freeman cannot be occupied without degrading himself. Such are those which particularly require bodily strength; but for these labours nature has created a special class of men. These special beings are those whom we subjugate, in order that they may take bodily labour in our stead, under the names of slaves or mercenaries."

Aristotle recognised only warriors and governors in the city; they alone composed the State in its political aspect. "It is true," he said, "that it cannot do without husbandmen and artizans, but these men have nothing to do with public business.[9] They are not worthy of the title of citizens.[10] They are incapable of greatness of soul. Their mercenary work is without virtue.[11] There is therefore only an external distinction between them and the slaves; they work for the public, slaves for private persons; they would be slaves if the State was rich enough to pay them, or strong enough to bring them under subjection.[12] From this it follows that the young people must not learn trades, which would degrade the citizen into the artizan." [13]

It also followed that the future orator was taught to despise the crowd, in order that he might address it fearlessly. "Which is he," said Socrates to one of his disciples, "which of all these people is he who overawes thee? Is it this shoemaker? Is it that other one, the public crier? Or is it this tentmaker? Is it not these who compose the Athenian people? But if thou thinkest so lightly of each individual, what hinders thee from despising them when massed?"[14]

The tone of the Roman citizen was equally haughty; it led him to regard "the crowd of artizans with supreme disdain."[15] After an interval of three centuries, Cicero reiterated the thought of Socrates. "What," he said, "can be more stupid than to respect the crowd of those whom one despises individually?"[16] The citizen must leave the mercenary occupations of commerce and manufactures to slaves or freedmen, because one is only free when not needing a salary; that is, when one is rich. According to Cicero, the citizen must avoid a salary as a mean and sordid gain, as the price of servitude, putting him who receives in the power of him who gives it. A profession which exchanges its products for money deserves no respect. Even intellectual work was despised. The freeman was degraded by acting as tutor or schoolmaster. Only the liberal arts, such as medicine, philosophy, architecture, commerce on a large scale, were honourable, and suitable to the position of citizen.[17] When Dio Cassius makes Mæcenas say that artizans who are engaged in a useful trade should be honoured, and those people who do nothing, or only evil, should be detested,[18] it is certainly not the debauched favourite of Augustus who uttered these words, so contrary to the ancient spirit; they belong solely to the historian, who had already felt the breath of a new spirit.

The contempt for labour had melancholy results for the ancient States. The artizan, who was despised by the rich, who was hardly considered as a citizen but almost as a slave whilst he worked for payment, also wished to attain the virtue of which he was said to be incapable, which was simply greatness of soul, or, in other words, the pride of the unoccupied man. He wished in his turn to exercise what has been called with equal wit and justice "the right of laziness." Thence arose the turbulence of the people in the Greek republics, their misery and venality, their successive reduction to slavery, and finally the dissolution of the State itself. Thence arose in Rome a seditious and hungry populace, who considered themselves as forcibly compelled to work which they hated, and who seized on the slightest excuse for rushing into tumults or to the bloody fights in the arena; whilst others, who thought themselves above the crowd, but who were no less degraded, became the flatterers and parasites of the rich, filled the vestibules of their palaces, submitted to all humiliations to be admitted to their tables, and swelled the train of ignoble servitors which illustrious Romans, lazy and debased, took with them into the streets.[19] Thence arose the pauperism which, already great under the Republic, became still more frightful under the Empire. Thence also came the unmeasured taste for pleasure and luxury, the influx to Rome of the sluggards of Italy and the provinces, the concentration of territorial property in the hands of a small number of rich men, carried to a point of which it is difficult to form to-day an exact idea. This evil, the inevitable result of pagan civilization, became one of the most active causes of its fall.

§ 2. *Poverty. The Poor.*

After our account of the contempt for work and workers, and the regard for riches as a chief cause of respect due to the citizen, we are bound to enter into some details of the manner in which antiquity looked at poverty, and treated the poor. If only the rich is honoured, if there is but proud disdain for the man who gains his living by labour, how much more must he be despised who is, for any reason whatever, deprived of the power of labouring. It must be important to add some particulars to complete the characterization of pagan society in this respect.

Throughout the whole of ancient times poverty was regarded as amongst the evils that should be most carefully avoided;[20] it was considered as a disgrace that could only be endured by the low and bad man.[21] The poor man was held to be incapable of wisdom and honesty. It was useless for him to swear by the gods; men were always inclined to think him a liar and perjurer.[22] If he married he was mocked as a senseless man; his children brought him disgrace and shame, even Plato holding that they could only be considered as vile bastards.[23] At a much later period a law which was then a strange anachronism was laid down; it treated those who married without dowry as not legally married, and branded them and their children with disgrace.[24] If a poor man, notwithstanding the weight of reprobation which he bore, proved himself respectable and wise, men were still hard of belief, and spoke of it with surprise, as an exceptional phenomenon;[25] and whilst stating it, still held the same opinion, that even great virtues could not prevent the dishonour which followed the simple fact of poverty.[26] If a rich man did not despise a poor one, he was thought to abase himself with rare condescension to a man who was placed naturally far below him.[27]

This was the general opinion about the poor, both in Greece and Rome. It is true we find poets and philosophers who speak of riches with contempt, and of success or poverty with indifference; but those who held this language generally took an imaginary standpoint. It was easy for them to despise in theory the fortune which they generally possessed in reality; yet even admitting their sincerity, they only confirm as an exception the general rule of antiquity. The poor, despised by virtue of this rule, were abandoned by ancient society to all the miseries of their lot. The rich citizen, accustomed to esteem a man only for his position in the State, his liberty and fortune, felt no sympathy for the poor. Antiquity, knowing nothing of respect for human personality could know nothing of beneficence. At the commencement of the fourth century, a Christian author was able to say with justice that pagan philosophers had given no precepts as to this virtue, which they ignored.[28]

The universal opinion was that we must do good only

to those who do us no injury,[29] and that personal interest must never be sacrificed. Ennius says that to direct a wanderer to the path is to rekindle his torch at mine, provided that mine will continue to burn after having served his turn.[30] Cicero, who quotes these verses without disapproval, sees that man is naturally inclined to generosity, even towards those who are unknown,[31] but he hastens to add the restriction that he must only yield to this sentiment when it can be done without detriment to himself. He must give only that which costs nothing, which he can spare without loss.[32]

Besides, what is the use of doing good to the poor? Reasons furnished by the most trifling egoism and the coldest harshness were given to show its uselessness. Not only, they said, does a man deprive himself of what he gives to the poor, but he needlessly prolongs his misery; for what is the use of life to him who is not rich? Why then, if unable to enrich him, help him to sustain his miserable existence? Is it not better to give him nothing, so that, with his useless life, his misfortunes may come more quickly to an end?[33] For that reason Plato desired that the poor attacked by illness should remain unhelped. If the constitution of an artizan was not strong enough to resist the malady, he could only die. The doctor might refuse his assistance without scruple, for the life of such a man can no longer be of any use when he is unable to exercise his calling. It is not so with the rich man, who has no occupation, which makes his life aimless when he can no longer work.[34]

Nothing is more revolting than the cold egoism of the wisest of ancient philosophers. But we must not accuse him alone, he was only the interpreter of an aristocratic society, above which it was impossible to rise. Truly nothing in this society was more melancholy than the fate of the poor who were invalided or broken down by illness. Instead of feeling sympathy, most people considered that it was a disgrace to be at the same time both ill and poor.[35] The poor, left without any kind of consolation, without religious hope and without material assistance, frequently died without any of those who had lived on their labour coming to their help. It has been alleged that there were institutions in antiquity analogous to the hospitals of Christian society, but there is no resemblance between a hospital founded and served by charity, and a temple of Æsculapius; where the sick man generally received magic formulas instead of advice, and amulets instead of remedies. The infirmaries established in the houses of the rich also do not deserve to be compared to hospitals; they were only apartments either for the master himself or for his slaves, when his own interest did not allow them to be deserted.[36] But the artizan who was not rich, the poor man who was not a slave, could find no refuge; it would have been contrary to the ancient spirit to care for them.

The citizen in comfortable circumstances added to his contempt of the poor a dread of death and an egoistical attachment to life. These essentially pagan sentiments were so powerful that the rich man often showed no greater care for the sick of his own household than for the sick poor.[37] In the great plagues, some saved themselves by flight, leaving their families to the ravages of death; others thrust their nearest relations out of the house. The unfortunate victims of the malady died, whilst the cowardly terror of men prevented any pagan from teaching or practising the devotion needful to help them. If any one visited the sick, it was for love of praise, to show his greatness of soul in despising the danger of death.[38] Those who survived, instead of becoming more serious, thought only of enjoying with greater ardour the wealth and pleasures of which an unexpected death might so quickly deprive them. The great plague of Athens, in the time of Pericles, and that of Carthage, seven centuries later, present the same picture of desolation and egoism.[39]

There are facts and passages which appear to contradict the statement we have just made, that antiquity knew nothing of beneficence. We shall easily see, when we examine them, that they do not at all modify our judgment on the general spirit of pagan society. Cicero is the one amongst ancient philosophers previous to Christianity who had the most to say of the duty of liberality, and who was perhaps the only one who saw that it was in conformity with our nature. He, however, speaks of it with great restrictions. "We must not," he says, "look in the same way on a man overwhelmed by adversity, and on one who without being unfortunate only seeks to increase his well-being. We shall incline to hold out a hand to these unfortunates, at least if they do not deserve their fate; if they do, we may leave them to perish. But who is to tell us at what point their misfortune is deserved?" Cicero continues, "The people who ask our help, not to support them in affliction, but that they may rise higher, ought not to be deserted by us; only we must use discernment in the choice of those who are worthy of our assistance."[40]

There again we find no pity inspired by misfortune. Aid is not given through love, but through the purely external motives of giving to an ambitious man the means of rising higher. It is true that Cicero calls him only truly liberal and praiseworthy who uses his fortune to ransom captives from the hands of pirates, to pay the debts of his friends, to help them to endow their daughters, to make a fortune for them, or to increase that which they possess.[41] But that is not universal, disinterested benevolence. It thinks only of Romans fallen into the power of barbarians, of friends impatient of gaining a position by a fortune. Mankind was not helped. Care was taken only to save a friend or countryman from the opprobrium of poverty, and to assure his rank of citizen; at the same time he would become a grateful client to his benefactor. Liberality so became a glory to him who exercised it, and contributed to the welfare of the Republic.[42] The Roman moralist appears to blame the largess given to the people, which necessarily disappeared with the fortune which they scattered. He gave a preference to the liberality which is shown by abilities and kind offices, as being more worthy of a distinguished man, and always possible.[43] He added, however, that largesses must not be forgotten, provided they were given within limits and with care, to men who were worthy of help.[44]

We see how vague and undecided are these views of Cicero upon benevolence. The most diverse sentiments are at strife. Natural benevolence leads him to help the poor and unhappy; and egoism, which never voluntarily renounces its possessions, lies hidden in the counsel to do good only to those who are worthy. Patriotic wisdom blames the interested and ruinous prodigality of the ambitious, and Roman pride will help first only friends who wish to rise higher, or citizens reduced to slavery. No higher principle rules this system of moral aristocracy, which like all the other ethical and political doctrines of Cicero, is intended only for people of the world and men of the State of Rome.

But did not the largess and distribution of money and food, made to the poor by the State or private individuals, witness in favour of the benevolence of the ancients? If we ever recognise the difference between the ancient and the Christian spirit, it is when we endeavour to use these facts as a proof that pagan society knew and practised charity. What were these gifts? Not means of existence given with benevolence and sympathy to men who were deprived of work by circumstances beyond their power, and who with all their efforts were unable to supply the needs of their families; they were a sop thrown to the crowd, without love or serious aim, but with interested views. Such were feasts for thousands of men, public distributions of wheat, wine, oil, and meat, spectacles, games in the arena, combats of men and beasts.[45] These prodigalities had found a defender in the moralist Theophrastus, who in his treatise on riches ceaselessly praises the magnificent splendour of the fêtes given to the people, in whose eyes such magnificence was the worthiest product of wealth.[46] Largesses were given by ambitious Greeks and Romans, who, whilst professing the greatest contempt for the crowd, wished for their suffrage and desired to conciliate their changing favour. Finally, they were resorted to by the State itself, to appease the lazy multitude, hungry and always ready for sedition.

In Athens, at the time of the decadence, when the citizens would no longer work, the Republic was compelled to come to their help. Already under Pericles there had been distributions of wheat, which in the end were often repeated. The public help, established by Pisistratus, for wounded men, was quickly extended to all who were, or professed to be, unable to work. Finally, the public treasury was exhausted, that the idle ones might be fed and amused by free repasts and spectacles.[47] In Rome especially, largess assumed enormous proportions; from the close of the Republic till the latter days of the Empire,[48] distribution of food, and spectacles, were the chief means of government. The entertainment of the populace, the *plebs urbana*, whose daily cry for bread and gladiators summed up their desires and expressed their deep degradation, was one condition of the existence of the State.

The distributions of food were regularly organized, a special administration being established for this branch of the public service.[49] Both in Rome and other large towns, Alexandria and Constantinople,[50] in the fifth and even in the sixth [51] centuries, the officers of the *civil wheat* were ordered to supply it to the whole male population, to all those who having forgotten work gloried in the name of citizen.[52]

Thinking men recognised at an early time that these distributions, far from putting an end to misery, were only another cause of corruption and decay.[53] They stopped the clamour of the crowd for a moment, and Aurelian pleased himself with saying that nothing could be gayer than the Roman people when they had eaten their fill,[54] but this also proved what is the result when society takes charge of feeding the poor. The Roman people had what is called in modern times the right of assistance; but this assistance given by the State was only an encouragement to idleness. After having been by turns a motive for sedition or a means of despotism, it became finally a cause of social dissolution.

Poverty advanced as rapidly in the provinces and in the country as in Rome itself. Depopulated by the wars, they exhausted their resources for the Romans, who amused themselves with spectacles and games. Agriculture had long fallen into the hands of slaves. Manufacture, held in contempt, had also fallen into servile hands. The small proprietors were ruined and hopelessly weighted with the taxes levied by the fiscal agents, who traversed the desolate country to find food for the Roman populace, or to pay the avaricious and undisciplined troops.[55] In vain they attempted by promises of immunities to induce new inhabitants to settle and cultivate the deserted lands; in vain they established colonies of barbarians in desolated provinces; in vain they gave to all inhabitants of the empire the title of Roman citizen, which, formerly a glory, was henceforward a mockery and burden; in vain they wished to enforce by law that the curials of the towns should sacrifice themselves and their fortune to the public good. It was not that which could arrest the universal misery and downfall. For this more was required than laws and privileges. It was necessary to give a new spirit to mankind, to restore work, or rather to restore man; to teach the rich to respect and love the poor, and the poor to be contented with his lot whilst ennobling it by the purity of his ways. Such were, in this respect, the conditions needful for the regeneration of the world.

§ 3. *Slaves. Slavery in General.*[56]

It is no part of our subject to seek for the origin and first causes of ancient slavery. We take it as an existing fact, as one of the most unjust rights of ancient States.

The slave, descended from former prisoners of war, or the son of races which yielded to conquering tribes, was the property, the chattel of his master, intended to do all the work which he despised as unsuited to the dignity of a free citizen.

Enthusiastic philologists are astonished at the existence of slavery in the ancient States whose freedom they love to vaunt. It is a blot which mars the harmony of their picture, but which nevertheless they cannot erase. It is in their opinion in perfect contrast to the spirit of personal independence by which the Greeks and Romans were animated. They cannot understand how it could be possible to find slaves amongst the nations who so carefully guarded their civil liberty and so heroically defended their national freedom.[57] But we have already shown that true liberty, individual right and respect for human personality, found no place in Greece or Rome. When this fact is admitted, ancient slavery may sadden but cannot astonish us; it accords perfectly with the egoistic spirit of ancient civilization. The argument by which the philosophers justify this iniquitous sale of man by man would appear to us even far stranger.[58] They knew not how to free themselves from the bonds of public opinion and the customs of their fellow countrymen. All their thoughts about social morality are governed by existing facts, instead of being enlightened by their natural conscience; or to speak more correctly, this light was extinguished by the pressure of the pagan atmosphere which surrounded it.

The sages said admirable things about the soul, its faculties, and some of its virtues; but they bestowed no attention upon the complete man. They made an abstraction of his external position in the world, and saw only the citizen. Citizenship is a characteristic of man. In their opinion civil liberty is not only an essential for the citizen, but a characteristic of man himself. All they say of man is spoken only of the freeman, of the member of the Republic. He who is neither a freeman nor a citizen is not looked upon by them as a man at all. The citizen alone is a person; he who is not a citizen has no personality; he is a chattel.

Even Plato has not risen above the social error of his

nation. If he hesitates sometimes, if his more generous feelings try to protest against the injustice of slavery, if he acknowledges that there have been slaves even more capable of virtue than the sons of the family, slaves whose faithful care has saved the life or fortune of their masters;[59] if he goes so far as to admit that this question is grave and embarrassing,[60] he is, nevertheless, not long before he falls back into the ideas of his time, proclaiming slavery to be a natural institution arising from the servility characteristic of a separate class of men. Nature, he says, made some to command, others to serve and obey.[61] In his ideal State, where he wishes to exclude everything which is contrary to reason, he introduces the elements of slavery by fixing men in hereditary and exclusive castes : on the one hand warriors and statesmen, on the other agriculturists and artizans. If he does not give to the latter the name of slaves, he assigns them the condition; for could his Republic have been realized, servitude would have quickly reappeared as a consequence of the dishonouring inferiority of the labouring classes. Besides, Plato expresses his opinion of slaves with unembarrassed clearness when he declares that there is nothing healthy in the servile soul, that it is incapable of goodness, and that a man of sense will never trust to this race.[62]

The logician, Aristotle, is equally unhesitating. Slavery is a natural state. A slave is so by nature. He is born with the destiny of service, as a free man is born with the privilege[63] of command; for if only he can be a citizen who need not work for a livelihood, and yet life without work is impossible, it must necessarily fall upon a special class, naturally destined to serve freemen, citizens.[64] Also, the citizen's house is perfect only when slaves are found there. In a well organized domestic economy two kinds of instruments are required for service, inanimate and living ones. The first are soulless slaves, the second are slaves having a soul.[65] But it is not a true soul, a complete spiritual nature like the master's; it is absolutely deprived of will.[66] The slave has no will but his master's; he is moved only by him; he is, in a sense, a part, a member of the master himself.[67] His virtue is absolute obedience, perfect assimilation of interests with those of him to whom he belongs. Between the two there can never be anything in common. Love is not required from the master, for how should he love an instrument employed in his service? At the furthest it might be possible to love his servant in so far as he was a man, but never in so far as he was a slave.[68] Doubtless very few masters would make this subtle distinction; the slave would be regarded always as slave, and but seldom as man. It is astonishing that Aristotle, after calling the slave an instrument, seems to admit that he is in a certain sense a man. We must not attach too much importance to this opinion, accidentally expressed by the philosopher, and contradicted by his whole system as well as by the universal sentiment of antiquity. If virtues and intelligence were discovered in the slave, he was regarded like the poor man as still incapable of rising above the natural opprobrium inherent to his state.[69] The terms servile and illiberal conveyed the idea of everything low, common, and ignoble.

The Stoics held opinions apparently different; they spoke of moral slavery and internal freedom. Zeno defined this to be the faculty of determining for one's self under the sole guidance of reason; so that the sage alone is free, and the true slave is he who is under the dominion of his passions and vices.[70] The remedy offered by this system to slaves consisted in the advice to rise above their condition by regarding it as an accident, indifferent in itself and unworthy to affect a man. The wise man will submit to it without a murmur; he will not feel the yoke, which is only hard to those who bear it with dislike. This theory was unpractical and fruitless. It did not prevent those who held it from continuing to keep slaves and to deny their possession of the intellectual faculties which make the philosopher and the citizen, and it was only a delusive comfort to those who had to bear all the misery of servitude.

The law showed no more humanity than the system of the philosophers; it also was only the expression and sanction of the deed. It also held that the slave was not a man. It regarded him as a thing, a *body*.[71] It refused him all civil right. It had for him only unjust severity, or humiliating indifference; and even where, as in Athens, it offered him some feeble guarantees, he had to submit to all the laws which decided the possession and transmission of *things*. The slaves were part of the patrimony, and passed by inheritance from one master to another. They were sold, lent, given, bequeathed, as if they were not men. They could neither acquire nor possess. If married, they had no right to complain if the master took their wives; it was neither adultery for them nor him, who was free to dispose as he would of his slaves. Their children, born for servitude, belonged first to the master, whose riches they increased, or who got rid of them if he did not wish to support them.[72]

The legal state of slaves was the same in Rome as in Greece: public opinion, with which the philosophers agreed, treated them in precisely the same way in Rome as in the Greek Republics. If the Roman citizen thought of the slave as a man, it was as a man of the lowest nature, as a second species of the human race.[73] He was one of three kinds of instruments necessary to cultivate a property, and this is how the three kinds were distinguished: one was mute, that is the plough, the cart, the whole of the implements; the other gave articulate sounds, that is the ox, the horse; the third spoke, that is the slave.[74] They do not trouble to reflect that language presupposes reason, which is inseparable from liberty.

Cicero speaks, like the Stoics, of moral slavery. He develops the proposition that the sage only is free, and every unreasoning man a slave.[75] But by the side of this paradox, as he calls it himself, he upholds real servitude, and distinguishes carefully between those who are the slaves of their passions, and those who are slaves in fact and law; he almost thought it a slight to the first to put them in the same rank with the second.[76]

We find here the same vagueness which we have already been compelled to charge on the ethics of Cicero. He calls servitude the obedience of an abject soul deprived of its free will.[77] The man who has no will is rightly a slave; there is injustice only in enslaving a freeman.[78] But who are those who have lost their liberty; that is, the power of deciding for themselves, and who are condemned to servitude by this absence of will? Is it the bad, the cowardly men degraded by debauchery and vice? Does Cicero desire that these men, who have become the slaves of their passions, should become also the slaves of those who govern themselves? Far from this, he leaves those who are born free in their liberty, and admits, *a priori*, as an undisputed fact, that those who are born slaves must for that reason lack a will. It would have been perfectly consistent if he had said, like Aristotle, that it is through their own nature that slaves are deprived of free will. He also justifies the necessity of servitude by the same reasons as Plato and Aristotle, and calls slaves the last class of men.[79] He does not think them capable of rising above the fatal limits of this state. If there are some who, by undoubted talent and fidelity, can acquit themselves with success in certain employments reserved for freemen, one must not trust them, in order to avoid blame. This would be a disgraceful thing in public opinion, and the sage—himself the slave of *decorum*—will avoid shocking the prejudices of the crowd.[80]

These prejudices retained their strength throughout the whole duration of Roman society. From time to time we find sophists and rhetoricians who, notwithstanding their religious incredulity or their hostility to new ideas, repeat that external servitude is only an accident of life, either because all men may be free if they can be philosophers, or because they are all alike slaves; some of despots, others of their own vices, and all, more or less, of events and circumstances.[81] But these declamations, which were not deeply serious, necessarily remained ineffectual. Ancient ideas about slavery continued to rule pagan society. They even resisted the efforts of those philosophers and emperors who, influenced by Christianity, tried to modify and improve the condition of slaves. Even under the Christian emperors a man's riches was reckoned by the number, often enormous, of his slaves; and those who, resisting the impulse which drew the world towards Christ, remained attached to the ancient worship, preserved also their ancient contempt for the servile class. Themistius, the friend of Julian, had only disdain for slaves, to whom he adds artizans, whose soul, according to him, is incapable of virtue and of noble ideas.[82] In the fifth century many people professed that the gods cared nothing for the slaves, and that the sage was dishonoured by intercourse with them.[83]

G

§ 4. *Treatment of Slaves.*

The treatment of these despised beings, of these instruments without will, corresponded to the idea held theoretically. It would perhaps be more correct to say that the opinion supported by philosophers and passed into law, was only an argument invented by ancient egoism to justify the way in which the freeman, the conqueror and oppressor, treated his slave.

If the fate of slaves in Athens seems to have been less hard than elsewhere in Greece, if they found there some legal protection against barbarous treatment, if their murder was punished as the murder of a freeman,[64] if they had the right of asylum in the temple of Theseus, if they could even purchase their freedom, we cannot see in all this the recognition of a natural right, or respect for human individuality in the persons of slaves; for it was in Athens, beneath the power of her institutions and the public opinion of her inhabitants, that Plato and Aristotle found the elements of their theories. We find the cause of this moderation rather in the character of the Athenians, who were more humane than the Dorians of Sparta, and perhaps also in the fear inspired by the large number of slaves in Attica.[65]

There was no Greek State where the slaves were more harshly treated than in Sparta. There was no law or asylum there to protect them from the cruelties of their masters.[66] The chase of the helots, of which so much has been said through inexact interpretation of the institution of the Crypteia, mentioned by Plutarch,[67] ought to be withdrawn from the history of Lacedemonian institutions. The researches of M. Wallon establish clearly that the intention of the Crypteia was only to prohibit the helots from leaving their habitations during the night, under penalty of death. This was a necessity for Sparta; the race that had conquered the soil could keep it only by oppressing the primitive inhabitants, by submitting them to the strictest oversight, and terrifying them with sanguinary laws like that of the Crypteia.[88]

In the olden time in Rome, when agriculture was still an honourable employment worthy of a citizen, the slaves formed part of the family circle; their position was less intolerable; the master, father of the family, lived in their midst, and took his meals along with them; whilst they often served him with more zeal and fidelity.[89] When the increase of luxury and egoism separated the master further from the servants, he treated them with greater barbarity in proportion to the greater distance between them. They were likened to beasts of burden,[90] and the distinction granted by theorists between these two kinds of domestic implements was effaced in practice. The law also punished with a like penalty him who killed a slave and him who killed an ox or a horse.[91] Whilst if a master was killed by a slave, the law took no trouble to discover the culprit, but slew all the slaves of the household together.[92] In the country, as in the town, the roughest labour was imposed on them during the day; whilst at night they were shut up in subterranean dungeons, which were damp and close.[93] The slave doorkeeper was chained to the door; he was sold with the house, as forming, in a way, part of the wall.[94] The master punished not only faults and forgetfulness, but the smallest movement, the slightest involuntary noise, if it displeased his momentary whim.[95] The punishment was often the infliction of frightful torture.[96] Sometimes when the master wished to pass sentence of death, he did not even seek for a pretext; his wish, his will, sufficed; for what more is required to kill a being who, though guilty of no crime, is not a man?[97] Emperors,[98] and even women, set the example of this cold and red-handed cruelty.

Even in Greece, that country of gentler manners, there were women who ill-treated their slaves, tiring them to death, refusing them food, and striking them so furiously that the blood flowed;[99] but it is amongst the Roman ladies of the decadence that we find the most revolting examples of this hardening of the feminine heart, and this odious contempt for human nature. One instance alone is enough to show this; the ladies armed themselves, during their toilet, with large pins, with which they pricked the bodies of the slaves if they neglected any detail of this complicated service; and in order that these pricks, inflicted without anger by women used to the sight of blood, might more certainly cause large wounds, the unhappy servants were not allowed to keep on their clothes above the waist.[100]

Roman harshness led the master to desert a slave whose age or infirmities rendered him useless for service; he had no longer any engagement with him. Truly, what could he do with a broken instrument which was good for nothing? Cato, who at first treated his slaves with more humanity, but who became hardened by the riches acquired in his civil and military calling, adopted the habit of ridding himself of those who were weakened by age. He was not inclined to support useless people. If he found any willing to buy, he sold his old slaves at a low price, like worn-out furniture; if not, he ordered them to be driven away, caring little for their fate.[101]

This custom became general. Sick servants, whose cure seemed hopeless, were exposed on an island in the Tiber, where they might be appropriated by the first comer. This was even humane, for many masters did not take any trouble, but hastened to kill the slaves who could no longer serve them.[102] The most distinguished men never shook off this indifference, which chills our most ordinary ideas of humanity. Cicero, in speaking of the Prætor Domitian, who had crucified a slave for having too eagerly killed a wild boar at the hunt, contented himself with saying, "that that will *perhaps* appear harsh";[103] and when a servant was taken away by death, for whom he had some affection, he defends himself from the charge of feeling sorrow, as though it was something unsuitable and contrary to decorum: "I am perhaps more grieved than it seems to me I ought to be for the death of a slave."[104]

We shall perhaps be told that this indifference and harsh treatment of slaves was an exception, and that generally masters were advised to treat their servants with humanity. Yes; they counselled moderation and prohibited too great harshness. But let us see for what reasons.

If Plato is unwilling that a man should be inhuman towards his slaves, it is because the wise man refrains from treating those unjustly towards whom injustice is so easy; because the well-bred man disdains to be angry with those whom he despises; and, above all, because a certain kindness is for the interest of the master himself.[105]

Aristotle holds the same opinion. According to him the master need not love his slave, and the slave has no right against his master.[106] The duty, or more correctly, the interest, of the latter commands him to bring up his slaves in virtue; that is, servile virtue, absolute obedience, the surrender of all opposing will to the master. This end is more easily attained by moderation than by harshness and violence.[107]

We see then that humanity is inspired only by greatness of soul, which forbids anger against a being placed so low, or by clearly discerned interest, which so manages the instruments as to be able to use them longer. Four centuries after Aristotle, a Roman economist formally repeated this advice. "We must be kind to slaves, in order that they may be docile; we must refrain from ill-treating them, in order that they may have no excuse for murmur and revolt, and that we may not by our own fault unfit them for labour."[108] The enfranchisement, which ought to be to some extent the corrective of slavery, was a very feeble remedy for so great an evil. We know with how many difficulties it was surrounded. If these difficulties were overcome, the slave did not gain true liberty; he received only a liberty which was disgraceful and despised. He did not gain all the rights of the freeman; he did not receive the respect accorded to the citizen of free birth. The freedman remained in an inferior position; he became either an artizan or the favourite of some great lord. If it chanced that he rose higher, he always retained in public opinion the taint of his original servitude.

The inevitable result of the attitude of the social morality of antiquity towards slaves and freedmen, was to debase and deeply pervert their moral sense. They were ceaselessly told they were instruments, bodies without will and incapable of virtue. Were not many of them sure to finish by accepting the situation without shame and conforming their conduct to it? Subjected to the contempt of their masters, the law, and society, they became cowardly, deceitful, cruel; their moral and intellectual powers were paralysed, and they too often justified the degradation of their condition by the degradation of their habits. In those who retained some feeling of human dignity, slavery produced the hot hatreds, revenges, and revolts of which there are so many examples in ancient history. The barbarity of the masters drove those slaves to despair who were not completely stupified, and they used cruelties against their oppressors which they had learned from them.[109] The ancient relation between the father of the family and his servants had changed to one of reciprocal and permanent hostility. There was a proverb under the Empire, "So many slaves, so many adversaries."[110] Thus when it was proposed in the Senate to distinguish slaves from freemen by their dress, the resolution was not carried; they foresaw with fear the danger which would threaten society, if the slaves could count their numbers and feel themselves more and stronger than their masters.[111]

§ 5. *Occupations of Slaves. Actors. Gladiators.*

In primitive times the slaves were occupied in the cares of agriculture under the orders of the master, or in fulfilling household requirements under the direction of the wife. In proportion to the increase of riches, luxury, and corruption, were the fresh services demanded from the slaves. The thousand requirements of an effeminate and debauched life, the toilette, cooking, festivities, baths, public walks, needed many special servants, who, as debased as their masters, lent themselves to all their desires.[112] On the other hand, the contempt for work felt by the free artizans threw on the slave those professional occupations that the free citizen thought beneath his dignity. Each rich house had workmen of every kind amongst its numerous servants, and trade, dishonoured as servile work, was left almost exclusively in the hands of slaves.

During the Empire, even works requiring intelligence were left to them. The master, whilst despising them, required of them more than material services, and expected from them the knowledge in which he was deficient himself. If he wished to sparkle with wit in the presence of his friends, his slaves were compelled to have it for him. Calvisius Sabinus bought some slaves at a great cost, one of whom knew Homer, another Hesiod, and a third lyrics. When at his banquets he wished to recite some verses, he asked for them from these people, who were placed behind his seat.[113]

These learned slaves were entrusted with the education of children, an education destitute of moral oversight, and turned at the best only to the development of the intellectual faculties. We have previously seen how fathers chose as tutors for their sons those slaves who were incapable of work which they thought more important.

But these were not the only services required from this despised race. They served also for the master's amusement in pleasures which were both disgraceful and barbarous. Here is presented to us one of the saddest aspects of ancient civilization. From amongst the slaves were taken the actors, dancers, players on the flute or lyre, male and female, an immodest band, whose task was to enliven the festivities of the rich, exciting the guests of these scandalous orgies to voluptuous pleasure.[114] The mimes and actors of all kinds, who amused both patricians and people at the theatre, also belonged to the servile class.

Formerly, in Greece, dramatic art had been untrammelled and important. The artist was esteemed by his fellow citizens because he only represented the greatest works of the immortal poets. Œschylus took part in the government of Athens after having been an actor and poet; the tragedian Aristodemus was sent as an ambassador to King Philip;[115] Sophocles was at the same time poet, priest, actor, and captain. This time existed no longer; the rapid and profound decadence of Greece had drawn art, and the esteem due to artists, into the common ruin of everything that had made the glory of this people. At the time of the appearance of Christianity, the ancient theatre, with its heroic tragedies and witty comedies, had vanished; the taste for theatrical representations was not less, but the art had become thoroughly immoral.

Throughout the duration of the Empire, after the time of Augustus, obscenity prevailed in the theatre. It was no longer a school of patriotism, recalling the traditions of the heroes of the earliest times, or criticising contemporary oddities; it had become a source of corruption to both actors and spectators. The only things represented were the adventures of deceived husbands, of adulterers, of the intrigues of libertines, of scenes in the *lupanar*. Only immodest women and effeminate men were seen there. Only the most disgraceful things were represented. Everything was debased that ought to have been respected. Virtue was made a mockery, and the gods were ridiculed.[116] The actor aroused a love of evil in the soul of the spectator. He inspired base or criminal passions,[117] and completely familiarized as he was with vice, he yet blushed sometimes at the disgraceful part he was made to play in the sight of the crowd.[118]

Notwithstanding this vileness, depraved pagan society still retained theatrical representations as ceremonials of worship.[119] The actors in Greece and Italy continued to form corporations with special privileges, and professing a priestly character.[120]

In the fourth century, Symmachus held that to give

games and preside at them was one of the duties of priests;[121] and Libanius, the pagan, who was a lover of physical beauty, vowed to the worship of form, defends and exalts the dance, from an artistic point of view, for its mental charm, provided that the dancer separates it from anything shocking to morality.[122] This sophistical distinction was impossible to enforce amidst a moral decadence so deep as that of the pagan world.

The parts which the actors had to play, the words they uttered, their impure pantomime, must have completely extinguished the last lights of moral conscience. These priests, by a strange contrast natural to the ancient character, were held in contempt even by those who could not do without them. Horace already reckoned them as amongst the lowest people, of the most doubtful morality.[123] Their ranks were recruited only from the lowest orders of society, especially from amongst slaves. Some contractor bought them for this service. For his own profit he devoted them to the gross amusement of the crowd, caring as little for the loss of their souls as for the infamy to which he condemned their persons.

The people attended their games with unwearied curiosity. They sought them out, and covered them with applause; but looking on them as beings destined for this by nature by the lowness of their condition, they felt for them neither the esteem which was doubtless unsuited to their character, nor the pity which they deserved as victims of the social order. They saw them pass from the stage to poverty or the tomb without compassion and without remorse. If the master raised a funeral stone to the child whose dance had delighted the spectators, he did it only to boast of the pleasure which his young slave had given the crowd.[124]

The law itself was hard on the members of this unfortunate class. Instead of making an effort to raise them by removing temptations to sin, it trampled them under foot, held them forcibly to the theatre, and chained them to vice. It was forbidden to actors and actresses to withdraw from the service of the people's pleasures; even their children were born mimes or actors, for they were born slaves. Notwithstanding their priestly character, the law called them immodest people, and qualified their profession as disgraceful.[125] It forbade them to wear certain luxurious clothing, and deprived them of rights which were enjoyed by freemen.[126] " They are condemned," said Tertullian, " to ignominy; the curial, the tribune, the senate, the equestrian order is far removed from them; they are interdicted from all honours and from the use of several ornaments. What perversity! the pagans love those whom they punish, and disparage those whom they approve; they exalt art, and brand the artists with infamy."[127] They were several times driven from Rome, either because their number embarrassed the despots,[128] or in the interest of public morality on account of their disorderly conduct.

Domitian prohibited public theatricals,[129] and Trajan wished to suppress entirely the practice of this effeminate art;[130] but scarcely were they expelled when they reappeared, more applauded than ever. Neither the nobles nor the people could live without them. Pagan society was thoroughly wearied of itself; it asked to laugh in the midst of the greatest perils, and required games and dances to enliven the last hours that separated it from its fall.

But this was not all: these immoral representations, these voluptuous dances and pantomimes, these naked women swimming in basins in the midst of the amphitheatre, in the presence of thousands of spectators of every age and sex,[131] were not enough for the Roman people, nor for the rich persons who indulged themselves in their orgies with the impure games of actors and musicians. This hardy race of Rome, eager for war, used to bloodshed, and remorselessly ill-treating those whom they despised, required something more. We allude to the spectacles of gladiators. Nothing throws the barbarity of the Roman world into stronger relief.

The origin of these spectacles was long before the time of the decadence. They are mentioned after the first Punic war.[132] They were intended to be then, as in the time of the Empire, a means of teaching courage to the Roman soldiers, whom historians represent as animated by the most intrepid patriotism. They knew no better way of accustoming them to the sight of blood, of teaching them contempt for suffering and death, than to make them assist at the combats of gladiators before they entered the field.[133] These bloody games soon became one of the dearest amusements of the people. Sometimes it was a fight of man with man, sometimes of men with wild beasts, which were called chases.[134]

The passion for these struggles was warm and general. No occurrence drew the people together in greater numbers; no solemnity inspired them with more interest; no recreation gave them more delight.[135] The Roman citizen, tired of idleness though he despised work, passed his days in the amphitheatre, viewing the combats with bears and lions, and filling the intervals between these chases with combats of gladiators, so that no time might be lost.[136] Was he pre-occupied?—he went to the amphitheatre to banish the thoughts which possessed him; melancholy?—he went to see men killed as a distraction.[137]

The great people, knights and senators, were to be seen there, along with the populace. The most important men presided;[138] the emperors claimed this honour as one of their privileges. Amongst the number we find, not only tyrants like Nero, Commodus, Gallienus, but princes renowned for their virtue, as Vespasian and Titus, taking pleasure in the combats of the arena. And what is even more difficult to understand, women of all ranks rushed there with an eagerness which was not exceeded by that of the most hardened warrior; even the vestals had a box of honour. None of the spectators had any pity for the combatants. The slightest feeling of humanity would have been enough to keep them from the amphitheatre; but this sentiment did not exist. They assisted at the *games* with ferocious curiosity. They judged the skill of the blows with the interest we should feel to-day in a game of chess. Eager to excite the combatants and insensible to the sufferings of the wounded, they burst into enthusiastic applause when one yielded in a skilful struggle, and they uttered cries of fury when they did not throw as much passion into the strife as the spectators—when they seemed willing to spare each other and to withdraw, so to speak, from their duty. It was to despise the sovereign people only to hesitate at killing one another for its amusement.[139] Women, virgins consecrated to the gods, as well as courtesans, had the same praises as men for him who bore the largest wounds or who fell with the greatest calm; it was they, ordinarily, who by graciously raising the hand gave the signal for the blow which should end the suffering of the wounded stretched on the ground.[140]

Ambitious men in Rome soon understood that to satisfy this thirst for bloodshed would be a more powerful means of popularity than distributions of oil or wheat, and that combats of gladiators would become the most efficacious largess.[141] Already in the latter days of the

Republic, the chiefs of different parties turned it into such an abuse that it was necessary to take measures against it. Cicero framed the Tullian law to prohibit any one who sought a public office from giving combats of gladiators.[142] This law was not made in the interest of humanity; the legislator only wished to prevent factions, and to take away from the ambitious man the surest way of gaining the populace. Augustus prohibited more than a hundred and twenty men to engage in combats. This decree was no more regarded than Cicero's law. Tiberius even ordered that there should be a great spectacle of gladiators every year at the expense of the citizens newly nominated as questors.[143] If Nero attempted to re-establish the Tullian law,[144] he was not led to do so by any care for the unhappy beings destined for the arena; his desire was that everything should depend on himself alone, and that no other should seek the people's favour.

The ardour of the Romans for gladiatorial combats never cooled so long as the Empire remained in existence. It was the same in the last moments of ancient society, already converted to Christianity, surrounded on all sides with barbarians; the people, pagan in custom though Christian in name, rushed to the Coliseum, greedy for bloodshed, but too cowardly to venture their own in defence of a dying country. From the commencement of the decadence of the Roman world to the fall of the Empire, the chief men in the State pandered to the most depraved instincts of the people. Games in the arena were the great means of ruling them. They were satisfied provided they received gladiators and bread. Emperors who were not monsters, Trajan, Philip, Constantine previous to his avowal of Christianity, even Theodosius, made the numerous bands of prisoners of war fight in the arena. The consuls and questors, by the law of Tiberius, were bound to give games with gladiators every time that they entered upon their office. It was a sort of tax of a joyful succession to office which they owed to the people.[145] Domitian, to change the spectacle, once made women fight.[146]

It was the most certain way of being held in remembrance by the grateful crowd; private people ordered in their will that gladiators should be made to fight at their cost, in order that the people might honour their name.[147] So great was the madness in this respect, that a rich Roman desired that after his death the beautiful slaves of his household should enter the lists; and another gave the same order as to the young boys who were his delight.[148] How can we describe such a state of mind? In the solemn hour of death, when the early Christians freed their slaves or bequeathed help to the poor and unhappy, the pagans coolly passed sentence of death on the poor creatures whom they had abused during their life, in order that an ignoble populace might applaud their name when they saw the flowing blood!

What appears perhaps even more horrible, was the combats of gladiators during the banquets of the rich. This barbarous custom, which is found in very early times in Campania,[149] soon spread to all places where Romans, rich enough to sacrifice men to the pleasures of their guests, were to be found.[150]

What a society was this of Rome, tolerating orgies where the blood of slaves mingled with the wine of their flower-crowned masters, where mortal combats alternated with impure pantomime, where the guests were offered in turns the grimaces of actors, the carnage of gladiators, and the kisses of courtesans,—where indeed the most monstrous cruelty was allied with the most shameless libertinism!

The introduction of combats in the arena was long resisted by the gentler temper of the Greeks; they received them only when the Romans, after having upset their liberty, taught them also to reverse the altar of mercy.[151] Gladiatorial games spread during the time of the emperors throughout the whole extent of Roman dominion, even into the East.[152]

The men destined for these combats were of different conditions, but generally slaves or men who were for any reason deprived of their liberty. Rich men who sought the suffrage of the multitude had amongst their troops of slaves *families* of gladiators.[153] Whoever owned the most and the strongest claimed the highest position, and boasted the most loudly of the combatants he supported.[154]

The practice of the gladiatorial art soon became a trade; there were contractors who bought slaves suited for this service. The depravity of the Roman populace went so far that they voluntarily sold themselves for the arena, preferring the chances of these sanguinary struggles to the labour which they despised. We should have expected these unhappy ones would go with horror and reluctance to the conflict; but so strong was their hatred of work and love of bloodshed, that they pressed forward to seek this service. They were tormented with the desire for applause. They wished to shine, whether by killing or yielding skilfully. Their honour consisted in never flinching, in uttering no cry in falling, in receiving the mortal blow with a smile, in saluting the spectators before rendering up the soul, in order to obtain a tomb which would tell posterity how many times they had conquered in the arena.[155] Cicero spoke of this courage with secret admiration as an instance of what exercise and habit could accomplish.[156]

Gladiators were bound to the *lanista* by a solemn oath. His duty was to feed, train, and exercise them.[157] He provided them for the rich man, who had none himself, and who wished to give the crowd a spectacle. The price was paid after the fight, so much for those who came out safe and sound, and so much for the wounded and dead. Sometimes disputes arose from these transactions. The jurisconsult Caïus has recorded an instance which shows strongly the cold indifference with which they trafficked in human blood for the amusement of the people. A *lanista* provided gladiators for a private person at the cost of twenty denarii for those who survived without serious wounds, and a thousand denarii for each one who should be killed or wounded in a way to unfit him for further combats. The question arose if this was a sale or simply a hiring; that is, if the man for whom the gladiators should have given their sweat (they said nothing of their blood) could keep them himself. Caïus resolved the question with perfect tranquillity of mind: "It is most probable," he said, "that those who remain safe and sound are hired; they must return to their first master. For the others, it is a sale; they belong to him who has made use of them; for what could the *lanista* do with corpses or mutilated bodies?"[158]

If the gladiators fought fearlessly, and killed one another according to the rules of science, part of the honour came to the contractor. When he was pleased with them, he gratified them with a tomb with an inscription. A certain Constance erected a stone to recompense his gladiators for being killed in such a way as to call forth the applause of the crowd.[159]

There were also public gladiators, supported and exercised at the expense of the State, and receiving pay from the fiscal. Caligula, when needing money, sold some by auction.[160] These gladiators, along with those belonging to the *lanistæ* and to private people, were so numerous that they threatened several times to break their chains, and became dangerous to the existence of the State. The revolt of Spartacus was so formidable that it was overcome only by the legions of Crassus and Pompey. At a later time the factions of the gladiators often disturbed public order in Rome. The emperors in several reprisals enrolled them in their armies, where they helped to introduce an undisciplined and ferocious spirit. Their numbers, and the feeling that they were indispensable both to the people and their rulers, gave them a great idea of their importance, although classed by the law amongst people without honour. This pride was singularly increased by the emperors mixing in their struggles. Commodus was proud only of his six hundred and twenty-six victories in the arena; one of his historians could even say, "that he was born rather to be a gladiator than to be a prince."[161]

Besides those who were gladiators by profession or taste, condemned culprits and prisoners were also compelled to fight. This seems to have been a primitive custom.[162] Emperors like Nero forced knights and senators, and even women of the noblest families, to descend into the arena.[163] One hardly knows which to wonder at the most, the despot who sought to dishonour everything in Rome that still shone with some lustre, or the cowardly Romans who had no longer enough energy to resist his sanguinary caprices. In the time of the persecutions of the Church, Christians were frequently condemned to the amphitheatre. The cruelty of this sentence was intentionally increased by forbidding them to receive payment from the public revenue, and forbidding them to learn the art of fencing to defend themselves from their attackers.[164] In the latter time of the Empire barbarian prisoners were the most frequent gladiators. If the Roman armies gained a victory, the captives were taken to Rome and given to the arena. The people who were seized with terror at the sight of the free Germans, gave themselves the cowardly pleasure of compelling them to kill one another whilst they were seated in safety on the tiers of the amphitheatre. They delighted to see these giant prisoners tremble, not with fear, but with rage and shame. The barbarians, to whom these fierce spectacles were unknown, wept at the idea of killing one another under the eyes of a populace who still boasted of being the people of Mars, but who, to merit this title, had only the harshness of their ancestors, without having their patriotic courage.[165]

If we are asked what enlightened men, those who passed for sages, thought of these games, we will content ourselves with quoting the opinions of two men, who, with an interval of four centuries between them, may be considered as organs of the pagan spirit. We will speak elsewhere of those who, obeying an impulse of their natural conscience, or a secret influence of Christianity, pronounced against gladiators. Just now it is important to show that defenders of the bloody amusements of the arena are found amongst the leaders of ancient thought, amongst those who expressed most exactly the mind and tendencies of pagan society.

Cicero did not condemn them. They were in his opinion an excellent school wherein to learn contempt for suffering and death. When he wished to show what could be attained by exercise, custom, deliberate determination, he cited the fearlessness and impassive courage.

of the gladiators, and their submission to the orders of the crowd; he restricted himself to adding only, that though these spectacles seem cruel to some people, he does not think that they are wrong, because only criminals condemned to death are compelled to fight in the arena.[166]

This reflection is not of much value, for the condition of those who are obliged to kill one another for the pleasure of the crowd does not change the nature of the spectacle; and further, to force criminals to kill one another proves a want of comprehension of the moral aims of chastisement. It is another proof of the harshness of the law and the egoism of Roman customs.

We will not linger with the panegyrist of Constantine, who in 313 praised this emperor for having turned a defeat of the barbarians into an amusement for the people, by giving the prisoners of this ungrateful and perfidious race to the beasts of the arena;[167] but we must refer to the sentiments of Symmachus, the last pagan, the active member of the college of high priests, who spoke eloquently in favour of the ancient national gods, and who was celebrated for his ancient virtues. After a victory of the Roman army over the Sarmatians, whose captives were reserved for the arena, he expressed a disdain, which was not thoroughly sincere, that these barbarians, so formidable in war, should be seized with fear when they found that they were obliged themselves to spill their own blood.[168] He gave gladiatorial games several times during his consulate.[169] On one occasion he arranged a combat of Saxon prisoners, which they escaped by killing themselves in their dungeons. Symmachus deeply regretted that "these despairing people, by killing themselves with impious hands," had deprived the Roman people of the sight of their death. He could console himself with nothing less than the example of Socrates, who was always tranquil even when fate was adverse to his wishes. He said that for the future he would not again choose for the arena these people, who were more villanous than Spartacus. He would have lions from Lybia, which were more docile than men.[170]

When we see such cold contempt for human life in the best of pagans, we no longer wonder at the passion of the crowd for displays of gladiators. At the same time we appreciate the terrible influence that these sights must have exerted over the mind and morals of the people. The last remnants of humane feeling were stifled, woman became as hardened as man, and parents by taking their children (who imitated the combats of the gladiators in their games) to the amphitheatre, prepared those cruel and cowardly generations which hastened the ruin of the Roman empire.

Through the applause bestowed on these conflicts by pagan society, it is sweet to distinguish some rare voices which, even before the time of the influence of Christianity, protested against this error of the human conscience. We find these examples in the poets. There is Ovid, who saw in the theatres and arenas only schools of corruption and barbarism, which he wished to see suppressed. There is Manilius, who expressed his indignation in energetic verse, representing the dangerous tendency of these sports in times of peace.[171]

The darkest touch of all in this picture of pagan egoism—which never dreamed that in debasing a slave a man equal in natural dignity was degraded—can be referred to by those who wish to consult the original authorities.[172]

(1) "ἀνελεύθερον." Arist., *Polit.*, III., 3, p. 75. (2) *Ibid.*, VIII., 2, § 1, p. 245. (3) Xenoph., *Œcon.*, c. 5, vol. v., p. 29 ff. (4) Xenoph., *Œcon.*, c. 4, § 3, vol. 5., p. 22. (5) *De Rep.*, II., p. 94 ff. (6) *O. c.*, p. 96. (7) *O. c.*, IV., p. 194. (8) Xenoph., *Œcon.*, c. 4, § 2, vol. v., p. 20. (9) *Politics*, VII., c. 8, p. 220. (10) *O. c.*, II., 1; III., 1, pp. 29-69. (11) *O. c.*, VI., 2, p. 191. (12) *O. c.*, II., 4; III., 2, 3; IV., 12, pp. 46, 74, 75, 136. (13) *O. c.*, VIII., 2, p. 245. (14) Xenoph., *Memorab.*, III., 7, vol. iv., p. 166. Ælian, II., 1, vol. i., p. 58. (15) Cicero, *Pro Flacco*, c. 8, vol. v., p. 61. (16) "An quidquam stultius, quam, quos singulos sicut operarios barbarosque contemnis, eos aliquid putare esse universos?"—*Tuscul.*, V., 36, vol. x., p. 573. (17) *De Off.*, I., 42, vol. xii., p. 65. (18) LII., 37, vol. ii., p. 25. (19) See, amongst other places, Lucian's *Nigrinus*, t. i., 32 ff. (20) *Theognis*, v. 177, *Gnomici*, p. 8. Cicero, *Tusc. Disp.*, V. 10, vol. x., p. 543. (21) *Theognis*, v. 631, 2, *Gnomici*, p. 26. (22) Juven., *Sat.* III., v. 37 ff., p. 45. (23) Menander, *Frag.*, p. 155 : "To what purpose, then, are the children which such parents are likely to bear? Are they not bastards and worthless? Most certainly so."—Plato, *De Rep.*, VI., p. 342. (24) *Majoriani Novella*, 8. (25) "A man of Phalerum, poor indeed and ignorant of politics, but otherwise not bad; nay, one might even say, a good honest fellow."—Demosth., *In Midiam*, § 83 ; *Oratt. Attici*, vol. iv., p. 487. Aristoph., *Plutus*, 976 ff., vol. i., p. 82. (26) *Fragment of Euripides*, ap. Stob., tit. 1, p. 82. (27) "Couldst thou possibly condescend so far as not to disdain the poor?"—Quintil., *Speeches*, 301, vol. iii., p. 17. (28) Lactant., *Div. Instit.*, VI., 10, vol. i., p. 457. (29) It is expressed by Cicero, when he says that " he is a good man who helps those whom he can, and harms nobody, unless provoked by some injury."—*De Off.*, III., 19, vol. xii., p. 141. (30) Ap. Cicero, *De Off.*, I., 16, vol. xii., p. 25. (31) *De Amic.*, c. 9, vol. xii., p. 219. (32) "Quidquid sine detrimento possit commodari, id tribuatur vel ignoto."—*De Off.*, I., 16, vol. xii., p. 25. (33) "It is but a poor kindness to give a beggar anything to eat or drink. For, both that which you give is lost, and the beggar's life is lengthened out for further wretchedness."—Plautus, *Trinummus*, Act II., Sc. 2, v. 58, 9, vol. ii., p. 159. (34) "Thus, then," said he, "ought a physician to act towards such a man " (*i.e.* an artizan). "Because, I suppose," said I, " he had a trade, and if he could not work at his trade, it was no use for him to live? Exactly," said he. "But the rich man, according to our view, has no such handicraft set before him, such that his life would be worthless, if he were compelled to abstain from it."—*De Rep.*, III., p. 168. (35) " 'Αισχρὸν γενέσθαι πτωχὸν, ἀσθενῆ δ'ἅμα."—Menander, *Fragm.*, 144. (36) Cf. Seneca, *Ep.* 27, vol. iii., p. 86; *De ira*, I., 16, vol. i., p. 20; *Natur. Quæst.*, I., præf., vol. iv., p. 153; Columella, XI. 1, and XII. 3, in *Scriptt. rei Rust.*, vol. ii., p. 418, 473. There were also infirmaries in the camps. See Forcellini's *Lexicon*. (37) Cf. Epict., *Dissert.*, I. 8, vol. i., p. 67. (38) Thucydides, in his description of the plague at Athens, says that there were some persons who went to tend their friends out of feelings of virtue and honour : ". . . οἱ ἀρετῆς τι μεταποιούμενοι, αἰσχύνῃ γὰρ ἠφείδουν . . ." II. 51, ed. Haack, Leipz., 1820, vol. i., p. 219. The scholiast explains ἀρετή by φιλανθρωπία καὶ ἀγάπης (kindly feeling and love) ; but ἀρετή, especially when contrasted with αἰσχύνη, ought not to be taken otherwise than in the old meaning of *fortitudo animi* (strength

THE LABOURING CLASSES.

of mind). (39) Thucyd., l.c., Pontius, vita Cypr., § 9 ; in *Opp. Cypr.*, p. cxxxix. (40) *De Off.*, II. 18, vol. xii., p. 98. (41) *De Off.*, II. 16, vol. xii., p. 94. (42) *Ib.*, 18, p. 98. (43) *Ib.*, 16, p. 94. (44) L.c. (45) Cicero, *De Off.*, II. 16, vol. xii., p. 94. (46) L. c. (47) Cf. M. Wallon, *Histoire de l'Esclavage*, vol. i., p. 150. (48) In the time of Julius Cæsar, 320,000 Romans shared in the distribution of corn ; by him the number was cut down to the half. It was not long before the number began to increase again. Augustus reduced it to 200,000. Under the Antonines it rose to nearly 600,000. (49) Curatoreo annonæ plebis, or annonæ frumentariæ populi.—*Inscrip. ap. Orelli*, vol. ii., pp. 81, 196, 201 ; *Cod. Theod.*, XIV., tit. 17, l. 1 ff. Even in Justinian's code there are regulations concerning the præfectus annonæ, which was entrusted with the distribution of the annonæ civiles.—*Corp. Jur.*, I., tit. 44; XI., tit. 22–24. (50) Euseb., *Hist. Eccl.*, VII. 21, p. 267; *Corp. Jur.*, l. c. (51) *Corp. Jur.*, l. c. (52) We regret that we have not been able to avail ourselves of M. Naudet's treatise " Sur les secours publics chez les Romains," in vol. xiii. of the *Mém. de l'Acad. des Inscript.* This volume is wanting in the collection of Memoirs in our town library. (53) Sallust, *Ep.* 2 ad C. Cæsarem de Republica Ordinanda, vol. ii., p. 207, and the passages from Cicero quoted above. (54) "Neque enim populo Romano saturo quicquam potest esse lætius."—Vopisc., *Aurel.*, c. 47 ; *Scriptt. Hist. Aug.*, vol. ii., p. 188. (55) Even Varro upbraids the Romans of his day : " they had rather busy themselves in the theatre and circus than in the cornfields and vineyards ; we contract for the corn that we live on, to be brought from Africa and Sardinia."—*De re Rust.*, II. præf. ; *Script. rei Rust.*, vol. i., p. 154; *Juvenal*, VIII. 117, 8, p. 99 ; Cf. Lactant., *De Mortibus Persecut.*, c. 7, vol. ii., p. 191. (56) See M. Wallon's classical work, *Histoire de l'Esclavage dans l'Antiquité*, 3 vol., Paris, 1847. (57) *e.g.* Becker, *Charicles, Bilder altgriech. Sitte*, Leipz., 1840, vol. ii., p. 20. (58) We use this expression here in its true meaning ; the modern meaning, invented by the Socialist schools, is exaggerated, and consequently false. (59) *De Leg.*, VI., p. 376. (60) Ibid. (61) *De Rep.*, I., p. 309. (62) *De Leg.*, VI., p. 376. (63) *Polit.*, I. 2, p. 10. (64) *O.c.*, II. 1 ; III. 1, pp. 29, 69. (65) *O.c.*; I. 2, p. 7; *Ethic. Nicom.*, VIII. 10, p. 161. (66) *O.c.*, I. 5, p. 25. (67) *O. c.*, I. 2, p. 12. (68) *Ethic. Nicom.*, VIII. 10, p. 161. (69) *Fragment of Euripides*, Ap. Stob., tit. 62, p. 237. (70) Diog. Laërt., VII. 1, No. 64, vol. ii., p. 784. (71) σώματα οἰκετικά, Æschin., *Adv. Timarchum*, § 16, vol. iii., p. 255 ; Σῶμα ἀνδρεῖον γυναικεῖον.—Bœckh., *Corp. Inscriptt. Græc.*, vol. i., No. 1607, p. 780 ; No. 1699, p. 825. (72) Cf. M. Wallon, vol. i., p. 288 ff. (73) "Homo vitissimus," *O. c.*, vol. i., p. 189 ; " Quasi secundum hominum genus."—Florus, III. 20, ed. Lemaire, p. 262. (74) Varro, *De re Rust.*, I. 17 ; in *Scriptt. rei Rust.*, t. 117. (75) *Parad.*, V., vol. xii., p. 260. (76) "For they do not call them slaves in the same way as bondslaves, who are made over to their masters by a bond or by some civil right."—*O. c.*, p. 262. (77) L. c. (78) " It is a kind of unjust slavery when those who can control themselves are placed under the control of another ; but when we make servants of those who cannot govern themselves, it is no wrong."—*De Rep.*, III. 19, ed. Lemaire, p. 315. (79) *De Off.*, I. 13, vol. xii., p. 21. (80) Ad Quintum fratrem, I., ep. l., vol. ix., p. 150. (81) Lucret., I., c. 456 ff., p. 18 ; Libadius, or. 31, *De Servitute*, vol. ii., p. 642 ff. (82) *Orat.*, 21,

p. 300 ff. (83) Macrob., *Saturnal.*, I. 11, vol. i., p. 244. (84) Xenoph., *De Rep. Ath.*, I. 10, vol. vi., p. 101. (85) The number is set down at 400,000. Hermann, *Griechische Staats-Alterthümer*, 2nd ed., Heidelb., 1836, p. 245; Becker, *Charicles*, vol. ii., p. 32. On the exaggeration of this figure, see M. Letronne's treatise, "Sur la population de l'Attique," *Mémoires de l'Académie des Inscriptions*, vol. vi. (New Series), p. 165 ff.; and M. Wallon, vol. i., p. 221 ff. (86) Xenoph., *De Republ. Athen.*, I. 11, vol. vi., p. 101; Plutarch, *Vita Lyc.*, c. 18, vol. i., p. 137. (87) Plutarch, l. c. (88) M. Wallon, *Explication d'un passage de Plutarque sur une loi de Lycurgue nommée la cryptie*, Paris, 1850. (89) Seneca, *Ep.* 47, vol. iii., p. 132. (90) ". . . Nec tanquam hominibus quidem, sed tanquam jumentis abutimur" (sc. servis). L. c. (91) *Dig.*, IX., tit. 2, l. 2. (92) Tacit., *Annals*, xiii. 32, vol. ii., p. 120. (93) Columella, *De re Rust.*, I. 6; in *Scriptt. rei Rust.*, vol. ii., p. 38. (94) "Thou porter, bound (O shame !) with chain of iron ! . . ."—Ovid, *Amores*, I. 6, 1, vol. i., p. 151. "It is said that Pilitus was once a slave, and even served as a doorkeeper, chained up as the old fashion was."—Sueton., *De claris rhetor.*, c. 3, p. 416. (95) Seneca, *Ep.* 47, vol. iii., p. 132; Plin., III., *Ep.* 14, vol. i., p. 97. (96) Seneca, *De Clem.*, I. 18, vol. ii., p. 26; *De Ira*, III. 40, vol. i., p. 103; Dio Cassius, LIV. 23, vol. ii., p. 68. (97) Juvenal, VI. 222-3, p. 71. (98) Macrinus, Aurelian, etc. Vid. Jul. Capitol., Macrinus, c. 13; Flav. Vopisc., Aurelius, c. 49; in *Scriptt. Hist. Aug.*, vol. i., pp. 218, 189. (99) Theano, *ad Callistonem;* in *Mulierum Græc. fragm.*, p. 232. (100) Cf. Böttiger, *Sabina, oder Morgenszenen in dem Putzzimmer einer reichen Römerin.* Leipz., 1806, vol. i., p. 40 ff. (101) Plutarch, *Cat. Mag.*, c. 4, vol. ii., p. 391. (102) Sueton., *Claudius*, c. 25, p. 238. (103) "Durum hoc fortasse videatur."—*In Verrem*, II., l. v., 3, vol. iv., p. 85. (104) "Sositheus decesserat, meque plus, quam servi mors debere videbatur, commoverat."—*Ad. Att.*, I., ep. 12, vol. viii., p. 93. (105) *De Rep.*, VIII., p. 448; *De Leg.*, VI., p. 378. (106) *Ethic Nicom.*, VIII. 10, p. 161. (107) *Politics*, I. 5, p. 24 ff. (108) Columella, I. 7; in *Scriptt. rei Rust.*, vol. ii., p. 43. (109) Seneca, *De Clem.*, I. 26, vol. ii., p. 33; *Ep.*, 107, vol. iv., p. 52; Plin., IV., *Ep.* 14, vol. i., p. 97. (110) "Totidem esse hostes, quot servos."—Seneca, *Ep.* 47, vol. iii., p. 132. (111) Id., *De Clem.*, I. 24, vol. ii., p. 31. (112) Seneca, *Ep.* 47, vol. iii., p. 132 ff. (113) Seneca, *Ep.* 27, vol. iii., p. 87. (114) Cf. Clem. Alex., *Pædag.*, III. 4, vol. i., 270. (115) August., *De Civit. Dei.*, II. 11, vol. vii., 32. (116) Tatian, *Or. contra Græcos*, c. 22, p. 263; Clem. Alex., *Pædag.*, III. 11, vol. i., p. 298. "All things are full of iniquity, of monstrosity, and of shame."—Chrysost., *Hom.* 37 in *Mat.*, § 6, vol. vii., p. 423. (117) Min. Felix, c. 37, p. 140. (118) "The very harlots, too, victims of the people's lust, are brought upon the stage, their misery increased as being there in the presence of their own sex, from whom alone they are wont to hide themselves; they are paraded publicly before every age and every rank—their abode, their praises and their gain are set forth, and that even in the hearing of those who should not hear such things. I say nothing about the rest. . . ."— Tertull., *De Spect.*, c. 17, p. 80. "Even those who have sold their chastity, blush to be seen there."—Cypr., *De Spect.*, p. 341. (119) According to Varro, ap. August., *De Civit. Dei*, IV. 31, vol. vii., p. 87. See too VI. 9, p. 121. (120) M. Wallon, vol. iii., p. 236 ff. (121) "Insigne ducitur sacerdotii vacare muneribus."—X., *Ep.* 54, p. 289.

(122) Or. 19, *pro saltatoribus*, vol. ii., p. 474 ff. (123) I. *Sat.* II. 1, 2, p. 208. (124) At Antibes the following inscription was found:—D. M. | Pueri Septentri | onis annor. XII. qui | Antipoli in theatro | biduo saltavit ex pla | cuit. " To the departed spirit of Septentrio, a boy aged twelve, who danced for two days in the theatre at Antipolis and was applauded."—Orelli, vol. i., p. 467, No. 2607. (125) Personæ inhonestæ. Munus turpe.—*Cod. Theod.*, XV., tit. 7, l. 4, 12. (126) *Ibid.*, l. 1 ff. (127) Tertull., *De Spect.*, c. 22, p. 82; *De Corona*, c. 6, p. 104. (128) Under Tiberius and Nero. Tac., *Ann.*, IV. 14, vol. i., p. 198; XIII. 25, vol. ii., p. 115; Sueton., *Nero*, c. 16, p. 265. (129) Sueton., *Domit.*, c. 7. p. 381. (130) Plin., *Panegyr.*, c. 46, vol. ii., p. 185. (131) Chrysost., *Hom.* 6 in *Ep.* 1 ad Thess., c. 4, vol. xii., p. 464. (132) Cf. Val. Max., II. 4, § 7, p. 97. (133) J. Capitol., Vita Maximi, c. 8; in *Scriptt. Hist. Aug.*, vol. ii. p. 66. (134) Cicero, *De Off.*, II. 15, vol. xii., p. 95; *Pro Sextio*, c. 64, vol. v., p. 431. (135) Cicero, *Pro Sextio*, c. 59, vol. v., p. 425. (136) "Interim jugulantur homines, ne nihil agatur."—Seneca, *Ep.* 7, vol. iii., p. 16. (137) "We desire at times to hide our grief and to stifle our groans, and yet the tears break forth despite the assumed composure of our countenance. At times we engage our minds with games or gladiators; but yet some slight hint of sorrow in the very games by which we are detached undermines our resolution. Therefore it is better to conquer our grief than to beguile it."—Seneca, *Consol., ad Helviam*, c. 16, vol. i., p. 138. (138) Tacitus, *Ann.*, I. 76, vol. i., p. 62. (139) Seneca, *De ira*, I. 2, vol. i., p. 6. (140) Prudent., in Symmachus, II., v. 1095 ff., p. 488; Tatian, *Or. contra Græcos*, c. 23, p. 264; Lactant., *Div. Instit.*, VI. 20, vol. i., p. 490. (141) Cicero, *Pro Sextio*, c. 64, vol. v., p. 430; *De Off.*, II. 15, vol. xii., p. 95; *Pers.*, VI. 48 sq., p. 25. (142) Cicero, *Pro Sextio*, l. c.; in *Vatinium*, c. 15, vol. v., p. 457. (143) Tacit., *Ann.*, XI. 22, vol. ii., p. 20. (144) *O. c.*, XIII., 31, p. 120. (145) Symmach., II., *Ep.* 46, p. 50. (146) Suet., *Domit.*, c. 4, p. 378. (147) Pliny, IV., *Ep.* 22, vol. i., p. 136. (148) *Athen.*, IV. 39, vol. ii., p. 100. (149) Livy, IX. 40. (150) *Sil. Ital.*, XI., 51–54; ed. Lemaire, vol. i., p. 648. *Athen.*, l. c., p. 99. (151) The philosopher Demonax told the Athenians when they were deliberating whether they should introduce combats with gladiators, that they ought to reverse the altar of mercy before adopting this custom. (152) In reference to the games of gladiators given for the first time at Berytus by Agrippa, who was otherwise so humane, see Josephus, *De Bello Jud.*, VII. 3, vol. ii., p. 406. (153) "Familiæ gladiatoriæ."—Cicero, *Pro Sextio*, c. 64, vol. v., p. 430; Tatian, *Or. contra Græcos*, c. 23, p. 264. (154) Tatian, l. c. (155) See the inscriptions ap. Gruter, vol. i., p. 333 ff. (156) Tusc. Disp., II. 17, vol. x. p. 435; Epict., *Dissert.*, I. 29, vol. i. p. 157. (157) Seneca, *Ep.* 37, vol. iii., p. 111; Petron., c. 117, p. 540; Cf. *Cod. Theod.*, XV., tit. 12, l. 2, 3. (158) *Instit.*, III., § 146, p. 271. (159) "Constantius, contractor for games, gave this tomb as a recognition to his gladiators for the favourable reception of his exhibition. A crown was given to the netfighter who killed Cœruleus, and himself fell, being killed; for both the fire was their death, both are covered by the tomb. The pursuer (*i.e.* light-armed fighter), hero of nine battles, who obtained a crown, left him dead on the field, to the grief of his wife Valera."— *Found in Istria*, Gruter, vol. i., p. 333, No. 4. (160) Dio Cassius, IX. 14, vol. ii., p. 182. (161) Herodian, I. 48, p. 36; J. Capitol., *Ant. Phil.*,

c. 19; in *Scriptt. Hist. Aug.*, vol. i., p. 66. (162) Cicero, *Tusc. Disp.*, II. 17, vol. x., p. 435. (163) Tacit., *Ann.*, XV. 32, vol. ii., p. 229; Suet., *Nero*, c. 12, p. 262. (164) Euseb., *De Martyr. Palæst.*, c. 7, 8, pp. 328, 330. (165) "Plebs Martia."—Symmach., *Epp.* X. 61, p. 295. (166) "What gladiator, even a man of ordinary standing, ever utters a groan or changes colour? Who ever shows cowardice when he takes his stand, or even when he succumbs to his foe? Who ever draws back his neck when he has succumbed to a foe and the people order him to be slain? Such is the force of training, practice, and custom." "To some the gladiatorial show appears cruel and barbarous, and I am not sure that it is not so in the present day; but when the criminals used to fight, no training could have been more effective to harden the eyes against pain and death."—*Tusc. Disp.*, II. 17, vol. x., p. 435. (167) "What can be more glorious than this triumph, when he gives us all a share of pleasure in the slaughter of our foes, and enhances the splendour of his spectacles with the remnant from the barbarian slaughter; when he throws so great a crowd of prisoners to the beasts, that those ungrateful and perfidious wretches feel as much pain for their own ridicule as for death itself."—*Incerti Paneg. Const.*, c. 23; in Pliny, *Opp.*, vol. ii., p. 335. (168) L. X., *Ep.* 61, to Theodosius, p. 295. (169) L. VIII., *Ep.* 4, p. 167. (170) L. II., *Ep.* 46, p. 50. (171) Ovid, *Tristia*, II., el. 1, v. 280 ff., vol. iii., p. 221. Manilius, *Astron.*, IV. 220 ff.; ed. Jacob, Berlin, 1846, p. 129. (172) *e.g.*, Fr. Jacobs, "Die Männerliebe" in his *Vermischte Schriften*, vol. ii., p. 212 ff. Xenoph., *Sympos.*, c. 8, vol. v., p. 206 ff.; *Athen.*, XIII., vol. v., p. 177 ff. Plutarch, *Flamin.*, c. 10, vol. iv. Cicero, *Tusc. Disp.*, IV. 33, vol. x., p. 524; *Philipp.* IV. 6, vol. vi., p. 280. Quintil., *Instit. Orat.*, VII. 4, vol. ii., p. 44. Sueton., *Domit.*, c. 8, p. 381; Juvenal, II. 43 sq., p. 36. Seneca, *Epp.* 47 and 95, vol. iii., pp. 132, 417. Colum., I. præf., in *Scriptt. rei rust.*, vol. i., p. 21. "'Υπὸ βαρβάρων διώκεται, προνομίας δὲ ὑπὸ 'Ρωμαίων ἠξίωται, παίδων ἀγέλας ὥσπερ ἵππων φορβάδων, συναγείρειν αὐτῶν πειρωμένων."—Tatian, *Or. contra Græcos*, c. 28, p. 267. *e.g.*, Sueton., *Tiber.*, c. 43, p. 153. Tacit., *Ann.*, VI. 1, vol. i., p. 259. Lamprid., *Heliog.*, c. 33; in *Scriptt. Hist. Aug.*, vol. i., p. 254. Aur. Victor, *De Cæsar.*, c. 28, p. 124. Lamprid., Al. Sev., c. 24, l. c., vol. i., p. 974. Euseb., *Vita Const.*, III. 55; IV. 25, pp. 512, 537. In the dialogue "Amores," vol. i., p. 873 ff. Amatorius, c. IV., vol. xii., p. 5.

CHAPTER IV.

CONSEQUENCES AND EXCEPTIONS.

§ 1. *Decline of Ancient Society.*

By uniting the different touches of the picture we have sketched, we can form some idea of the spirit which animated pagan society. Though somewhat roughly drawn, it will suffice for our aim.

Egoism was the ruling principle of antiquity: sometimes it was the egoism of the State, sometimes of the individual. The personality of man, his liberty and natural rights, were unknown; the State only recognised the citizen, whose physical and intellectual forces she absorbed. The citizen, beyond his relation with the State, saw only inferior beings whom he might use for his enjoyments, as the State used him for political needs. The respect due to man as man was forgotten; he was valued only in proportion to his external position. Social rank was the measure of individual worth.

The family and marriage were only political institutions, with no moral aim for individuals. Woman was deprived of her natural rank in society. The child was only a future citizen, and was the property of his father until he entered upon the enjoyment of his rights. The poor and workers were despised, because no one could be a citizen unless he was rich enough to do without work. The conquered became the slave of the conqueror, and as a slave lost all personality and sank into a mere chattel. To sum up, egoism reigned supreme everywhere and changed all social relations by its despotic requirements.

We have heard much of the polished manners and the humanity of the Greeks, of the exact justice and even the clemency of the citizens of Rome. If the picture we have drawn is faithful, we shall know what to think of these exaggerated opinions. Where the individual has been swallowed up in the State, where individual life has no other rule of conduct than earthly success, there can be neither true humanity nor true justice. Cicero himself acknowledged, "We have neither true right nor true justice; we have only a shadow, a feeble reflection;"[1] because there could be no justice where there was neither love nor respect for man.

Public egoism, far from being tempered by the conduct of individuals, was re-asserted in all its strength. It could not be otherwise; for the political morality of antiquity was only the fruit and expression of the mind of each of those who composed it. The individual had made society in his own image; he had no ideal which he could use as a type. The vague remembrances of a better state, of a lost golden age, had been banished to the region of myths. The freeman owed himself to the State because the State was his workmanship, in a way his property, and it guaranteed him the means of realizing terrestrial happiness. But if he had duties towards the State, he had none towards humanity. Antiquity did not recognise humanity, but saw in people living beyond the national frontier nothing but barbarians or enemies, persons to whom no duties were owing beyond political relations. It followed from this that the citizen, in all other relations than those to the Republic, was master of his own actions, and yielded to his individual egoism. The more he esteemed obedience to the laws, submission and devotion to the State, the more he felt free to follow his passions and desires when not restrained by political considerations.

Whilst the civic virtues were strong they bridled the egoism of men. Grecian and Roman citizens, compelled to fight in defence of their country, stimulated by the desire to increase her glory and greatness, found in their patriotism the secret of the admirable things that they accomplished. But there came a time when these virtues were weakened. In proportion as they grew rich and incurred the dangers of a purely external civilization, they asked only to enjoy their fortune. Public interest yielded to personal interest, and individual egoism triumphed over that of the State.

The institutions of the pagan world were powerless to stop this fatal progress; ancient society entered the time of its decadence; the vices of its social morality caused its fall. The decadence began in Greece when Rome was still strong and great. The Romans, victorious over the Greeks, despised them for their triviality, their perfidy, their effeminacy, their proverbial debauchery. Cicero did not exaggerate when he said that there were but few Greeks who were worthy of their former glory.[2]

However, it was not long before the Romans imitated them. At the very time when they made a mockery of them, they were already descending the steep incline leading to moral decadence and the dissolution of society. In the time of the Empire, political virtue, which had been shaken by the civil wars, quite disappeared; the rich no longer took any interest in public business. The despotism of the emperors paralysed all energy. Those who still kept a remnant of ancient patriotism took refuge in the resignation of stoical philosophy, and allowed the vessel of the Republic to drift, contenting themselves with shivering at the perils which threatened it. With the greatest number absolute indifference had replaced ancient civic devotion. In pagan society no one thought of anything but utility or passing pleasure. Interest alone, as Epictetus said, became the father, brother, parent, country, god of men.[3]

Many Romans sought both nourishment and pretext for their egoism in the materialistic philosophy of Epicurus, which they eagerly embraced. This system, destitute of moral principle, knowing no other law than enjoyment and indifference to public misfortunes, smiled on men of the world at a time when a Nero or Heliogabalus reigned. It was invoked on all sides to justify the vilest excesses and to give permission for a cowardly withdrawal from the duties of citizen.[4] The "pigs of Epicurus" were the subject of the contempt of the most elegant libertines, as well as of those who still kept a remnant of ancient patriotism.[5] If the rich and great, those whose community really represented the ancient State, abandoned the State and broke the ties which united them to it, what virtues could be expected from the population of the towns? Degraded, debased, despising work as much as they were themselves despised, living by the daily distributions, rushing to join in the tumults or in the amusements of the arena, they precipitated themselves into the abyss with the same carelessness as the rich.

The Empire was abandoned to tyrants or to troops of prætors. Neither law nor the systems of philosophers could rekindle in their hearts the power needful to save a falling world. Rome was no longer, as in primitive times, the abode of all ancient virtues.[6] These virtues had vanished; both those of the citizen and those of the individual had perished in the universal ruin. Egoism in its most disgraceful form, with its cowardice and harshness, its libertinism and indifference, was everywhere rampant. It was bound to be so, for egoism was the root of ancient morality, and could produce finally only the death of society.

§ 2. *Purer Opinions.*

But, we shall be asked, was there nothing good in this classic world, without a knowledge of which no modern education is thought to be complete? Did human conscience never speak? Do we find no moral idea rising above the universal level? We have no idea of answering these questions with an absolute negative. Whilst we maintain that the general spirit was essentially egoistic, and without respect and love for man, we recognise with pleasure that there were sages who looked higher, who made efforts—of which perhaps they took no account— to break the bonds of pagan morality, and protested, at least by implication, against the tendencies which ruled their countrymen.

We find in several eminent men purer ideas about social relations than those which constituted the public opinion, the social spirit of antiquity. It will be enough to mention some of these witnesses, whose number could be easily increased. We will choose the most striking, to show that we have not carelessly disparaged ancient civilisation by setting forth only the darkest sides.

There were some who held ideas contrary to custom and accepted opinion in reference to woman and marriage; they approached those which a little later were introduced by Christianity. Socrates affirmed that woman is not inferior to man by her nature, and that if she lacks thought and strength, it is his duty to raise her by education to his own level.[7] Plato, notwithstanding his errors as to the position and destiny of woman in the Republic, seems to have foreseen a higher aim for marriage than the political one; for he said it served also to bring servants of the gods into the world.[8] Aristotle has a still stronger feeling of the moral aim of marriage. He speaks of the duty of husband and wife to help one another, to be reciprocally complete, each one having individual gifts. The children seemed to him to strengthen the bond between father and mother.[9] We find also in some of the poets this idea of marriage as a union of mutual service, a community of duties placed under the protection of the gods.[10] For example, Theognis says that the purest happiness consists in the home life with a good wife.[11]

There were also in Greece and Rome, even after the heroic ages, some marriages founded upon mutual esteem,[12] where peace and devotion reigned; where the wife was chaste and modest, finding her happiness in managing her household, full of deference for her husband and of tenderness for her children. We know the beautiful tribute of Xenophon to the virtues of the wife of Ischomachus.[13] We know also the Roman matrons of the time of the Republic, whose noble type was perpetuated to the middle of the decadence in such women as Helvia, the mother of Seneca.[14]

The children of these families were not treated with the harshness which was authorized by custom and law. We are astonished to find that even Aristotle, who counsels abortion and exposure, requires fathers to love their children, and thus recognises the duties of natural affection.[15] Menander in one of his comedies teaches that a good father does not aggravate his son, and that kindness is the best means of education.[16] This feeling was sometimes carried to the length of weakness; and whilst antiquity shows us touching examples of true and grateful filial piety,[17] we also find sons who abused the too great indulgence of their fathers.[18]

We also find juster opinions as to slavery scattered throughout the ancient writers. We do not speak of the purely speculative opinions of the Stoics, for it was not a sufficient protest against slavery to call it an accident deserving the contempt of sages; it was needful to proclaim also the dignity of work, and the natural equality of slave and master; but this idea itself, so foreign to the genius of antiquity, was expressed by some philosophers. Socrates asked if it is honourable for freemen to be more useless than slaves; if it is nobler to dream in inaction of the means of living, than to seek them by working.[19] According to the testimony of Aristotle, there were in his time men who maintained that it is law, not nature, which distinguishes the freeman from the slave, that the master's power is the result of violence, and consequently that servitude is an injustice.[20] Aristotle does not adopt this opinion himself, probably because it seemed to him dangerous for the institutions of Greece. We find it again in Philemon the comedian. Though any one is a slave, he is not the less made of the same flesh as the master; for no one is a slave by nature, it is only the body that ill-fortune can bring to servitude.[21] Theano, the wife of Pythagoras, desires that masters shall treat their slaves with kindness, because by their nature they also are men.[22]

It is equally pleasant to be able to state that the idea of benevolence was beginning to dawn in some of the greatest minds. Socrates was in this respect, as in so many others, before his age. Notwithstanding the contradictions in his ethical views, he wished that men should do good to the poor, not from personal interest, but to keep them from falling.[23] Aristotle expressed afterwards the beautiful thought, though without divining all its depth, that there is more happiness in giving than in receiving.[24] He also said that the happiness of love does not consist in the possession of the object which is loved, but in the act of love itself, because it is an energy of the soul. He felt that there existed a benevolence less restricted than friendship, a love due also to the unknown.[25]

Socrates had vaguely foreseen this idea of a more universal bond between men. When asked on one occasion as to his country, he replied, "I am a citizen of the world."[26] We say he had vaguely foreseen, because we do not think that this expression had the same meaning in the mouth of the philosopher that it would have if spoken by a Christian. It was the protest of an individuality which felt its rights, against the oppressive egoism of the ancient State. Cicero reveals the meaning attached to these words by many of those who repeated them, when he approaches them with the thought that a man's country is where he finds himself well off.[27] Political virtues had become weak. The individual sought to withdraw from his duties towards his country in order to live only for himself. He thought himself at home wherever he found that he was comfortable. Love of country, exclusive though it was, had made the greatness of the ancient world. The weakening of this virtue, unreplaced by a purer feeling, was not a moral progress. It was a progress in the egoism of individuals. We admit with pleasure that Socrates had felt instinctive impulses of this purer and more humane sentiment;

Cicero also was not a stranger to it. He foresaw a city higher than the earthly one, a natural community embracing all men on earth. He was the first to pronounce the name of charity to designate the tie of love which in this city should unite the whole human race.[28]

We may also mention, as showing a better spirit at the time of the decadence of Roman society, the sadness of Tacitus and the indignation of Juvenal over the widespread corruption of their time. These two noble minds, although they remained strangers to the influence of Christianity, rose to a great height above degenerate pagan society. The historian had a warm feeling for the strong Roman virtues, and was filled with hopeless sorrow by the degradation of his contemporaries. The poet placed moral purity of heart above outward respectability of conduct.[29] He knew that the bad thought, though untranslated into outward action, is wrong, and he pitilessly castigated the irregularities of his age.

Besides, what more signal proof can there be that in the midst of the moral decadence of the Roman world there remained better souls, than the conversion of so many men to Christianity? They were filled with trouble at the sight of the lax morality in all classes of society, whilst the conviction of the powerlessness of laws, philosophic systems, and pagan worships, to change the world by benefiting individuals, made them conscious of their own weakness, and led them to the Gospel. Without this gospel some would have fallen into doubt and despair; others, to stupify themselves, would have rushed with greater eagerness into material enjoyments. Society would have been dissolved. Humanity would have perished hopelessly in a bottomless abyss.

We must look upon the more humane ideas about social relations and duties which we find in some ancient authors, as well as on the examples of devotion and generosity recorded in history, not inspired by patriotism or self interest, as isolated facts! They are exceptions in the life of nations or individuals, often dictated by motives which it is not easy to unravel. They do not flow from one sole source, a moral principle which rules the life.

The opinions given by philosophers are also only exceptions in their moral and political systems; instead of being the necessary result or logical development of these systems, they are in opposition to the premises. More than once the same man expresses the most contradictory opinions upon the same subject, as he obeys his conscience or his politics. These contradictions are the most common in the finest minds : we have noticed them several times in Socrates and Cicero. It was the protest of conscience against the results of reflection, falsified by the general spirit of the times. The ancients themselves were sometimes struck with the difference between a man's principles and his conduct.[30]

What we have said of the activity of moral conscience that pagan life had not entirely stifled, proves sufficiently that we are not of the opinion of St. Augustine, when he maintains that a believing sinner is more pleasing to God than a virtuous pagan, in whose virtues he sees only splendid vices, or the semblance of good.[31] It seems to us that the purer opinions in the midst of paganism are rays of the light which naturally lights every man. They are made to see as St. Paul says, "For when Gentiles which have no law do by nature the things of the law, these, having no law, are a law unto themselves; in that they show the work of the law written in their hearts, their conscience bearing witness therewith, and their thoughts one with another accusing or else excusing them; in the day when God shall judge the secrets of men, according to my gospel, by Jesus Christ." [32] "God," says Origen, "has imprinted on the souls of all men ideas and moral rules for their direction in life, in order that they may not have the excuse at the day of judgment that they knew not the law." [33]

When we find the ideas of these rules expressed by pagan authors, it is neither polytheism nor the civil institutions which has inspired them. They are the efforts of conscience to make her voice heard, but as individual and isolated opinions they could never have become general precepts for society. A higher sanction was lacking. It was needful that they should be acknowledged as being of Divine origin. Here, where they should have found their firmest support, they met only with obstacles. The prevailing religion was not with them. This supreme authority, instead of giving help, contradicted them flatly by sanctioning the abuses, and favouring—by the example of the divinities—the vices which it ought to have known how to overcome.

We must therefore examine in a general manner the moral influence which paganism, through its own nature, was bound to exert.

(1) "Nos vero juris germanæque justitiæ solidam et expressam effigiem nullam tenemus; umbra et imagiuibus utimur; eas ipsas utinam sequeremur."—*De Off.*, III. 17, vol. xii. p. 139.   (2) Sallust., *Ep.* 1 *ad Cæs. de rep. ordin.*, c. 9, vol. ii. p. 182.   Horace, II. *Sat.*, II. 10, 11. Cicero, *Ad Quintum fratrem*, I. *Ep.* 1, vol. ix. p. 150; *In Verrem*, II. lib. I. 26, vol. iii. p. 261.   Plin., *Hist. Nat.*, XV. 5, ed. Lemaire, vol. v. p. 382.   Juvenal, III. 60 ff. p. 43.   (3) *Dissert.*, II. 22, vol. i. p. 314. (4) Cicero, *De finibus*, I. 7; II. 14, vol. x. pp. 148, 192.   (5) Horace, *Epist.*, I. 40 ad fin., p. 298.   (6) "Virtutum omnium domicilium."— Amm. Marc. XIV. c. 6, vol. i. p. 21.   (7) Xenoph., *Sympos.*, c. 2, vol. v. p. 161.   (8) *De Leg.*, VI. p. 370.   (9) *Ethic Nicom.*, VIII. 12, p. 163. (10) Stob., vol. lxvii. p. 272.   (11) *Gnomici*, p. 49, v. 1177 sq.   (12) Coum., XII. præf.; in *Scriptt. rei Rust.*, vol. ii. p. 467.   (13) *Œcon.*, c. 7 vol. v. p. 40 ff.   (14) Seneca, *Consol. ad Helviam*, c. 14 ff., vol. i. p. 135 ff.   (15) *Ethic. Nicom.*, VIII. 12 p. 162.   (16) " υἱὸς δ' ἀμνείων

ἐστὶν εὐνοίᾳ πατρός."—p. 238.   (17) Val. Maxim., V. 4 and 5, p. 264 ff.
(18) *e.g.* the Hautontimoroumenos of Terence. Cf. M. Saint-Marc.
Girardin, *Cours de litt. dram.*, vol. i. p. 212 ff.   (19) Xenoph., *Memor.*,
II. vol. iv. p. 118.   (20) " For according to the law one man is a slave
and another man is free ; but by nature there is no difference. Therefore
it is an injustice, for it is the power of force."—*Polit.*, I. 2, p. 7.   (21)
Philem., *Fragm.*, ed. Meineke. Berl., 1823, p. 410.   (22) *Ep. ad Callistonem;* in *Mul. Græc. fragm.*, p. 232.   (23) Xenoph., *Sympos.* c. 4, vol.
v. p. 174.   (24) *Eth. Nicom.*, IX. c. 7, p. 177.   (25) Ibid.   (26) Cicero,
Tusc. Disp., V. 37, vol. x. p. 375.   (27) Ibid.   (28) " For when a
soul, after learning and imbibing all the virtues, enters into a fellowship
of charity with its friends, taking as such all who are allied by nature ;
when it adopts a pure worship and religion : . . . what can one
imagine or describe more blessed than such a state ? Then, moreover,
let it not consider itself hedged in by the walls of a single town, but
acknowledge itself a citizen of the whole world, as though one city.
. . ."—*De Leg.*, I. 23, vol. xi. p. 360.   "Fellowship with the human
race, charity, friendship, justice."—*Acad. Quæst.*, IV. 46, vol. x. p. 131.
(29) "Nam solus intra se tacitum qui cogitat ullum facti crimen
habet."—XIII. 209, 210, p. 143.   (30) Cicero, speaking of Epicurus,
whose life was better than his system, says : " We must inquire not
into his private character, but the spirit shown in these treatises."—*De
finibus*, II. 25, p. 209.   (31) *Contra Julianum Pelagianum*, IV. 3 ;
Contra duas epp. Pelagianorum, III. 5, vol. x. pp. 391, 301.   (32)
Romans ii. 14, 15, 16.   (33) *Contra Celsum*, I. 4.

CHAPTER V.

THE RELATIONS OF ANCIENT MORALITY WITH PAGANISM.

§ 1. *Moral Impotence of Paganism.*[1]

WE are far from agreeing with many of the early Christians in saying that pagan religions were inventions of the devil for the ruin of men, by keeping them in error and evil. However imperfect they were, we see in them a faint reflection of eternal truth; they were manifestations of the religious need innate in the soul of man.

Amongst the philosophers and poets of ancient times, who were gifted with greatest genius, we meet here and there with bursts of pious feeling, aspirations towards God and Divine things expressed in sublime terms. The same conscience which revealed its life by proclaiming parts of the moral truth, showed itself also in foreseeing the truth about God.

The popular religions themselves recognised the presentiment of the true relation between man and divinity. What were the sacrifices, unless they were acts testifying to the need of reconciliation, and the desire of sinful man to be at peace with God? What these religions lacked, besides complete truth about the nature of God, was moral power, the necessary authority to lead men to good, and the indispensable help to sustain their weakness. "The pagan religion," said Montesquieu, "forbade only some flagrant crimes; it stopped the hand and neglected the heart." [2] This moral impotence was inherent in the nature of polytheism. If there is a plurality of gods, there can be neither unity nor energy in religious belief. The spiritual life of the soul is divided. This division became a source of torment to thinking minds, and of carelessness or superstition to the frivolous or ignorant multitude. To which of these gods of unequal power, and jealous of one another, must a man address his prayers? Is he certain to be upheld or protected by the one he has invoked? Is it suitable to pray to them all at once, or is it not simpler to pass them all by? These are questions that must have been asked many times by reflecting men as to their relations with the divinities. Still further, these gods, on account of their number, were necessarily limited in wisdom and power. They were too much like man. They resembled him too much in his imperfections. Therefore their moral influence could not be very efficacious. Their anger might be feared, but how could they be respected or loved?

They were generally personifications of the forces or phenomena of nature, or deifications of the faculties or affections of man. Thus paganism chained man to nature, and did not raise him above himself. It never showed him a higher world beyond the visible one. It knew nothing of the immortality of the soul, or had only an imperfect foreshadowing of it. It followed therefore that life upon earth was the sole aim of man, and the search for terrestrial happiness his only occupation during a fleeting existence, terminated by death. Especially amongst the Greeks, who were an impressible and lively race, man was lost in external nature. He yielded with delight. Physical beauty was the object of his enthusiastic worship, and physical enjoyment his supreme happiness. He was restrained by no true religious principle. The examples of the gods, on the contrary, impelled him forwards.

The character of the divinities was the greatest hindrance to the moral influence of paganism. It offered to its followers no ideal of perfection. Mythology has no type of holiness, of purity, of perfect love. Gods, like men, hated and fought one another, returning evil for evil. They had no forgiveness for their equals; how should they have it for men, except for those who bought it by their offerings? When we add to that their unregulated passions, their unbridled sensuality,[3] we shall be convinced that a religion which supports hatred and voluptuousness by the example of the gods must have a melancholy effect on morality. Besides, this was an unregretted influence; immorality was sanctioned and made a means of honouring the gods.

Xenophon of Corinth promised Venus fifty courtesans if he carried off the victory at Olympia, and Pindar celebrated this vow by an ode.[4] There were temples which were served by *hetæræ*, or built with the tax that they payed to the Republic. These women dedicated to the goddess of love precious gifts bought with the price of their dishonour. The generative power was worshipped under the name of Phallus, to whom worship was given in impure mysteries.

Art, the powerful helper of ancient religions, also contributed to weaken their authority over men. Some have thought that it was a great means of moral education amongst the Greeks; that the contemplation of the majesty of the Olympian Jupiter, of the ideal beauty of Apollo, of the harmonious regularity of the forms of Venus and the Graces, must necessarily inspire similar feelings, and strengthen the moral sense by gratifying æsthetic taste.[5] Others have seen in art only the product of an ardent and sensual imagination, and have certainly reckoned it amongst the most active causes of the decay of religion and morality amongst the Greeks.[6] We do not go so far. We doubt not that beautiful and noble feelings were aroused by the sight of the great works of nobly inspired genius; but that depended on the subject represented, as well as on the individual disposition of the spectator. Art could not modify or create dispositions where they did not exist; it had not the power to regenerate men. This is the more true because even in its best period it lacked a solid and certain moral principle. The decline of art followed the decline of Greece; from that time the artists chose impure subjects, the loves of the gods, their debauches and quarrels. There was no longer anything represented on pictures, vases, bowls, and bass-reliefs but immoral mythological scenes, exciting to evil.[7]

The religion of the Romans had at its commencement a more serious character; the people had more fear and respect for the gods than the Greeks. In the earliest times they had no idols, they only consecrated temples and woods to their divinities. Thence came also greater gravity in life, more of external virtues. Besides the causes of decay inherent in the nature of paganism, the ruin of Roman religion was hastened by the invasion of the art and myths of Greece. The moral fall accompanied the fall of their worship. Greek mythology, disseminated by poets and artists, exercised a pernicious influence upon Roman morality. In the last two centuries of the Republic, Roman painters ornamented the interior of the houses with voluptuous scenes from the history of the gods,[8] and gave the goddesses the features of their own courtesans.[9]

ANCIENT MORALITY AND PAGANISM.

Thus paganism, both in its essence and in the art which it inspired, was incapable of arousing and satisfying the moral and religious needs of the heart; on the contrary, it aided all the egoistic passions. The sight of the loves of the gods was sure to produce licentiousness; whilst that of their wars was not calculated to inspire men with a love of peace. The histories of Greece and Rome supply a thousand proofs of this conclusion. The works of the ancients abound in passages, where not only is the licentiousness of the gods given as an excuse for that of men, but where this is represented as inspired by the gods themselves.[10] When the man of slight morality saw the fables of his divinities reproduced by the arts under a thousand forms, he discovered always beneath the harmony of the verses, or under the grace of the statues, beings whose conduct was no better than his own. Instead of being turned towards improvement, he was led to sin with more assurance, his conscience being sheltered by the examples of vice in his gods. Imagination and moral feeling were completely changed, and mythological deeds, instead of filling the soul with calm, excited bursts of violent passion.[11]

The wisest men had not overlooked these dangers. Plato mocked at these fables and the genealogies of the gods. He blamed the poets for having invented them, and wished to banish their immoral rites from his ideal republic.[12] The more practical Aristotle wished for their suppression in the existing republic, but he had to limit his demands to the removal of statues, images, and immoral ceremonial from the sight of youth.[13] The poets themselves mourned the ill effects of mythological knowledge. Ovid expressed himself very strongly in verse on the dangers of frequenting the temples where only scandals about the gods would be learned.[14] Propertius shuddered when he thought of the hand that had first painted obscene pictures to pollute the chaste looks of the maidens.[15] Varro declared that both worship and life are purer when man worships invisible gods. He thought that those who first made images destroyed respect for the divinity which they lessened, so plunging the people into miserable error.[16] He recognised that a religious soul is powerfully impressed by the invisible and infinite only; a sculptured god will never be the object of either love or fear. The educated man will see in it only a beautiful statue, without believing it a god; the common man will be led to superstition, or confirmed in vice.

This was not all. Pagan rites tended to harden instead of softening the heart. Amongst the Romans the sports of the amphitheatre were accompanied with ceremonies and sacrifices; in invocation and honour of the gods, the blood of gladiators and wild beasts was caused to flow. It was one of the functions of the Roman pontiffs to give these sports. To this must be added the human sacrifices, which were not used only by the nations of Asia or Africa, or by the peoples of Germany and Gaul, but were also offered by the Greeks and Romans to their divinities in the period of their highest civilization.[17] These were not always solemn acts of expiation,[18] or the best means of appeasing angry gods,[19] but they were acts of national hatred towards conquered prisoners,[20] perhaps even simple pretexts for disposing of men and children who were not wanted.[21] Whatever was the aim, they were acts of useless barbarity, mad rites which proved at the same time the little respect that the ancients had for man, and the little care felt by them for the life of prisoners taken in battle, and inferiors. According to Porphyry, human sacrifices were suppressed everywhere in the time of the Emperor Adrian,[22] but again at the commencement of the fourth century the Romans, according to the testimony of Lactantius, offered bloody worship to Jupiter of Latium, by sacrificing a man in his honour every year.[23]

§ 2. *Weakening of Religious Beliefs.*

It is easy to foresee the results of this cruel and impure religion, and the moral effects that it must produce upon its followers. In proportion as men reflected, their reflections estranged them from their gods. The progress of civilization led to the decay of religious faith. Incredulity replaced the ancient worship given to the gods; but this did not make men better. The moral effects were the same as those of superstition. Men could sin in as much comfort when not believing in the gods, as when conforming their lives to the fables which they held as true. The first impression would necessarily be that these divinities, limited in their power, and always occupied with rivalries and amorous intrigues, cared very little for the affairs of mankind. Some verses of Ennius expressing this thought were recited in Rome amidst the applause of the people.[24] The poet Lucilius, the friend of Scipio, mocked at the gods and at those who prostrated themselves before empty images believing that there was life in their brazen statues.[25]

This spirit spread through all classes of society. It found an interpreter, in the time of the decadence, three centuries later, in Lucian, whose dialogues of the gods, more witty than the satires of Lucilius, are also bolder, because incredulity had made rapid progress. The gods were given to the laughter of the crowd in gross comedies.[26] The pagans, after making their heaven a theatre for ignoble intrigue, mocked at their own work by transporting it to the stage, and making actors take the part of gods.[27] Augustus himself, though externally a severe guardian of their worship, parodied the adventures of Olympus in his orgies with his courtesans.[28] It was thought honourable no longer to believe in "the ignoble mob of gods."[29] The fables awoke the respect of none, not even women and children.[30]

The most eminent men proclaimed this incredulity. Cæsar and Cato said calmly, in full senate, that they did not believe in the immortality of the soul.[31] Philosophers had long taught these principles. Three centuries before Christ, Stilpo of Megara had affirmed that the Minerva of the Parthenon was not a divinity, but the work of a man. The life of this philosopher accorded with his absence of faith,—he had a taste for wine and women.[32] Nearly at the same time, Euhemerus wrote a book to prove that the gods were only men, whose sepulchres might still be seen, and who consequently deserved no extraordinary respect.[33] Ennius translated this book, which was much relished in Rome, where philosophy early took a direction hostile to the popular religion. Cicero thinks it probable that men may arrive by reflection[34] at the conclusion that there are no gods; for himself, he thinks he does a good thing in combating superstition, belief in the silly fables invented by poets and painters; with the reserve, however, that the wise man does not seek to disturb the institutions and rites of his fathers.[35] Cicero, notwithstanding this reserve made as a statesman, contributed greatly by his works to weaken the belief of his fellow-citizens. Several of his dialogues show clearly the uncertainty and inefficacy of his faith in the existence of a divinity.[36] There were others with less caution than he. Lucretius wrote a poem with the avowed intention of destroying religion, which he looked upon as the cause of all evils.[37] These atheistic and materialistic philosophers, indifferent to public misfortunes, assisted, calm and careless, in the ruin of ancient liberties. "It is," said Lucretius, "a pleasant sight for the wise man, seated on the sea shore, to see a ship struggling with the angry waves, or to view in safety the movements of two armies upon the battle-field."[38]

The philosophers, far from replacing the superstitions they assailed with a purer faith, in which moral conscience and ancient virtue should have regained their extinguished energy, made themselves contemptible by sharing the debauchery and libertinism of their time.[39] At their death, tombs were raised by their friends, consecrated to eternal sleep.[40] Thus wisdom, dishonoured even by those who called themselves her disciples, fell into the same contempt as religion. Paganism, according to the expression of a pagan himself, furnished some with arguments in favour of incredulity, and others with excuses for their vices.

Still, the statesmen who saw this evil influence were also aware of the moral power of religious faith, and felt compelled to save it as a means of government; they tried to purify it from what they called the inventions of the poets. The high-priest Scævola, a hundred years before Christ, who himself disbelieved the fables and held by philosophic theology, tried to re-establish the disturbed national worship by separating it both from the mythological and speculative elements, which were, in his opinion, unsuitable for the people. Varro had the same aim. He believed that there were many true things of which the people ought to know nothing, and many untrue ones which it was useful that they should believe. He thought, like Cicero, that the ancient

Roman religion, freed from successive additions, should be preserved, as much on account of its antiquity as because of its usefulness to the Republic.[41] He even allowed philosophers to confess that religion was only an arbitrary invention of statesmen, in order to restrain, through fear of the gods, those who would not otherwise submit to the laws.[42] These politic philosophers observed the forms of worship in order to set an example of obedience to the people, "because the laws prescribed them, and not because they are said to be pleasing to the gods." They rendered customary honours to "all that vile populace of gods that the superstition of several ages had infinitely increased"; but it was only done to conform to national customs.[43] These customs were protected by law, which also forbade the exercise of unapproved religions. The emperors were high-priests; they claimed and obtained divine honours. Domitian commenced his decrees with these words: "Such is the will of our lord and god."[44] Heliogabalus paraded the streets of Rome in a chariot drawn by lions or tigers, and was saluted in turns as Bacchus, or as the mother of the gods.[45]

This politic hypocrisy and sacrilegious ambition answered no end. An official worship given to gods in whom men had no longer any faith, was a melancholy method of bringing back the crowd to the faith of their fathers. Religion, brought down to be an expedient for more thoroughly oppressing the people, lost its remaining influence. The Romans, seeing the gods ridiculed in the theatre, despised by men of the world, deserted by philosophers; seeing also heaven invaded by the most unworthy tyrants, who were placed in the rank of gods, sank deeper and deeper in an abyss of corruption and impiety.

Strange to say, in the midst of this general incredulity, the need of putting man in relation with invisible and superior powers made itself felt anew; so true is it that the human heart cannot live without religion. But, instead of going to the living spring that Jesus Christ had put into the world, men addressed themselves to the divinities of foreign nations. They had recourse to many ceremonies. They consulted magicians, diviners, priests of all kinds. They were initiated into all mysteries, and, in order to sin comfortably in the midst of this revival of superstition, they introduced into Rome the most impure worships of Oriental countries. Women, especially, followed this path eagerly; but it was even more astonishing to see grave and educated men deny divine providence and the immortality of the soul, whilst they believed in all auguries.[46]

The emperors were no less credulous. Some prohibited foreign ceremonials, whilst themselves practising them secretly; others opened temples in Rome for all the Asiatic and Egyptian divinities. At the same time philosophers tried to revive faith in polytheism by their speculations or their phantasies. Apollonius of Tyana, a contemporary of Christ, offered a singular mixture of magic and theosophy to unsatisfied souls. He was reverenced as the equal of God by some emperors of the third century; but his extraordinary system had no influence on mankind.[47] More serious efforts were made by the new Platonists. They wished by mystic interpretation and subtle allegory to give power to the religious ideas, which in the schools were only vague abstractions, powerless to influence the heart, and in popular worship were only absurd or immoral fables. They discovered everywhere divine manifestations beneath the imperfect forms. They hoped to revive faith in the gods by restoring mythology to what they called its primitive purity.

This system, often profound and ingenious, was the last sign of life in paganism before its fall; the last ray of a light, feeble in its own nature, and ready to be extinguished for ever. Their ideal enthusiasm had no power over the masses. The people could not understand this mixture of mysticism and superstition which was offered to them as the final remedy. They could not rise to the cloudy heights of their metaphysics, which was less powerful the less it was occupied with moral questions. Pagan society remained idolatrous or incredulous, with uncorrected morality; a new principle of faith and a new principle of life were needed to change and save it.

Conclusion.

After having sought to understand the spirit which, in the ancient world, men breathed towards each other in their mutual relations, we have found that the pagan religion was powerless to change this spirit and arrest the universal ruin. It was necessary for the Roman world to be completely destroyed to make room for a new order of things.

Ancient society, in the time of its greatness, shows of what human nature is capable through its inherent forces. It represented humanity with its natural qualities, energetic vices and incomplete virtues. It gave us immortal examples in literature and art; it produced heroes and thinkers worthy of eternal admiration. But it had neither protection nor encouragement for the weak; it had no comfort for the sorrowful, no real restraint for the wicked.

This civilization was the first step on the ladder of

progress ascended by humanity, under the eye of God, through ceaselessly renewed sorrows: the period of its greatest glory marks the highest point which can be reached by men without the sense of God's guidance and without knowledge of His law. Society, having attained this, is compelled to stop; it has no force to carry it farther. Whatever just admiration we may have for antiquity studied in all its bearings, we could not say with a celebrated historian that the ancient Republics produced men whose moral greatness has never been surpassed on earth;[48] for this greatness of the ancients was cold and proud. Love, forgiveness, humility, were not its essential elements. It lacked what is deepest and most spiritual in principle, religious principle. In the time of the decadence no one in pagan society attained even to the greatness of the early ages. This greatness had belonged only to the citizen, and there remained but debased subjects under despotic emperors. Patriotism had vanished beneath the freezing breath of of the lowest and most egoistic interest. Men hated or despised each other. They ridiculed their gods. They were occupied with base or barbarous pleasures. Society was united only by external bonds, and these bonds were so loosened that they would break with the least strain.

Where can the remedy for all these evils be found? Must we seek it in the institutions and social principles of the ancient world? These institutions were worn out, and these principles were themselves the cause of the universal decadence. A society founded upon an unjust fact—that is, contempt for the human personality—can be saved only by a new fact. A tyrant, a contemporary of Christ, after having spoken of the powerlessness of the laws to arrest corruption, of which he was himself a shameful instance, uttered these memorable words: "We must seek the remedy in the recesses of the soul itself."[49] Truly it was through the soul that the cure of the human race must come; the individual conscience must be regenerated before society could be raised. For this the world required a new leader, as the Roman augurs had predicted,[50] though with another meaning, in the time of Nero.

(1) Cf. M. Villemain, "Du polythéisme dans le premier siècle de notre ère." *Nouv. mélanges*, Par. 1837, p. 201 ff.; M. Filon, "Mémoire sur l'état moral et religieux de la société romaine à l'époque de l'apparition du christianisme." *Mém. de l'Acad. des sciences, mor. et polit., Savants étrangers*, vol. i. p. 769 ff.; Tholuck, *Ueber das Wesen und den sittlichen Einfluss des Heidenthums*; ap. Neander, *Denkwürdigkeiten aus der Geschichte des Christenthums*. Berlin, 1823, vol. i. (2) *Esprit des lois*, XXIV. 13. According to Benj. Constant (*Du polythéisme romain*, vol. i. p. 55), this statement is not altogether accurate, for, "when polytheism has reached a certain stage of perfection, it takes account of the heart's emotions as well as the outward actions." This opinion does not seem to us so true as Montesquieu's, which is based on a deeper and fuller knowledge of the nature of polytheism. (3) See amongst others the *Protreptictus* of Clem. Alex., vol. i. p. 1 ff. (4) *Athen.*, XIII. 33, vol. v. p. 72, where too the fragment of the ode is found. (5) Fr. Jacobs, "Ueber die Erziehung der Hellenen zur Sittlichkeit," in his *Vermischte Schriften*, vol. iii. (6) Tholuck, the treatise above quoted. (7) Plin., *Hist. Nat.*, XXXV. 36, §§ 4, 24, ed. Lemaire, vol. ix. pp. 329, 342. Cf. too Grüneisen, "Ueber das Sittliche in der bildenden Kunst der Griechen," in the *Zeitschrift für historische Theologie*, vol. iii. bk. 2, p. 1 ff. (8) Terence, *Eunuchus*, Act III. Sc. 5, v. 34 ff., vol. i. p. 151. (9) Plin., *Hist. Nat.*, XXXV. 37, § 6, vol. ix. p. 365. Seneca, *De Superstit.*, ap August., *De Civit. Dei*, VI. 10, vol. vii. p. 123. (10) Eurip., *Hippol.*, 451 ff., vol. i. p. 319. Isocrat., *Paneg.*, § 46 ff.; in *Oratt. Att.*, vol. ii. p. 241. *Athen.*, XIII. 20, vol. v. p. 44. Martial, XI., *Ep.* 43, vol. ii. p. 149 ff. (11) Terence, *Eun.*, l.c. Plin., *Hist. Nat.*, XIV. 28, § 3, vol. v. p. 362. (12) *De Rep.*, II. p. 108 ff. *Euthyphron*, c. 6, vol. viii. p. 64. *De Leg.*, XII. p. 365. (13) *Polit.*, VII. 15, p. 241 ff. (14) *Tristia*, II., *El.* 1, 287 sq., vol. iii. p. 222. (15) *Eleg.* II. 5, 19 sq. p. 206. (16) Ap. August., *De Civ. Dei*, IV. 31, § 2, vol. vii. p. 87. "If we impute the origin of sin to the gods, what else is it but giving an incentive to our sins? It is just using the example of deity to give unbridled licence to moral iniquity".—Seneca, *De Brevit. Vitæ*, c. 16, vol. ii. p. 68. (17) Porphyrius, *De Abstin. ab esu Animalium*, II., Venice, 1547, qto. fol. 51. Clem. Alex., *Protrept.*, c. 3, vol. i. p. 36. 18) Sueton., *Octav.*, c. 15, p. 63. Dio Cassius, XLVIII. 14, vol. i. p. 441. (19) Dio Cassius, XLVIII. 48, vol. i. p. 462. (20) Plutarch, *Arist.*, c. 9,

vol. ii. p. 352. (21) Tertull., *Apolog.*, c. 9, pp. 34, 35. (22) Porphyrius, *ibid.* (23) Tatian, *Or. Contra Græcos*, c. 29, p. 267. Min. Felix, c. 30, p. 114 ff. Tertull., *ibid.* Lactant., *Div. Instit.*, I. 21, vol. i. p. 92. (24) Ap. Cicero, *De Divinat.*, II. 50, vol. xi. p. 284. Cicero adds, "magno applausu, assentiente populo." (25) ". . . veri nihil, omnia ficta."—*Fragm. ex. sat.*, lib. 20; in *Persius and Juven.*, p. 216. (26) Tertull., *Apolog.*, c. 15, p. 54. (27) Clement of Alexandria, addressing the pagans, exclaims : "Alas! what iniquity; ye have made heaven into a stage, and divine things are become to you a play; things holy ye have turned into buffoonery with the masks of devils, and true religion ye have travestied with superstition."—*Protrept.*, c. 4, vol. i. p. 52. Firmicus Maternus, c. 13, p. 28, also says : "Ye have turned heaven into a stage." (28) Sueton., *Octav.*, c. 70, p. 100. (29) "Ignobilis deorum turba."—Seneca, *De Superst.*, ap. August., *De Civit. Dei*, VI. 10, vol. vii. p. 122. (30) *Juvenal*, VI. 149 ff., p. 40. Cicero, *Tusc: Disp.*, I. 5, vol. x. p. 363. (31) Sallust., *De Bello Catil.*, c. 51, 52, vol. i. pp. 80, 87. (32) Cicero. *De Fato*, c. 5, vol. xi. p. 313. (33) Id., *De Nat. Deor.*, I. 42, vol. xi. p. 52. Athenag., *Legatio*, c. 28, p. 305 ff. Clem. Alex., *Protrept.*, c. 2, vol. i. p. 20. August., *De Civit. Dei*, VII. 27, vol. viii. p. 140. (34) *De Invent.*, I. 29, vol. i. p. 170. (35) *Pro Cluentio*, c. 61, vol. iv. p. 355 ; *De Nat. Deor.*, II. 2, vol. xi. p. 60. *Tusc., Disp.*, I. 5, 6, vol. x. p. 363; *De Divinat.*, II. 72, vol. xi. p. 302. (36) See M. Villemain, *Du Polythéisme*, etc., p. 208 ff. (37) I. 931, p. 34. (38) II. 1-6, p. 44. (39) Seneca (*Ep.* 29, vol. iii. p. 92) says that he has no hope of getting a certain Marcellinus to be a philosopher, and this is the reason : "He will examine our schools, and accuse philosophers of bribery, adultery, and gluttony; he will show me one in a brothel, another in a cookshop, another in a noble's court. He will cast in my teeth these charlatans who would have done better never to have touched philosophy than thus publicly defame it." See, too, Juvenal, *Sat.* II. 1 ff., p. 35. (40) "Somno æternal. | C. Matrini | Valen- | ti, philosophi Epicur. vix. ann. XXXIX."—"To the eternal sleep of Caius Matrinus Valentius, Epicurean philosopher. He died aged 39," etc.— Ap. Orelli, vol. i. p. 262, No. 1192. (41) Ap. August., *De Civit. Dei*, IV. 27-30, vol. vii. p. 84 ff. Cicero, *De Divinat.*, II. 33, vol. xi. p. 269. (42) Cicero, *De Nat. Deor.*, I. 42, vol. xi. p. 52. (43) Seneca, *De Superst.*, Ap. August., *De Civit. Dei*, VI. 10, § 3, vol. vii. p. 123. (44) Sueton., *Domit.*, c. 13, p. 386. (45) Lamprid., *Heliog.*, c. 38; in *Scriptt. Hist. Aug.*, vol. i. p. 250. (46) Plin., *Hist. Nat.*, II. 5, vol. i. p. 234. (47) Caracalla built him a temple.—Dio Cassius, LXXVII. 18, vol. ii. p. 415. Alex. Severus placed his bust in his private chapel.—Lamprid., *Al. Sev.*, c. 29; in *Scriptt. Hist. Aug.*, vol. ii. p. 278. Julia Mammæa, especially, held him in great esteem. (48) Sismondi, *Histoire de la chute de l'Empire Romain*, vol. i. p. 18. (49) Tiberius: "reliquis intra animum medendum est."—Tacit., *Ann.* III. 54, vol. i. p. 167. (50) ". . . parari rerum humanarum aliud caput."—Tacit., *Ann.* XV. 47, vol. ii. p. 212.

BOOK II.

CHAPTER I.

FUNDAMENTAL PRINCIPLES OF CHRISTIAN MORALITY.

§ 1. *The Kingdom of God and its Founder.*

THE human race had forgotten God, but He willed that men should not perish. He had not turned from them. He desired by recalling them to Himself to bring them back to the path of truth and happiness. There was no man to whom this mission could be entrusted. No son of the preceding generations was pure enough to carry out the plans of Divine wisdom and love; therefore God sent His Son to save the world, and Christ was born.[1]

The nation in whose midst Christ was born was almost unknown, and was despised by those who knew it; but in it was still preserved the tradition of one only true God, and the promise of a Redeemer. A great legislator had laid down a code of pure morality, and a series of inspired men had enforced obedience after each transgression, and revived hope when the sorrow of public calamity was heavy on the people. At the time of the birth of Christ, this nation had fallen under Roman rule. Their morality was lowered, their pious zeal was cooled, but in the midst of this decadence they looked for the Messiah to renew and restore all things. This hope of a Saviour arose vaguely in the world at a time when, beneath its material power, pagan society showed symptoms of inevitable dissolution. A mysterious unrest disturbed humanity. A prophecy, already called ancient, was repeated amongst the nations, that the East should arise, and a new power, coming from Judea, should govern the world.[2]

It is here that Jews and pagans had their thoughts fixed on temporary interests and a splendid earthly kingdom. They dreamt of nothing but a temporal saviour, a powerful king, a victorious conqueror. But suffering and fallen humanity required other remedy than this. Every form and phase of earthly power had been tried without finding either liberty or peace, and especially without finding true happiness for the soul. The essential thing was, to teach man to love his brother and sacrifice himself for his sake; to humiliate himself in order to respect others, in spite of their bodily weakness or lower rank; to recall the equality of all men in misery and dignity, because all are equally sinners destined for eternal salvation; to show the realized type of moral purity and perfect love which was thought impossible. It was to draw them back to the fear of a God of justice and to confidence in His mercy. It was to found a kingdom not of this world, a reign of God, with different characteristics, laws, and conditions from the earthly ones. It was for this that Christ came into the world, beginning with the cradle and ending with the cross, living a life of obedience to God and love to man. It was for this, also, that His life and teaching formed such a contrast to all that antiquity was accustomed to hear and see.

At the birth of Christ, shepherds heard heavenly voices announcing great joy for all people: "Glory to God in the highest, peace on earth and goodwill to men."[3] On the banks of Jordan, in the deserts of Judea, a man of austere manners prepared the way for Him, more powerful than himself, who[4] "shall throughly cleanse His threshing floor; and He will gather the wheat into His garner." He said to men of all ranks, " Repent, for the kingdom of heaven is at hand."[5] He who should found this kingdom was to be mighty in "words and works," as Moses was;[6] of humble birth, belonging to a workman's family, poor, but of royal descent, He united in His own person the two extremes of pagan society. Touched with the misery and sins of men, seeing their hatred, rancour, violence, and mutual harmfulness, He determined to deliver them from the yoke under which they groaned, whose burden was heavier than they could lift. But first He felt, like them, temptations to egoism and pride. It was not till after He had triumphed[7] over these, that He taught men, like John, His forerunner, "Repent, for the kingdom of heaven is at hand."[8] He preached the gospel, the good news of the reign of God."[9] Though without a place to lay His head, He taught with authority, astonished the people, perplexed the sages, and ruled the winds and sea.[10] He then describes the kingdom which He invites all to enter, in which those who are admitted enjoy perfect happiness and a peace more real and durable than the world can give.[11] They find the only true liberty, and throughout the world there is no other real slavery than the service of sin, no other servitude than submission to the evil which reigns in the hearts of men.[12] The kingdom of God does not come with outward splendour, like earthly empires which are founded on egoism and maintained by force:[13] it is internal and spiritual, and will endure for ever and ever. In opposition to this kingdom, Jesus Christ set the sins and miseries of the world. He testified against the world that its works were evil,[14] so that the sinner was left without excuse.[15] He aroused the wish to enter the peaceful kingdom of God, by awaking in the weary and heavy-laden soul the knowledge of the sin which was in itself and the evil it suffered here below.[16]

The head of this new kingdom is not an arbitrary and capricious man, but God Himself; as to whose nature Christ teaches truths which are at once profound and simple: God is a spirit,[17] He is not a visible, limited, imperfect being; He is not a jealous God, yielding to evil passions; He is the Father of all men, without distinction.[18] He calls all men to His kingdom; they are received, not for their social position, but for their individual worth; dignity must be in the soul itself, for "what shall it profit a man to gain the whole world and lose his own soul? Or what will a man give in exchange for His own soul?"[19] A time will come when all men must give an account to God, not of their rank and fortune, but of their personal worth, their inmost feelings, and the actions which have resulted from these feelings.[20] The poor and afflicted, neglected by the ancients, are called happy by Christ, who promises them eternal consolations.[21] "To the poor is the gospel preached" was His answer to John's disciples who asked if "He was He who should come." He thanked God that *these things* were hidden from the wise and prudent, and revealed unto babes.[22] Women, as well as men, have their place in His kingdom. Christ gives them the same help, and insures for them the same salvation.[23] He did not exclude even little children, but blessed them, and said to His disciples, "Forbid them not to come to Me."[24]

We must not think that Christ shut the doors of His kingdom on the wise, the great, the rich; for though in their pride they despised and oppressed their inferiors, they were also men, with souls of not less worth than those of the poor. If He said, "It is easier for a camel to go through the eye of a needle than for a rich man to enter the kingdom of God," it was only to show the hindrances which love of worldly wealth places in the way of religious desires; He added also that "what is impossible with men is possible to God." [25] Jesus Christ came "to seek and to save all that were lost." [26] He declares it to be "the will of God that no one shall perish, but that all shall be saved"; [27] He invites all sinners to come to Him, He seeks all the wandering sheep, He re-opens the doors of His Father's house for those who were far off.[28] All men without exception bear the yoke and penalty of sin; rich and poor, strong and weak, are under its power, but all may be saved; all alike are in sin and misery, and all alike may hope for the same salvation.

Jesus Christ broke the narrow bonds of ancient patriotic exclusiveness, and addressed His appeals to other nations than His own. He invited all the nations of the world, without distinction, to enter His spiritual kingdom. "Jews and Samaritans,[29] pagans from the east and west,[30] must all be *one* in God and in Him." [31] Mankind must form "one flock under one Shepherd." [32]

The laws of this kingdom must be different from the ancient laws, which, founded on egoism, were summed up in *talion* and the right of the strongest. The Jewish law gave no other measure of love than self-love. Its morality was better than that of the pagan law, and commanded love to one's neighbours; but it considered as neighbours only those who would do us no injury, or at furthest those who were fellow-countrymen.[33] Moral obligations were reduced to negative advice, "Do not to others as thou wouldest not that they should do to thee." *Talion* itself was sanctioned in its harshest form. "Thou shalt love thy neighbour and hate thine enemy." [34] "An eye for an eye, a tooth for a tooth." [35] Thus Christ said that He gave a new commandment.[36] This new unknown commandment is perfect, disinterested love; love capable of sacrificing personal interest for a brother's good;[37] such love as He Himself practised, and of which there was previously no example. "A new commandment I give unto you, that ye love one another; even as I have loved you, that ye also love one another."[38] This is the greatest commandment, equal to the one "to love the Lord thy God with all thy heart and soul and mind."[39] To keep this faithfully is the mark of a disciple and member of the kingdom of Christ.[40]

We may be surprised that love is turned into a command, imposed with the authority of a law. How can this spiritual and spontaneous feeling be imposed, and why has Christ commanded it? The ancient order of things had a fundamental law, a principle which united its morality and institutions; the new order must also have its principle and law. It is not a law like that laid down by an earthly State, but a condition that is to be freely fulfilled. It is a virtue of the soul, and in this view love becomes a duty for the Christian. We are only Christian whilst loving. He who will not love, who refuses to obey this greatest commandment, is not a member of the kingdom of God.

Everything is comprised in this law of love; for when we love, everything is easy. The entire moral teaching of Christ is summed up in love. If He enters into little details about other virtues, it is only because they are different manifestations of this fundamental one. One of the Apostles said truly that love is the fulfilment of the law, that all precepts are summed up and abbreviated in that of love.[41]

No idea of this new love had dawned on the ancient world. It is universal. Men are no longer separated by differences of nationality or worship. They are, without distinction, brethren.[42] It is an active, devoted, untiring love. The rule is no longer to refrain from doing evil, but "to do to all men whatsoever ye would that they should do to you."[43] Who is there that does not always like, especially in misfortune, to receive proofs of kindness and sympathy? Therefore it is a love doing good to all who are in need; it restrains its own wants that it may help and clothe the poor, satisfy their hunger, and relieve them in illness.[44] This love is humble, free from pride. If the pagan gave largess through ambition, if the Pharisee sounded the trumpet when he went in the street to give alms, the orders of Christ to His disciples are not to let their gifts be seen of men. "When ye give alms, let not your left hand know what your right hand doeth."[45] Finally this love is a complete renunciation of egoism; for it banishes hatred, rancour, and the wish to return evil for evil. Where the loving Christian sees discord, he tries to re-establish peace;[46] he hopeth all things, and so refrains from judging his brother. Remembering his own weakness, he is indulgent to the faults of others, and refrains from throwing the first stone. He no longer says, "an eye for an eye," but he offers no resistance to evil done to him. "Whosoever smiteth thee on the right cheek, turn to him the other also."[47] He has nothing to do with vengeance (though it was permitted by the law of the Jews, and was considered a sign of greatness of soul in pagan society), for he knows a diviner and purer greatness of soul, the forgiveness of injuries, always and unconditionally.[48] In the kingdom of God it is not enough to avoid external violence, the heart must be free from hatred. God refuses the worship of those who cherish hatred in their heart. "Before laying thy gift on the altar, be reconciled to thy brother." If he should refuse, Christian love, far from being cooled, displays fresh energy. "Ye have heard that it was said, Thou shalt love thy neighbour, and hate thine enemy. But I say unto you, Love your enemies, and pray for them that persecute you; that ye may be the sons of your Father which is in heaven: for He maketh His sun to rise on the evil and the good, and sendeth rain on the just and the unjust. For if ye love them that love you, what reward have ye? do not even the publicans the same? And if ye salute your brethren only, what do ye more than others? do not even the Gentiles the same? Ye therefore shall be perfect, as your heavenly Father is perfect." [49]

Christ has expressed the essence of this love in the idea of *service:* " Whosoever would become great among you shall be your minister; and whosoever would be first among you shall be your servant."[50] Thus what the Jews and pagans had the most thoroughly despised and debased becomes the highest standard of moral greatness in the new order; servitude is ennobled and re-instated, loving service is the social law of the kingdom of God.

There remains still a final step: the loving Christian gives up interest, fortune, pleasure to help a brother; but will he sacrifice his life? The pagan would sacrifice himself for his country, but not for *man*. Jesus Christ places the sacrifice of life as the supreme proof of love, not for a vanishing terrestrial State, but for the immortal soul of man, even the least on earth. " Greater love hath no man than this, that a man lay down his life for his friends." [51] We see, by the example of Christ, that these friends are men.

It has been said that the universal love that Christ taught to His people excluded a deeper special love; that the Christian, who was devoted to the human race, was cooler in his own relationship—he had no longer family, friends, or country. This error is contradicted both by the entire spirit of the new law and by the precise teaching of Christ Himself. He, who honoured with His presence the wedding at Cana in Galilee, also asserted that marriage is a Divine institution. He thus sanctified conjugal union and affection, and strengthened the marriage bond which was held as loosely by the Jews as by the pagans.[52] He was the first to forbid divorce, the separation by man of those who had been joined together by God.[53] He was the first to reduce the grounds of separation to the sole ground of adultery; whilst He added further, that "whoever married her who was put away, also committed adultery."[54] By this He reserved for the divided pair the possibility of repentance, pardon, and reconciliation. He loved and blessed little children, and held them up as models, that the love of their parents might be thereby increased; He trusted them to their care, He desired them to be received in His name,—that is, brought up to faith in Him; He threatened those who despised them and led them to sin and perdition.[55] He had a special love for His disciple John,[56] and delighted in the society of the family of Bethany, thus sanctifying friendship in its purest sense. Lastly, He gave the most explicit teaching as to the duties of His disciples towards their country, when He Himself paid the public tribute[57] and added the words, "Render therefore unto Cæsar the things that are Cæsar's; and unto God the things that are God's."[58] He clearly showed the relation between His kingdom and all earthly ones; He came to found a spiritual reign, whose bond and law are love; an alliance of soul, notwithstanding the barriers of rank and nationality. When Pilate asked Him, "Art Thou a king then?" He answered, "Thou sayest that I am a king," but "my kingdom is not of this world."[59] This kingdom however is not necessarily in antagonism to the terrestrial State; it does not suppress it, and can subsist in the midst of the world. Citizens of the kingdom of God remain earthly citizens and fulfil these obligations obediently and faithfully. It is only when Cæsar trenches on the domain of God, and asks for what does not belong to him, that the citizen of the heavenly kingdom, whose conscience has been wounded, gives unhesitatingly to God what belongs to Him alone, and obeys Him rather than man.[60]

Such are the new laws of the kingdom of Christ. The love of God and man is its foundation, as the love of self was the base of ancient society. But the salvation of men will not be accomplished by giving them a new and unknown law, and ordering them a love contrary to their passions and habits; it must be presented to them in living realization to prove its possibility. Antiquity had sought in vain for such a type, but it was given by Christ Himself. His life was pure and holy, filled with love and sacrifice. He went from place to place, moved by compassion for the afflicted, "healing all manner of disease and all manner of sickness,"[61] doing good to all, without regarding "the person of men,"[62] without asking to what nation or worship those who asked help belonged.[63] He sought the society of the poor and despised, even of sinners; for "it is they who are sick who need a physician."[64] He showed the difference between the justice of God and that of man; and in His Father's name gave pardon to the repentant sinner, however low his lot. He forgave the impure woman after she had washed His feet with her tears; He confounded the accusers of the woman taken in adultery, and said,

"Neither do I condemn thee; go, and sin no more"; in the midst of His suffering on the cross, He gave to the penitent thief the assurance that he should be with Him in Paradise.[65] It may seem perhaps that it was easy for Christ to say, "I forgive you," to these people, who had not injured Him; but He went further, and accomplished the most difficult and astonishing thing the world had ever seen. Notwithstanding the proofs of His love, His people did not receive Him.[66] The crowd accepted His benefits, sat down by Him, pressed round His pathway to bring the sick to Him; but whilst admiring Him remained deaf to His tenderest appeals. The great people, powerful by influence and authority, guardians of the ancient law, hated him as a dangerous innovator, and sought to kill Him after each miracle of His love. And yet, notwithstanding the indifference of the people and the hatred of the powerful, He never ceased to love them all. Each day He renewed His efforts to gather together the children of Jerusalem, "as a hen gathereth her chickens under her wings"; [67] He forgives both those who forsook and those who persecuted Him; He has only a sorrowful look for the friend who in a moment of weakness denied Him, and when he repented, He asked only for increase of love.[68] He wept over His unhappy country "which killed the prophets" and was blind to the things that "belong unto peace."[69] When He hung upon the cross, ready to give up His soul to God, beaten, spit upon, and crowned with thorns, no murmur escaped His lips; but for the murderers who insulted Him He prayed, "Father, forgive them; for they know not what they do."[70]

Throughout His life He remained thus "meek and lowly in heart,"[71] indignant only with the profaners of the temple, denouncing woe only on those hypocrites who "cleanse the outside of the cup and of the platter, but within they are full of extortion and excess."[72] Seeking no glory from men,[73] desiring always to do His Father's will, "He humbled Himself, becoming obedient even unto death, yea, the death of the cross."[74] He said that "whoever would become great" amongst the brethren must be their "servant"; that He Himself came "not to be ministered unto, but to minister."[75] To these words He added His own touching example, He performed for His disciples a service reserved for slaves; He washed their feet, and showed in this symbolical act that there can be no service too lowly for love to render.[76] Lastly, He taught that there can be no greater proof of love than the sacrifice of life for the loved ones, and proved His words by dying for His friends. And who were these friends? Not the disciples only, but all men, sinners, those who hated and persecuted Him. All are His sheep, and the good Shepherd seeks the lost sheep, and does not rest until it is brought back to the fold. "He layeth down His life for the sheep. He that is a hireling, and not a shepherd, whose own the sheep are not, beholdeth the wolf coming, and leaveth the sheep and fleeth." Mark well the contrast: "I lay down My life." Doubtless He might have escaped by flight the plans for His death, of which He knew; but it would have been like a hireling to prefer His own life to the salvation of men. He, who was all love, was incapable of this, which would have been egoism, and He had previously taught, "he who would save his life shall lose it." So He gave Himself up to His enemies, not through unreflecting and enthusiastic fanaticism, but as a proof of the greatest love. Christ loved men, notwithstanding their hatred and indifference; He wished to save them from the sin which hindered their love to Him. They crowned their sins by killing the innocent and holy One, who had only love and pardon for them. This enormous crime re-awakened their conscience and produced a repentance which was the starting-place of a new life. It was for this that Christ gave Himself and God allowed the sacrifice. It was thus that he died a victim of the sins of the people, which at the same time He expiated and effaced. It is thus that His death, the most startling proof of His love, is the necessary development, indispensable to His whole work, which thus becomes the cause of salvation to those who penetrate the mystery; and thus He fulfils His words, "'The Son of Man" gave "His life a ransom for many."

The death as well as the life of Christ is an example to be followed by all members of the kingdom of God. He said expressly, "I have given you an example, that ye also should do as I have done to you."[77] "A new commandment I give unto you, That ye love one another; even as I have loved you."[78] And this must be so far carried out as to make His people willing to sacrifice life itself for each other. The power of this new love taught by Christ, but unknown to the ancients, is that it embraces all men and is willing to sacrifice itself for them.

It will be said, it was easy for Christ to love thus, who was sinless, and one with the Father,[79] but what of us? The weakness of our nature, our circumstances, the prejudices of our time and age, our sins, offer insurmountable obstacles; how can we follow in His footsteps? The work of Christ would have been very unfinished if it had not shown to sinful man the way to copy Him, and become through love a citizen of His kingdom. He explains what gave Him the power of loving men: He loves them because He keeps His Father's commandments and abides in His love.[80] The love of God is thus the reason and source of the love of man; the new social order is founded on the purest religious principle. It is however not easy to the egoistical heart to love God. To attain this Christ emphatically repeats His precepts: Mend your ways. Leave the path of pride and vice, which leads to the death of the soul. Give up the service of the world; for no man can serve two masters at the same time.[81] Put the love and requirements of God before attachments to wealth or earthly friends.[82] Humble yourselves; do not think yourselves righteous; do not forget that "One there is who is good," and He alone.[83]

Still new obstacles arise in the heart: man has good desires, but no power to carry them out; he wishes, but thinks that he is unable. Christ shows how to conquer these difficulties, and the way of victory is still through the power of love. This time it is love for Himself, love which produces trust and fidelity, or as it may be called, faith.[84] Nothing is more powerful to kindle the flame of love in the human heart than love shown by another; and where could there be a greater act of love than the death of Christ? Who could resist its power? In picturing His sufferings and unmerited death, who could help feeling like the multitude who returned from Calvary "smiting their breasts."[85] Conscience is awake, and troubled with a sensation of complicity in the death of the just, for who could say that he would not have been one of the crowd who cried, "Crucify Him, crucify Him"?[86] This feeling of guilt, which accompanies gratitude for the love and holiness of Christ, leads to the wish to obtain His forgiveness and favour, and thus, through His sacrifice, to be reconciled with God. Christ wills that they who love Him shall be with Him where He is. He is their Advocate with the Father, who holds them justified because they have believed in His Son.[87]

Man feels in the depths of His conscience that He, who was capable of so much love, must have been without error and sin; that is, that He was not merely a man, like all others. Not from the human heart, with its egoism, pride, and anger, could come such a pure, devoted, humble, forgiving love. Our own inner experience tells this every day, and all ancient history confirms it. We no longer hesitate to affirm that it was needful for God to reveal Himself in a second Adam, and what to many minds seems contrary to reason, presents itself as perfectly rational and necessary. From the time we feel drawn to Christ by the Divine love He manifested, we are compelled to acknowledge, with the apostles, that the eternal Word became flesh in Him, full of truth and grace; that He is the image of the invisible God, whose fulness dwells in Him; that He can rightly appeal to the witness of His works, and say that God worked in Him; that the Father loved Him and is one with Him; that He came on earth to save, and to give peace and happiness; that He alone is the Way, the Truth, and the Life. Filled with this conviction, we say with Peter, "Lord, to whom shall we go? Thou hast the words of eternal life. And we have believed and know that Thou art the Christ, the Son of God." [88]

Then also we wish to show the grateful love aroused by His benefits and sacrifice; to do this we shall live in Him, we shall hold fast to His doctrine, obey His commandments. Trying to love all men as He did, we shall seek to do the same works of charity. We shall be truly free, having the certainty of God's love, possession of salvation, the commencement here below of eternal life.[69]

These are individual acts and states. The first aim and effect of Christ's work was to regenerate the individual. He addresses the individual conscience to awaken the sense of sin, need of pardon, and desire for a new life. Repentance, conversion, faith, love of Christ, admission into the spiritual kingdom of God, are essentially interesting to the individual who is re-established in his dignity and rights. Christ never helps the division and isolation of men. In pagan society, in spite of the despotism of the State, each citizen lived only for himself and his own interest, without a care for the fate of others. But Christ teaches that each must care as much for his neighbour's salvation as for his own; for when He gave the precept and example of love, He united believers by the strongest and sweetest ties into a family of brothers. When He thought all men worthy of His conversation, even of His sacrifice, the Christian who follows in His footsteps can feel neither hatred nor contempt for any one, however humble he may be. He will respect man, to whatever rank he belongs, seeing in him an immortal soul, the object of Divine solicitude. Full of love, he will serve his neighbour, without asking from whence he comes or how rich he is. Christ desires to establish human society on a fresh foundation, that of reciprocal respect and love. The regeneration of the individual is a necessary condition of the regeneration of society. The external kingdom of God is only possible as each becomes individually a child of God. In proportion as men give up sin and accept the work of Christ, a stronger social tie is formed than was ever dreamed of by legislators or philosophers, and they realize through love that Church, against which, according to the Master's promise, the gates of Hades shall not prevail.[90]

§ 2. *The Apostles and the Apostolic Church.*

To propagate His principles and continue His work, Christ chose several disciples, who, in intimate daily intercourse with Him, had gained such unchangeable confidence in Him, that He considered them worthy to be His apostles. They recognised Him as Christ, the Son of God, who alone has the words of eternal life.[91] Though different in disposition and character, they agreed in this faith, which became their common soul, by which they lived the life of their Master,[92] being one with Him.[93] They were chosen from amongst the poor, the simple, the despised of the ancient world, in order to prove that the renovation of society did not require for its accomplishment the help of the powerful and wise.[94] Christ, through His love, raised them to Himself, not calling them servants, but friends and brethren.[95] He showed thus that every man is capable of the Divine life, and that virtue, reserved by antiquity for the free and important citizens, may be the heritage of all, because all are equal before God. He sent them amongst people who " were distressed and scattered, as sheep not having a shepherd," [96] to reveal to them the kingdom of God.[97] They were to be His " witnesses unto the uttermost part of the earth." [98] He did not conceal from them that they would have persecutions and suffering for His Name, but He promised them the help of the Holy Ghost, the Comforter, and a heavenly crown when the strife was ended.[99]

The apostles received, in a special measure, the gift of the Holy Ghost, whereby they were taught all truth, and enabled to bear an eternally true testimony to their Master. Thus endowed they went about the world, proclaiming everywhere that the crucified Jesus is the Lord and Christ, who alone can save men from sin and its miseries.[100] They cured the sick through faith in Him, and brought to Him people of all ranks; the poor and slaves,[101] as well as foreign lords,[102] Roman officers,[103] and ladies of quality.[104] They founded communities amongst Jews and pagans, in Asia, Greece, and Italy. Neither persecution nor torture repulsed them. They conquered all by the love of Christ.[105] Those of the apostles who have left us writings, where the power of the Holy Spirit who inspired them is shown on every page, are the surest and most faithful interpreters of the Divine thought of Christ. We must see how they kept and developed the principle of love which, by changing men, would transform the world.

Saint Peter denied his Master in a moment of weakness, but confessed Him by his preaching in western Asia and his martyrdom at Rome. He recognised that Christianity is universal, "that God is no respecter of persons, but in every nation he that feareth Him and worketh righteousness is acceptable to Him."[106] He taught that man's dignity comes from intrinsic worth alone, that God will not judge him according to his rank, but his works; that compared with the title of Christian, all honours and privileges are passing vanities; whilst Christians can claim to be "a chosen race, a peculiar people, a holy nation." United amongst themselves with the bond of fraternal love, each employing his gift for the service of his brother, they ought to lead a pure life filled with love, in the midst of pagan corruption, in order that those who know not Christ may learn to love and glorify God because of the good works of His disciples.[107]

The apostle *Saint James* calls the law of love the royal law. He also proclaims the great principle that in the kingdom of God there is no difference of persons. He says the esteem of Christians for men is not measured by their outward condition; they do not prefer the rich to the poor, for they know that they are also brethren.

He insists on the need of man's proving his faith by incessant and active charity. He must not judge others, must refrain from anger, and show that he has wisdom from on high by being chaste, peaceable, moderate, just, gentle, and merciful. In order to bear these "fruits of justice," unruly desires must be subdued, for it is when a wished-for thing is not possessed that dissensions and hatred arise. To triumph over passion and sin he must humble himself "in the presence of the Lord," and receive His word with faith.[108]

Saint John, the disciple whom Jesus loved, endeavours in his touching epistles, as well as in his gospel, to show the close and deep connection between love to God and love to men. The starting-point of all his teaching is " God is love." This love of God was manifested in that " He sent His only begotten Son into the world, that we might live through Him." To show more strongly the greatness of Divine love, unknown to antiquity, and which, from a human point of view, could never have been merited because of corruption, St. John adds, " Herein is love, not that we loved God, but that He loved us, and sent His Son to be the propitiation for our sins." This love of God for sinful man ought to claim his in return. " We love Him, because He first loved us." The Christian who loves God will keep also, through love to Him, His chief commandment to love all men, "not in word, neither with the tongue, but in deed and truth." He who has known the whole force of love will follow in the footsteps of Jesus. " He laid down His life for us, and we ought to lay down our lives for the brethren." Such a love for our neighbour is the brightest proof of love for God and His Son. " He that abideth in love abideth in God, and God abideth in him." " He that loveth not knoweth not God; for God is love;" and "If a man say, I love God, and hateth his brother, he is a liar: for he that loveth not his brother whom he hath seen, cannot love God whom he hath not seen. And this commandment have we from Him, That he who loveth God love his brother also."

He who most completely developed the principle of love in its different applications is the last chosen apostle, *Saint Paul,* who, from a violent persecutor, became by faith and love the equal of the disciples who had enjoyed the happiness of living in intimacy with their Master. Let us linger a little over the grand and beautiful figure of Paul. It shows us to what the love of Christ may inspire the soul. His warm and eager nature, when enlightened by grace, is struck with the vice and iniquity prevailing in the world. Notwithstanding the law which God had given to the Jews, and which the pagans had in their own conscience,[109] they both turned from God to follow " the lusts of their hearts."[110] Paul saw men divided, corrupt, full of hatred and evil desires. He found amongst them neither natural affection nor mercy,[111] and in energetic language he draws a picture of the society of his time, which is confirmed in every line by the unanimous testimony of historians. " God gave them up unto vile passions: for their women changed the natural use into that which is against nature; and likewise also the men, leaving the natural use of the woman, burned in their lust one towards another; men with men working unseemliness, and receiving in themselves that recompense of their error which was due. And even as they refused to have God in their knowledge, God gave them up unto a reprobate mind, to do those things which are not fitting; being filled with all unrighteousness, wickedness, covetousness, maliciousness, full of envy, murder, strife, deceit, malignity; whisperers, backbiters, hateful to God, insolent, haughty, boastful, inventors of evil things, disobedient to parents, without understanding, covenant breakers, without natural affection, unmerciful."[112]

Paul sees that suffering creation sighs for deliverance from this "bondage of corruption." Moved by the sight, filled with love for men, his brothers, he desires that they should share this gospel which has given him this strength of love, as well as happiness and peace. Freed from ancient exclusiveness, which saw an enemy in every foreigner, he knows that "there is no respect of persons with God," that in Jesus Christ there is no more Greek nor Jew, neither barbarian nor Scythian. There is no longer a privileged nation, nor others left outside, but all are fellow-citizens, heirs together of the kingdom of God.[113] For this reason he must preach the gospel "both to Greeks and to barbarians."[114] He is not disheartened by the knowledge that the gospel is "unto Jews a stumbling-block, and unto Gentiles foolishness." He cannot be ashamed of this Gospel, for he knows by his own deep experience that it is the power of God unto salvation to every one that believeth, a force and power destined to conquer the world.[115] Armed with this force, which makes him triumphant in the midst of afflictions,[116] he attacks paganism and its morality in its most celebrated strongholds, in learned Athens, immodest Corinth, and even in the capital of the world, in the palace of the Cæsars.[117] The Stoics, who also deplored the universal corruption, wrapped themselves proudly in their own egoistical virtue, whilst the Apostle of Christ went from town to town, from danger to danger, to beseech men, in Christ's name, to be reconciled with God.[118] He pointed out their sins, and desired that their own eyes should be opened to them; then he led them to Christ, who died for them, and who will pardon them if they believe in Him. Paul was never dazzled by social distinctions. Master and slave, Roman governor and man of the people, wise and ignorant, are all equal in sin and responsibility before God.[119] Also, when they are converted, they are equal in reconciliation and salvation. Paul wished men to be filled with these ideas, that in the humiliation of their common feeling of misery, they may learn to respect and love each other, as equally called to the liberty of the children of God.[120]

Like all the other apostles, he insists on humility, though this idea must have been astonishing to the pagan world. It is one of the principal characteristics which distinguish the morality of Christianity from that of pagan antiquity. Humility, considered by the pagan an indignity unworthy of a free man, is to Paul no degradation at all, but a deep feeling of dependence on God, joined to a sense of the insufficiency of external and passing things. It is the consciousness of being nothing, and doing nothing, but by God.[121] This feeling, which bows the pride of man, is accompanied by another, which raises him to his true dignity: if man can do nothing without God, he can do everything through Him. Through the love of Jesus Christ he enters into union with God; the chains of egoism are broken; he recovers his liberty, and acquires a power of which ancient pride, with all its manly virtue, was incapable. He no longer wishes to be raised above his brothers, towards whom he feels neither contempt nor hatred. Being humble towards God, he is modest towards his neighbour; he respects and patiently bears with his weaknesses, because he loves him.[122] In this way humility becomes the principle of respect, which is allied to love. Love to those around is the means by which Christians prove their love to Him who, in His mercy, first loved them in spite of their sins, giving them life in Christ Jesus.[123] Paul gives love, or charity in its widest sense, the highest place amongst virtues. It is the sign of perfection. All mental gifts are useless without it,—it gives them their value, and endures when all other virtues have passed away.[124] Paul proclaims the great principle that it is love that will establish justice, and consequently peace, in the world. "He that loveth his neighbour hath fulfilled the law. For this, Thou shalt not commit adultery, Thou shall not kill, Thou shalt not steal, Thou shalt not covet, and if there be any other commandment, it is summed up in this word, namely, Thou shalt love thy neighbour as thyself." Love worketh no ill to his neighbour; love therefore is the fulfilment of the law.[125] Love will draw together the different classes of society, separated by pride and violence. Love will unite individuals who are made free by Christ and restored to their personal worth. Paul, faithful to his Master, adds that free submission is the crown of love. The more completely Christians are made free, the more completely they are bound to serve one another in love.[126] On every occasion, and under all forms, Paul recommends this charity that the members of God's kingdom owe to one another as brothers, members of one body, of which Christ is the head. He exhorts them to care for the interests of others rather than their own, to be forbearing one towards another, to give up in unimportant matters rather than disturb the weak, to avoid divisions, to sympathise with others in their joys and griefs, to be united amongst themselves, and as far as possible to live in peace with all the world. He reminds them that love is always ready to forgive, as God forgives sinners for the love of Christ. Render to no man evil for evil; bless those who persecute you; revenge not yourselves, but if thine enemy hunger, feed him; if he thirst, give him drink.[127]

Such are the general traits of the principles that were to serve as the basis of a new society, and to determine the relations between the members of the Kingdom of God. We find them propagated and transmitted by the apostles as pure and powerful as they received them from Jesus Christ. Like their Master, they appealed to the individual man to submit his conscience to faith, and his will to the supreme command of charity. But they were not content with general exhortations. They elaborated and developed fundamental principles. They gave direct instruction as to the social influence of the Gospel spirit. Redress of the social injustice of the ancient world must follow the application of the principles of love and respect taught by Christ and His Apostles. Woman must be raised from her inferior position; the child restored to the parents' tenderness, whilst remaining under their authority; work and workers reinstated in their dignity; the poor and destitute commended to the care of the rich; the weak guarded against the oppression of the strong, the slaves made free.

Impatient enthusiasts would have asked to realize these applications at once, careless of the evils wrought by sudden changes in society; for the sake of putting their absolute theories in practice, they would have made changes contrary to human nature. To raise woman, they would have killed her sweetest virtues. To establish fraternity and equality, they would have abolished the right of private property. To honour work, they might have tried to render it attractive. To abolish slavery, they would have broken at one blow all the ties between master and servant. And lastly, to carry out all these reforms, they would have appealed to force, and would

CHAP. I.] FUNDAMENTALS OF CHRISTIAN MORALITY. 161

have aroused a furious war. Under the pretext of introducing the religion of peace and love into the world, individual egoisms would have taken the reins, and society would have been destroyed. But the apostles were not enthusiastic dreamers, solely occupied with the success of a Utopian system. Christianity is not a socialistic chimera, intended to renew the customs of the world before changing individuals. If this had been the view of the apostles, they would have understood neither the teachings of the Saviour nor the needs of human nature. It would have been contrary to the law of love to introduce it brusquely and violently into the world. Love is a free, spontaneous, individual feeling; it excludes constraint and will not be imposed by force. Jesus Christ Himself, after saying that His kingdom was not of this world, commanded His too eager disciple to "put back his sword into the scabbard." The kingdom of God develops slowly, without appeal to arms, and without external brilliancy. The number of members grows by the voluntary accession of converted souls. It must be realized by the attractive power of Christ's love; and this power is exerted first on individuals, whose regeneration must precede that of society, of which it is the indispensable condition. It is for this reason that the apostles, whilst firmly holding the new principles as to social relations in the kingdom of God, respect the established order, and forbid Christians to make violent changes in their earthly position.

The Apostle Peter, he who put his hand to the sword to defend his Master, advises submission to all men, "not only to the good and gentle, but also to the froward. For this is acceptable, if for conscience toward God a man endureth griefs, suffering wrongfully." [123] Paul adds his solemn exhortations to these, for obedience to the powers established by God to maintain order and justice in the world, for payment of tribute, and prayer for kings and magistrates. Saint Paul and Saint Peter desire Christians to submit to the established order, not from fear of punishment, but as a conscientious duty for the love of God.[129] Too zealous Christians, wounded by contact with a corrupt world, wished for authority to separate from it. Paul gives them another rule of conduct. He desires that they shall refrain from mixing with impure men; but instead of leaving the world, they are to become, by the example of their holy and loving life, an element of the regeneration of the society amidst which they live.[130] This is the high aim of the Christian community on earth; it is the yeast of humanity, destined to give it the fruitful and indestructible principle of a new life, without laying violent hands on established institutions. Ardently desiring individual conversions, the apostles waited patiently for social reforms. They left it to the work of time, and the irresistible power of the Spirit of Christ. They always respected existing laws, though they pointed out the principles destined to modify them, by conforming them to the character of the kingdom of God. These principles are the consequences and application of Christian love.

The apostles commenced their work of social reform through love by raising woman, to whom was given so high a place in the example of holy women in the gospel history. But they did not ask a hurried and unnatural emancipation. They recognised them as belonging to the weaker sex, and only considered them the equal of man in spiritual things. They are with him inheritors of life-giving grace; whilst in Christ Jesus "there can be no male and female." The apostles, seeing the deep depravity of pagan women, taught those sweet and touching virtues which are the beauty of the maiden and the wife, modesty, gentleness, piety, purity of heart.[131] These virtues give woman respect in the eyes of man; she can no longer be the plaything of his brutal passions. Paul rebuked, more vigorously than antiquity had ever done, those who carried on disgraceful relations with unhappy prostitutes.[132] Marriage is no longer only a civil union, contracted with a worldly or political aim; it becomes a union of souls, represented by the type of Christ and His Church. The apostles continue to require the submission of the wife to the husband, but it is a free obedience through love, and no longer a servile dependence; the man is head and protector of the woman, as Christ is Head of the Church. The woman is the glory of the man, for he is nothing without her, as she is nothing without him, though she may exercise the best influence upon him. The husband then must love his wife, as Christ loves His Church, by sanctifying her; he will treat her with honour and discretion.[133]

It is hardly necessary to say after this, that the apostles insisted on the duty of reciprocal conjugal fidelity, and that they considered a union as sacred as marriage indissoluble. Even in this early time there were married Christians who thought it was their duty to separate, in order to live, as they expressed it, solely for God. This was not approved of by Paul, who forbade separation for ascetic reasons, unless by mutual consent, and only "for a time," that they might not expose each other to temptation. If husband and wife were separated for grave causes, they might not enter into other marriages, but were to seek a reconciliation. Paul even forbids separation on account of one being a pagan. If they are willing to live together, the Christian must hope that the infidel may be saved and sanctified. The woman, at her husband's death is free to marry whom she will, provided it be "in the Lord," though Paul thinks her happier if she remain a widow.[134] Widows are surrounded with an atmosphere of solicitude unknown to the pagan world.[135] There are certain passages in which Paul prefers celibacy to marriage, but he explains this by referring to the dangers and afflictions of the times.[136] Also this idea was in itself a step in advance. Christianity, which sanctified marriage, also re-asserted its freedom, as opposed to the political materialism of the pagan state in its punishment of celibacy.

The same new spirit is shown in the precepts on the relations between parents and children. Whilst children are taught to honour, obey, and assist those who brought them to the light of day, parents are also commanded, "Provoke not your children, that they be not discouraged," but "nurture them in the chastening and admonition of the Lord." The father who does not care for his family is worse than an infidel. The family is thus established on a new foundation—respect for the immortal soul, and the members are allied by a new tie —that of reciprocal love. All family duties are only different manifestations of this unique love.

When we pass to the despised classes, the poor and unhappy, we see that the apostles do not take away the property of the rich to relieve the poor, but they do better; they raise him, in the rich man's eyes, as a brother disinherited for this world, but an inheritor of heaven. Riches and poverty are indifferent to the humble Christian, who does not seek to amass wealth, and who knows that the love of God does not depend on outward condition.[137] Paul says, "Not that I speak in respect of want; for I have learned, in whatsoever state I am, therein to be content. I know how to be abased, and I know also how to abound; in everything and in all things have I learned the secret both to be filled and to be hungry, both to abound and to be in want. I can do all things in Him that strengtheneth me."[138] Besides this lesson of contentment for the poor, he impresses on those who are well off the duty of almsgiving and mercy, using this illustration: the body of man is composed of various members, which regard each other whilst uniting in one aim; and so in the Church, Christians, who are members of the body of Christ, owe a mutual care to each other. Whilst following their common aim, they must bear one another's burdens, relieve one another's necessities, for "if one member suffer, all the others suffer with it."

In collections, the rich were to make up for the poverty of those who could not contribute; but this must not be done with regret or constraint, but from sincere charity, freely, voluntarily, joyfully, with gratitude to Christ, who "though He was rich, yet for your sakes became poor, that ye, through His poverty, might become rich." In this way Paul attempts to establish equality between rich and poor, through love. He does not ask for a division of fortune, or that some shall be overburdened to relieve others, but he desires that through spontaneous charity, the rich from their abundance shall relieve the needs of the poor, and thus "there may be equality."[139] To do good to brethren in need is one way of showing love to God and Christ; whilst the unrelieved misery of the poor is an accusation of egoism against those who parade their faith.[140] To these exhortations to almsgiving, the apostles added their advice to work, enforcing their precept by their practice. Paul with his hands ministered to his necessities, "and to them that were with" him.[141] He says, "Rather let him labour, working with his hands the thing that is good, that he may have whereof to give to him that hath need." And he adds also, "If any will not work, neither let him eat." Christian charity is not to provide a stimulus for the idleness of the lazy beggar.[142]

We have still to show the application of these principles to the greatest social iniquity of the ancient world, slavery. Here again we find nothing hasty or violent in the apostles' teaching, but a wise patience unites a serious respect for the rights of men with an active charity. Placed in the midst of society in which slavery was so deeply rooted, they did not attack the property which, to the masters, had become an established right; but they prepared for the recognition of natural right, grounded on justice and love. The strange reproach has been brought against the apostles of not having roused the slaves to immediate freedom. They have been called no better than the pagan Stoics, because, instead of breaking the chains of the slaves, they were contented to teach them a barren theoretical liberty. Some have even gone so far as to accuse them of cowardly compliance with the wishes of the powerful of the world; yet it was they who, after preaching unpleasing truths, submitted joyfully to prisons, tortures, and death.

If they had acted with the violence of impatient innovators, they would not have been disciples of Him whose kingdom is not of this world. If they had been only philosophers, they would not have made voluntary servitude the supreme degree of Christian love. They also agree with the Stoics that the true slavery is the moral bondage of sin, but they teach that man is made free by Christ, not by a simple effort of his reflection or will. "If therefore the Son make you free, ye shall be free indeed." "Where the Spirit of the Lord is, there is liberty."[143] Man, freed from the yoke of sin, takes on himself that of just obedience; he exchanges a debasing slavery for an ennobling one. The free Christian becomes the servant of God, and through charity the servant of his brothers.[144] The apostles delight to call themselves the servants of God and Christ, servants of all Christians through love of their Master.[145] All Christians, without distinction, are called to liberty; but this must not serve as a pretext for living according to the flesh, nor as a veil to hide evil deeds; each must live in the state to which God has called him. The Christian slave is not oppressed with the penalties of his condition, for he also can obtain the glorious liberty of the children of God. This liberty of freedom from sin is more precious and more really possible than the barren metaphysical liberty of the Stoics. The Christian slave has been freed by Christ, even as the Christian freeman becomes His servant; in Christ "there can be neither bond nor free, there can be no male and female, for ye are all one in Christ Jesus."[146] This is the ground of the reiterated commands addressed to slaves to be obedient to their masters, "in singleness of heart as unto Christ; not in the way of eyeservice as men-pleasers; but as servants of Christ, doing the will of God from the heart; with goodwill doing service, as unto the Lord, and not unto men." They must also honour them, "that the name of God and the doctrine be not blasphemed," and they must give willing obedience "not only to the good and gentle, but also to the froward."[147]

It would be a mistake to imagine that the apostles spoke thus through weakness, to gain favour with the masters. They clearly recognise that liberty is better than slavery. Paul says to a Christian slave, that if he can become free he may use the liberty;[148] but the apostles only enforced freedom through charity. Besides, whilst they exhort slaves to submission, they exhort masters to treat them with humanity. Paul makes the appeal in the name of justice : "Masters, render unto your servants that which is just and equal; knowing that ye have a Master in heaven." Whilst the great apostle was living in Rome, he met with Onesimus, an escaped slave, belonging to Philemon, one of the Colossian Christians. He taught him the Gospel, and made him promise to return to his master, whom he also exhorted to receive him "no longer as a servant, but more than a servant, a brother beloved, both in the flesh and in the Lord."[149] The Epistle of Philemon was preserved in the Churches to teach the apostolic lesson to both masters and slaves.

All the social principles that we have just mentioned from the apostolic writings were realized in the primitive Churches, which are eternal types of the purity of Christian society, with all the members united by active love, and a vivid and sincere faith. After Christ had left His disciples, they still dwelt in Jerusalem with the apostles and the women, Mary the mother of Jesus, and his brethren, who were all " of one accord."[150] They met frequently, had brotherly repasts, accompanied with prayer, and at the end distributed bread and wine in remembrance of the last communion of Christ.[151] Each repast was thus sanctified and became a symbol of Christian fellowship and a remembrance of Christ's death. This custom spread rapidly in all the communities founded by the apostles, and of one heart and mind amongst themselves. But the greatest glory of these Churches was the charity shown to the poorer brethren; the world had seen none so strong, watchful, and devoted. The first Christians in Jerusalem " had all things common ; and they sold their possessions and goods, and parted them to all, according as any man had need."[152] "And the multitude of them that believed were of one heart and soul: and not one of them said that aught of the things which he possessed was his own. . . . For neither was there amongst them any that lacked, for as many as were possessors of lands or houses sold them, and brought the prices of the things that were sold, and laid them at the apostles' feet: and distribution was made unto each, according as any one had need."[153] In accordance with this, Joseph surnamed Barnabas, originally from the island of Cyprus, sold his lands and brought the price to the apostles.[154] A man named Ananias, with his wife Sapphira, sold their property and gave part of the money to the apostles with the assurance that it was the whole. They had thought to be honoured for their beneficence, but Peter reproached their falsehood with severity, and God punished them for it.[155]

It has been sometimes thought that this account in the Acts of the Apostles, of the Church at Jerusalem ought to be understood as an authoritative community of goods, intended as a model for all time. Some dimly enlightened minds have endeavoured from these facts to realize a like community, but each of their experiments has ended in disorder and confusion. An attempt to explain the passage in the Acts in this way is met by insurmountable historical and psychological difficulties. It is as contrary to human nature as to established opposing facts. The first Christians did not form an ascetic association, separating themselves from the world and giving up personal property. They continued to live in society and to maintain the civil relationships which they had accepted before their conversion; and though brotherly love was their great law, the apostles never imposed on them as a necessary obligation the sacrifice of all their wealth for the good of the community. There is the strongest proof of this in the voluntary collections, the frequent exhortations to almsgiving, and the formal words of Peter to Ananias, " Why hath Satan filled thy heart to lie to the Holy Ghost, and to keep back part of the price of the land? Whiles it remained, did it not remain thine own? and after it was sold, was it not in thy power?"[156] Can there be a more explicit consecration of the rights of property?

The example of the Church at Jerusalem proves only one thing, but it is a thing worthy to be the model for Christians in all ages: it proves the deep feeling of charity and devotion with which the first believers were animated. The love of Christ had conquered all their egoism. They considered their fortune as belonging also to their poorest brothers, and they brought gifts to the apostles which were often large, but always voluntary and spontaneous. Several of the richest people, impelled by an ardent charity, sold part or the whole of their goods for this end; but it was not a rule for all. Christianity does not attempt to abolish the rights of property. If we permit ourselves to imagine an ideal State, where, without distinction of rich and poor, the needs of each are supplied, we must also add that this cannot be brought about by outward laws; it can only be established by the power of love and regeneration of heart in both rich and poor.

From the voluntary gifts of the faithful a common fund was formed for the needs of the Churches. To this was added the collections made in the communities, which were very often poor themselves. Already, when there was a famine, in the time of the Emperor Claudius, the Christians of Antioch sent help to those in Jerusalem.[157] Several years later, those of Achaia and Macedonia, in spite of "their deep poverty," gave from "the riches of their liberality"; "according to their power, yea, and beyond their power, they gave of their own accord."[158] Paul asked the Churches of Galatia and Corinth to tax themselves for the very poor community of Jerusalem; he wrote to the Corinthians to organize the collections, "Upon the first day of the week let each one of you lay by him in store, as he may prosper, that no collection be made when I come."[159] The apostles or the Churches sent messengers through the provinces to collect these gifts. Paul during his travels had them sent to himself.

The poor who were helped from this common fund were those who could not do enough work to gain a sufficient livelihood, and especially aged widows who had married only once, and who had led a charitable and holy life, belonging to families who were too poor to support them.[160] They also sent help to Christians imprisoned for their faith, and provided for the wants of the apostles, whom, in all their travels, they entertained with eager and respectful hospitality.

The Church in Jerusalem chose seven deacons for the administration of this common fund, and the service of the poor. They were to be men of pure, austere, devoted life. Being entrusted with the administration of what might be called the inheritance of the poor, the strictest honesty was enforced upon them. Paul writes to Timothy that they must not be "greedy of filthy lucre."[161] Their wives assisted in their ministry. There were even already deaconesses, properly so called.[162]

Pastors generally, as well as those *servants* of charity who worked under their direction, set an example of the new life, of love, peace, patience and charity.[163] The morality of both pastors and flocks astonished the pagans, who found it easier to hate or rail at what they did not understand, than to comprehend its cause. St. Peter writes, "They think it strange that ye run not with them into the same excess of riot, speaking evil of you."

Thus came into the world a new principle of life,—love—presented in its most perfect form by Christ, and realized in primitive Christian society. They do through love, freely and joyfully, what they would not be constrained to do; for they rejoice in what no law could command, the power of sacrifice. External position no longer measures the worth of the human soul. Man, who till now was lost in nature or absorbed by the State, is established in himself. His individuality, first humiliated by the consciousness of sin and dependence on God, regains its true dignity through the salvation promised equally to all men. In the time of Christ ancient society asked two questions which it could not answer, What is the truth? and Who is my neighbour?[164] The answers to these questions are found: The Gospel of the love of God is the truth; and, Any man whatever, regardless of social position, is thy neighbour. Love is the foundation of the kingdom of God. This kingdom is not established by temporal institutions, nor by force of arms; it does not come from without, and is only visible in the world as it lives in the soul.

We have seen the apostolic Church in its humble, though pure and sublime, commencement. We must follow its progressive development by the side of the decadence of pagan society. We must show how, in religious society, charity was taught in all its applications by the representatives of Christian thought, and realized by institutions and deeds that contrasted strongly with those of paganism. Thus we shall learn the life and system of social morality of the Christians. We say system, though none of the writers in the early ages

CHAP. I.] FUNDAMENTALS OF CHRISTIAN MORALITY. 173

formulated the social consequences of charity into a logical whole; but we may unite their ideas under some principal heads. We can show, with fairness and fidelity, that all these ideas rest on the great principles established by Christianity, those of respect for human nature and the charity which is inseparable from it. This respect and charity were never found in antiquity, but we shall now find them everywhere; in the doctrine of the Fathers on social relations and classes of mankind, as well as in the institutions of the Church, and the individual conduct of her members.

(1) It will be understood that we cannot here enter into the strictly theological question; we are compelled by our subject to keep to the lines of history. (2) Tacitus, *Hist.*, V. 13, vol. iii. p. 399. Suet., *Vespas.*, c. 4, p. 348. (3) Luke ii. 10, 14. (4) Matt. iii. 11, 12. (5) Matt. iv. 17. (6) Acts vii. 22. (7) Matt. iv. 1 sq. (8) Matt. iv. 17. (9) Matt. iv. 23. (10) Matt. vii. 28, 29; viii. 27. (11) Matt. v. 3 sq.; vi. 33; xi. 29. Luke xv. 28; John xiv. 27. (12) John viii. 32–34. (13) Luke xvii. 20. (14) John vii. 7. (15) John xv. 22. (16) Matt. xi. 28–30. (17) John iv. 24. (18) Matt. vi. 9; xxiii. 8. (19) Matt. xvi. 26. (20) Matt. xxv. 31 sq. (21) Matt. v. 3–5; see too Luke xvi. 19 sq. (22) Matt. xi. 5; Luke x. 21. (23) Luke vii. 48–50; viii. 42 sq.; Matt. xv. 21 sq.; Cf. Matt. xxii. 30. (24) Matt. xix. 13–15; Luke xviii. 15, 16; Cf. Luke ix. 48. (25) Matt. xix. 23–26; Cf. Luke xiv. 19 sq. (26) Matt. xviii. 11; John iii. 17; xii. 47. (27) Matt. xviii. 12–14. (28) See the parables of the Lost Sheep and the Prodigal Son. (29) John iv. 21 sq. (30) Matt. viii. 11; John x. 16. (31) John xvii. 21. (32) John x. 16. (33) Lev. xix. 18. (34) Matt. v. 43. (35) Matt. v. 38–40; Exod. xxi. 24, 25. (36) John xiii. 31. (37) John xiii. 31; xv. 12–17. (38) John xiii. 34. (39) Matt. xxii. 37–40. (40) John xiii. 35. (41) Rom. xiii. 8–10. (42) Matt. xxiii. 8; Luke x. 29 sq.; the parable of the Good Samaritan. (43) Loc. cit. and Matt. vii. 12. (44) Matt. v. 42; Luke xxi. 1; Matt. xxv. 34 sq. (45) Matt. vi. 3, 4. (46) Matt. v. 9. (47) Matt. v. 39–41. (48) Matt. vi. 12–14; xviii. 21 sq. Luke xvii. 3, 4. (49) Matt. v. 43–48. (50) Matt. xx. 26, 27; xxiii. 11; John xiii. 14. (51) John xv. 13. (52) The law of Moses, too, regarded marriage simply as a political institution. (53) Matt. xix. 6. (54) Matt. v. 32; xix. 9. (55) Matt. xviii. 2–10. (56) John xiii. 23; xxi. 7. (57) Matt. xvii. 23 sq. (58) Matt. xxii. 17–21. (59) John xviii. 36, 37. (60) Acts v. 29. (61) Matt. iv. 23; ix. 35. (62) Matt. xxii. 16. (63) *Vide* Matt. viii., xv. etc. (64) Matt. ix. 10–13. (65) Luke xxiii. 40–43. (66) John i. 11. (67) Matt. xxiii. 37. (68) John xxi. 15 sq. (69) Matt. xxiii. 37; Luke xix. 41, 42. (70)

Luke xxiii. 34. (71) Matt. xi. 29. (72) Matt. xxiii. 23 sq. (73) John v. 41; viii. 50. (74) Phil. ii. 8. (75) Matt. xx. 28. (76) John xiii. 3 sq. (77) John xiii. 15. (78) John xiii. 34; xv. 12. (79) John viii. 46. (80) John xv. 9, 10. (81) Matt. vi. 24 sq. (82) Matt. xix. 16 sq.; x. 37. (83) Matt. xviii. 4; xix. 7; Luke xviii. 10 sq., the parable of the Pharisee and the Publican. (84) The word πίστις has both these meanings. (85) Luke xxiii. 48. (86) Luke xxiii. 21. (87) John xvii. 24; 1 John ii. 1; Rom. x. 4, 10; Gal. iii. 24, etc. (88) Matt. xvi. 16; John i. 14; iii. 15; v. 20; vi. 39 sq.; x. 25 sq.; xiv. 6-10; xvii. 21; 2 Cor. iv. 4; Col. i. 15-19; ii. 9. (89) John v. 24; vi. 47; viii. 31-36; x. 9-28; xiv. 12 sq.; xv. 4; xvi. 27. (90) Matt. xvi. 18. (91) John vi. 68, 69. (92) Gal. ii. 20. (93) John xvii. 23. (94) Matt. ix. 17; xi. 25. (95) John xv. 14, 15; Matt. xii. 49, 50. (96) Matt. ix. 36. (97) Matt. x. 7. (98) Acts i. 8. (99) Matt. x. 16 sq.; John xiv. 16-18; xv. 20; xvi. 2, 13. (100) John xvi. 13; Acts ii. 36; iii. 19; iv. 12. (101) Acts iii. 1 sq., and St. Paul's Ep. to Philemon. (102) Acts viii. 27 sq., the eunuch of the queen Candace. (103) Acts x. 1 sq., the centurion Cornelius; xiii. 7 sq., the proconsul Sergius Paulus. (104) Acts xvii. 5-12. (105) Rom. xiii. 37-39· (106) Acts x. 34, 35. (107) 1 Pet. i. 17; ii. 9, 12; iii. 8, 9; iv. 3, 10. (108) Jas. i. 19 sq.; ii. 1 sq.; iii. 17, 18; iv. 1 sq. (109) Rom. ii. 15. (110) Rom. i. 24; ii. 9; iii. 12. (111) Rom. i. 31. (112) Rom. i. 26-31; cf. Gal. v. 19-21. (113) Rom. ii. 11; Col. iii. 11; Gal. iii. 28; 1 Cor. xii. 13; Eph. ii. 19; iii. 6. (114) Rom. i. 14. (115) Rom. i. 16; 1 Cor. i. 25. (116) Rom. viii. 35 sq. (117) Acts xvii. 15 sq.; xviii. 1 sq.; 1 Cor. v. 6; Phil. iv. 22. (118) 2 Cor. v. 20. (119) 1 Cor. xii. 13; Gal. iii. 28; Rom. i. 24; ii. 6; xiv. 12; Acts xxiv. 25. (120) Rom. viii. 15, 21. (121) 1 Cor. iv. 7; Phil. ii. 12, 13. (122) Eph. iv. 2; Col. iii. 12, 13. (123) Eph. ii. 4, 5. (124) 1 Cor. xiii. 1 sq.; Col. iii. 14. (125) Rom. xiii. 8-10; Gal. v. 14. (126) Gal. v. 13; Eph. v. 21; Phil. ii. 6 sq. (127) Rom. xii. 5 sq. (128) 1 Pet. ii. 13, 14, 17. (129) Rom. xiii. 1-7; 1 Tim. ii. 2; Titus iii. 1; 1 Pet. ii. 13. (130) 2 Cor. v. 10; 2 Thess. iii. 6. (131) 1 Pet. iii. 3-5; 1 Tim. ii. 9, 10, 15. (132) 1 Cor. vi. 15, 16. (133) 1 Cor. xi. 2 sq.; Eph. v. 22 sq.; Col. iii. 18, 19; 1 Tim. ii. 12; 1 Pet. iii. 7. (134) 1 Cor. vii. 39, 40; 1 Tim. v. 14. (135) 1 Tim. v. 3 sq. (136) 1 Cor. vii. 7-9, 26 sq. (137) Rom. ii. 11. (138) Phil. iv. 11-13. (139) 2 Cor. viii. 13, 14. (140) 1 Cor. xiii. 1 sq.; 1 John ii. 17; 1 Pet. iii. 8; Jas. ii. 13 sq. (141) Acts xx. 34. (142) Acts xx. 35; Eph. iv. 28; 2 Thess. iii. 10. (143) John viii. 36; 2 Cor. iii. 17. (144) Rom. vi. 17, 18; viii. 21; Gal. iv. 1-7; 1 Pet. ii. 16. (145) Rom. i 1; Gal. i. 10; Phil. i.1; Jas. i. 1; 2 Pet. i. 1; 2 Cor. iv. 5. (146) Gal. iii. 28; v. 13; 1 Cor. vii. 20-22; xii. 13; Col. iii. 11; 1 Pet. ii. 16. (147) Eph. vi. 5-8; Col. iii. 22; 1 Tim. vi. 1, 2; Titus ii. 9, 10; 1 Pet. i. 18 sq. (148) 1 Cor. vii. 21. Sacy's translation does not seem to us accurate, though it is supported by the authority of several old commentators. The original runs: "εἰ καὶ δύνασαι ἐλεύθερος γενέσθαι, μᾶλλον χρῆσαι." Some commentators supply τῇ δουλείᾳ, others τῇ ἐλευθερίᾳ; in our opinion the latter interpretation ought to be taken. (149) Philemon 10-18. (150) Acts i. 14. (151) Acts ii. 42. (152) Acts ii. 44, 45. (153) Acts iv. 32, 34, 35. (154) Acts iv. 36, 37. (155) Acts v. 1 sq. (156) Acts v. 1. Cf. Mosheim, "On the true nature of the community of goods in the Church at Jerusalem," in *Dissert. ad Hist. Eccles. pertin.* 1743, vol. ii. p. 1 sq.; M. Sudre, *Histoire du Communisme*, 3rd ed., 1850, p. 43 sq. (157) A.D. 44. Acts xi. 28-30 ; cf. Josephus *Antiquit. Jud.*, xx. 2 § 6, vol. 1. p. 960. (158) 2 Cor. viii. 2, 3 ; Rom. xv. 25-27. (159) 1 Cor. xvi. 2. (160) 1 Tim. v. 9, 10, 16 ; Acts vi. 1. (161) Acts vi. 1 sq.; 1 Tim. iii. 8 sq. (162) 1 Tim. iii. 11; Rom. xvi. 1. (163) 1 Tim. iii. 1-5; 2 Tim. ii. 24, 25 ; Titus i. 6-9. (164) Pilate, ap. John xviii. 38 ; the lawyer, Luke x. 29.

CHAPTER II.

CHRISTIAN SOCIETY IN GENERAL, AND IN ITS RELATIONS WITH THE STATE.

§ 1. *Equality. Brotherly Love.*

ANCIENT social order rested on the reputed natural inequality of men. Even the wisest of the ancients never rose above this fundamental injustice. Christianity alone threw its celestial light on the long hidden doctrine of equality. We can hardly understand to-day, how what seems to us so simple and elementary could have remained hidden from Plato and Aristotle, whilst only a Divine intervention could teach it to mankind. The proclamation of equality was a revolution in the domain of mind which has led progressively to a modification of the whole social order. The writers of the Church, interpreters of Christian thought, unanimously expressed this idea, and upheld it, not only by the new arguments of religion, but by those that are discovered by reason when freed from external bondage. In the midst of oppression and persecution, as well as after the triumph of the Church, the Fathers taught the natural equality, the common origin and destiny, of all men. Sprung from the hand of the same Creator, all men bear the same image of God. Being descended from the same first parent, their bodies are made alike. They are born alike feeble and unclothed, and the same death is in store for all. They are alike gifted with immortal souls capable of receiving the Holy Ghost. They are, without exception, the objects of God's mercy.[1] The distinctions in the world are not founded by nature; they are accidental, and due to purely external causes. It is not birth which ennobles; the true nobility is of the soul. Men are great only through their faith, virtue, and piety. As little as the lowliness of external condition is an obstacle to moral worth, so little is the dignity of that position in itself a cause of true greatness.[2] "Thou sayest that thy father is consul and thy mother holy and good," says Chrysostom; "what does it matter to me? Show me thine own life, for it is only by that I can be able to judge of thy nobility."[3]

Human nature must be respected also, even where virtue and faith are not yet found, for man is always "a great thing."[4] All deserve naturally the same respect.[5] The tie of an original parentage unites them together, to whatever nation or family they belong. The pagan and Jew are brothers of the Christian, because they are men. They are *neighbours*, even before conversion, because they also belong to God. It may be that he whom we ridicule for bowing down to idols will some day adore God with greater fervour than we do.[6] As Tertullian says, "The world is a vast republic, a great family of God's children."[7] The consciousness of this parentage gives rise, not only to respect, but to a deeper feeling also. All men, being brothers, are led to mutual love; Christians, more than all men, should feel this universal love towards bad and good. They must embrace all in their enfolding charity, alike regardless of worldly position or spiritual sentiments. The writings of the doctors of Christianity constantly describe and recommend this in innumerable forms. We feel a deep

N

conviction that this new principle, which always opposes the egoism of the pagan world, is the power that will change mankind, that it will be the source of new light and warmth for endless ages. All the Fathers assert the truth that charity is the mother of all virtue, the principle which makes all duty easy.[8] Polycarp says, he who loves is far from sin,[9] and as Augustine adds, he follows both what is clear and what is veiled in the Word of God.[10]

The *whole* of Christianity is comprised rather in charity than in hope or faith.[11] Its practice is decidedly better than the ascetic life. Chrysostom gives it the preference over fasts, abstinences, solitary penances. He does not advise retreat from the world to the solitude of deserts or mountains, but a chaste, pure, and charitable life in the midst of society; for he pronounces love, gentleness, and almsgiving to be greater than celibacy.[12] If any one feels impelled to give himself to a solitary life, he must sanctify it by love, or it will be worthless.[13]

The greatness of Christ's love, the happiness of reconciliation with God by it, the conviction that spiritual union with the Saviour gives Divine life, are the springs of this active and devoted charity. In proportion as a man is pervaded by this love will he lead a holy life, abounding in deeds of love. He will be impelled to follow the footsteps of Christ, to imitate His ineffable goodness, His wonderful gentleness. He will love like Him, and bear his neighbour's burden.[14] This will be done with the purest motives, without thought of earthly profit or heavenly recompense.[15] By a natural reaction this love of man becomes a stimulus to further advance in the love of God, in which it first originated.[16] If the Christian owes respect and love to every man, he is united by still closer ties to his brethren in faith; special reasons, inherent in the nature of the kingdom of God itself, are added to general motives. Participation in the same Holy Spirit, a common salvation, an assured hope of reunion after death, establish a spiritual brotherhood amongst Christians, which, even when it is not objectively visible, unites them in one body of which Christ is the Head.[17] Some of the Fathers, in the early ages, expressed the corelative idea of the universal priesthood of Christians. In distinction from Jews and pagans, who reserved pontifical privileges for special families or classes, Christians form one Church, whose members are equal in spiritual dignity and are all priests in heart.[18]

This is why all Christians called themselves brethren, whether they were poor or rich, masters or slaves. Gregory Nazianzen says we are all one in the Lord; rich and poor, strong and weak, servant and freeman, have one only Head, from whom everything comes, Christ Jesus. What the members of the body are for each other, each amongst us is for his brothers, and all for each.[19] This brotherly love, which led Christians to live, strive, and suffer together, was the subject of constant exhortations by the Fathers and doctors of the Church.[20] It was only perfect, according to their teaching, when they had learned the supreme lesson of willingness to die for their brethren, according to the Divine example of Christ.[21] This was symbolised in the repast called *agape*, and in the Holy Communion, which, besides being the sacrament of communion with the Lord, is also for those who partake of it a proof of their common love and faith. Originally the eucharist and *agape* were united.[22] Later they were only celebrated separately, either on account of increasing numbers, or to avoid the calumnies of the pagans, who brought absurd and odious reproaches against the Church on account of the *agape*.[23] The *agape* became a method of benevolence, somewhat analogous to the pagan largess; but whilst the ambitious Romans feasted the lazy crowd whose suffrages they desired, the charitable Christians brought in the poor to these brotherly repasts where piety and meditation presided.[24] However, it was found impossible to avoid disorder in these gatherings, which were even perverted from their aim. Consequently they fell into disuse and were forbidden by the Church. It is to be regretted that human frailty hindered the perpetuation of an institution so beautiful in its origin.

The ideal of brotherly love, which was symbolised in the *agape*, strove to realize itself in Christian friendship, and in monasteries. It is easy to understand that the Fathers would not say much of friendship, of which the philosophers had said so much. They rise to universal love, which neither excludes nor hinders friendship, but which subordinates it to the general duty of charity towards all. This friendship in its perfection must serve as a type of union with all the faithful in God's kingdom. Friendship, with the Fathers, as with the pagan philosophers, is a community of manners and feelings, strengthened by mutual service, but they also add the religious motive of communion by faith in one Saviour, and a common hope of eternal life. Friendship, thus purified and sanctified, is truly disinterested and capable of sacrifice; whilst philosophic friendship, which never rose above the level of use and interest, always remained more or less egoistical.[25]

Monasteries, according to the wish of their founders, ought to be schools and shelters for this perfect friendship, typical of holy and brotherly harmony of soul. To the monks were ordered, in a more special manner, the duties of love, peace, and fellowship of interest and feeling. Even community of wealth, impossible in the larger society of the world, was realised in these monastic associations, but this was only done with the free consent of the giver. It was a condition of admission, but no one was obliged to seek entrance. Those who joined the monastic order laid down their worldly honours, or were raised from the degradation of a servile and inferior condition. They kept only the characters of man and Christian, under a rule which was alike for all. These associations realised, in this way, Christian equality and brotherhood. Men, deceived by the glitter of the world, sought refuge there, as well as freed slaves, artisans, and labourers who were reduced to misery and could no longer find an honourable place in the midst of society in its decline.[26] The men who retired from the world to live in holy friendship, sheltered from all trouble, were open to the charge of leaving the world through egoism, for the Christian owes himself not only to his friends, but to all his brethren; it is to avoid this that the monks had such strict orders to exercise charity in all forms towards the outside poor. Monasteries were meant to be schools of brotherly love for their inhabitants, homes of charity for the unhappy to whom their gates were open, and a type of Christian communion in its perfection for the Church.[27]

§ 2. *Relations of Christian Society to the Ancient State.*

The Christian communion, grounded upon reciprocal love and respect, necessarily joins the Christians scattered over the world into a society whose members, though personally unknown to each other, are united by spiritual ties. Augustine calls it "a spiritual republic in the midst of pagan society."[28] It is the city of God upon earth. This city is not, we emphatically assert, to be established by a violence which upsets the existing order of things. It respects established forms and requires its members to do the same. The Christian life may be manifested in all social positions and in all circumstances; therefore the Church does not touch civil and political institutions, but prepares for their alteration by giving a new spirit to individuals. It was in this sense that an ecclesiastical author, about the beginning of the second century, wrote, "Christians are not distinguished from other nations either by language, dress, or habits. They do not shut themselves up in particular towns, but live where they were born, in the midst of Greeks or barbarians. They are different from pagans in conduct, and their life is altogether distinct."[29] They obeyed the laws and paid tribute and taxes with a readiness which was a model to the pagan, who ought to have been the most interested in upholding the ancient laws.[30] They honoured the magistrates, whom they looked upon as appointed to maintain civil order. They prayed for them, and for the emperor who was their earthly head, as Jesus Christ was Head in the kingdom of God.[31] They asked their Master to give the emperor a quiet reign, faithful counsellors, honest and peace-loving subjects.[32] These prayers were offered in the midst of persecutions. Even the cruelest tortures did not prevent them from asking the protection of God for the emperors. During this whole period, which was full of sedition and revolt, arising often from the most trifling excuses, there was never one headed by the oppressed Christians. They continued resigned and submissive, although treated as public enemies and rebels against the Cæsars. Christianity sanctifies all established order which is not in open contradiction to the law of God. It even teaches its members to submit to what is false and irrational, provided their conscience is clear. "They triumph over the laws," says the author of the Epistle to Diognetus, "they triumph over the laws by their life, leading the life of citizens of heaven whilst upon earth." [33]

The Christians, quiet and desirous of peace, did not irritate the authorities by refusing obedience to the laws, unless it was to something which compromised their faith in the Lord Jesus Christ.[34] For this reason they would not consent to give Divine honours to the emperors, to adore them, to bow themselves and sacrifice before their statues, to swear by their genii, for this would have been to deny the only true God. They saw in the emperor only a man, inferior to God, like other men, ordained by Him to govern in earthly things, but not to receive a worship due only to the Creator and His Son.[35] On this point they showed inflexible firmness. The aged Polycarp, summoned by the proconsul, who felt pity for his age, to swear by the genius of Cæsar, refused to do so, but expressed his willingness to obey in anything else. "Understand," he said, "that we have learned to honour the magistrates whom God has instituted." [36] The pagans could not understand this obstinacy, which they thought more suitable to more austere times, which demanded sterner characters, but which was altogether out of place in milder, or to speak more correctly, more effeminate and indifferent times.[37]

It is easy to see that in a State where the citizens, and especially those in office, were compelled to render such honours to the emperor, where public life was closely connected with the rites and sacrifices of paganism, Christians found themselves obliged to refuse offices in the State, or they would have been compelled to take part in pagan ceremonies contrary to their conscience.[38] This was a natural and lawful feeling, justified by the intolerance of pagan society towards Christians. When in later times the Church spread, and followers of the Gospel were found in all classes of the empire, these regulations were modified, paganism became less exacting, and Christian functionaries were not so rigorously compelled to sacrifice to the emperors or the gods. Thus in the reign of Diocletian, Christians filled high positions, both in the army and in the imperial household.[39] When under the growing influence of Christianity the emperors surrounded themselves with Christians, whose life and principles inspired them with greater confidence than they felt in the followers of the former gods, the doctors of the Church did not forbid the acceptance of public employment, which they regarded as a means of glorifying the name of Christ, and they gave advice full of wisdom and charity to the Christian imperial officers. Theonas, Bishop of Alexandria, exhorted Lucian, who held an important post in the household of Constantine Chlorus, to avoid everything that could cast a shadow on the Christian name, to practise the strictest justice towards both rich and poor, to take no money for permission to see the emperor, to be always kind, affable, humble, and to obey and serve the emperor with fidelity in everything which did not interfere with his faith.[40] This remarkable fact that the pagan emperors preferred to trust Christians rather than their own co-religionists, proves that they felt confusedly the power of Christianity for the salvation of men and society. Even before the triumph of the Church, it filled the Christians with courage to know that, by their spirit of peace and love, they were more useful than the pagans to the Republic, which was better protected by the strength of charity than by strength of arms.[41]

Whilst they submitted without murmur or revolt to

the established order, they had the firm assurance that the kingdom of God, the heavenly city, founded on love of God and man, would one day replace the earthly city whose foundation, according to Augustine, was love of self carried to the length of contempt for God.[42] They declared loudly that the ancient social state was iniquitous and violent, because it was founded on the inequality of men. "Neither Romans nor Greeks," said Lactantius, "can carry out justice, because with them men are divided into too many classes,—from the poor, the humble, the subjects, to the rich, the powerful, the kings. Equity does not exist. Inequality excludes justice, whose power consists in looking on all men as equals."[43] Augustine expresses the difference between pagan and Christian society in this pithy saying, which tells all: "Justice is impossible where charity does not rule."[44] The re-establishment of justice, the freedom of men kept in iniquitous dependence, could come from charity only.[45] It was through this alone, the respect and care of man for man, that despised persons and classes could have their dignity restored. From the origin of Christian society the new spirit, learned from the apostles' teachings, showed itself in the treatment of those of inferior rank, whom antiquity had contemptuously overlooked or considered as hostile to the citizen.

(1) Cyprian, *Ad Demetr.*, p. 218, *Ep.* 59, p. 98. Lactan., *Div. Instit.*, V. 15, vol. i. p. 399. Greg. Nyss., *De Hominis Opificio*, c. 16, vol. i. p. 89. Ambrose, *Sermo 8 on Ps.* cxviii. § 57, vol. i. p. 1077. "We are all born alike, both emperors and beggars; and we all die alike, for the lot of each is alike."—*Breviarium in Psalt.;* in Opp. Hieron., vol. ii. p. 233. (2) Min. Felix, c. 37, p. 139. "In short, no one can be truly 'most excellent' but he who is good and innocent; no one can be truly 'most illustrious' but he who has wrought with generous heart the deeds of mercy; no one can be truly 'most perfect' but he who has fulfilled satisfactorily all degrees of virtue."—Lactan., *Div. Instit.*, V. 15, vol. i. p. 399. (3) *Or. in terræ motum et Lazarum*, § 6, vol. i. p. 782.

Ambros., *Exhort. Virginit.*, c. 1, § 3, vol. ii. p. 278. (4) "Μέγα ἄνθρωπος."—Basil, *Hom. in Ps.* xlviii. § 8, vol. i. p. 184. " Magnum opus Dei es, homo."—Ambros., *Sermo* 10 *in Ps.* cxviii. § 11, vol. i. p. 1090. (5) Basil, *Ep.* 262, vol. iii. p. 403. (6) Ambros., *De Noe et Arca*, c. 26, § 94, vol. i. p. 267. August., *Enarr.* 2 *in Ps.* xxv. § 2, vol. iv. p. 82; *Sermo* 359, § 9, vol. 1. p. 979. (7) "We look on the world as one universal commonwealth. . . . Moreover, we are your brethren by right of nature, being of one mother; although ye [the pagans] may scarcely be called men, because ye are bad brethren."— *Apol.*, XXXVIII. and XXXIX., pp. 117 and 121. (8) Clem. Rom., *Ep.* 1 *ad Cor.* c. 49, p. 176. Hieron., *Ep.* 82, vol. i. p. 521. (9) *Epist.*, c. 3, p. 187. (10) *Sermo* 351, § 2, vol. v. p. 940. (11) Zeno *Veron.*, b. I. tract 2, p. 111 sq. (12) "Τὸ γὰρ μέγιστον ἀγάπη καὶ ἐπιείκεια καὶ ἐλεημοσύνη, ἣ καὶ παρθενίαν ὑπερηκόντισεν."—*Hom.* 1 *in Matth.*, § 7, and *Hom.* 46 *in Matth.*, § 4, vol. vii. pp. 116 and 486. (13) Petrus Chrysol., *Sermo* 42, p. 177. (14) Clem. Rom., *Ep.* 1 *ad Cor.*, c. 49, p. 176. *Ep. ad Diogn.*, c. 10, p. 239. (15) Orig., *Contra Cels.*, I. 67, vol. i. p. 382, (16) "Passing on from the love of man to the love of God."—Hilar. Pictav., *Comm. in Matth.*, c. 4, § 18, p. 626. (17) Clem. Alex., *Strom.* II. 9, vol. i. p. 451. Min. Felix, c. 31, p. 122. Tertull., *De Monog.*, c. 11, p. 531. August., *Sermo* 58, § 2, vol. v. p. 236. (18) "For all saints have the priestly dignity."—Iren., *Adv. Hær.* IV. c. 8, p. 237. "Are not we laymen also priests?"—Tertullian, *De Exhortat. Castit.*, c. 7, p. 522. (19) Greg. Naz., *Or.* 16, vol. i. p. 243. (20) *Hermas.* II., Mand. 8, p. 96. Ignat., *Ad Polyc.* c. vi. p. 44. (21) Tertull., *Apol.*, c. 39, p. 121. August., *Tract.* 51 *in Joh.*, § 12, vol. iii., P. II., p. 463. Ambr., *De Excessu Fratris*, Bk. II., § 44 sq. vol. ii. p. 1145. (22) See Acts ii. 42, 46. Pliny in his letter to Trajan seems to refer to it: "They had a custom of meeting together to partake of food, ordinary food, however, and harmless."—*Ep.* X. 97. Translator's reference, Dean Stanley's *Christian Institutions*, ch. iii. pp. 43, 44. (23) Athen., *Leg.* CXXXI., p. 308. Tertull., *Ad Uxorem*, II. 4, p. 168. Orig., *C. Cels.* I. c. 1, p. 319. (24) *Constit. Apost.*, II. 28, p. 243. Tertull., *Apol.*, c. 39, p. 123. Clem. Alex., *Pædag.*, II. 1, vol. i. pp. 165, 166. August., *Sermo* 178, § 4, vol. v. p. 591. *Contra Faustum*, XX. c. 20, vol. viii. p. 246. (25) Clem. Alex., *Strom.*, II. c. 9 and 19, vol. i. pp. 450, 483. Chrysost., *Hom.* 1 *in Col.*, § 3, vol. xi. p. 315. August., *Ep.* 258, vol. ii. p. 669. Hieron., *Ep.* 53, vol. i. p. 270. (26) "Now also men from the class of slaves frequently come forward to profess service to God, or even freedmen, either having been set free by their masters for this very purpose, or soon to be set free,—from agricultural life too, from the artizans' trades and the common working people; at any rate, if they have been roughly trained, so much the happier their choice. If these be not admitted, it is a great mistake: God has chosen the weak things of the world."—August., *De Opere Monach.*, c. 21, vol. vi. p. 360. *Ibid.* c. 25, p. 362. (27) Cf. Cassian., *Collat. Patrum*, coll. 16, c. 1 sq. p. 476. (28) "Omnium Christianorum respublica est."—*De Opere Monach.*, c. 15, vol. vi. p. 363. (29) *Ep. ad Diogn.*, c. 3, p. 237. (30) Just. Mart., *Apol.*, I. c. 17, p. 54. Tatian, *Or. Contra Græcos*, c. 4, p. 246. *Constit. Apost.*, IV. 13, p. 302. (31) Polyc., *Ep.*, c. 12, p. 191. Just. M., l. c.; Athenag., *Leg.*, c. 37, p. 313. (32) Tertull., *Apol.*, c. 30, p. 101. (33) c. 3, p. 237. (34) Orig., *C. Cels.*, VIII., 65, p. 790. The *Constit. Apost.* enjoin obedience to the worldly authorities "in those things which God wills."—IV., 13, p. 302. (35) Tat., *Or. c. Græcos*, c. 4, p. 246. Theoph., *Ad Autol.*, I. c. 2, p. 344. Tertull., *De Idol.*, c. 15, p. 95; *Ad Scapulam*, c. 2, p. 69; *Ad Nation.*, I. c. 17, p. 51. (36) Euseb., *Hist. Eccles.*, IV. 15, p. 132. (37) Tertull., *Ad Nat.*, I. c. 18, p. 52. Later on, it is true, under the Christian emperors, there were some Christians who paid a superstitious worship to the images of the emperors, when the pagans themselves reminded them of the inconsistency of this practice with their principles. —See " *Consultationes Zachæi Christiani et Apollonii Philosophi*," I. c. 28, in D'Achéry, *Spicil.*, vol. i. (new ed.) p. 12. (38) Tertull., *De Idol.*, c. 17 and 18, p. 96. Orig., *C. Cels.*, VIII. 5 and 6, p. 747. (39) Euseb., *Hist. Eccl.*, VIII. c. 1 and 6, pp. 269, 292. (40) Theonas, *Ep. ad Lucianum Præpositum Cubiculariorum*, in the *Bibl. PP. Gallandi*, vol. iv. pp. 69, 70. (41) Orig., *C. Cels.*, VIII. 74, vol. i. p. 798. (42) ". . . Amor sui usque ad contemptum Dei."—August., *Dei Civit. Dei*, XIV. c. 28, vol. vii. p. 286. (43) *Div. Instit.*, V. c. 15, vol. i. p. 399. (44) "Ubi caritas non est, justitia non esse potest."—*De Serm. Domini in Mont.*, I. § 13, vol. iii. P. II. p. 122. (45) "Lex libertatis, lex caritatis est."—August., *Ep.* 167, § 19, vol. ii. p. 457.

CHAPTER III.

THE FAMILY.

§ 1. *Woman. Marriage.*

THE restoration of woman, which was taught by the apostles, was achieved by the Church. In the pagan world woman was degraded by the laws and debased by her own habits. Christianity held out to her a lifting hand. The Fathers remembered that degradation only to resist it with all their energy. It is true that instead of finding the cause of her inferiority in the State's materialistic egoism and man's pride in his strength, it was sometimes regarded as a consequence of the curse on women after the fall, as a punishment whose penalties Christ came to destroy.[1] When Chrysostom and Augustine express this opinion, they do not explain why woman only is punished, and placed to atone for her fault, in dependence on him who sinned as she did. This explanation satisfies neither intellect nor faith. Many of the Fathers enlarged their ideas in this respect. Ambrose said expressly that it is wrong to accuse woman alone of causing the fall. If she fell, ought not stronger man to have been able to resist and to guard his weaker companion? The fall of man, so to speak, absolves that of woman. Also God has willed that through her salvation came into the world.[2]

This is the necessary point of view really to raise

woman from her ancient inferiority, which Chrysostom and Augustine had otherwise no intention of maintaining. Jesus Christ freed the whole of humanity; in the kingdom of God there is no chosen sex. All the Fathers are unanimous on this point. They teach the perfect equality of man and woman; that both are alike formed of dust, after the same image of God; that they must cultivate the same virtues, obedience, chastity, charity; that they have the same struggles against the same temptations; that they will both rise again to appear before the tribunal of the same judge, who will judge them without respect of persons.[3] Their natures are therefore equally honourable. "The Saviour," says Augustine, "gives abundant proof of this in being born of a woman."[4]

What then could be more iniquitous than the pagan laws intended to keep women in an inferior position, and depriving them of the most natural rights?[5] Hereafter woman herself must no longer plead weakness when difficult virtues are required of her! This weakness is only in her flesh; in her soul is a force as strong as in that of man. If God has given her a gentleness which is impressed more easily than the manly will, He has done it the better to dispose her to compassion and sympathy. Besides, in circumstances which require courage, she often shows more than man. Gregory of Nyssa, in his beautiful picture of the virtues of a Christian woman says, "Where is he who can compare with her in trial, who equals her in piety, constancy, and devotion?"[6]

These teachings necessarily had an immense influence on women. All the feelings which the ancient social order had repressed or degraded were freely drawn out by Christianity. Christian women showed from the first a charity, sweetness, and modesty that paganism had never known. It has been said that, feeling more vividly than men the benefit of spiritual freedom through Christ, they wished to show their gratitude to their Saviour by more absolute devotion. The Church, deeply feeling the reserve becoming to women, maintained the apostolic precept that they must not speak in the public assemblies of believers;[7] but this exclusion from preaching did not hinder them from fulfilling a mission in society suited to their character. We shall find later that the ancient Church gave them humble, gentle duties in harmony with their natural virtues. Let us remember here, that in times of persecution they were models of charity and courage. They consoled the prisoners, dressed the wounds of the tortured, prayed with the martyrs, and according to the expression of Chrysostom, "showed themselves more courageous than lions."[8] They bore in their own persons cruel tortures with a quiet heroism which, more than all the rest, proves the superiority of Christian to pagan woman.

In later times, when persecution had ceased, woman continued to be distinguished by a more active piety. Whilst men were occupied in the forum or amused with the games of the amphitheatre, they went to the churches or led in their own homes a life of consecration to Christ. Chrysostom delighted to hold them up as an example to men. "They surpass us," he says, "in love to the Saviour, in chastity, in compassion for the miserable."[9] History has preserved the names of several of these holy women. We will mention only some belonging to the latter days of the empire, to show the contrast between Christians in high rank and pagans belonging to the same classes. Melania the younger, who had large estates in all parts of the empire, gave them all to the Church for the poor. She dedicated herself to the service of the unhappy. She went through the country seeking everywhere to relieve distress, to help the sick and comfort the afflicted.[10] Paulla, of the family of Scipio, and Paulus Æmilius, widow of Toxotius, a descendant of the Julian line,[11] and Fabiola, of the family of Fabius,[12] followed this example. They added a new and sweeter fame to the line of warriors from whom they were descended. At the same time the Princess Priscilla visited the hospitals, where with her own hands she rendered the humblest services to the sick poor.[13] The Empresses Pulcheria and Eudoxia were not less distinguished for high mental power than for the gentleness and purity of their manners.

Ideas about marriage were altogether altered by the elevation of woman and the subordination of the earthly interests of the State to the spiritual interests of the reign of God. In the State men are united for temporary needs; in the kingdom of God they are united by love for eternity. The Saviour had already given its true character when He represented it as a Divine institution, and a union of soul. These great principles were developed by the Church, and increased the contrast between Christian and pagan civilization. According to the Fathers, marriage with one wife was instituted by God Himself when He created the first couple. It is not a passing union for the temporary satisfaction of carnal desires or the needs of the State. It is rather an association of souls than bodies, intended to glorify God and to last beyond this life.[14] It is a mystery, for it is a type of the union of Christ and His Church.[15] Thus sanctified, it becomes a school of virtue, and of mutual duties between husband and wife, for their education, with their family, to eternal life. Each household, each family, ought to be an image of the Church; for where two or three are united in the name of Christ, He is there in the midst of them.[16] Because of the deep meaning given by Christianity to marriage, it received for the first time the sanction of the Church. Blest by the priest in the presence of the congregation, it became one of the most solemn religious acts.[17] Clandestine marriages, unconsecrated by the Church, were looked upon almost as illegal unions.[18]

Another consequence of the religious feeling in reference to Christian marriage was to make it a matter of choice. Paganism could not understand this freedom; it inflicted penalties on him who refrained from the duty of furnishing the State with citizens. Christianity founded marriage, not on passion or interest, but on true love.[19] This is a spontaneous sentiment; therefore he who does not feel it must be allowed to remain unmarried. When individual rights are recognised, the wish to remain unmarried must be respected; it can no longer be punished as contrary to the interests of the Republic. We find, in very early times, Christians who chose to remain unmarried; they are even held up for special esteem, as knowing how to resist the desires of the flesh.[20] This esteem, in its principle, was homage given to Christian liberty.

In later times some Fathers, such as Ambrose and Augustine, thought the cares of married life a hindrance to holiness, and gave to celibacy the exaggerated importance of a more perfect virtue. They were willing to say that marriage might be good and honourable, but they only advised it for those who could not otherwise live in chastity.[21] Methodius, an enthusiastic admirer of virginity, admits however that marriage ought not to be abolished; for although the moon, to which he compares the celibate, is greater than the stars, they nevertheless shed a little light in the sky.[22] By the side of this ascetic tendency, the truer and more Christian idea was also upheld,—that marriage is not a hindrance to piety, and that consequently it is no less holy than virginity and celibacy. This was the opinion of Chrysostom. This great-minded man often tries to prove that the sacred union of marriage, instead of being a hindrance, is for Christians a means of mutual help in spiritual life. Domestic cares, household rule, the education of children are noble duties; as such, if well fulfilled, they cannot hinder progress towards perfection. Such a Christian husband and wife show a holier life than the inhabitants of many a monastery.[23] It often happened that one wished to leave the other, from devotion to the ascetic life. Chrysostom represented to these thoughtless pious people that fasts and abstinences are worthless if the tie of love is broken.[24] Besides, it is to expose the one who has no vocation for asceticism to temptation. The union between husband and wife is so holy that it creates a solidarity, a mutual responsibility, which compels them to guard it with the most inviolable fidelity.[25]

In the natural and close union of Christian marriage, woman seems at a first glance to occupy a subordinate position, analogous to that assigned to her by pagan society. It is true that the Fathers repeat from the Old and New Testaments, that woman submits to man on account of her weakness; but it is a free submission, for the wife is equal to the husband by nature and by her rank in the conjugal union. If she must serve, it is in the Christian sense, through love.[26] She must be as a sister, placed in his sight as the Church is in sight of her Head.[27] She and her husband do not form two separate beings; they only make together one person, of whom the husband is the head.[28] It is no longer the olden slavery of woman; she is raised, and equals the husband in dignity, whilst seeing in him the head of the family. Christianity could never have proclaimed an emancipation of woman as it was carried out by the Roman ladies of the decadence, or as it is taught by modern socialism. With marvellous intelligence of the needs of nature and life, two domains are divided between husband and wife, so as to claim the whole activity of each. Human life has two sides, public and private; God has given to each sex the limits which none pass without penalty. Neither men nor women ever leave their own sphere without wounding the universal conscience of the human race. According to the Fathers, outside business is given to man, the forum, the senate, the camps; whilst to woman are given internal household duties. Chrysostom says, "She can neither carry arms, nor vote in the assemblies, nor manage the commune, but she can weave thread, give better advice than her husband about domestic matters, rule and keep order in her household, superintend the servants and bring up the children. Each sex has its special vocation; God has not given all to one, He has wisely divided it."[29] Thus the wife, instead of being the servant of the husband, is his companion and helper; she is, according to the beautiful ideas of the Fathers, his indispensable complement. It is only through her that he becomes all that he ought to be in accordance with the intentions of God.[30] It is woman who comforts man and gives him calm and courage. To quote again from Chrysostom: "Nothing," he says, "can better mould man than a pious and wise woman. It is proved, because many violent, harsh, passionate men have been led to gentler feelings through the influence of their wives."[31]

The Fathers, knowing how woman pities and compassionates more easily than man, give to her, besides household duties, a mission away from home. They do not refuse to widen the sphere of her activities, but they do not call her to mix in the struggles of men, or to take any occupation contrary to the genius of her sex. Her appointed task is one of consolation and charity, caring for the poor, visiting the sick, consoling the afflicted.[32] The Christian wife, as drawn by the Fathers, is modest, pious, fearing the voluptuous or barbarous spectacles of paganism, seldom leaving her house, where, instead of receiving lovers or actors, she hospitably entertains those who are unhappy, and poor foreigners. When she goes out, it is not to the circus or bath, pompously with a troop of slaves; but, covered with a veil, she goes quietly to church, or the dwelling of a poor person. It was rightly said that she forms the most beautiful ornament of her husband, and the joy of her family. Briefly, she is admirable.[33] We may be permitted to add the portrait drawn towards the end of the fourth century by Bishop Asterius, of Amasia: "She is thy member, thy helper, thy aid in the trials of life. She attends thee in sickness, comforts thee in affliction; she is the guardian angel of thy home, the keeper of thy wealth. She suffers the same evils as thou and enjoys the same pleasures. If thou hast riches she takes care of them, if thou art poor she will make the most of thy small means. She resists misfortune with strength and courage. Thanks to the tie which unites her to thee, she bears the painful burden of educating her children. If thou shouldest lose thy fortune, thou wilt hide thyself in discouragement. Thy false friends, whose affections vary with the vicissitudes of thy lot, disappear; thy slaves leave thee. The wife alone remains, as the member of an afflicted body, as a servant of the ills of man, to give the care he needs. It is she who wipes away his tears, and who dresses his wounds when he has been tortured.

It is she, finally, who goes with him when he is led into captivity."[34]

To attain the happiness of possessing such a wife, the Fathers exhort Christians not to think lightly of marriage, this most important event of life, on which all worldly happiness or discomfort depends.[35] They desire that the choice shall not be made without serious consideration. As Christian marriage is the union of souls, typically illustrated by the union of Christ with the Church, it is necessary, above all, that there shall be a common feeling about what is most essential—about faith. They decided, therefore, to prohibit mixed marriages of Christians and pagans, and began by pointing out the inconveniences which would necessarily result from unions of this kind, where the pagan husband would hinder his Christian wife from giving herself to prayer and the inspirations of charity.[36] Before long they were absolutely forbidden. Tertullian had already reproved them as improper.[37] A little later the Fathers unanimously condemned them, and the councils excommunicated those parents who consented to them.[38] If a husband or wife became Christian after marriage, that was no reason for breaking the bond. On the contrary, it ought to be sanctified by the efforts of the Christian to lead the one still in idolatry to the Saviour.[39] The converted woman was advised to be still more gentle, humble, and peace-loving, because she had more to fear from the hastiness of her pagan husband.[40]

After requiring joint faith as the first condition of a happy marriage, other counsels, full of wisdom and charity, were added. We just mention these to mark still more clearly the difference between the Christian spirit and that of pagan civilization. The wife must not be chosen for beauty or riches, but only for her virtues and the graces of a good disposition. Therefore it is wise to find out what her previous conduct has been, and above all, if she has faithfully fulfilled her duties to her parents.[41] "A wise and pious young girl," says Chrysostom, "is more precious than all the gold in the world."[42]

The young girl was advised to take for husband the one chosen for her by her father.[43] This was a remnant of the ancient paternal right, but it was mitigated by the acknowledgment that for a happy union the girl must love him who seeks her, and not be forced to marry against her wishes. Augustine even desired that when she had arrived at years of discretion, she should be allowed to choose her husband herself.[44] This was an immense progress from the customs of antiquity.

Lastly, to preserve the ties of family love still more completely, the Fathers asked that marriage between relations should be prohibited, or at least that the relationships fixed by Roman law as hindrances should be increased.[45] This was not a barrier imposed contrary to the respect of Christianity for the rights of individuality; it was a natural consequence of the principle of love. It was desired that the family, which partly represented the Church of God, and which had lost its power in pagan society through the loosening of the most sacred bonds, should be united more closely by a charity free from all personal desires. Ambrose wished to attach these prohibitions to a special Divine law,[46] but although that utters no voice in the matter,[47] they are still in accordance with the spiritual laws of the kingdom of God.

When the union is concluded, the Church, contrary to pagan custom, does not impose duties on the woman only. She requires them also from the husband. She says the wife must be amiable; by chastity, by gentleness of manners, by simplicity of character, by charity towards all, and by submission to him to whom she has voluntarily given herself before God, she must venerate and seek only to please him.[48] A Christian poet of the fourth century has given these counsels to a young girl in verses full of truth and delicacy.[49] On the other hand, the Fathers require that the husband shall respect his wife, that he shall surround her with his care, that he shall treat with gentleness and goodness the companion of his life, the mother of his children;[50] that he shall love her more than his own parents, even to death if need be, as Christ gave Himself for His bride, the Church; that he shall protect and instruct her, that he shall correct her with love, and if unfortunately she remains deaf to his counsels, he shall bear it patiently, without sending her away or ill-treating her.[51]

The conjugal union, in which husband and wife are united by such great duties, was originally looked upon as too close to be dissolved by death; an alliance of two immortal souls ought to last throughout eternity. For this reason, several of the early Fathers pronounced against second marriages.[52] According to Athenagoras, the man who marries again commits a decent kind of adultery.[53] Tertullian, after he had adopted the rigid system of the Montanists, absolutely condemned second marriages. His reasons are not generally of great weight, though he expresses very pure feeling, as when he says that the husband being near God, the surviving wife will be more closely united to him when she sanctifies her remembrance by prayer. She will thus live with him in spiritual communion and holy harmony that nothing can disturb.[54] Tertullian had been less decisive before he accepted the tenets of Montanism. In his two books to his own wife, he begged her not to re-marry if he died first; however, he added that if this did not suit her inclinations, a second marriage was not contrary to the law of God.[55] This was the opinion held by the apostles, founded on the idea that in the heavenly world perfect love will be no longer fettered by difference of sex, according to the words of Christ, "For in the resurrection they neither marry nor are given in marriage, but are as angels in heaven" (Matt. xxii. 30).

This more lenient doctrine, already held by Hermas and by Clement of Alexandria,[56] finally prevailed in the Church. Widowers and widows were advised not to marry again. To the last were plainly pointed out the difficulties inseparable from a second marriage, in the education of the children of two mothers, as well as in the remembrance retained by the husband of his last wife, which might shadow the happiness of the new union. Ambrosius, and especially Chrysostom, treat this subject with as much charity as delicacy.[57] Neither they, nor the other Fathers who advise voluntary widowhood, condemn second marriages. They do not find them forbidden by the law of God, and consequently it is not sinful to engage in them. Often they ought even to be advised. According to Jerome a young and rich widow, exposed to a thousand temptations, ought to marry again if she is not sure of herself; for a second marriage is preferable to a disorderly life.[58] It is true that some Councils caused widows who re-married to submit to temporary punishment, but they did not excommunicate them.[59] After the time of Augustine it was a heresy to condemn second marriages.[60]

The same high idea of the holiness of marriage that we have been endeavouring to bring out, ruled the Christian belief as to divorce, which was so frequent and so easy in paganism. The Church unreservedly condemned these causeless separations, so many scandalous examples of which were to be seen in pagan society.[61] Adultery was the only admitted cause of separation. When the Fathers commanded chastity in marriage, and made reciprocal fidelity one of the holiest conjugal duties, they at the same time reminded the world that adultery is one of the gravest violations of the law of God. The councils excommunicated those who were guilty of it, and they were only received again after long penitence.[62] From a general point of view this was only to reinforce the reprobation in which the adulterer was held even in pagan society; but we know that that society made exceptions in regard to the transactions of men with a certain class of women. These exceptions the Church could not allow to exist. Contrary to pagan laws and customs, and in consequence of Christian respect for reinstated woman, it is no longer she alone who is thought capable of committing adultery. The doctors of the Church vigorously attack the pagan pride which accused woman alone, whilst man claimed to be free. Henceforth the unfaithful husband was held to be as guilty as the wife who violated her duty. He is even blamed the most, for he has not the excuse of weakness. He has power, and should employ it well. He ought to give his protection to her who is trusted to him, and to set an example of virtue, that he may not give her au excuse for vice.[63]

The lightness with which the pagans treated concubinage was strongly condemned by the Fathers. How could they admit the distinction made by Roman society between the concubine and the prostitute? For them, according to Augustine, without excuse for bachelor or widower, any person besides the wife with whom man has to do, falls into the category of prostitutes, with whom only a disgraceful and illicit union can be formed.

Jerome says on this subject, "The laws of the Cæsars are different from the laws of Christ. What Papinianus ordered differs from what Paul taught. The pagans loosen the reins which restrain men's unchasteness. Violation and adultery are forbidden with free persons, but are allowed with slaves or at the *lupanar*, as if the sin did not depend on the wish of the person who sins, but on the position of the person with whom he sins! With us, on the contrary, what is not permitted for women is also forbidden for men."[64]

Adultery, being in its own nature a rupture of the conjugal bond, ought to entail separation, but according to the opinion of the Fathers this should not be an absolute rule; at least, it need not be carried to the length of divorce. There are only a few isolated voices in favour of divorce after adultery. Epiphanius holds that the innocent wife sent away without reason by the husband, or compelled to leave him on account of his unfaithfulness, may marry again without sin.[65] Hilarius of Poictiers and Asterius are of the same opinion.[66] The greater part of the Fathers, feeling the scandals of pagan society, and wishing to increase the gravity of conjugal engagements, always give their opinion against another marriage after a separation, although this power was still allowed by the civil laws. If it is a sin for a husband to live with his wife when he knows that she has committed adultery, he becomes guilty of the same crime if, after having sent away his unfaithful wife, he marries another. This opinion, which had been already expressed by Hermas,[67] became that held by nearly all the Fathers.[68] It was founded on the purest Christian feeling. The holiness of marriage necessarily made it indissoluble. If one of the two violated it, the fault should be punished by separation, but this should only be temporary, until the repentance of the guilty one. The opening for reconciliation is there, and the penitence of the one and the pardon of the other should ensure redoubled affection and fidelity.

The Councils by their decisions sanctioned the advice of the Fathers. That of Elvira, 305 A.D., excommunicated the woman who, after leaving her husband on account of his adultery, should marry another. She might not receive absolution until the death of her first husband.[69] Some years later the Council of Arles limited itself to asking, under the form of advice, that those husbands who had adulterous wives should not marry again, in the hope of a mutual reconciliation.[70] The prohibition soon became, notwithstanding, the general law of the Church.[71]

We should not have said all on this subject without speaking of the teaching of the Church in reference to fallen women. On the one hand she insisted on the duty of men to be chaste, as much for the sake of their own morality as for the sake of the women that pagan morality put defenceless in their hands. In the midst of the unbounded licentiousness of the latter age of the empire, the Fathers continually taught that impurity is a crime against God, defiling His noblest creatures, destroying both the soul and physical beauty, whose worth consists in virgin purity.[72] On the other hand, the Church, following the example of the Saviour, who held out His hand to the adulterous woman, called to her bosom those unfortunates whom paganism degraded and held in the ways of vice. She purified them, and gave them pardon and peace in the love of Christ. Forbidden baptism, or excommunicated, as long as they lived in infamy,[73] they were forgiven and received when, giving up their profession, they gave proofs of penitence.[74] The

Church gained glorious martyrs from amongst these rescued ones. Afra died for the Saviour, in Augsburg, with three servants, who, having followed her in vice, followed her also in conversion.[75] Pelagia, a celebrated actress and courtezan at Antioch, was converted, and retired into a convent, from whence the prefect, assisted by the law of his time, vainly tried to drag her back to the theatre. She spent the remainder of her life in this retreat, showing her gratitude to Christ by the humble piety of her conduct.[76] These facts prove the power of Christianity to arouse the deadest souls, and also the energy of woman's nature, which can be raised by the hand of Christ from the deepest abyss; whilst the charity of Christian society receives and welcomes the sinner whom the world first abused and then despised.

§ 2. *Children.*

The Christian spirit, by raising woman and sanctifying marriage, changed the family (which till then had only had a civil importance) into a religious institution. It modified the relations between parents and children, without weakening the authority of the first or the respect and obedience of the second.

In our first part we saw that the pagan father only accepted his child if he promised to become a robust and useful citizen, and if he was not too poor to bring him up. The pagan mother, on her side, freed herself by abortion or exposure from the result of her too often criminal loves. From the earliest times the Christians reproved these barbarous customs. The Church, animated by a touching solicitude, blessed and protected little children because "of them is the kingdom of heaven."[77] She respected human nature even in the child which had not yet seen day, and desired that when born he should be the object of his parents' tenderness, whatever might be his physical state. The Fathers declare that to cause a child to perish by abortion is to destroy the work of God. It is to become a murderer, as much as if the child was born into the world. It is to take life from a creature who is already the object of Divine goodness. God, who has no respect of persons, who judges them neither by appearance nor age, is the Father of all life, however incomplete it be.[78] The Apostolic Constitutions also compare abortion to homicide. Those guilty of it are excluded for ten years from the Church, although the civil law did not yet punish this crime.[79]

The Church holds the custom of the exposure of children in equal horror. The Christians bring it as a severe reproach against pagan society. Justin Martyr sees in it one of the proofs of the hardening of heart which comes from idolatry; for if it is not killing the the children, it is at least debasing human nature; knowing that those who are saved are generally destined for shame or slavery.[80] A hundred and fifty years after Justin, Lactantius expresses himself with vigorous eloquence against this custom, which was so deeply rooted in ancient morality. "How can any one imagine that fathers have given to them the right to kill their newborn children? It is an act of the greatest impiety. If God sends souls into the world, it is for life, not death. However, there are men who believe that it does not soil their hands to take from these hardly formed beings the life they have not given them. Do not hope that they will spare the life of the stranger, these men who do not spare their own blood! Without contradiction, they are deeply perverted. What shall I say of those who are led by false affection to expose their children? Can we consider those innocent who offer their own bowels as prey for dogs, and kill them more cruelly than if they were strangled? Who can doubt that it is impious, thus to trust one's own to the pity of others? Even when it happens that the exposed child is taken by some one who will feed him, it is still the father who is guilty of having sold his own blood to servitude or prostitution! . . . He may as well kill his child as expose him. It is true these murderous fathers complain of their poverty and imagine they have not enough to bring up a family; as if the wealth of this world was completely in the power of those who possess it, as if God did not every day bring the rich to poverty, and raise the poor to plenty! If then a man cannot feed his children through poverty, it is better that he should keep away from his wife, than that he should destroy with impious hands the work of God." [81]

The Fathers not only attacked the cruel excesses of paternal powers amongst the pagans, but tried to sanctify the feelings of affection that Christianity had unlocked in the heart. The child, from his earliest days, is brought into the kingdom of God; he is received into the Church by baptism; he cannot be excluded from the grace of which that sacrament assures to him the possession. "If old sinners," said Cyprian, "are received in the Christian community, with how much greater reason shall the newborn child be received, who has not yet committed sin?" [82] This care was not confined exclusively to legitimate children. Natural children, even those of adulterers, are equally creatures of God; they are under His paternal protection, and consequently worthy of the charity of the Church. [83]

Children are souls trusted to parents who are responsible for them; the blame will fall on the parents if the children are lost.[84]

This tightening of the bond which unites them, brings fresh sources of happiness in fulfilling their duties towards their children, their fellow-citizens in the kingdom of God. The old, inflexible harshness of the Roman father must disappear, to be replaced by an authority tempered with love. The father must think of his son as his equal in natural dignity, and destined to continue the race of children of God in the world. Certainly he must teach him respect and obedience, but not by treating him like a slave. In teaching him to know and love the law of God, he will cause him to learn also to submit his will to that of his parents.[85]

This religious education is strongly enforced by the Fathers, particularly Chrysostom. This great man and eloquent interpreter of the Christian spirit sees in the absence of religious education, as much as in the misery and needs of humanity, the cause of the decadence of the world. Men occupy themselves, he says, in gaining honour and riches, that they may leave reputation and fortune to their children, for whose souls no one cares. This neglect is a great sin, for it gives the children to eternal death, and helps to ruin society. What has upset the whole world is, that man has not cared more for his own "children."[86] Chrysostom and all the other Fathers see no salvation but in religious education. They speak of this continually in the most emphatic terms. They wish that at an age when the will is still flexible the children should be led in the good way; that they should receive pious impressions at an early age; that they may grow up through fear of God and love of Christ, to wisdom, faith, humility, and charity; that in their earliest years the great principles of the Christian life may be impressed upon them.[87] To bring this about, parents should undertake the education of their children themselves, instead of leaving it to ignorant and often irreligious slaves.[88]

It was chiefly to the mothers that the Church gave the care of the earliest religious education. The father, engaged in other things, could not always consecrate to this duty the time it claimed; besides, the mother, by her sweeter, more patient and loving nature, is more likely to awaken pious feeling in the childish soul. Pagan moralists knew nothing of the mother's influence; they did not say much of the education of daughters, to which maternal solicitude is first directed by the doctors of Christianity. Chrysostom and Jerome insist on the duty of mothers to train their daughters in pious and simple manners, that they may some day make good wives, capable of ordering a household, and in their turn training children for heaven.[89] The Christian mother must also influence her sons. Whilst in pagan society they were soon taken from their mother, who was restricted to her own part of the house, or who freed herself only to enter the paths of vice, we see them trusted by the Church to maternal tenderness, from whence in their earliest years they drew the germs of spiritual life. Several of the most illustrious doctors owed their greatness to their pious mothers. History has preserved the memory of Monica, the mother of Augustine; of Nonna, mother of Gregory of Nazianzus; of Anthusa, mother of Chrysostom.

In the early time of the Church, Christian children were taught only in their own families. This could not be otherwise whilst Christian society was surrounded by dangers and persecutions. It has been asked whether Christians sent their children to pagan schools, or whether they refrained through conscientious scruples.[90] There is no historical evidence on the subject, but it is allowable to suppose that those who refused to hold public office because they would not join in idolatrous rites, would also refuse to trust their children to masters who, whilst teaching them the fables of paganism, would at the same time have familiarised them with its morality. In proportion as the Churches were organized, there were doubtless schools for children, as well as for adults who were being prepared for baptism or the ministry. The first traces of schools that may be called primary are met with in the fourth century.[91] The schools were kept by priests. Children went there after the age of five.[92] The monks had made meritorious efforts for the education and instruction of youth. Basil, during his rule, made it a most essential duty; he gave valuable counsel on the method of treating children, and accustoming them to a wise discipline.[93] It would lead us away from our subject to give more ample details relating to the establishments for the literary and religious instruction of adults. It must suffice us to have proved that under the influence of Christianity education took a religious, and consequently an infinitely more moral, character than in the ancient world.[94] When the Fathers refused to separate instruction from education, into which they introduced the Christian element, they rendered a service to humanity that only blind spirits will refuse to recognise. Yet even to-day there are men who wish to banish from education the element which irritates them; we must hesitate at no sacrifice to preserve its influence; the salvation of the world is at stake.

(1) Chrysost., *Hom.* 13 *in Eph.*, § 3, vol. xi. p. 309. August., *De Genesi ad Litteram*, IX. § 50, vol. iii. p. II. p. 220. (2) "The woman has some excuse for her sin, the man has none."—Ambr., *De Institutione*

THE FAMILY.

Virginis, c. 4, § 25, vol. ii. p. 255. Cf. Gen. iii. 15. (3) Clem. Alex., *Pædag.* I. 4, vol. i. p. 103 Greg. Naz., *Or.* 31, vol. i. p. 502. Greg. Nyss., *Or.* 1 *in Verba Fac. Hom.*, vol. i. p. 151. (4) *Sermo* 190, § 2, vol. v. p. 621; *Sermo* 51, § 3, p. 199. (5) Augustine, speaking of the Voconian law, says :—" I do not know that anything more unjust than this law could possibly be devised or expressed."—*De Civit. Dei*, III. c. 21, vol. vii. p. 63. (6) *Or.* 1 *in Verba Fac. Hom.*, vol. i. p. 151. (7) Tertull., *De Virg. Vel.*, c. 9, p. 178. Cypr., *Testim. adv. Jud.* III. 46, p. 318. Chrysost., *Hom.* 37 *in* 1 *Cor.*, § 1 sq. vol. x. p. 343. (8) "Λεόντων Θερμοτέραι."—*Hom.* 29 *in Rom.*, § 2, vol. ix. p. 747. (9) Chrysost., *Hom.* 42 *in cap.* xviii. *Gen.*, § 7, vol. iv. p. 433 ; *Hom.* 13 *in Eph.*, § 3, vol. xi. p. 100; August., *Sermo* 9, § 12, vol. v. p. 40. (10) Palladius, *Hist. Lausiaca*, c. 119, p. 226. (11) Hieron., *Ep.* 108, vol. i. p. 693. (12) *Id.*, *Ep.* 77, vol. i. p. 464. (13) Theodoret., *Hist. Eccl.*, V. 19, p. 223. (14) Athenag., *Leg.*, c. 33, p. 311. Asterius, *Hom. an Liceat Dimittere Uxorem*, p. 64. (15) Chrysost., *Hom.* 12 *in Col.*, § 5, vol. xi. p. 419. Paulin. Nol., *Poem.*, 22, pp. 124 sq. (16) Clem. Alex., *Strom.* II., vol. i. p. 502. (17) Ignat., *Ep. ad. Polyc.* V. 41. Clem. Alex., *Pædag.*, III. 11, vol. i. p. 291. Tertull., *Ad Uxorem*, II. 8, p. 172; *De Monog.*, c. 11, p. 531. (18) Tertull., *De Pudic.*, c. 4, p. 557. (19) August., *Sermo* 51, § 21, vol. v. p. 205. (20) Athenag., *Leg.*, c. 33, p. 310. (21) August., *De Bono Conjugali*, vol. vi. p. 233 sq.; *De Nuptiis et Concup.*, I. 1 sq., vol. x. p. 187. Ambr., *De Viduis*, c. 12, § 72, vol. ii. p. 205. (22) *Convivium Decem Virginum*, Or. 2; in Combelis., *Bibl. Græc. PP. auctarium noviss.*, vol. i. p. 71 sq. (23) Chrysost., *Hom.* 1 *in Rom.*, xvi. 3, vol. iii. p. 175. Greg. Naz., *Or.* 11, vol. i. p. 180. (24) " Τί τὸ κέρδος τῆς νηστείας καὶ τῆς ἐγκρατείας, ἀγάπης διερρηγμένης ; οὐδέν." —*Hom.* 19 *in Cor.*, § 1, vol. x. p. 160. (25) August., *De Conj. Adult.*, I. 1, vol. vi. p. 285. (26) August., *Quæst. in Gen.*, I. quæstio 153, vol. iii. P. II., p. 311. Chrysost., *Hom.* 26 *in* 1 *Cor.*, § 2, vol. x. p. 229. Hieron., *Comm. in Tit.*, c. 2, vol. iii. p. 427. (27) Hermas I. vis. 2, c. 2 and 3, p. 77. Paul. Nol., *Poema*, 22, vv. 167 sq., p. 128. Asterius, *Hom. an Liceat Dimittere Uxorem*, p. 64. (28) Chrysost., *Hom.* 12, *in Col.*, § 5, vol. xi. p. 419. (29) Clem. Rom., *Ep.* 1 *ad Cor.*, c. 1, p. 147. Clem. Alex., *Pædag.*, III. 11, vol. i. p. 288. Ambr., *De Paradiso*, c. 11, § 50, vol. i. p. 167. Chrysost., *Quales Ducendæ sint Uxores*, vol. iii. p. 127. (30) Chrysost., l.c. ; *Sermo* 4 *in Gen.*, § 1, vol. iv. p. 659. Ambr., *De Instit. Virg.*, c. 3, § 22, vol. ii. p. 254. (31) Chrysost., *Hom.* 61 *in John*, § 3, vol. viii. p. 365. (32) Nilus, *Peristeria*, § 1, c. 3, p. 87. (33) " Κάλλιστον γὰρ ἔργον γυνὴ οἰκουρός," etc.—Clem. Alex. *Pædag.*, III. 11, vol. i. p. 293. Tertull., *Ad Ux.*, II. 8, p. 172. Paul. Nol., *Poema* 22, p. 124 sq. (34) *Hom. an Liceat Dimittere Uxorem*, p. 65. (35) " πρᾶγμα τοῦ ἀνθρωπίνου βίου κεφάλαιον."—Asterius, l.c. p. 62. (36) Tertull., *Ad Ux.*, II. c. 4, 6, pp. 168, 170. (37) *O. c.*, c. 3, p. 168 ; *De Coronâ*, c. 13, p. 109; *De Monog.*, c. 11, p. 532. (38) Cypr., *Testim. adv. Jud.*, III. 62, p. 323. Ambr., *Exp. Ev. Luc.* viii., § 2, vol. i. p. 1410, etc. Council of Elvira, 305, can. 15 ; of Arles, 314, can. 11 ; Mansi, vol. ii. pp. 8 and 472. (39) Tertull., *Ad Ux.*, II. 7, p. 171. August., *De Conjug. Adult.*, I. 17; *De Fide et Operibus*, c. 19, vol. vi. pp. 291, 136. (40) *Constit. Apost.*, I. 10, p. 212. (41) Clem. Alex., *Strom.*, IV. 20, vol. i. p. 621. Chrysost. *Quales Ducendæ Sint Uxores*, vol. iii. p. 211 sq. (42) Chrysost., *Hom.* 20 *in Ephes.*, § 8, vol. xi. p. 155. (43) Nauma-

P

chius in *Gnom.*, p. 122. (44) August., *Ep.* 254, vol. ii. p. 668. (45) August., *De Civit. Dei*, XV. 16, vol. vii. p. 301. (46) *Ep.* 60, vol. ii. p. 1017. (47) *August.*, l.c., note 1. (48) Clem. Rom., *Ep.* 1 ad Cor., c. 21, p. 161; *Constit. Apost.*, I. c. 8, 9, VI. 29, pp. 209, 360. (49) Naumachius in *Gnom.*, p. 122 sq. The date of this poet, who is so little read, is not fixed. Erasmus, Scaliger, Voss, and others feel sure that he is Christian. Such is also the opinion of M. Schoell (*Hist. de la Litt. Grecque*, 2nd ed., vol. vi. p. 76). (50) Asterius, *Hom. an Liceat Dimittere Uxorem*, p. 66. (51) *Ignat. ad Polyc.*, c. 5, p. 41. *Const. Apost.*, I. 2, p. 203. (52) Just. Mart., *Apol.*, I. 15, p. 52. (53) Athenag., *Leg.*, 33, p. 311. (54) Tertull., *De Monog.*, c. 10, p. 531; *De Exhortat. Castit.*, c. 2 sq., p. 519. (55) *Ad Uxorem*, II., p. 161 sq. (56) Hermas, II. Mand. 4, c. 4, p. 91. Clem. Alex., *Strom.* III. 12, vol. i. p. 548. (57) Chrysost., *Hom. de Viduis*, vol. iii. p. 345. Ambr., *De Viduis*, c. 2, § 10, c. 11, § 68, c. 15, § 88, vol. ii. pp. 188, 203, 210. August., *De Bono Viduitatis*, c. 4, vol. vi. p. 273. Hieron., *Ep.* 54, vol. i. p. 294. (58) Hieron., *Ep.* 79, vol. i. p. 507. (59) Council of Neo Cæsarea, A.D. 315, can. 3 ; of Laodicæa, 4th cent. A.D., can. 1; Mansi, vol. ii. pp. 540, 564. Bas., *Ep.* 188, can. 4, vol. iii. p. 271. (60) August., *De Hæres.*, c. 28, vol. viii. p. 8; *De Civit. Dei*, XVI. 34, vol. vii. p. 338. (61) Council of Elvira, A.D. 305, can. 8 ; Mansi, vol. ii. p. 7. (62) Ib., can. 64, 69 ; Council of Ancyra, A.D. 315, can. 20, l.c., p. 16, 519. (63) Lactant., *Div. Instit.*, VI. 23, vol. i. p. 500. August., *De Conjugiis Adulterinis*, II. 7 sq., vol. vi. p. 299 sq.; *Sermo* 9, § 11 sq., vol. v. p. 40. (64) *Ep.* 77, ann. 399, vol. i. p. 459. (65) Epiph., *Adv. Hær.* II., vol. i. *Hær.* 59, § 4 ; and III., vol. ii. *Exposit. Fidei Cath.*, § 21, vol. i. p. 497 ano 1103. (66) Asterius, *Hom. an Liceat Dimittere Uxorem*, p. 64. Hilar. Pictav., *Comm. in Matt.*, c. 4, § 22, p. 627. (67) Bk. II., Mand. 4, c. 1, p. 87. (68) Clem. Alex., *Strom.*, II. 23, vol. i. p. 507. Tertull., *De Monog.*, cpp. 9, 10. p. 530. Orig., *Comm. in Matth.*, vol. xiv. § 24 ; vol. iii. p. 648. Lactant., *Div. Instit.*, VI. 23, vol. i. p. 501. Greg. Naz., *Ep.* 181, vol. i. p. 884. Hieron., *Comm. in Matth.*, c. 19, vol. iii. p. 87. August., *Sermo* 392, § 2, vol. v. p. 1054. (69) Can. 9 ; Mansi, vol. ii. p. 7. (70) Can. 10 ; l.c., p. 472. (71) *Canones Eccl. Afric.*, can. 102 ; l.c., vol. iii. p. 806. (72) Athenag., *Leg.*, c. 34, p. 311. (73) August., *De Fide et Op.*, c. 18, vol. vi. p. 136. Council of Elvira, A.D. 305, can. 12; Mansi, vol. ii. p. 7. (74) August., *O. c.*, c. 15, 19, pp. 131, 136. Council of Elvira, can. 44, p. 13. (75) Ruinart, *Acta Mart.*, p. 455. (76) Chrysost., *Hom.* 67 *in Matt.*, § 3, vol. vii., p. 665. (77) Cf. *Ep. ad Zenam et Serenum*, c. 17, in *Opp. Just. Mart.*, p. 416. (78) Barn., *Ep.*, cpp. 19 and 20, vol. i. pp. 51, 53. Athenag., *Leg.*, c. 35, p. 312 ; Min. Felix, c. 30, p. 114. Tertull., *Apol.*, c. 9, p. 36; *Ad. Nat.*, I. 16 ; p. 51. Cypr., *Ep.*, 59, p. 98. (79) *Const. Apost.*, VII. 3, p. 366. (80) Just. Mart., *Apol.* I., cpp. 27, 29 ; pp. 60, 61; *Ep. ad Diogn.*, c. 3, p. 236. Min. Felix, c. 30, p. 114. Arnob., II. 75, vol. i. p. 105. (81) *Div. Instit.*, VI. 20, vol. i. p. 491. Cf. August., *De Nuptiis et Concup.*, I. 15, vol. x. p. 193. (82) " . . . Quanto magis prohiberi non debet infans, qui recens natus nihil peccavit."—Cypr., *Ep.*, 59, p. 99. (83) Methodius., *Conviv. X. Virginum*, or. 2, in Combelis., *Biblioth. Græcorum PP. auctar. noviss*, vol. i. p. 75. (84) Ambr., *De Bono Mortis*, c. 8, § 35, vol. i. p. 404. (85) Chrysost., *Hom.* 21 *in Eph.*, § 1, vol. xi. p. 159. (86) " καὶ τοῦτό ἐστιν, ὃ τὴν οἰκουμένην ἀνατρέπει πᾶσαν, ὅτι τῶν οἰκείων ἀμελοῦμεν παίδων."—*Hom. de Viduis*, vol. iii. p. 317. (87) Barn., *Ep.*, c. 19, p. 51. Polyc., *Ep.*, c. 4, p. 187. Clem. Rom., *Ep.* 1 *ad Cor.*, c. 21, p. 161; *Constit. Apost.*, IV. 11, p. 301. Chrysost., *Hom. de Viduis*, vol. iii. p. 319. (88) Chrysost., *Hom.* 9 *in Col.*, § 2 vol. xi. p. 392. (89) Chrysost., *Quales Ducendæ sint Uxores*, vol. iii. p. 227. Hieron., *Comm. in Tit.*, c. 2, vol. iii. p. 427; *Ep.*, 107, 128, vol. i. pp. 681, 961. (90) Cf. M. Lalanne, *Influence des Pères de l'Eglise sur l'éducation publique*, Paris, 1850, p. 7. (91) "Philip the hermit, and priest of the schools."—Palladius, *Vita Chrys.*; *in Opp.*, vol. xiii. p. 77. (92) Chrysost., *De Mutatione Nominum*, 2, vol. iii. p. 109. (93) Basil., *Regula Fusius Tract.*, interrog. 15 et 23, vol. ii. p. 355 sq. (94) As to the Homily on education, which is ascribed to Chrysostom, see the work of M. Lalanne, p. 209 sq.

CHAPTER IV.

THE LABOURING CLASSES.

§ 1. *Work. The Free Workman.*

CHRISTIANITY, which is a heartfelt and spiritual religion, does not offer to those whom it invites to become members of the kingdom of God material means of earthly prosperity. It was not in its nature to furnish an external remedy for the misery which pressed upon pagan society, and which was the fatal result of contempt of work and those who worked. Christian charity, whilst helping all in misfortune and sorrow, had something else to do than to point out the way to fortune to the degraded multitude, who only cared to be fed and amused at the public expense. The Gospel sought first to raise man from his degradation, by breaking the pride of laziness in some and the servile chains of others. How different from those utopians who upset society whilst writing on their flag the *rights of labour!* The Fathers transformed it by proclaiming the *duty of labour.* Work no longer conveys the ancient idea of being unworthy of the man who desires to be respected; it is dignified and held worthy of all ranks of men. Christianity raised the despised and impoverished working classes, through this elevation of work, more effectually than gifts or division of property could have done. Society was imbued with a new spirit, which was to become the first condition of the progress and industry of modern civilization.

The early Christians did not think manual labour ignominious. They neither felt themselves to be miserable nor disgraced because they were obliged to gain their living by the sweat of their brow.[1] They protested against the contempt in which the pagans held them when they practised a profession. Their doctors represented work as the common law for all men, as the condition of earthly existence. Unless this had been the will of God, He would have made the requisites of life produce themselves spontaneously. It is true that the Fathers speak of work as a punishment for, or rather an expiation of, the fall of man;[2] but they also state that it received a new meaning, because it was honoured by Christ, who was the son of a workman, and by the apostles, who worked with their own hands.[3] Work so ennobled is no longer a penalty but an honour for man; it is worthy of the highest praise.[4] Every profession is held to be honourable, only excepting those which destroy body and soul. No work is thought degrading, however humble it may be, provided it can be carried on without sin. The Church laboured to suppress only degrading or criminal industries.[5]

The consequences of this doctrine are that work is looked upon as a duty, and idleness meets with energetic reprobation. The suppression of slavery must also follow. We shall have a separate article on this, and now limit ourselves to what concerns the freeman.

"Work with your hands" had been already written by Barnabas to the Christians to whom he addressed his epistle.[6] The Apostolic Constitutions forbid a man to mix with the idle crowd, always ready for evil, and advise him to engage in useful work, having his soul turned towards

God. The rich who need not work to live are exhorted to avoid inaction, and to take advantage of their position to increase their knowledge by study and intercourse with pious men.[7] The young are especially warned against idleness as contrary to human nature and the law of God. Chrysostom looked on this vice as the cause of decay and ruin for the individual, as well as for the family. He might have added that it was injurious to the whole of society.[8] Consequently, the necessity of teaching useful trades to children was strongly insisted upon.[9] In the schools of the monasteries they were taught handicrafts in wood, stone, and metal, and in preference to all else agriculture, which had regained its true and ancient dignity.[10]

The Fathers of the Church restored the dignity of work, not only for the personal interest of the worker, but also for the sake of its connection with charity. This idea, peculiar to Christianity, is one of the strongest arguments in favour of the dignity of work. On the one hand they appeal to the sympathy of the healthy and robust poor man to help those who are more unfortunate than himself. They point out that he must work that he may not become a charge on his brethren, and deprive the feeble and infirm of the alms which are due to them only.[11] On the other hand they proclaim the great principle of Paul, that man must work to gain the means of doing good.[12] Nothing would more completely raise work than offering it to the rich as a means of charity, as well as to the poor. The same respect for useful occupations makes the Fathers desire that benevolence may not be carried to the extent of encouraging idleness. Restrict yourselves, they say, in the alms you give to the poor; find them means of gaining their own living; give them work, and teach them to honour it by their integrity and energy.[13]

With the same intention the founders of monasteries imposed work, particularly agriculture, on those who were seeking for more perfect piety. The monks found in the tilling of the ground means to supply their charity and hospitality, and also a preservative against the dangers of a solitary life passed in inaction. In the fourth century Augustine addresses severe remonstrances to certain Christians who wished to give up the world in order to escape work, under the pretence of giving themselves to a life of contemplation. He reminds them of the precepts of Christ and His apostles, the universal need of work, the not less universal duty of charity, and the disgrace which is merited by him who is willing to live luxuriously on the products of the toil of his brothers.[14] At the same time, some illustrious priests and bishops confounded these lazy monks by their example. Hilary of Arles, one of the most pious and learned prelates of the French Church, and descended from an important family, worked himself in the field.[15] There were others who also employed themselves in other professions not unsuitable to their ministry, in order that they might be able to help the poor without becoming themselves a burden on the faithful.[16] These priests set a noble example to the egoistical Christians, and also showed to pagan society that manual labour does not injure man's dignity. That which is despised by the pride of the world can be sanctified by charity.

§ 2. *Slaves.*[17]

There is no room for slavery in a society which is founded on respect for human personality, and on charity, and which has restored work to its dignity. Christianity never suddenly destroyed any institution which was closely linked with the laws and customs of the ancient world. If the representatives of the Church had proclaimed the immediate freedom of slaves, they would have infringed the rights of the masters, which, although founded on injustice, were in accordance with the general spirit of the time, and they would have thrown thousands of men who were unprepared for freedom upon society. If emancipation had been effected roughly, with a sudden and violent vindication of the rights of man, this violence would not have been in accordance with the spiritual nature of the religion of Christ. It came about without sudden overthrow, simply through the slow and gentle power of charity. The most urgent thing was to free souls. They must be raised to internal spiritual liberty, and shown that the divisions of the earthly city do not exist in the city of God, where all are united by the same respect and love.

For this reason the Scriptural doctrine of the natural equality of all men was applied specially to slavery. The Fathers of the Church pronounced, on every occasion and at all times, during the period with which we are engaged, against the theory of the natural inequality of the slave. Barnabas, expressing the apostolic thought, had already said that God did not call men according to their rank as master or servant.[18] "No one is a slave by nature," says Clement of Alexandria, and Basil.[19] Chrysostom, when examining the origin of slavery, goes back to that of the human race, and recalls that God who created the two first beings free and equal, never created slaves to serve them.[20] He also says, "The slave has the same natural nobility as the master, the same soul, the same gifts of God."[21] Augustine also says that master and servant are only different names, and the men who bear them were originally equal.[22] The two last-mentioned Fathers wished to prove that slavery is a consequence of the fall of man, a punishment for the bad use he made of his liberty.[23] But this opinion was open to a very grave objection. If slavery is a penalty for original sin, why should God punish only one half of mankind, why should freemen be exempt? Chrysostom tried to set aside this objection by maintaining that the masters are not less enslaved than their servants to their own passions and vices.[24] This argument does not seem to us to have much weight, for it still leaves the masters a great advantage; they have only one burden to bear, whilst their slaves submit to two, that of external servitude, as well as that of sin, which they share with their masters. This opinion of the Fathers is only partially true. If they had limited themselves to referring slavery, like all the other evils of the ancient world, to the fall of man through sin, without making it a special punishment for one class of mankind, we should have been unable to object to a doctrine which would have seemed to us incontestably true.

By the side of this rather confused idea of slavery represented as a punishment, we find, held by the Fathers, the clearer and more historical view that the distinction between masters and servants is the result of the tyranny and egoism of mankind. Augustine declares that the cause of servitude must be sought in the wickedness of some and the misfortunes of others.[25] The soul may remain free whilst the body is subjected to this condition. The doctors of the Church speak, like the Stoics, of slavery of body and freedom of soul. Whilst the philosophers, hardly knowing it, borrow from them some Christian ideas, they on their side take the arguments and terms of the philosophers, to which they give a deeper and truer meaning by applying them to Christianity. Ambrose says, in similar language to that used by Epictetus, "It is not nature, but the lack of wisdom, which makes a man a slave. Also he cannot become free by manumission, but through discipline. He alone has true freedom who possesses it in himself, in his own soul. That man is called free whom nothing can hinder from carrying out his will. The wise man is therefore free, because there is no obstacle that he need fear." [26] Christianity raises this theory of internal freedom to a greater height than philosophy, by showing that it is not one or other of the vices which holds certain individuals in bondage, but that *all* men are alike slaves of general sin. Sin is the only servile work, the only real universal slavery, common to master and servant. Civil liberty gives no exemption from it, and emancipation will free no one.[27] In this sense the slave who has conquered sin will be freer than the master if he still remains in the bondage of egoism. "I call noble and lord," says Chrysostom, "the slave who is covered with chains, if it accords with his life; I call him low and ignoble who in the midst of dignities retains an enslaved soul." [28]

But how can we attain this freedom from sin? Who is he who will deliver us? It is Christ. To become truly free we must acknowledge that we are under the power of evil. In the consciousness of this misery we must humiliate ourselves and enter the service of Christ, who alone is our Liberator, Protector, and Redeemer.[29] Christ took the sting from external slavery and destroyed its essence. When He destroyed the consequences of sin, He, the Lord of all, took the form of a servant, that the servant might be raised to an equality with the master; equally freed by Him, men are equal in Him, and there is no longer a difference between master and slave.[30]

In the Church, therefore, slavery could exist only in name; it is an accidental external condition which does not affect the moral worth of man. A Christian could not be a slave, in the ancient meaning of the word; though the world separated and subordinated some to others, they were united by the ties of brotherhood.[31] Disgrace is no longer attached to the office of slave; it is not even disgraceful to serve a bad master.[32] The Christian bears servitude without a murmur, as also, if free, he refrains from pride." The laws of the kingdom of God go further still: it is not only no dishonour to serve, but it is the highest form of charity. It is a complete reversal of pagan ideas. If the pagan was astonished to hear the Christian proclaim that work is honourable, how much more surprise still will he feel to hear him speak of the dignity of a state of service! All men are limited and finite creatures, equally dependent on God; no one is absolutely free; all carry out the ends of God, who, alone free, is the universal Master, having supreme authority over all. Their glory and destiny are to acknowledge and accept this dependence, serving God neither constrainedly nor thoughtlessly, but through love, with a clear understanding of what they are doing.[34] This free submission to God, which is the fulness of human perfection, was shown by Christ, who gave an example of perfect obedience.[35] He thus raises those who were bowed down, at the same time that He teaches that the greatest love consists in obedience to God and free consecration to the service of men. Nothing more assisted in raising the condition of slaves than this deeply Christian idea, that charity consists in *serving* others, an idea that is realized in the life and death of Christ.[36] Christ asks that men shall love Him, and through love become obedient to His commandments.

The greatest love therefore consists in serving Him and acknowledging Him as Master. This is true spiritual liberty, the greatest dignity and the only real power.[37] Tertullian even said that the world had altered the meaning of words, by giving the name of liberty to a state which does not differ from slavery, and servitude to that which is the cause of true freedom.[38] This name of servant, so despised by pagan society, became for Christians the most honourable title; they wished to be called only servants of God and Christ.[39] Those who, by their functions in the Church, occupied the most important positions, begged for this title by preference, adding that they were at the same time servants of the family and of the Church of Christ.[40] For to serve men, as Christ had done, was the chief means of serving Him; it was a gift from God, and Christians should glory in being called, for Christ's sake, servants of all men.[41]

In view of the principles just stated, it is no longer matter of surprise that the early Christians did not attempt the immediate abolition of slavery. In a society where all men are equal by nature and in Christ, where free service is the highest form of love, slavery is only an accident, in an infinitely truer sense than with the Stoics. It is truly an accident which ought to disappear, for it is the result of injustice, of a want of respect and love for man; but the Church can leave to that charity which triumphs over all the duty of some time suppressing an institution so incompatible with the kingdom of God. This gentle influence of charity was working in both slaves and masters, and drawing them together. If the first Christians continued to have slaves, they must not therefore be accused of contradicting their theory by their practice: the contradiction was effaced by charity. The external distinction remained, but only as the result of custom. In fact, the brotherly love of master and slave for each other practically annulled it; they were both brothers in spirit, and equally servants of Christ.[42]

The early Fathers, faithful to the apostolic precept that each should remain in the condition where God placed him, and full of the thought that spiritual freedom is more precious than all worldly advantages, desired the Christian slaves to wait patiently for their emancipation, that they might prove themselves not to be the slaves of their own desires. Ignatius writes, "Let them continue to serve without murmuring, and God will give them a better than earthly liberty."[43] Some centuries later the Council of Gangra, in Paphlagonia, anathematized those who under the pretext of piety taught the slaves to seek freedom, and to cease their respectful service to their masters.[44] There were also Christian slaves who complained of the harshness of their masters, and of servitude in general. They professed that having recognised their true Lord, they ought not to be subject to any other.[45] But the strongest arguments were used to recall them to obedience. If the slave is in the household of a Christian master, he should love him like a father;[46] he is doubly attached to him, by the temporary office of slave and by the spiritual tie of eternal love.[47] If the master is a pagan, and therefore harsher in his treatment of those who believe in Christ, the duty of obedience still remains, unless the master attempts to enforce acts which are contrary to their faith or conscience.[48] They are exhorted in general to gentleness, endurance, submission. Their conduct must show how the virtue inspired by Christianity excels that of the philosophers.[49] They are recommended to bear servitude in this passing world of exile, where none is free, and beyond which the Christian expects deliverance and heavenly glory.[50]

To these exhortations, which in the anarchy of the last ages of the empire were not always heeded, prohibitions were added which prove how Christianity respected acquired rights whilst it held the doctrine of inward freedom. Thus in 451 the Council of Chalcedon forbade the convents to receive slaves without the consent of their masters, " in order that the name of God be not dishonoured "; that is to say, that Christianity may not be charged with preaching disobedience.[51] It was not that the Fathers were blind to the melancholy of the servile state : " It is a hard office," said Hilary of Poictiers, and Augustine declares that "all servitude is full of bitterness"; but they teach the slave an inward freedom : first to humiliate himself that he may conquer the desire to emancipate himself, and then to rise above his condition, which is not in itself disgraceful, to attain true nobility of soul; for they say, bondage of soul is infinitely harder and more miserable than that of the body.[52]

Thinking only of the desire of the natural man, we should expect to find that these exhortations to obedience hindered the progress of Christianity amongst slaves; but it was not so. We know that after the second century many servants in great houses embraced the gospel.[53] These slaves presented a touching picture of one of the most beautiful effects of Christianity : in the midst of pagan depravity they did not attempt violently to break their yoke; they quietly remained slaves on earth, because they knew they were citizens of the kingdom of God. A fact belonging to this early time shows us the sentiments with which faith inspired the slave. Euèlpistus, a servant of the imperial household, was taken with Justyn and others before the tribunal of the Prefect Rusticus, who questioned him as to his condition. He answered, "I am a slave of the Emperor, but I am a Christian. It is Jesus Christ who has given me liberty, and I have the same hope as my brothers." [54] The stoical resignation of Epictetus is admirable, but the spiritual freedom of this Christian slave is nobler still, for it is purer and holier. This despised race, believed by the ancients to be incapable of manly virtue, numbered in their ranks many of the most glorious martyrs of the Church, who chose death rather than renounce their faith or consent to disgraceful propositions from their masters. The Potamiæna Eutyches, Victorinus, Maro, Nereus, Vitalis, and many others, bore striking testimony to their freedom of soul through Christ, and their love for their Divine Liberator.[55]

The Church not only gave counsels of patience to the slave, but had also precepts of humanity and gentleness for the master. If she could not tell the one to free himself by force, she did not allow the other suddenly to send away his slaves. To make use of the expression of the wise historian of slavery, "It never seemed urgent to take away the slave from the master, but it was needful to detach the master from slavery by a feeling of the dignity of man." [56] And, as we believe we ought to add, by a feeling of charity towards the slave, who must be respected both as a man and as a member of the kingdom of God. In the Church, slaves are no longer instruments without will, permitted by antiquity to be used or abused according to the wishes of the master; they are men who merit our sympathy as being brought to servitude by a tyranny which had destroyed natural equality.[57] Still further, they have a right even to our respect, because if a hard fortune has deprived them of outward liberty, it must be an energetic will that preserves their spiritual liberty.[58] They are brothers, called to the same salvation, to the same participation in the blessings of the kingdom of heaven, as freemen. One cannot then despise them,[59] and treat them as beasts of burden,[60] or refuse to them law and justice.[61] Chrysostom says, "Do not imagine that an injury to a slave will be regarded as indifferent, because it is only to a slave. The laws of the world see a difference between the two races, but the laws of the commonwealth of God ignore it."[62] Masters must remember that they, as well as their servants, are slaves. They have civil freedom, but they are under the yoke of sin, from which Christ redeemed them for His service; and this Divine Redeemer became humble that He might serve men, and give them an example to follow.[63] They must not disdain to call brothers those whom the Lord Himself has honoured with this title.[64] They must love them as equals, as sons to whom they are united by faith.[65] They must renounce pagan harshness, and show their love by gentleness and benevolence, by gratitude for their services, and willingness to forgive their faults.[66] The Church treated masters who were deaf to these counsels, not appreciating the principles of the gospel, with the same severity that she used towards slaves who refused their obedience. She declared them unworthy to be her members. She refused to accept the gifts of the master who ill-treated his slaves by blows, hunger, or too hard work.[67] The woman who in anger beat a servant to death was excluded from the communion of the faithful.[68]

They sought to establish a *family* in its true significance. Ancient Rome sought to realize it by the strict subordination of all its members to the power of the father and head; in the Church it was to be united by mutual charity. "The master," said Ambrose, "is called the father of his family, so that he may govern his slaves as though they were his sons."[69] Augustine requires that they shall be treated in the master's dwelling as though it were a father's house; that they shall be treated as sons, except as to the right of inheritance.[70] This brought a flow of duties on the owners unthought of by antiquity, which had only recognised those of the slave, without imposing any upon the master. Henceforward the master, being brother to the servant, must care for his soul. He is partly responsible for his salvation. He must overlook and correct him, and above all set him the example of grave, modest, faithful, loving conduct. He is bound to raise him to virtue and piety.[71] In the earliest ages of the Church there were such households, where masters and servants formed one family, in the Christian sense.[72] When Thecla was cited to appear before the tribunal, fifty of her slaves, urged by gratitude, bore testimony in her favour.[73] Paulla, a descendant of Paulus Æmilius Leo, and Fabiola, are spoken of as being rather the servants than the mistresses of their women.[74]

There remains one further step: civil emancipation must be gained. The Fathers did not confine themselves to counsels of gentleness and humanity to the masters; they tried to convince them that slavery is contrary to the nature of man, and to that of the kingdom of God, and to persuade them to free their slaves. They wished to obtain this result by persuasion, that the bestowal of freedom might be a free act of charity, a result of the virtue imparted to man by Christianity. The doctors of the Church insisted so strongly on the duty of masters to educate their slaves in piety, because in their eyes it was the surest way of preparing for their emancipation and making them worthy of it.[75] Gregory Nazianzen shows the masters that to give freedom to their slaves is only to re-establish the order of nature.[76] Chrysostom uses all his eloquence to obtain this aim, notwithstanding the murmurs of some members of his Church. He desires that they shall limit the number of their servants to such as are most needful, that they shall free the others after having taught them useful trades, that they shall only buy new ones to instruct, and afterwards give them their liberty.[77] He expresses his wish that slavery may disappear by the mutual services which the faithful render to one another through charity. The true Christian community ought to be a family of brothers, all free, and all servants one of another. "Let there be," he says, "a mutual exchange of service and submission, and there will be no more slavery. One will no longer rank amongst freemen, and another amongst slaves. It is better that masters and slaves serve each other; such servitude will be far preferable to any other liberty."[78]

These ideas did not remain fruitless. Long before Chrysostom had raised his voice in favour of slaves, there had been glorious examples of Christian masters freeing their slaves. The earliest known of these is Hermes, Prefect of Rome under Trajan, who embraced Christianity with his wife, children, and 1,250 slaves. On Easter day, the day of their baptism, Hermes gave them all freedom and ample assistance to enable them to gain a livelihood. Shortly afterwards he suffered martyrdom with Bishop Alexander, who was the means of his conversion.[79] Another Prefect of Rome, under Diocletian, Chromatius, was celebrated in the Church for his zeal and charity. He set free 1,400 slaves, and gave them abundant means of support; he said that those who had God for their Father ought not to be the servants of man.[80] Melania, with the consent of her husband Pinius, gave freedom to 8,000 slaves; Ovinius, a French martyr, to 5,000.[81]

These great examples were followed by Christians who were not so rich. In the early part of the fourth century three brothers set free their seventy-three slaves.[82] Augustine told the people in one of his homilies that several clerks of the Church of Hippo were going to emancipate some slaves they possessed.[83] We cannot doubt that many others did the same, though the historians, struck only with what shows in large proportions, have preserved no account of the less startling facts. Whilst rich pagans directed in their will that the blood of their slaves should be shed in combats in the arena, Christian masters, taught by the Church, gave freedom and legacies to their slaves, by their will.[84]

The giving of freedom assumed a solemn ecclesiastical character. From the third century slaves were emancipated in church, in the presence of the clergy and congregation, without the ancient formalities.[85] African councils, held at the beginning of the fourth century, asked the emperor to decree that enfranchisement should be always concluded in church, so that this pious custom should be established.[86] He who wished to free a slave led him by the hand before the altar, where the act of manumission was read, by which the master gave his servant liberty, because he had found him faithful in everything.[87] The priest added his benediction, and the act raised to this religious elevation had a more real value than civil emancipation in pagan society. The Christian freed slave regained a complete and honourable liberty. He entered the community of his brothers surrounded by as much respect as if he had never been in servitude.

§ 3. *Gladiators and Actors.*

The Church took still further means to abolish slavery, by endeavouring to diminish the number of people whose lives were spent in service. With this aim she recommended a more simple life to Christian masters. She warmly blamed the pagan luxury of having many useless slaves, as dangerous to morality. She strove to suppress disgraceful occupations to which some of the servile race were condemned. Clement of Alexandria, although he did not formally disapprove of slaves, thought it blamable to keep them for every slight service of pleasure or luxury.[88] " Why have you so many slaves ? " said Chrysostom, a little later, in one of his homilies addressed to Christians at Constantinople; " you ought, as with food and clothes, so also with slaves, to limit yourselves to what is necessary. And what necessity is there for so many ? I cannot see it. One master should be content with one servant; even further, one servant should be enough for two or three masters. If this seems hard to you, think on those who have none, and who serve themselves better and more quickly; for God has created us capable of helping ourselves, and even of helping others. . . . If you doubt it, listen to Paul, 'My hands work for myself and those who are with me.' This teacher of the world, worthy of heaven, did not blush to serve so many thousands of men; and you, you think yourselves disgraced unless you have troops of slaves in your train, not knowing that therein lies your dishonour. For God has given us feet and hands that we may not need servants. What will you do with these swarms of slaves ? We see the rich walk like shepherds with their sheep, or like sellers of men, to the baths and on the public walks. But I will not lay down too strict a law : have a second servant. If you add more, it is not from care for them, but in the interest of your own luxury." [89]

Throughout the whole duration of the empire the Church fought with energetic severity against the abuses to which pagan society subjected slaves; she strove to suppress the vices and passions of the masters, in the double interest of their own salvation and that of the unhappy one she would snatch from their hands.

The vice of παιδεραστία was rigorously condemned, and those who yielded to it were excommunicated without hope of remission of the sentence.[90] Those also were chidden who kept gladiators or actors, and who went to the spectacles and games in the circus.

A thousand times the doctors and preachers pictured the danger of the public games to those who aspired to be citizens of the kingdom of God. The combats of gladiators or of beasts filled them with profound horror. They saw no difference between a homicide and the spectator who, seated on the tier of the amphitheatre, eager and pitiless, watched a deadly struggle; it was becoming an accomplice in shedding of blood.[91] The Christian, who loves every man as a brother and respects life because it is the gift of God, who alone has the right to take it back, ought to shun these bloody sights, which are only schools of barbarism, or as Tatian energetically calls them, "horrible feasts where the soul is fed on human flesh and blood."[92] The Fathers could not understand how the magistrates could authorize these combats, or civilized men enjoy them.[93] To those who pleaded in their justification that the men were condemned criminals, they answered, that it is no longer justice when, instead of punishing the guilty, the law compels him to add a second crime to the first by shedding the blood of his neighbour for the savage pleasure of the crowd. If the object of punishment is improvement, what an improvement to be compelled to kill a man![94] But this excuse of the pagans was not sincere, because we know that there were gladiators by profession. The Church endeavoured to suppress this barbarous calling. She refused baptism to gladiators, without deep penitence and an engagement to give up their profession. She also exhorted the rich to consecrate to works of charity the sums they spent in support of combatants. "Instead of buying and feeding wild beasts," said Lactantius, "ransom prisoners and feed the poor; instead of bringing together men to kill each other, go and bury the innocent dead. What advantage is it for your luxury to enrich the gladiators and uphold them in crime? Use well and with sacrifice your perishable wealth, in order that for your true well-doing God may give you an eternal recompense." [95]

There are persons who, whilst approving the vigour shown by the Church in opposition to these homicidal games, have blamed her for forbidding with equal energy the other spectacles, dances, and theatrical representations. They say it was an excess of strictness; it was despising art and suppressing genius, whilst it threw a gloomy and melancholy shade over life, by depriving it of legitimate amusement. This reproach is unfounded. If in these spectacles they did not kill the body, they killed the souls of both actors and spectators. We need not refer again to the deep immorality which was unblushingly exhibited on the Roman stage in the ages of the decadence. If we recall the picture that was sketched in our first book, we find that the dislike of Christian doctors for spectacles of dancers or actors was extremely well founded. To guard the members of the Church from almost inevitable corruption, they were exhorted to refrain from the theatre, where their eyes would have seen only pictures of effeminate voluptuousness, and their ears have heard only impure or criminal words. They were reminded of the direful influence which the sight of the wickedness of gods and men had exerted on morality.[96] Those who, in spite of these warnings, still frequented the theatres, now become so impure,[97] were declared unworthy of Christian communion. Those who were naturally eager for sights were pointed, not only to the beauties of the Bible, but to the magnificence of the world, to the rising and setting of the sun, to the heavens resplendent with stars, to the immensity of the ocean, to the beauties of the mountains and rivers. " What theatre constructed by the hand of man," says the author of a treatise on spectacles, " can equal these wonders of creation ? "[98]

If these exhortations were not enough, the Church issued formal prohibitions. It would have endangered the future of Christian society if she had not joined severity to persuasion to attain this end, as far as accorded with the new spirit of love she desired to spread in the world. No one was compelled to enter the Church ; but once having done so, it became his duty to submit to the rules she imposed. Therefore she had the right to forbid the Christians to attend these spectacles, at least on Sundays and festivals.[99] They were absolutely prohibited to catechumens and priests. The latter had even to leave festivities, at which actors were expected, before their arrival.[100]

Till now we have spoken of the efforts made to hinder the attendance of spectators at the theatre, but there was an equal wish to lessen the number of actors themselves. The Church desired, not only to prevent the degradation of the faithful, which would result from the sight of infamous pictures and contact with degraded men, but to withdraw those unfortunate ones from this disgraceful profession who had adopted it in despair, and, sold to the theatre, were kept there by the fatality of their condition. She condemned the profession of actor, and excommunicated those who followed it;[101] at the same time she tried to persuade them to leave it, by showing them the spiritual dangers to which they exposed themselves and the spectators. "Nothing can be worse," say the Fathers, "than to feign vice; one ends by becoming one's self accustomed to the point of view of the personages whose parts one takes; and if one does not do this, the fiction, which is a lie, should for that alone be condemned."[102] To this consideration Christian preachers add earnest appeals to the dignity of those who act. "What can be more dishonouring," says Chrysostom, "for a man, and especially for a woman, than to give themselves for a spectacle to the public, to excite the laughter of the crowd, and the bad passions of impure men! This is to debase human nature, and to prove that the soul is no longer considered worthy of care."[103]

If actors, touched by these motives, consented to give up their profession, the Church opened her arms to receive them, showing more charity than pagan society, which held them pitilessly in their abject state. The councils decided that they might receive baptism on condition of leaving their profession.[104] If that had been their only means of gaining a livelihood, Christian charity provided them with sufficient means to begin a new and more honourable life. Cyprian wrote to Euchratius that a converted actor must be aided from the funds of the Church.[105] These men, who were so indignantly refused admission into pagan society, sometimes attained the clerical office. Such was the old man Cardamus, formerly a mime and drunkard, who became sober and humble after his conversion, was accepted as priest and honoured with the esteem of Paulenus of Nolæ.[106] The Church even found martyrs amongst former courtesans, as she had done amongst actors. Genesius, who in the time of Diocletian, had to play in Rome in a satirical piece against Christianity, felt his soul enlightened by grace at the moment when in his part he asked for baptism. He was converted, and as he refused to continue in his calling to which he was bound by pagan law, he was put to death, glorifying his Redeemer.[107]

These proofs of spiritual freedom are the most powerful argument in favour of the ideas which we enunciated at the beginning of this chapter about slaves. We said that emancipation did not need a reversal of the established order for its accomplishment, and we have seen what it could do in the soul. In this as in all social reforms, Christianity effects the transformation of society through the regeneration of individuals.

(1) "It is not right to feel ashamed, if people consider us wretched or helpless because we work with our hands."—*Ep. ad Zenam et Serenum*, c. 17 in *Opp. Just. Mart.*, p. 416. (2) Gen. iii. 17-19. (3) Ambr., *De Jacob et Vita Beata*, I. 6, § 24, vol. i. p. 452. Chrysost., *Hom.* 33 et 66 *in Mat.*, vol. vii. pp. 378 and 655. August., *De Opere Monach.*, § 3, vol. vi. p. 349. (4) See the encomium on work, Theodoret., *Or.* 7, vol. iv. Pt. 1, p. 598 sq. (5) Chrysost., *Hom.* 1 *in Rom.* xvi, 3, vol. iii. p. 178. (6) *Ep.*, c. 19, p. 52. (7) Bk. I. c. 4; Bk. II. c. 68; Bk. IV. c. 11, pp. 205, 275, 301. (8) Chrysost., *Hom.* 1 *in Rom.* xvi., 3, vol. iii. p. 178 sq. (9) *Constit. Apost.*, IV. 11, p. 301. (10) Basil., *Regula Fus. Tract.*, interrog. 15, vol. ii. p. 355. (11) *Constit. Apost.*, IV. 2, p. 295. Ambr., *De Offic.*, II. c. 16, § 76, vol. ii. p. 88. Cassian., *Collatio* 24, c. 12, p. 617. (12) *Constit. Apost.*, VII. 12, p. 369. (13) Chrysost., *Hom. de Eleemosyna*, vol. iii. p. 279. (14) This is the subject which Augustine treats in his work, "*De Opere Monachorum*," vol. vi. p. 797 sq. (15) Gennad., *De Viris Illustra.*, c. 69, p. 32. (16) Epiph., *Adv. Hær.*, III. t. i. hær. 80, no. 6, vol. i. p. 1072. (17) Ref. to M. Wallon's 3rd vol., and Möhler, *Bruchstücke aus der Geschichte der Auftrebung der Schlaverey durch das Christenthum.*—Tübingen, 1834, p. 61 sq. (18) *Ep.*, c. 19, p. 52. (19) Clem. Alex., *Pædag.*, III. c. 12, vol. i. p. 207. Basil., *De Spir.* s., c. 21, vol. iii. p. 42. Lactant., *Div. Instit.*, V. 15, vol. i. p. 399. (20) *Or. in Terrae Motum et Laz.*, § 7, vol. i. p. 782; *Hom.* 22 *in Eph.*, § 2, vol. xi. p. 167. (21) *Hom.* 15 *in Eph.*, § 3, vol. xi. p. 114. (22) *Enarr. in Ps.* cxxiv. § 7, vol. iv. p. 1058. Cf. Clem. Alex., *Pædag.*, III. 6, vol. i. p. 274. (23) Chrysost., *Serm.* 4 *et* 5 *in*

Gen., vol. iv. pp. 659, 665. August., *De Civit. Dei.* XIX. 15, vol. vii. p. 423. (24) *Hom.* 22 *in Eph.*, § 1, vol. xi. p. 165. (25) *Quæst. in Gen.*, l. I. quæstio 153, vol. iii. p. II. p. 311. Greg. Naz., *Carm. Varia*, carm. 52, v. 29 sq. vol. ii. p. 127; *Or.* 16 *et* 24, vol. i. pp. 256, 428. (26) *Ep.* 37, § 9 sq., vol. ii. p. 932; *De Joseph Patr.*, c. 4, § 20; *De Jacob et Vita Beata*, II. 3, § 12, vol. i. p. 490, 462. (27) Tatian, *Or. c. Græcos*, c. 11, p. 253. Tertull., *De Coronâ*, c. 13, p. 109. Cypr., *De Opere et Eleem.*, p. 241. Ambr., *Ep.* 37, § 24, vol. ii. p. 936. Chrysost., *Sermo* 4 *in Gen.*, § 2, vol. iv. p. 660. August., *Sermo* 134, § 3, vol. v. p. 455. Hilar., *Tract. in Ps.* cxxxv. § 6, p. 485. Paul. Nol., *Ep.* 9, p. 44. Macarius, *De Libertate Mentis*, c. 31, p. 222. (28) *Or. in Terræ Motum et Laz.*, § 7, vol. i. p. 782. (29) Jesus Christ is our " manumissor."— Ambr., *De Jacob*, etc. Bk. I. (30) Chrysost., *Hom.* 29 *in cap. ix. Gen.*, § 77, vol. iv. p. 290. (31) Id., *Hom.* 22 *in Eph.*, § 24; *Hom.* 1 *in Philem.*, § 1, vol. xi. pp. 166, 774. (32) Theodoret., *Or.* 8, vol. iv., P. I. p. 694. (33) Tatian., *Or. c. Græcos*, c. 11, p. 253. (34) August., *Enarr.* 3 *in Ps.* ciii. § 3, vol. iv. p. 867; *Sermo* 21, § 6, vol. v. p. 79. Bas., *De Spirit.* s., c. 21, vol. iii. p. 43. (35) Ambr., *De Fide*, V. 8, § 109, vol. ii. p. 570. (36) Id. *Ep.* 37, § 23, vol. ii. p. 936; *De Joseph Patr.*, c. 4, § 19, vol. i. p. 490. (37) "To the wise man even service is freedom."—*Id. Ep.* 37, § 24, p. 936. Paul. Nol., *Ep.*, 8, v. 33 sq. p. 41. Petr. Chrysol., *Sermo* 115, p. 499. (38) *De Coronâ*, c. 13, p. 109. (39) It has been thought that this title was only applied to priests and monks; this is a mistake. Hermas calls all the Christians "servants of God" (Bk. I. vis. 1, c. p. 76). Tertullian, speaking of the Christian wife of a pagan husband, calls her "the handmaid of God" (*Ad Ux.*, II. 6, p. 170); with him Christians in general are "servants of God" (*De Spect.*, c. 1, p. 72). The Christians of Vienna and Lyons, writing to the Christians of Asia, style themselves "δοῦλοι Χριστοῦ (Euseb., *Hist. Eccl.*, V. 1, p. 154). Both children and women were so called. See the inscriptions, Muratori, vol. iv. p. 1834, No. 10; p. 1856, No. 3; p. 1892, No. 7 etc.; and Reinesius, p. 1004, No. 449. (40) This custom was introduced in the 4th century. August., *Ep.*, 155, 220, vol. ii. pp. 406, 618. (41) "Δούλους τε πάντων ἀνθρώπων ἑαυτοὺς εἶναι λογίζονται. Macarius, *De Carit.*, c. 3, p. 138. Ambr., *De Paradiso*, c. 14, § 72 vol. i. p. 178. (42) Lactant., *Div. Instit.*, IV. c. 16, vol. i. p. 401. (43) *Ad Polyc.*, c. 4, p. 41. (44) Canon 3, Mansi, vol. ii. p. 1101. (45) Chrysost., *Hom.* 4 *in Tit.*, § 3, vol. xi. p. 753. (46) *Constit. Apost.*, IV. 12, p. 301. Cypr., *Testim. adv. Jud.*, III. 72, p. 324. (47) Hier., *Comm. in Phil.*, vol. iii. p. 451. (48) Id., *Comm. in Tit.*, 2, vol. iii. p. 429. (49) Chrysost., *Hom.* 22 *in Eph.*, § 1, vol. xi. p. 166. (50) August., *De Agone Christiano*, c. 7, vol. vi. p. 181; *De Civit. Dei.*, XIX. 15, vol. vii. p. 423. (51) Canon 4; Mansi vol. vii. p. 360. (52) "Onerous work, it is true, but not necessarily unhappy for a man . . . yet how wretched is the bondage of the soul."—Hilar., *Tract in Ps.*, cxxv., § 4, p. 408. All slavery is full of bitterness."—August., *Enarr. in Ps.* xcix., § 7, vol. iv. p. 806. Orig., *C. Cels.*, III. 54, p. 483. (53) *Acta Martyrii Justini*, c. 3; in *Opp. Just. Mart.*, p. 586. Orig., *C. Cels.* III. 55, p. 484. (54) *Acta Mart. Just.* l. c. (55) Cypr., *De Laude Martyrii*, p. 345. (56) M. Wallon, vol. iii. p. 318. (57) Nilus, *Perist.*, sect. x. c. 6, p. 165. (58) Isid., *Pelus.*, I. ep. 306, p. 68. (59) Ignat., *Ad Polyc.*, c. 4. p. 41.

(60) Clem. Alex., *Pædag.*, III. 11, vol. i. p. 295. (61) Nilus, l. c. note 1. (62) Chrysost., *Hom.* 22 *in Eph.*, § 2, vol. xi. p. 167. (63) Ambr., *De Jacob*, etc. I. 3, § 12, vol. i. p. 448. (64) August., *Sermo* 58, § 2, vol. v. p. 236. (65) *Constit. Apost.*, IV. 12, p. 302. (66) Barn., c. 19, p. 52. Basil., *Moralia*, req. 75, vol. ii. p. 311. Petr. Chrysol., *Sermo* 26, p. 111. (67) *Constit. Apost.*, IV. 6, p. 197. (68) Council of Elvira, A.D. 305, can. 5; Mansi, vol. ii. p. 6. (69) *Ep.* 2, § 31, vol. ii. p. 762. (70) August., *De Civit. Dei*, XIX, c. 16. vol. vii. p. 424. (71) Clem. Alex., *Pædag.*, III. 11, vol. i. p. 296. Chrysost., *Hom.* 40 *in* 1 *Cor.*, § 5, vol. x. p. 385.—Hieron., *Ep.* 130, vol. i. p. 989. (72) M. Wallon, III. p. 339, and inscriptions there quoted. (73) *Acta SS.*, Jany., vol. i. p. 601. (74) Hieron., *Epp.* 23, 108, vol. i. pp. 127, 705. (75) Nilus, *Perist.*, sect. x. c. 6, p. 165. (76) *Or.*, 16, vol. i. p. 256. (77) *Hom.* 40 *in* 1 *Cor.*, § 5, vol. x. p. 385; *Hom.* 11 *in Act.*, § 3, vol. ix. p. 93. (78) *Hom.* 19 *in Eph.*, § 5; *Hom.* 1 *in Philem.*, § 1, vol. xi. pp. 141, 775. (79) *Acta SS.*, May, vol. i. p. 371. (80) *Acta SS.*, Jany., vol. ii. p. 275. (81) Pignorius, *Comm. de servis*, Padua, 1674, qto. præf. Palladius, *Hist. Laus*, c. 119, p. 226. (82) *Acta SS.*, May, vol. vi. p. 777. (83) *Sermo* 356, § 3, vol. v. p. 966. (84) Chrysost., *Hom.* 13 *in Mat.*, § 6, vol. vii. p. 176. (85) Constantine found this custom already for a long time established; "Jam dudum placuit ut," etc. . . . A.D. 316. *Corp. Jur.*, l. 1, tit., 13, l. 1. (86) *Canon. Eccl. Afric.*, can. 64; Mansi, vol. iii. p. 770. (87) August., *Sermo* 21, § 6, vol. v. p. 79. (88) Clem. Alex., *Pædag.*, III. 4, vol. i. p. 268. (89) *Hom.* 40 *in* 1 *Cor.*, § 5, vol. x. p. 384. (90) Barn., *Ep.* c. 19, p. 51. Athenag., *Leg.*, c. 34, p. 311. *Constit. Apost.*, VI. 28, p. 359. Arnob., I. 64, vol. i. p. 44. Chrysost., *Hom.* 12 *in* 1 *Cor.*, § 5, vol. x. p. 103; *Hom.* 5 *in Tit.*, § 4, vol. xi. p. 762.—Council of Elvira, A.D. 305, can. 71; Mansi, vol. ii. p. 17. (19) Athenag., *Leg.*, c. 35, p. 312. Theoph., *Ad Autol.*, III. 15, p. 389. Min. Felix, c. 30, 37, pp. 117, 140. Arnob., II. 41, vol. i. p. 78. (92) Tatian, *Or. c. Græcos*, c. 23, p. 264. Cypr., *Ep.* 1, p. 3. (93) Tertull., *De Spect.*, c. 18, p. 81. Lactant., *Div. Instit.*, VI. 20, vol. i. p. 490. Chrysost., *Hom.* 12 *in* 1 *Cor.*, § 5, vol. x. p. 203. (94) "It is a good thing when the guilty are punished: Who but the guilty man will deny this? And yet an innocent man cannot take pleasure in the punishment of another. . . . As to those, too, who are condemned to the games, what thing is this, if from some less serious crime they turn out murderers by way of improvement?" —Tertull., *De Spect.*, c. 18, 19, p. 81. (95) *Div. Instit.*, VI. 12, vol. i. p. 470. (96) Tatian, *Or. c. Græcos.*, c. 22, p. 263. Theoph., *Ad Autol.*, III. 15, p. 389. Clem. Alex., *Pædag.*, III. 11, vol. i. p. 298. Tertull., *De Spect.*, p. 72 sq. Lactant., *Div. Instit.*, VI. 20, vol. i. p. 492. Ambr., *Sermo* 5 *in Ps.* cxviii., vol. i. p. 1025. Basil, *Comm. in Ex.*, c. 5, § 156, vol. i. p. 490. (97) Chrysost., *Hom. contra Ludos et Theatra*, vol. vi. p. 275 sq. (98) *Tract. de Spect. in Opp. Cypr.*, p. 312. (99) *Can. Eccl. Afr.*, can. 61; Mansi, vol. iii. p. 767. (100) August., *De Symbolo, Sermo ad Catechum.*, § 5, vol. vi. p. 407. Council of Laodicæa, 4th cent., can. 54; Mansi, vol. ii. p. 573. (101) Council of Elvira, A.D. 305, can. 62; Mansi, vol. ii. p. 16. Council of Arles, A.D. 314, can. 5, p. 472. (102) Tatian, *Or. c. Græcos*, c. 22, p. 263. August., *Enarr. in Ps.* cxlvii. § 7, vol. iv. p. 1233. *Sermo* 51, § 42, vol. v. p. 197; *Sermo* 198, § 3, p.

632.   (103) *Hom.* 37 *in Mat.*, §§ 6, 7, vol. vii. p. 422 sq.   (104) Council of Elvira, A.D. 305, canon 62 ; of Arles, A.D. 314, can. 5 ; Mansi, vol. ii. pp. 16, 472 ; *Can. Eccl. Afric.*, can. 63, vol. iii. p. 767.   (105) *Ep.* 61, *De Histrione*, p. 101.   (106) Paulin. Nolan., *Ep.* 15, 19, 21 ; pp. 87, 108, 115.   (107) Ruinart., *Acta Marti*, pp. 2-70.

CHAPTER V.

THE POOR AND UNFORTUNATE.

§ 1. *Riches and Poverty.*

THE observation which closed the preceding chapter solves the great problem of riches and poverty in Christian society. Jesus Christ had said, "To the poor is the Gospel preached." The Church inherited this teaching, and, in conformity with her principle of the equality and spiritual union of all men, calls and receives to her bosom men of all conditions. Whilst the pagan State gave the poor man an inferior and dishonourable position, Christianity ensured for him as good a place in the kingdom of God as the rich man; for as we constantly repeat, the worth of man is not estimated there by the accidental circumstances of his external state. For those who were deceived by a hollow civilization, for the rich and learned, uncertain of their future and vainly seeking a solution of their doubts,[1] as well as for those whom this civilization despised on account of their poverty, the Gospel became the source of truth and peace.

The Divine wisdom of the Saviour was accessible to all. Unlike that of the philosophers, who taught only a small number of unoccupied men in the leisure hours of an easy life, it might be grasped by all—the poorest and most ignorant, by women and even children; for, as Tatian says in his discourse to the Greeks, "The energy of the soul is the same, whatever be the weakness or privation of the body she inhabits." [2] The pagan philosopher never came down to the level of the people, whilst amongst the Christians, he who aspired to wisdom came to the ignorant and sinners to lead them through knowledge of the truth to a purer life. God made men to live in society; they desire to help one another. This consideration proved to the Fathers the need of giving this help first to those who required it the most. The Christian, inspired by the charity of Jesus, will seek those who are in outward circumstances beneath him, that he may raise them to the rank reserved for them in the kingdom of God. "We are separated," said Origen, answering one of the representatives of pagan egoism, "we are separated from the animals, which have no intelligence, but not from men of an inferior position. They are our brothers equally with those who fill a more distinguished rank." [3] The Fathers repeat frequently that the poor man is made in the image of God, the same as the rich; he hopes for the same heavenly inheritance. In the eyes of the supreme judge the beggar is not less than the emperor. To give visible proof of this in the eyes of men, Christ became poor and humble, without a place to rest His head. He sent His disciples to conquer the world, telling them not to provide gold or silver.[4] In this way, in His own person and that of His apostles, He ennobled that which had been the object of such profound contempt in the pagan world. The poor man, then, is worthy of the same respect, and ought to be received with the same love, as those who have not to struggle with misery: whoever despises him despises and offends God.[5]

Thus, as we have seen with the slaves, Christianity tends to raise the poor, by representing poverty and riches as external conditions, indifferent in themselves, and independent of the personal worth of man. The Stoics professed to hold an analogous theory; but it was less complete than that held by the Church, for she alone taught that there are imperishable treasures superior to any earthly ones.[6] The rich and poor come into the world and go out of it in the same nakedness.[7] Riches are only lent by God, in whose power she trusts, and who can in an instant raise whom He will, and cast down him who glorifies himself.[8] Poverty is no more an evil than wealth is a good : they may be equally honourable or equally contemptible, according to the use made of them.[9] The only real riches or poverty is what exists in the soul. "No one," said Lactantius, "is poor before God but he who lacks justice, and no one is rich but he who abounds in virtues"; [10] or, as Ambrose expresses it, "It is not the census, but the qualities of the soul that show the rich man." [11]

But, it has been asked, was the Gospel only preached to the poor to offer them the derisive consolations of a sterile theory ? Can the man who is the prey of suffering and misery be contented with a speculative equality, without real results to himself ? What relief can he find in the abstract idea of the indifference of poverty or riches ? Should not Christians hasten to redress the wrongs of the social order by a more equal division of worldly wealth; that is to say, by taking away the superfluities of some, to improve the position of others ?

There are some passages in the Fathers which apparently support these ideas. Some of the most celebrated doctors seem to speak of the sin of personal property and the justice of community of goods, but, on weighing their words, we see easily in what sense they ought to be understood. Barnabas, in warmly recommending the duty of charity, says that we ought not to consider anything as belonging to ourselves alone, but to share everything with our neighbour; for if there is communion in spiritual and everlasting things, with how much greater right ought it to exist in these temporary things.[12] Filled with enthusiasm by the example of the first Christians in Jerusalem, amongst whom none were in poverty because they had all things in common, Chrysostom expresses the wish that the faithful in Constantinople should imitate this "republic worthy of angels," by introducing amongst themselves community of goods. Rich and poor would be happier. All would be able to live comfortably, which would be a great blessing. It would be heaven on earth, and a strong means of attracting pagans to a society where they saw the reign of so much love.[13] About the same time Ambrose of Milan tried to argue the question on the ground of natural right. "Nature," he says, "created everything for common use. If then there are men who are excluded from the enjoyment of the products of the earth, it is contrary to nature. The unequal division of this wealth is the result of egoism and violence. Nature is the mother of common right, usurpation is the mother of private right."[14] Augustine, by different reasoning, arrives at a like result. He writes to one of his friends, "that the faithful alone can possess his wealth justly and worthily, for no one has a right to wealth of which he will not make a good use. The ownership of unbelievers is impious and unjust, because they make use of their property for evil. Pious Christians therefore ought to possess everything, because they alone know how to use it rightly."[15]

These passages seem explicit, but it appears to us that the strength is only in the expression, and that they are intended to depict an ideal State, or to give a more earnest exhortation to Christians to practical charity. Barnabas himself, a little before the passage just quoted, recommends a man not to covet his neighbour's goods. That pre-supposes that the neighbour has the greatest right of possession. How can we explain the contradiction between this precept and that of sharing with the poor, if the latter was not simply advice addressed to charity, leaving it entirely free? Chrysostom limits himself to the wish that the ideal formed by his imagination may be realized some day, and Augustine emphatically declares that what he believes to be right cannot be applied in practice. He adds, that the injustice of the ownership of the impious must be tolerated in this world, because it is guaranteed by the civil law, which ought to be observed by the citizens of the kingdom of God; the principles of the Christian prohibit him from taking away the possessions of a wicked man, whatever may be his right to them. Ambrose had no other intention than to inspire the faithful with more entire devotion to the poor. When he shows that everything is created for the use of all, that the poor man has a natural right to the necessities of life, he intends that no one shall look at his property as being absolutely for himself alone. He wishes charity to be regarded as a just duty towards one's neighbour. Besides, the frequent exhortations to almsgiving that these same Fathers addressed to the well-to-do members of their churches, are the surest proof that they did not strive to realize these Utopian theories. To invite some one to give for charity—that is, to practise a free and voluntary virtue—is to acknowledge that what he gives belongs to him, that he is the master of it and can use it as he will.

As slavery was not abolished by violence, nor woman

emancipated by a sudden reversal of social order, so also the poor must not be enriched by the spoliation of the wealthy. On the contrary, property, which was as carefully guarded by the laws of Moses as by those of Rome, is never grasped at by the Church, nor by her institutions and principles. She never attacks the right of each man to own what he acquires by legitimate means. Positive facts, and many passages from the Fathers, even from those whom we have quoted as apparently contradictory, prove the respect of Christianity for property. The Fathers knew nothing of the ancient Roman distinction between property absolute, supposed to be derived from the State, and property not absolute (*res mancipi* and *res non mancipi*). For Christians there is only one kind of property,—true, natural, individual ownership of things lawfully possessed, because they have been gained by just means.[16] The State and the Church have no power. Christianity, which has re-established the rights of a free personality, does not deduce the right of property from a professed concession of a society superior to the individuals; it derives it from God alone, the Creator of all, who, according to Augustine, is the Father of the family, whose children and servants we are. What we possess is only a loan of which we are allowed the use.[17] He lends it to us that we may use it in accordance with His will. Each of us is responsible for what he has received, but no one has the right to call our ownership in question.[18]

We have seen before that the possession of earthly wealth is regarded as indifferent by Christianity, as adding no real merit to the owner. We can be citizens of the kingdom of God without having the smallest possession. The poor man is, from one point of view, exposed to less temptation than the rich; it should be less trouble to him to rise above earthly things. At a very early time there were Christians who exaggerated these ideas, and considered riches as a hindrance to salvation. This arose with some from a lack of intelligence, or the desire of attaining greater perfection by absolute renunciation; with others it was jealousy of riches. From the time that these tendencies showed themselves, the Fathers opposed them with the eternal truth of the principles of the Gospel. Already Clement of Alexandria had written a special treatise to prove that poverty is not essential to salvation, that riches are not a reason for exclusion from the kingdom of God, that it would be irrational to suppose that Christianity demands the renunciation of property, because in that case beggars would be the best of the faithful, which is contradicted by experience.[19] Augustine, Ambrose, Jerome, Paulinus of Nola, and many other writers of the Church, teach that riches are not to be condemned in themselves. They may become very useful, according to what is done with them. On the other hand, poverty alone does not make a man holy and pleasing to God. Every poor man is not just, as every rich man is not condemned. Poverty and the renunciation of riches are useless if the vices are retained.[20]

The Church, then, neither teaches that riches are a hindrance to salvation nor that the poor have rights over the possessions of the rich. Far from exciting the passions, she seeks to calm them by raising the thoughts from earth and uniting human hearts in the bonds of love. The early Christians, filled with these thoughts, did not feel humiliated by their poverty. They accepted their despised condition as a glory, and answered the pagans who reproached them with it: "We are not poor, for we have need of nothing; we do not covet the wealth of others ; we are rich in God. He who possesses much, if he desire more, is poorer than we." [21] In later times, men filled with different sentiments were to be found amongst Christians. Egoism and envy reappeared. There were rich people with very slight leanings to charity, and poor ones who repeated with murmurs these words, so often heard again in our own days, " God ought not to have made the poor ; there should have been only the rich." [22] This bad spirit was energetically opposed by the doctors of the Church. In the midst of pagan society, in the presence of universal misery and poverty, there was a strong temptation to carry effort on behalf of the poor to extremes; but the Church, which realized justice only through charity, knew how to refrain. Her writers and preachers ceaselessly reminded the poor of their duties as citizens of the kingdom of God. Besides the considerations which raised them from their low estate, they are exhorted to bear their poverty with courageous resignation, and not to be led away by the example of the pagans into sin against the rights of property.[23] " The hand of the Christian," said Asterius, in one of his homilies, "ought only to be held out to give alms, never to seize what does not belong to him. He may protect his own fortune, but he must not touch that of another.[24] " Why are you to be pitied ? " said Ambrose. " The bird of the air is not richer than you, and still it is joyful; it does not despair; it sings, for God takes care of it. Be then, as it is, without fear for your life, cast your care on Divine goodness." [25] This trust in God must lead the poor to be contented with their lot. They are exhorted to the work which Christianity had restored to its dignity, that they may gain a livelihood; and if their labour was insufficient, or their hands were weakened by illness or age, charity was ready to fill up the gap.

§ 2. *Christian Beneficence towards the Poor in General.*[26]

We have seen that the Church did not desire to abolish the rights of property. She honours man in every state. She respects his personality and all belonging to it. She does not favour pretensions which would cause the overthrow of society. Still, that brotherhood may be realized, men separated by the difference of their position in the world, are told to approach one another. This cannot be brought about by force; it is charity alone which is destined to bridge the abyss which separated the classes in the ancient world.

The Fathers represent active and helpful charity, kindness towards the poor and unfortunate, as one of the greatest Christian duties. It is a mark by which the true members of the kingdom of God are distinguished from the world; for as Ignatius says, "The pagans leave those who cannot protect themselves; they have no care for those who are hungry and thirsty."[27] The writers and orators of the Church employ all the resources of their faith and talents to press Christians to be charitable in all circumstances. Charity is the object of their most eager solicitations in every epoch,—in the days of the infant Church, in the midst of persecutions, and after triumphs; when the Roman world was still rich and powerful, as when, after its fall, it was impoverished and sold to barbarians. All are without distinction the apostles of almsgiving; and if some amongst them, as Chrysostom or Augustine, merit this title in a higher degree, it is only that, placed in the midst of special circumstances, they had occasion more frequently to exhort their hearers to charity.[28] "Bounty," says Cyprian in his eloquent treatise on alms, "is true riches. It is a great blessing given by God to be in a position to do good to others.

It is a Divine thing, a crown of peace, to be able to soothe sorrow and to dry tears. The beneficent man is a living representation of God upon earth.[29] It is he who gives to God the worship most pleasing in His sight;[30] for it is better to do the works of charity than to ornament churches or to enrich them with precious vases."[31]

The Fathers addressed these exhortations specially to those to whom God had given wealth. It is through the free charity of the rich, aiding the work of the poor, that inequalities of fortune should gradually disappear. "The rich and strong," said a Christian poet of the third century, " ought to be the support of the poor and weak, as the tree supports the vine."[32] We have seen that Ambrose represented charity as a duty of *justice*. Chrysostom said with the same meaning that "the rich are only the administrators of goods for the poor; to refuse their necessities is to rob them, to deprive them of what is theirs by nature and right. Starting with the idea that they are united by the ties of a spiritual parentage, they ought to have a share in the inheritance that each father leaves to his family."[33] Salvian goes further still. Looking at riches as an obstacle to salvation, he says, " It is wrong to leave them to men who may make a bad use of them. The father should only leave part of his possessions to his children, and that on condition that they are pious and charitable; all the rest ought to return by right to the poor."[34] That was an exaggerated demand, in accordance with the character of the man who formulated it. It ignored family rights and the free nature of charity, therefore it could not become a general law of the Church. The Fathers do not hesitate to ask that a man shall willingly sacrifice everything to rescue a desolate brother from misery; but this sacrifice, inspired by love only, must always be free. If this were not so, the Fathers need not have combated so vigorously the excuses of the rich as to the need of supporting their rank or leaving a fortune to their families. These considerations, that are brought forward to dispense with the duties of beneficence, ought to disappear before the imperious duty of helping men in loss and peril.[35]

With the same motives the Fathers energetically denounce usury, a destructive scourge of Roman society. According to Chrysostom it is a double sin : it increases the misery of the poor and feeds the avarice of the rich.[36] "The usurer," he says elsewhere, "helps the poor man only to ruin him afterwards, like one who holds out his hands to a wrecked struggler in the waves, only to plunge him more certainly into the depths."[37] The doctors of the Church, placed in a world full of abuses to which they must continually oppose the ideal perfection of the kingdom of God, held the opinion that all interest on a loan was usury, an unlawful gain. If a brother needed money for a pressing want, it ought to be lent to him without interest, for there can be no charity in the desire to gain personal profit from it.[38] The poor are also exhorted not to go to usurers, that they may not embarrass their personal freedom by obligations above their strength, but to provide their livelihood by work and economy.[39] If, notwithstanding these exhortations, pressed by need they fall into the hands of usurers, rich Christians ought to free them ; for to pay the debt of the poor is one of the most beautiful deeds of charity.[40]

It is not only the rich who are exhorted by the Fathers to help the poor and unhappy; they desire every one to give according to his means. The spiritual brotherhood of the kingdom of God imposes equal obligations on all. The misery of the beggar accuses the harshness of all who own property. It is a severe warning intended to remind us of the will of God.⁴¹ Sympathy with misfortune ought not to depend on the amount of one's possessions. The preachers of the Church present their touching pictures of the misery of the poor to all Christians, to arouse all alike to benevolence. When each gives, however little it may be, the united charity of several will relieve miseries which one alone could not accomplish. He who has no money to give must not refrain through false shame from serving those as destitute as himself. In default of material help, he can give them counsel, and comfort them with proofs of affection, especially by the example of his own resignation to the will of God.⁴²

The priests should head their flocks in the practice of this universal charity, as setting an example of the virtues they taught. They were to be considered as the protectors and keepers of the poor and of all those unhappy ones in respect to whom pagan society was utterly merciless.⁴³ Bound to a simple and temperate life, that they might be able to be more charitable,⁴⁴ their house and table were open to the poor of all kinds,⁴⁵ whom they received without sharpness, avarice, or distinction of persons, with equal kindness for all.⁴⁶ The bishops were above all called to serve all Christians, their brethren. There must be for them neither poor nor rich.⁴⁷ Their glory was to be the providence of the poor, whilst to enrich themselves was ignominious.⁴⁸ The Apostolic Constitutions lay down their duties in these words: "To orphans take the place of a father; to widows give the protection they would have had from their husbands; help young people who desire to marry with your counsels; find work for the artizans; have pity on the infirm; receive strangers beneath your roof; give food and drink to those who are hungry and thirsty, and clothes to the naked; visit the sick and help the prisoners." [49]

What we have said in reference to Christian beneficence in general would be enough to show the new spirit with which Christianity was replacing ancient egoism, but we shall add still some traits that mark the difference still more clearly between the Christian and pagan spirit. The pagan repulsed the poor with contempt, which he considered to be greatness of soul. If he chanced to help him, it was with secret dislike and nearly always with some egoistical motive. The Christian, on the contrary, gave with joy, without murmur or regret; he was happy to be able to relieve a brother.[50] The pagan, if he gave, gave only what he could spare without harming his own interests; the Christian should give, not only of his superfluity, but of his necessities.[51] The pagan gave only to those from whom he hoped to receive some benefit himself, or who needed help to raise their position in the world; all the others, those particularly whom he thought useless to the State, were unworthy of his egoistical and political benevolence. The Christian, on the contrary, ought to give without distinction to all who held out their hand, without asking if they are worthy of help, what use they will make of it, or if they are still useful to society.[52] The pagan gave most frequently through ostentation or ambition; he ruined himself with largesses to gain the favour of the populace, without benefit to the crowd whose miseries increased with idleness, or to the really miserable who perished deserted by all. The Fathers of the Church raised their voice energetically against these excesses of pagan pride and degradation.[53] The kindness inspired by compassion for a neighbour's sorrows is not to be found there. It is almost a sacrilege to give what ought to return to the poor to those who are not such. There is only one true benevolence: it is through love to cherish those who want everything, even when they can no longer render service.[54] When Christians still imbued with pagan pride wished to appear holy before men by giving largesses to the poor, or providing them with *agapæ* or repasts in memory of the dead, the Fathers rebuked them severely; they reminded them that almsgiving is nothing without the grace of charity.[55] In the kingdom of God external work has no intrinsic value. Egoism must be replaced by love. It is vain to give up wealth, to give to the poor, to free the slaves, if it is done to get honour from men; it is not charity. It is easier to strip one's self of riches than of pride. Only the man regenerated by faith in Christ can be charitable, for he only knows how to be humble and disinterested.[56]

In Christian society charity did not remain a sterile though beautiful theory, but realized itself in facts. It inspired the faithful and their pastors, and communities and individuals vied with one another in love and benevolence to the poor. In the misery of the times of the decadence Christians found numerous occasions to exercise their charity. No period of the Church showed so many and such touching examples of devoted love. This had never been seen in antiquity, because it was thoroughly incompatible with its spirit, but it was realized by Christianity. The Churches formed a special administration for the support of their poor. They regulated the application of their bounty, whilst leaving to individual charity its spontaneity.

The custom of making oblations for the poor was introduced very early. These were offerings laid on the altar after a religious service, or brought to the priest every month. They were entirely voluntary; every one contributed according to his means.[57] When these were insufficient, they willingly imposed privations on themselves which were not prescribed by any rule. Justin Martyr had said already that those who before their conversion loved riches, joyfully made sacrifices for the poor.[58] They fasted for a day and gave the money saved to the offertory.[59] Many Christians imposed on themselves these voluntary fasts for this reason.[60] After the death of any member of the family the survivors continued to give oblations or alms in the name of the dead, who was not thought of as absent, but as still making part of the spiritual community of the kingdom of God.[61] The Church never accepted offerings from every one. She refused those which were not prompted by a pure heart; she wished that to aid the poor should be considered an honour as well as a duty. She therefore refused the oblations and alms of men who had acquired their wealth unjustly, or who were known to be harsh in their dealings. She refused to accept them from the excommunicated or penitents.[62]

A special fund was soon formed from the oblations,[63] which was increased by legacies left to the churches[64] for the help of the poor. According to the ancient Fathers, this fund was the patrimony of the poor and unfortunate.[65] To steal or waste it was considered a sacrilege which exceeded highway robbery in cruelty, for it was to kill the poor.[66] The Church also anathematized the unfaithful priest or the powerful man who could be guilty of this crime.[67] To guard the patrimony of the poor from the needs and depredations of rapacious lords, she asked and obtained from the Christian emperors special lawyers who were charged to defend the interests of ecclesiastical wealth.[68] The supreme administration of this wealth belonged to the bishops, born guardians of the poor.⁶⁹ Under their oversight the gifts were received and distributed by deacons, who were charged to keep a list of the poor, to visit them, find out their needs, and watch their conduct.⁷⁰

Deaconesses were appointed to aid poor women. This was a touching institution, springing from delicacy, and entirely in accordance with the kind and sympathetic spirit of Christian women. To have sent the deacon to visit the women would have given rise to pagan calumnies; the deaconess alone could freely enter the women's apartments to carry help and consolation to her sisters.⁷¹ These servants of Christ were chosen ordinarily, and in accordance with apostolic custom, from widows of one husband, aged at least sixty years. This double condition was fixed because of the experience and serious disposition of widows. Having felt the sorrow of losing the companion of their life, they were led to sympathize with the griefs of others.⁷² As however devotion and compassion are not the privilege of aged women alone, unmarried and younger women were also taken for deaconesses.⁷³ It even came to pass that this ministry was given exclusively to married women whose husbands were still living.⁷⁴ It appears, however, that there was not a uniform rule in all the churches in this respect. We are ignorant of the reasons that led the French councils to be the first to suppress an office so useful to the Church, and so much in accordance with the spirit of gentle charity the Saviour gives to women.⁷⁵

If the laity ought to give indiscriminately to all who asked, the bishop and deacon, who were responsible for the patrimony of the poor, should only bestow it with discernment. They were bound to refuse alms to those who had the means of a livelihood, and especially to those whose poverty was their fault. Those whose age or infirmities hindered them from working, or who through temporary maladies or the great number of their children were reduced to destitution, were the only ones who ought to receive assistance.[76] The number of the poor was very great. The figures known to us, whilst showing the greatness of the misery, prove also the greatness of the charity of Christians in these times. Under Bishop Cornelius, towards the close of the third century, the Church of Rome, already celebrated by Ignatius for its goodness and kindness, supported more than 1,500 poor people.[77] The Church of Antioch, in the time of Chrysostom, maintained more than 3,000.[78]

The Churches did not limit their help to their own poor. United by the spiritual tie of a common faith and love, those who were prosperous sent abundant help to the more unfortunate. The Church of Rome, under Bishop Soter, in the second half of the second century, as a hundred years later under Bishop Stephen, sent money collected in distant provinces, sometimes to help the populations wasted with famine, sometimes to lighten the fate of the persecuted faithful in the churches. Eusebius relates that this custom was followed in his time.[79] In the fifth century Atticus, Bishop of Constantinople, sent 300 pieces of gold to aid the poverty of the Church in Nice.[80] In these pressing cases, when the ecclesiastical funds were exhausted, the bishops asked for collections from the faithful, which rarely failed to be plentiful.[81] Pious prelates even sold the vases and ornaments of their churches. This was done by Cyril when there was great want in Jerusalem,[82] by Acacius, Bishop of Amida,[83] and by Deogratias, Bishop of Carthage.[84] Augustine and Ambrose did the same, to ransom captives enslaved either by barbarians or by the Romans themselves. Some Christians, caring more for external splendour of worship than for the fate of their brothers, blamed these acts which they thought necessity itself could not justify. Ambrose defended them with the energy of his charity: "If the Church," he says, "possesses gold, it is not to preserve it, but to use it for the needs of its members; what is the use of saving that which in itself is good for nothing? Will not the Lord ask some day, Why did you leave so many poor to die with hunger? You have gold, why did you not provide them with food? Why did you leave so many captives without the ransom that would have saved them from slavery or death? Would it not have been more charitable to preserve the living vases rather than those which were made of inanimate metal? Is there no answer to these reproaches, or will you say: 'I feared lest the temple of God should be destitute of ornaments'? The Lord will answer you, 'My Sacraments can be celebrated without gold, for it is not with gold that they were bought. Their ornament is the redemption of captives. There are no vases so precious as the salvation of souls from death; that is the gold which stands the test, useful gold, the gold of Christ." [85] Jerome also said that it was more important to help the poor than to beautify the churches; for after all, if the temple remains without ornament, where is the harm? This poverty was consecrated by that of Christ Himself.[86]

To the benevolence practised by Christian communities must be added that of the monastic associations. The convents at this time were homes of charity, especially in poor and desert countries. It is told that the monks of Egypt, dividing their time between prayer and agricultural labour, found food for the numerous poor of the surrounding country.[87] They sent help to the barren districts of Lybia, and freighted ships with provisions for the provinces suffering from the frequent famines of these unhappy ages.[88]

This collective charity of the churches and monasteries was only possible through the individual charity of the faithful. We do not need further proofs of their entire devotion, but we will mention one or two examples to show the difference in this relationship between the spirit of the citizens of the kingdom of God and that of the pagans at the period when paganism and its civilization were rapidly approaching their fall. In strictness we ought to mention all the names whose remembrance has been transmitted by Christian antiquity. All the Fathers rendered illustrious by their learning, all the martyrs, lay or clerical, men or women, were models of charity. We can only select a few; they must represent the rest. They show in the East as in the West, in Africa as in Italy and France, the same spirit animating both the members and principals of the Church. Cyprian dedicated a large share of his inheritance to the relief of the poor. His house was open to every one; no unhappy person went away without comfort or relief. In an extraordinary case, when the ecclesiastical funds were insufficient, he wrote from his exile to his priests to supply the deficiency from his personal property.[89] The martyr Laurence, when the pagan governor asked for the treasures of his church, showed him the poor.[90] Basil the great, wishing to retire into solitude, whilst still young, gave his paternal inheritance to the poor. When there was a great famine in Cappadocia later, by his exhortations and example he persuaded the rich to open their granaries to the poor. Throughout his career the austere simplicity of this remarkable man, celebrated for his eloquence and great knowledge, equalled the magnificent profusion of his alms.[91] His contemporary, Ephraim, who preferred a solitary life to a bishopric, left his retreat when Edessa was desolated by dearth and epidemic. He appealed to the benevolence of the richer members of his Church. With the help of their gifts he established a hospital beneath a portico of the town. He begged the poor who were still well to assist their invalid brothers under his direction, thus giving to some a safeguard against famine, and to others the care which lessened their sufferings.[92] It is useless to speak of charity so well known as that of Chrysostom, of Augustine, of Ambrose. These eloquent apostles of alms would not have excited such a powerful influence if their words had not been sustained by the force of their example. Paulinus of Nola and Hilary of Arles sold their large estates for the poor.[93] Martin of Tours even sacrificed his sacerdotal robes.[94] The Bishop Escupère, of Toulouse, went hungry, and used only basket and glass for the bread and wine of the Eucharist, in order to help the poor.

These noble examples of the bishops were followed by the laity, filled as they were with the love of Christ. At the time of the decline of the Roman world, there were in the highest classes of Christian society men and women, with their families, living simply, that they might be able to spread more benefits around them. We have before given the names of some of these model women; we will only mention here the names of two or three men of illustrious rank, distinguished by their inexhaustible charity. Pammachius, after having been pro-consul, spent his large fortune in alms, and wished his house to be considered a refuge open to all the poor.[95] Nebridius, son of the prefect of the prætor of the Empire of the East, and of a sister of the wife of Theodosius, used his position at court to protect the oppressed, and dedicated his revenue to the relief of the poor and the ransom of prisoners.[96] Peter, the tax gatherer, in the time of Justinian, expiated the harshness towards the poor into which his office had led him, by selling himself to a slave merchant for their benefit.[97]

These facts, which might easily be multiplied, prove better than any arguments the power of the new spirit which Jesus Christ bestows on those who give themselves to Him with all their heart.

§ 3. *Widows and Orphans.*

All who were unhappy were, without any distinction, the objects of the charity of Christians. If there were any that appealed to them in a special manner, it was those who required a special kind of help and protection; above all, widows and orphans. Through the feeling of the brotherly union of all men (hardly divined by antiquity), the Christian widow who had lost her husband, the child who had lost his parents, regained a family in the Christian community. Deprived of their natural helpers, they were surrounded with more care than other miserable ones, who were often satisfied with material and temporary help. They ought, to quote the expression of the Apostolic Constitutions, to occupy a high place in the temple of God.[98] Few precepts are repeated oftener or more emphatically than the duty of caring for widows and orphans and sacrificing self in their aid.[99] During the persecutions there was added to general motives the consideration that the husbands or parents could suffer martyrdom with greater courage, knowing that those whom they loved would never be deserted.[100] The faithful who received orphans into their houses were asked to encourage their marriage with their own children rather than with others, in order that they might soon have a new family around them.[101] The advice to care for orphans and widows is addressed specially to priests and bishops; they were to provide for their support from the funds of the Church or by collections.[102] The bishop took care that these children, bereft of their parents, were brought up in the Christian faith and instructed in useful arts, to enable them to gain their livelihood or to marry suitably, without remaining too long dependent on the Churches.[103] He defended rich orphans and widows, and protected them from the avarice of their families, and from powerful adversaries who were tempted by their position to infringe their rights.[104] "Your ministry," said Ambrose to the clergy, "will shine with a lovely light if your efforts hinder a powerful man from oppressing the widow and orphan, if you lead him to see that you value the precepts of God more highly than the favour of men." For their encouragement he recalls his own conflicts with the emperor when he refused to give up the property entrusted by widows to his charge.[105]

The monks received poor orphans into the monasteries, where they were taught and fed without charge, and looked upon as the common children of all the brothers.[106] From the fourth century Christian charity erected public establishments for these members of the Church who deserve so much sympathy. It is told of Bishop Eleusius, of Cyzicus, that he took the pagan temples and made them into hospitals for old widows.[107] The first orphan houses date apparently from the same period. They were under the direction of priests, who were afterwards legally empowered to be the tutors and guardians of the children committed to their care.[108]

§ 4. *The Oppressed and Captives.*

Amongst the unfortunate people recommended to the care of the Churches and the faithful, we must not forget the captives and those who were unjustly oppressed. In this respect opportunities were not wanting for the Christian charity of the early ages. Personal liberty remained insecure. Notwithstanding the protective laws and efforts to increase the vigour of the administration of the empire, it was subject to the whims of the emperors and their officers, to the cupidity of the soldiers and agents of the fiscal, to the tyrannical caprice of rich and powerful men, and to the brutal savagery of barbarians. Violence has perhaps never reigned under so many forms, or made so many victims, as in these times of social dissolution; but Christian benevolence has never shown more ingenious perseverance.

During the persecutions, Christians who were thrown into prison or sent to the quarries, were visited by their friends, who prayed with them and brought them assistance. Special collections were made for them, the poor denied themselves a day's food to enable them to contribute.[109] The funds of the Church were used to ransom brothers sentenced to public works or to the arena, and Christians incurred all kind of dangers to come to their aid.[110] The law of the tyrant Licinius, which inflicted the same penalties on those who visited Christian prisoners as on themselves, did not prevent even women from facing the peril in order to console them and to dress their wounds.[111]

The right of asylum in the Churches was introduced by degrees, as it had existed in the pagan temples, to shelter the victims of despotism, cupidity, or popular fury. Ministers or functionaries proscribed by the emperor or chased by the crowd,[112] noble widows exposed to the intrusion of powerful and greedy men,[113] the poor who were pursued by their creditors,[114] slaves ill-treated by their masters, or threatened for their faith,[115] found in the churches or monasteries a refuge from their persecutors. If there was a poor man who sought to free himself from the harshness of a usurer, the faithful made a collection, paid his debt and set him free. If a slave came, he was intreated to have patience, whilst at the same time the master was advised to show more humanity. He was only allowed to remain when a return to servitude would have exposed his conscience to serious peril.[116] Even the barbarians respected this right of asylum. After the taking of Rome, Alaric spared all those who had taken refuge in the churches.[117]

Besides the asylum open to them in religious houses, the oppressed of all sorts had an equally certain refuge with the bishops, whose protecting charity was never sought in vain by the innocent. In the midst of universal anarchy, they alone raised their voice to utter a protest on behalf of outraged humanity. It was one of their special duties to save defenceless men from the hands of powerful oppressors, and to intercede with the emperors and magistrates on their behalf, to undertake long journeys and brave all wrath, provided the cause of those in whom they were interested was just.[118] The humblest person was sure to find his bishop ready to hear and defend him. Sometimes we find men unjustly condemned who have been delivered by Ambrose from exile, prison, or torture.[119] Sometimes there is a deserting soldier recommended, on account of his repentance, to the pardon of his chief by Gregory Nazianzen.[120] Sometimes we find revolted slaves for whom Basil has interceded with their masters.[121] Most frequently we find assistance given to the country people, who suffered from the rapacity of the fiscal agents, the ruinous avarice of the usurers, and the oppression of the great proprietors. These last, although Christians in name, are represented by the preachers of the time as worse than barbarians. They allowed their peasants who cultivated their vast domains to perish of want. As indifferent to their moral destiny as to their earthly lot, they intentionally kept them in paganism, because they levied a tax on the temples.[122] Chrysostom and Augustine, on several occasions, spoke energetically in favour of these oppressed tillers of the ground. They sternly remonstrated with the rich men who oppressed them, reminding them how unsuitable such harshness was in Christians who feared God's anger and desired to obtain His pardon.[123] When entire populations, unable to endure these intolerable exactions, rose in revolt against the imperial officers, the bishops, without defending either sedition or tyranny, had sufficient influence to recall the people to obedience, and the agents to humanity. Gregory Nazianzen, in a discourse given in the presence of a Roman governor who had come to punish a revolt, began by quieting the people, and then gave counsels of indulgence and pardon to the governor.[124] When the population of Antioch, exasperated by a new tax, ill-treated the officers of Theodosius and upset his statues, and when he sent commissioners to severely punish the guilty, the Archbishop Flavian, notwithstanding his great age, started at once to endeavour to allay the anger of the emperor. During his absence Chrysostom gave his celebrated discourses to cheer the people, who were as alarmed now as they had before been prompt to revolt. Some hermits of the neighbourhood hastened to implore mercy from the commissioners.

In Constantinople Flavian appealed so warmly to Theodosius, that the emperor, touched, consented to a general pardon.[125]

If intercessions remained fruitless, the Church, justly regretting to see her charitable efforts of no avail, unhesitatingly declared these harsh and violent men to be unworthy of Christian communion. Athanasius excommunicated the Governor of Libya on account of his cruelty and debauchery.[126] The emperors themselves were solemnly reminded that the possession of supreme power does not dispense with humanity. Theodosius having in a fit of anger massacred seven thousand inhabitants of Thessalonica, Ambrose wrote him a letter expressing the sorrow he felt to see a Christian emperor condemn so many men to death, without distinguishing between the innocent and guilty. He told him that, blood-stained as he was, he must not present himself before the altar. When he wished to enter the Church at Milan, the courageous bishop stopped him on the threshold, imposing a penance, to which the emperor submitted, confessing his sin.[127] It is true, as stated by M. Villemain, that ambition has often used this example for its own end; but it is also true that at the end of the fourth century it was a fine sight to see a Christian bishop stand up alone to defend the rights of justice and charity against the master of the world.

The wars which were continued throughout the whole duration of the Roman empire, civil troubles, contests between competitors for the crown, and the invasion of barbarous tribes, often put Christian charity to the test. Besides the prisoners taken in battle, entire populations were carried into captivity, after having seen their dwellings ruined and their fields laid waste. To ransom these unfortunates was shown by the Fathers to be a proof of supreme love, and a noble act of justice which must be undertaken at any cost; for it was to redeem brothers not only from death or slavery, but from the danger of falling back into idolatry; to give back children to their parents and citizens to their country; or to save Christian women from the brutal passions of barbarians.[128] The necessary money was given by rich Christians or taken from the funds of the Churches; special collections were often made for this object. It even happened that men, inspired with ardent charity, sacrificed their own freedom to give back a husband or son to his family. In very early times we find examples of this sublime devotion. Clement of Rome writes to the Church at Corinth : " We have amongst us many who have given themselves to servitude in order that others might be set free." [129] Bishop Denis, in the name of the Church of Rome, sent money to Cappadocia to ransom captives doomed to slavery.[130] The hordes of Numidians having invaded Roman Africa and carried off many prisoners, the bishops of the province appealed to the Church at Carthage for help; and Cyprian then made a collection to which both rich and poor eagerly contributed.[131] The captives taken by the Goths in Italy were ransomed by the Christian communities of the country. Ambrose disposed of the sacred vases of the Church for this purpose, convinced that it was more in the spirit of the Gospel to save these unfortunates from misery, shame, and death, than to preserve the ornaments.[132] Augustine set the same example.[133] He was followed, about the middle of the fifth century, by Deogratias, Bishop of Carthage, who, after the invasions of the Vandals, ransomed the prisoners with the price of the holy vases. When they returned to Carthage and there was no room to lodge them, he placed two churches at their disposal, and himself presided over the needful care for their wants.[134] We must add that it was not brothers in faith only whom they ransomed from captivity. Compassionating all suffering, respecting liberty for all, they imposed sacrifices on themselves to send back to their own country foreigners and pagans who had been made prisoners by the Romans themselves. Acacius, Bishop of Amida, about 420, sold the consecrated vases to ransom and send back in freedom 7,000 Persians who had fallen into the hands of the Roman army.[135]

§ 5. *The Sick.*

The pagan, who loved the world and had no hope of a future life, dreaded illness and avoided invalids. He hardly cared for the members of his own family, and in epidemics his fear and terror led him to desert them without scruple. The sick poor were abandoned both by society and individuals, who considered them as useless to the State. Sickness increased their previous uselessness; it was an additional opprobrium, added to the disgrace of poverty.

In Christian society all was different. Illness was regarded as in itself a sorrow. It was a trial for those whom it attacked, and a reason for brethren to redouble their charity and compassion. Jesus Christ had called those blessed of His Father and inheritors of the kingdom of heaven who had visited Him in sickness in the person of the least of His brethren.[136] The Church established it as an imperative duty not only for bishops and priests, but for all Christians, both men and women.[137] This duty was shown to be so much the greater when, hindered from working, the sick poor were less able than before, to provide for their living.[138] Besides food and remedies for the body, they gave them also the best reasons for keeping up their courage, or inspiring resignation. They told them of the love of God, who does not wish a single soul to be lost; of the duty of submission to His will, which is as wise as it is good; of the happiness of being delivered by death from the sorrows of this world; of the hope of a better life, where they may meet again those whom they have cherished here below.[139]

There was a class of sick people who needed peculiar sympathy: this was the lepers, who are so numerous in all eastern countries. These unfortunates were driven from all inhabited places, forsaken by their families, forced to retire to caverns on the mountains, unable to show themselves lest they should be pitilessly stoned, and rather objects of terror and hatred than of a helpful pity. Basil advises with warmth that they shall not be deserted, that Christ, whose members they are, may not be saddened: they must be loved the more for the miseries of their desolation.[140]

The great epidemics, which terrified the pagans, were for the Christians opportunities of showing their charity. "The Lord," said Cyprian, "wishes to be sure whether those who are well will serve the sick, whether the members of the same family love one another, whether the masters will take pity on the slaves, whether the doctors dare face their duty, and whether the danger of death will restrain the harshness of violent men, and the cupidity of avaricious ones."[141] It requires courage to conquer the horror and dread of contagion, but Christian charity must not be daunted, "Let no man excuse himself," says a writer in the second century; "let no one refuse the service of the sick, with the excuse that he has not learned how to attend on them, or that he cannot bear the sight. Let him who so speaks learn that he may himself fall a victim to the malady and wish for the help of his brothers."[142] The same idea was developed in touching words, two centuries later, by Gregory Nazianzen and Gregory of Nyssa.[143] "If the poor," says a writer on the other side, "are overcome by illness through want of help, it is regarded by the Christians as the gravest accusation."[144]

These precepts of charity were observed by individuals as well as by Churches. Everywhere in the earliest ages, the faithful, especially the women, visited the sick, to pray with them and give them aid. We have already mentioned Fabiola, Placilla, Ephraim, and nothing would be easier than to lengthen the list of these devoted and heroic Christians. The care of the sick was also the special charge of the deacons and deaconesses; they distributed amongst them the money from the collections and oblations.

During the plague of Carthage, about 250 A.D., the Christians who lived there willingly obeyed the exhortations of their bishop, Cyprian, some going themselves to minister to the sick poor, and others bringing gifts for them.[145] The same self-sacrifice was shown during the plague at Alexandria; priests, deacons, rich and powerful laymen, visited the sick or carried the dead to the cemetery. The blanks left by the death of many of these devoted men, victims of their charity, were soon filled by other brothers, notwithstanding the almost certain peril to which they were exposed.[146] The care of the Church for the poor who were suffering from sickness or want soon raised institutions for them, the very idea of which had never entered the pagan mind. Christian society, instead of repelling the man incapable of helping the State or himself, took the sick poor under its charge, and opened various hospitals for them, knowing that if one member suffer, all the others suffer with him. It was in the early part of the fourth century that the first of these institutions was founded; they are both the effect and the glory of Christianity.[147] From the latter half of this century they became numerous everywhere: in the East and in the West houses of refuge were raised for the infirm or invalid poor, hospitals for the sick, refuges for needy travellers.[148] Some were founded by private persons; others by bishops with the help of the funds of the Church and collections; others were established near the monasteries.

The most important of these hospitals was that founded by Basil in the town of Cæsarea, where this great theologian filled the office of bishop from 370 to the time of his death, 379. He founded it with the help of gifts from the faithful of his Church who were roused by his eloquence as well as by his example.[149] This hospital, which, according to Gregory Nazianzen, rose like a new town at the gates of Cæsarea, provided lodgings for travellers, rooms for invalids, for whom there were doctors and nurses, and workshops for the poor who were able to work.[150] There was a special hospital for lepers.[151] Gregory Nazianzen, the friend of Basil, calls this institution the beauty of piety, where illness becomes a school of wisdom, where misery is changed into happiness, where Christian charity shows its most striking proof.[152] It bore the name of Basilias until the fifth century, in memory of its founder.[153]

The untiring Bishop of Cæsarea established similar hospitals in each diocese of the country. He recommended them, especially those for lepers, to the care of the clergy, and arranged for their oversight by suffragan bishops.[154] He asked the civil governors to free these houses consecrated to charitable uses from taxes.

He bound them to visit them personally, in the hope of interesting the lay element of Christian society in them, and he had the happiness of being eagerly assisted by them.[155]

Chrysostom, who preached almsgiving so ardently, followed the example of Basil. He founded hospitals himself in connection with his various churches, or by his appeals to their charity stimulated the faithful to raise them. He set priests over these houses and provided them with doctors. He chose nurses and servants from amongst the aged poor who had no family and no work, in order to provide them with occupation and a home.[156] The erection of the hospital at Antioch is doubtless due to him,[157] as well as those at Constantinople, which were afterwards said to have been founded by one Zoticus.[158] In the time of the Emperor Theodosius, most of the Churches, especially in large towns, had these charitable houses belonging to them.[159] Macarius founded and directed one at Alexandria;[160] the hermit Thalassius, who lived near a village on the bank of the Euphrates, built a hospital for the blind of the country, and devoted himself to their service.[161]

In the West, the earliest known hospitals were founded by rich persons. Gallicanus, a patrician, and former consul under Constantine, established one at Ostia;[162] towards the end of the fourth century Pammachus, and his wife Paulina, of the family of Paulus Emilius, founded one at Porto, near Rome;[163] and about the same time Fabiola, of the race of Fabius, built a hospital, where she attended herself on the sick poor.[164]

The hospitals founded by private people were generally adopted by the Churches, and governed like those which they had themselves started. The administration was placed under the oversight of the bishops, the funds were provided either by endowment or from the possessions of the Churches.[165] The houses themselves were placed under the direction of special clergy.[166] The Church of Alexandria, from the time of Theodosius the Great, had a special priest charged with the office of *xenodochus*.[167] Even the attendants had a clerical character. They were named by the bishops and formed one of the inferior orders of the hierarchy.[168] The Church thus left her impress on everything relating to the exercise of charity. She claimed as one of her greatest privileges the right of caring for the suffering part of society. She wished to be a refuge for physical sorrow and misery, as well as for weary and heavy-laden souls. In taking on herself this duty, she did not release ordinary Christians from it. The charity of Christian society never has been and never can be the result of anything but individual charity. This is free and cannot be ordered by the law; it is only possible through the new spirit which transforms and animates individuals, and which teaches them to love one another, because it teaches them to respect each other.

In the early ages of the Church this respect for man extended even to the dead. In the corpse itself Christians recognised the work of God. It was in their eyes a habitation, temporary only, but ennobled by the soul which had dwelt therein.[169] They detested the Roman custom of burning the dead as sullied by paganism.[170] The practice of throwing the dead bodies of the poor and slaves to the dogs or to birds of prey was a greater cruelty in their sight. The corpses of the martyrs were so treated during the persecutions, and this insulting contempt distressed the Christians as much as the tortures that they were made to endure.[171] They returned to the ancient custom of burying the dead practised by the Israelites and the Romans themselves.[172] Funeral ceremonies became a religious service in which the whole community was interested. As they formed in a manner only one family, no one could remain indifferent to the loss of one member. They accompanied the dead to the cemetery with prayers and chants. The priest pronounced a blessing on the soul which had just left the earthly communion to enter the spiritual communion of the heavenly kingdom.[173] After the fourth century a distinct order of clergy was entrusted with the duties of burial; they formed, under the name of sacristans, the last order of the clergy.[174]

The poor were buried with the same prayers as the rich. Ecclesiastical funds or private charity supplied the expenses of the ceremony.[175] To render the last duty to a poor man was looked upon as one of the greatest requirements of charity.[176] For death re-establishes the natural equality between those who were separated in life by their external condition. The same earth covers them; the same salvation blesses their souls if they have believed in the Saviour and walked in His footsteps. Amongst the Christian virtues which astonished the pagans, this care for the dead, especially amongst the poor, was one of the things they least understood.[177] It was in truth the witness of a spirit profoundly different from that of paganism; and when we see Seneca reckon amongst works of true benevolence the burial of the bodies even of criminals, we find another proof that he was not a stranger to the influence of the new ideas.[178]

(1) Tertull., *Apol.*, c. 21, p. 78. Orig., *C. Cels.*, III. c. 74, vol. i. p. 496. Arnob., II. 15, vol. i. p. 49. (2) Just. Mart., *Apol.* 1, c. 60, p. 79; *Apol.* 2, c. 10, p. 95. Tat., *Or. c. Græcos*, c. 32, p. 296. Athenag., *Leg.* c. 11, p. 288. (3) Orig., *C. Cels.*, VIII. 50, p. 778. Lactant.,

Div. Instit., VI. 10; vol. i. p. 456. (4) Matt. x. 9. (5) Greg. Naz., *Or.* 16, vol. i. p. 247. Greg. Nyss., *Or.* 2, "De pauperibus amandis," vol. ii. p. 53. August., *Sermo* 239, § 6, vol. v. p. 696. Ambr., *Ep.* 63, § 87, vol. ii. p. 1043. (6) *Ep. ad Zenam et Serenum*, c. 14, p. 415. Clem. Alex., *Quis Dives Salvetur*, vol. ii. p. 935. (7) Ambr., *Hexæm.*, VI. 8, § 51, vol. i. p. 133. August., *Sermo* 61 § 9. vol. v. p. 247. (8) Lactant., *Div. Instit.*, V. 16, vol. i. p. 402. (9) Clem. Alex., *Quis Dives Salvetur*, vol. ii. p. 935. Chrysost., *Hom. in Jes.*, 45, 7, vol. vi. p. 150. Theodoret., *Or.* 6, vol. iv. P. 1, p. 563. (10) *Div. Instit.*, V. 15, vol. i. p. 399. (11) *Ep.* 63, § 89, vol. ii. p. 1044. (12) C. 19, p. 52. (13) *Hom.* 7 *in Act.*, § 2; *Hom.* 11 *in Act.*, § 3, vol. ix. p. 58, 93. (14) *De Off. Ministr.*, I. 28, § 132, vol. ii. p. 35; *Sermo* 8 *in Ps.* cxviii. § 22, vol i. p. 1064. (15) *Ep.* 153, vol. ii. p. 405. (16) Cf. M. Troplong, *De l'infl. du Christ. sur la Legislat. Civile des Romains*, p. 121. (17) "A wealthy slave, belonging to the household of a certain great Father." —*Enarr. in Ps.* 38, § 12, vol. iv. p. 238. (18) Cf. Luke xix., 12 sq., the parable of the ten pounds. (19) *Quis Dives Salvetur*, vol. ii. p. 935. (20) "Neither is the rich man's wealth a hindrance, if he use it well; nor does the poor man's poverty make him more acceptable, if he avoid not sin in the midst of his parsimony and indigence" (Hieron., *Ep.* 79, vol. i. p. 498). "Therefore neither is every poor man a saint, . . . nor is every rich man condemned" (Asterius., *De Divite et Lazaro*, p. 13). August., *Sermo* 14, § 4; *Sermo* 36, § 5 sq., vol. v. p. 59, 124. Ambr., *Ep.* 63 § 92, vol. ii. p. 1044. Paul. Nol., *Ep.* 40, p. 252. Petr. Chrysol., *Sermo* 28, 121, pp. 119, 521. (21) Min. Felix, c. 36, p. 133. (22) "Non debuit Deus facere pauperes, sed soli divites esse debuerunt." August., *Enarr. in Ps.* 124, § 2, vol. iv. p. 1056; *Sermo* 14, § 5, vol. v. p. 59. (23) Asterius., *Hom. de Divite et Lazaro*, p. 13. (24) *Hom. de Œconomo Iniquo*, p. 23. (25) *Hexæm.*, V. 17, § 57, vol. i. p. 102. Lactant., *Div. Instit.*, VI. c. 12, vol. i. p. 469. (26) Cf. Launoius, " De Curâ Ecclesiæ pro Miseris et Pauperibus" (very incomplete).—*In Opp. Col.* 1731, fol. vol. ii. pt. ii. p. 568 sq. (27) *Ad Smyrnæos*, c. 6, p. 36. (28) M. Villemain, *Tableau de l'éloq. chrét. aue* 4e *siècle*, p. 181. (29) Clem. Alex., *Strom.*, II. 19, vol. i. p. 483. Greg. Nyss., *Or.* 1 *in Verba. Fac. Hom.*, vol. i. p. 151. (30) Greg. Naz., *Or.* 16, vol. i. p. 242. (31) Hieron., *Ep.* 130, vol. i. p. 991. Chrysost., *Hom.* 80 *in Matth.*, § 2, vol. vii. p. 768. (32) Commodianus, v. 460, 461, p. 631. (33) Chrysost., *De Lazaro, concio* 2, § 4, vol. i. p. 732; *Hom.* 2 *de Verbis Apost. habentes eundemspir*, § 9, vol. iii. p. 278. Hieron., *Ep.* 66, vol. i. p. 399. (34) *De Avaritiâ*, III. 2, p. 265. (35) Clem. Rom., *Ep.* 1 *ad Cor.*, c. 38, p. 169. Cypr., *De Opere et Eleem.*, p. 237. Basil., *Hom. in Divites*, vol. ii. p. 51 sq. (36) *Hom.* 41 *in Gen.* xvii., § 2, vol. iv. p. 413. Cypr., *Testim. adv. Jud.*, III. 48, p. 318. (37) *Hom.* 5 *in Matth.* § 5, vol. vii. p. 82. (38) Lactant., *Div. Instit.*, VI. 18, vol. i. p. 483. Ambr., *De Tobiâ*, c. 3, vol. i. p. 593. Basil, *Hom. in Partem Ps.* xiv. vol. i. p. 107. Greg. Nyss., *Or. contra Usurarios*, vol. ii. p. 225. August., *Enarr. in Ps.* liv. § 14, vol. iv. p. 230; *Sermo* 239, § 5, vol. v. p. 696. (39) Basil., *Hom. in partem Ps.* xiv. vol. i. p. 109. (40) Ambr., *De Off.*, II. 14 § 71, vol. ii. p. 87. August., *Ep.* 268, vol. ii. p. 683. Nilus, *Perist.*, sect. 9, c. 1, p. 134. (41) "Frequently some beggar at the door, begging for a single coin, repeats God's precepts in thine ear."—August., *Sermo* 32, § 23, vol. v. p. 116. Chrysost., *Hom.* 30 *in Ep.*, 1 *ad Cor.*, § 4, vol. x. p. 274. (42) Greg. Nyss., *Or.* 1, *De Pauperibus Amandis*, vol. ii. p. 239. Chrysost., *Hom. de Eleem.*, vol. iii. p. 253. August., *Enarr.* 2 *in Ps.* xxxvi. § 13, vol. iv. p. 203. Ambr., *De Off.*, II. 15, § 73, vol. ii. p. 87. (43) Polyc., *Ep.*, c. 6, p. 188. *Ignat. ad Polyc.*, c. 4, p. 40. *Const., Apost.*, II. 25 sq. p. 238. Cypr., *Ep.* 5 & 36, pp. 10, 49. (44) Hieron., *Ep.* 52, vol. i. p. 265. (45) *O. c.* p. 259. (46) Polyc., *Ep.*, c. 6, p. 188. (47) *Constit. Apost.*, II. 5, p. 217. (48) "Gloria Episcopi est pauperum inopiæ providere. Ignominia omnium sacerdotum est, propriis studere divitiis."—Hieron., *Ep.* 52, vol. i. p. 264. (49) Bk. IV. 2, p. 295. (50) Barn., c. 20, p. 53. Clem. Alex., *Pædag.*, III. 6, vol. i. p. 275. Chrysost., *Hom. de Eleem.*, vol. iii., p. 254. (51) Ambr., *De Off.*, II. 28, § 136, vol. ii. p. 102. (52) "Give to all in need with a single heart, nothing doubting as to whom thou benefitest. Give to all. They therefore who take a gift shall render an account to God, why they have taken it, and for what end. They also who take alms by feigning want, shall render an account; but he who gives shall be guiltless" (Hermas, II., Mand. 2, p. 86; I. vis. 3, c. 9, p. 81). Lactantius, in refuting Cicero, says: " Give rather to him from whom thou hast nothing to hope. Why dost thou choose persons? Why dost thou scrutinise his body? Thou oughtest to treat him as a man, whoever begs of thee, because he supposes thee to be a man. . . . Give freely to the blind, the infirm, the maimed, the needy; for they, if thou give not, must die. They are useless to men, but useful to God, who still keeps them alive, who gives them breath and grants them light. . . . He who can help a dying man, and helps him not, is that man's murderer."—*Div. Instit.*, VI. 11, vol. i. p. 462. (53) The rich pagan " seeks empty honour from men, and, in order to win it, gives them displays and games full of wicked lust; he buys shows and bears, he gives his riches to the lion-fighters, whilst Christ is dying from hunger amongst the poor."—August., *Sermo* 32, § 20, vol. v. p. 116. (54) Lactant., *Div. Instit.*, VI. 11, 12, vol. i. pp. 464, 466. Hieron., *Ep.* 66, vol. i. p. 399. Ambr., *De Off.*, II. 21, § 109, vol. ii. p. 96. (55) Ambr., *De Pœnit.*, II. 9, § 83, vol. ii. p. 434. (56) August., *Tract.* 51 *in Joh.*, § 12, vol. iii. Pt. II. p. 468. Hieron., *Ep.* 77, vol. i. p. 458. Macarius, *Hom.* 27, § 14, p. 383. (57) Just. Mart., *Apol.* 1, c. 67, p. 83. Tertull., *Apol.*, c. 39, p. 120. (58) *Apol.* 1, 14, p. 51. (59) *Constit. Apost.*, V. 20, p. 331. (60) Origen quotes and approves the apocryphal passage: " Blessed is he who also fasts that he may have to feed the poor."—*Hom.* 10 *in Levit.*, vol. ii. p. 246. (61) Tertull., *De Coronâ*, c. 3, p. 102; *De Monog.*, c. 10, p. 531. (62) *Constit. Apost.*, IV. 6 sq., p. 297. August., *Sermo* 178, § 4, vol. v. p. 591. (63) *Constit. Apost.*, III. c. 4, p. 279. (64) Greg. Naz., *Ep.* 80, vol. i. p. 833. (65) "Possessio Ecclesiæ sumptuo est egenorum."—Ambr., *Ep.* 18 *ad Valentinianum*, vol. ii. p. 833. (66) Hieron., *Ep.* 52, vol. i. p. 269. (67) Council of Vasense, A.D. 442, can. 4; Mansi, vol. vi. p. 440. (68) Council of Carthage, A.D. 401 and 407; Can. Eccl. Afric., can. 75; Mansi, vol. iii. p. 773. (69) *Constit. Apost.*, II. 25, p. 238. August., *Ad Bonif.*, ep. 185, c. 9, vol. ii. p. 500. (70) *Constit. Apost.*, II. 25, 31, 32; III. 19; pp. 238, 246, 292. Cypr., *Ep.* 4, p. 9. (71) *Constit. Apost.*, III. 15, p. 290. Epiph., *Adv. Hær.* III. vol. ii. *hær.* 79, § 3, p. 1060. *Exposit. Fidei. Cath.*, § 21, p. 1103. (72) Tertull., *De Virg. Velandis*, c. 9, p. 178. Vidua, χήρα, are often used as synonyms for deaconess (Hieron., *Ep.* 123, vol. i. p. 904). (73) *Constit. Apost.*, VI. 17,

p. 350. Cf. Ignat., *Ad Smyrn.*, c. 13, p. 38. (74) An epitaph of a married deaconess has been discovered at Verona, she died at the age of forty-five.—Orelli, vol. ii. p. 362, No. 4872. (75) Council of Orange, A.D. 441, can. 26; of Epaone, A.D. 517, can. 21; of Orleans, A.D. 553, can. 18. However, it appears that even subsequently there were deaconesses in Gaul; Radegonde, wife of Lothaire I. was ordained deaconess by Médard (*Acta SS.*, Aug., vol. iii. p. 70). (76) *Constit. Apost.*, II. 4; IV. 3, pp. 217, 296. (77) Euseb., *Hist. Eccl.*, VI. 43, p. 244. (78) Chrysost., *Hom.* 66 *in Matth.*, § 3, vol. vii. p. 658. (79) *Hist. Eccl.*, IV. 23; VII. 5, pp. 145, 252. (80) Socrat., *Hist. Eccl.*, VII. 25; p. 365. (81) Just. Mart., *Apol.* 1, c. 14, p. 51. Cypr., *Ep.* 4, p. 9. Possidius, "Vita August.," c. 4, § 48; in *Act. SS.*, *Aug.*, vol. vi. p. 435. (82) Sozomen., *Hist. Eccl.*, IV. 25, p. 583. (83) Socr., *Hist. Eccl.*, VII. 21, p. 359. (84) Victor Vit., I. 8, p. 41. (85) *De Off.*, II. 28, § 136 sq., vol. ii. p. 102. (86) *Ep.* 52, vol. i. p. 265. (87) Chrysost., *Hom.* 8 *in Matth.*, § 6, vol. vii. p. 128. August., *De Moribus Eccl. Cath.*, I. 31, vol. i. p. 529. (88) Palladius, *Hist. Laus.*, c. 76, p. 179. (89) *Ep.* 36, p. 49. Pontius, "Vita Cypr.," § 3; in *Opp. Cypr.* p. cxxxvi. (90) Ambr., *De Off.*, II. 28, § 140, vol. ii. p. 104. (91) Greg. Naz., *Or.* 20, vol. i. p. 340 sq. (92) Sozomen., *Hist. Eccl.*, III. 16, p. 527. (93) Prosp. Pomerius, *De Vita Contempl.*, II. 9, p. 51. Gennad., c. 59. p. 32. (94) Sulp. Severus, "Dial. de Vita B. Mart.," c. 2.; in *Opp. Leyde*, 1654, p. 488. (95) Paulin. Nol., *Ep.* 13, p. 73. Hieron., *Ep.* 66, vol. i. p. 395. (96) Hieron., *Ep.* 79, vol. i. p. 501. (97) *Acta SS.*, Jan., vol. ii. p. 506. (98) Bk. II. c. 26, p. 242. (99) Barn., c. 20, p. 53. Hermas, II. mand. 8, III. simil. 1, p. 96, 103. Lactant., *Div. Instit.*, VI. 12, vol. i. p. 466. (100) Lactant., l. c. (101) *Constit. Apost.*, IV. 1, p. 295. (102) Polyc., c. 6, p. 188. Just. Mart., *Apol.* I. c. 67, p. 84. Tertull., *Apol.*, c. 39, p. 120. Cypr., *Ep.* 36, p. 49. *Constit. Apost.*, III. 1 sq., p. 277. Chrysost., *Hom. de Viduis*, vol. iii. p. 311. (103) *Constit. Apost.*, IV. 1, 2, p. 295. (104) Council of Sardica, A.D. 347, can. 10; Mansi., vol. iii. p. 28. August., *Sermo* 176, § 2, vol. v. p. 584. (105) *De Off.*, II. 22, § 149, vol. ii. p. 106. (106) Basil., *Reg. Fus. Tract.*, interr. 15, vol. ii., p. 355. (107) Called χηροτρόφια, Sozomen, *Hist. Eccl.*, V. 15, p. 615. (108) Called "Orphanotrophi." Laws of Leon and Anthemius, A.D. 469; Corp. Jur., I. tit. 3, l. 32, 35. (109) *Constit. Apost.*, V. 1, p. 304. Just. Mart., *Apol.* I. c. 67, p. 84. Tertull., *Apol.*, c. 39, p. 120; *Ad Mart.*, c. 1, p. 136. Lucian., *De Morte Peregr.*, vol. ii. p. 567. (110) *Constit. Apost.*, V. 3, p. 305. (111) Euseb., *Hist. Eccl.*, X. 8, p. 396; *Vita Const.*, I., 54, p. 435. Cf. Tertull., *Ad Uxorem*, II. 8, p. 172. (112) Eutropius, the minister of Arcadius; Cf. M. Villemain, *Tableau de l'Eloq. Chrét.*, p. 167. The husband and wife of Rufinus, Josim., V. 8, p. 256; see too IV. 40, p. 222. Amm. Marcell., XXVI. 3, vol. ii. p. 74. (113) Greg. Naz., *Or.* 20, vol. i. p. 353. (114) August., *Ep.* 268, vol. ii. p. 683. (115) Basil., *Reg. Fus. Tract.*, interr. 11, vol. ii. p. 353. Isid. Pelus., *Epp.*, Lib. I. ep. 142, p. 36. (116) Vide note 114, 115. (117) August., *De Civit. Dei*, I. 1 vol. vii. p. 3. (118) Ambr., *De Off.*, II. 21, § 102; 29, § 149, vol. ii. pp. 94, 106. Council of Sardica, A.D. 347, can. 10; Mansi, vol. iii. p. 26. (119) *Ep.* 41, ad Theodosium, § 25, vol. ii. p. 953. (120) *Ep.* 78, vol. i. p. 832. (121) *Ep.* 73, vol. iii. p. 167. (122) Zeno Veron., I. tract. 15, p. 130. (123) August., *Ep.* 247, vol. ii. p. 663. Chrysost., *Hom.* 60 *in Matt.*, § 3 vol. vii. p. 614. (124) *Or.* 17,

T

vol. i. p. 265. (125) Chrysost., *Homiliæ* 21 *de Stat.*, vol. ii. pp. 1, 3.
Ambr., *Ep.* 41, ad Theodosium, § 32, vol. ii. p. 955. Villemain, *Tabl. de
l'Eloq. Chrét.*, p. 164 sq. (126) Bas., *Ep.* 16, vol. iii. p. 155. (127)
Ambr., *Ep.* 51 ad Theodosium, a. 390, vol. ii. p. 998. Theodoret, *Hist.
Eccl.*, V. 17, p. 219. Sozomen, *Hist. Eccl.*, VII. 25, p. 743. (128)
Lactant., *Div. Instit.*, VI. 12, vol. i. p. 466. Ambr., *De Off.*, II. c. 15, §
70, 71, c. 28, § 138, vol. ii. pp. 86, 103. (129) *Ep.* 1, ad Cor., c. 55, p.
178. Tradition records a similar deed of Paulinus of Nola. Gregory
the Great tells (in his " Dialogi de vita et miraculis Patrum Italicorum,"
III. 1, in *Opp.*, ed. Bened., Paris, 1705, fol., vol. ii. p. 127) how when he
had exhausted all his means in ransoms for the people carried captive
into Africa by the Vandals, Paulinus gave himself up to a poor widow
who begged him for the ransom money for her son ; the widow accepted
his offer, and both together set out for Africa ; there Paulinus won the
good opinion of the Vandal king, and obtained from him the freedom of
all his captive fellow-countrymen. This story is not confirmed by any
historical record of the time. " Everything in the writings of Paulinus tends
to show that he never left Italy ; and Augustine, who praises his virtue, and
invites him several times to visit Africa, would not have forgotten an act of
devotion like that."—Villemain, *Tabl. de l'Eloq. Chrét.*, p. 371. (130)
Basil., *Ep.* 70, vol. iii. p. 164. (131) Cypr., *Ep.* 60, p. 100. (132) Ambr.,
De Off., II. c. 28, § 136, vol. ii. p. 102. (133) Possidius, "Vita August.," c. 4.
§ 48 ; in *Acta SS.*, *Aug.*, vol. vi. p. 435. (134) Victor Vit., I. 8, p. 10.
(135) Socrat., *Hist. Eccl.*, VII. 21, p. 359. (136) Matt. xxv. 36, 40.
(137) "For this is the part of the first greatest commandment, to visit the
sick."—Basil., *Ep.*, 263, vol. iii. p. 405. (138) *Epist. ad Zenam et Sere-
num*, c. 17, p. 416. Commodianus, v. 1120 sq., p. 647. (139) Cypr., *De
Mortalitate*, p. 229 sq. (140) Greg. Naz., *Or.* 20, vol. i. p. 359. (141)
De Mortal., p. 233. (142) *Ep. ad Zenam et Ser.*, c. 17, p. 416. Lactant.,
Div. Instit., VI. 12, vol. i. p. 467. (143) Greg. Naz., *Or.* 16, vol. i. p. 244.
Greg. Nyss., *Or.* 1 et 2, de Pauper. Amandis, vol. ii. pp.56, 238. (144)
Commod., v. 1132, p. 647. (145) Pontius, "Vita Cypr.," § 9, in *Opp.*,
p. cxxxix. (146) Euseb., *Hist. Eccl.*, VII. 22, p. 269. (147) August.,
Tract. 97 *in Joh.*, § 4, vol. iii. P. II. p. 538. Julian., *Ep.* 49, p. 89.
(148) Πτωχοτροφεῖα, νοσοκομεῖα, ξενοῦνες, ξενοδοχεῖα. (149) Greg. Naz.,
Or. 20, vol. i. p. 359. (150) Basil., *Ep.* 94, vol. iii. p. 187. (151)
Greg. Naz. l. c. (152) L. c. (153) Sozomen, *Hist. Eccl.*, VI. 34, p.
693. (154) Basil., *Ep.* 143, vol. iii. p. 235. (155) Id., *Ep.* 142, p.
235. (156) Palladius, "Dial. de Vita Chrysost.," in *Opp.*, vol. xiii. p.
19. (157) Chrysost., *Hom.* 66 *in Matt.*, § 3, vol. vii. p. 658. (158)
" There is a house shared in common by the Church . . . and set
apart by the Church, which we call a ' hospital.'"—Chrysost., *Hom.* 45 *in
Act.*, § 3, vol. ix. p. 346. See too *Ad Stagirum*, III. 13, vol. i. p. 223. Law
of Leon and Athemius, A.D. 469 ; Corp. Jur. I. tit. 3, l. 45. (159)
Theodoret., *Hist. Eccl.*, V. 19, p. 223. (160) Pallad. *Hist. Laus.*, c. 6,
p. 24. (161) Theodoret, *Hist. Relig.*, c. 22, vol. iii. P. II. p. 1256.
(162) Baronius, *Martyrol. Rom.*, p. 267. (163) Hieron., *Ep.* 66, Ann.
397 ; *Ep.* 77, vol. i. pp. 401, 465. (164) Hieron., *Ep.* 77, p. 461.
(165) Chrysost., *Hom.* 66 *in Matt.*, § 3, vol. vii. p. 658. (166) " οἱ
κληρικοὶ τῶν πτωχείων." Council of Chalced., A.D. 451, can. 8 ; Mansi,
vol. vii. p. 361. (167) Pallad., *Hist. Laus.*, c. 1, p. 14. (168)
Παραβολανοί (from their risking, παραβάλλεσθαι, their lives), " those

appointed to tend the bodies of the sick."—Corp. Jur., I. tit. 3, 1. 18, Cod. Theod., XVI. tit. 2, l. 42, 43. (169) August., *De Civit. Dei*, I. 13, vol. vii. p. 11. (170) Min. Felix, c. 11, p. 33. (171) Euseb., *Hist. Eccl.*, V. 1, p. 165. (172) Min. Felix, c. 34, p. 130. Cf. Plin., *Hist. Nat.*, VII. 54, vol. iii. p. 218. Macrob., *Saturn.*, VII. 7, vol. ii. p. 233. (173) *Constit. Apost.*, VI. 30; VIII. 41, p. 361, 423. (174) Κοπιάται, fossarii. De VII. Ordin. Ecclesiæ, in *Opp.* Hieron., vol. v. p. 100. Cod. Theod., l. XIII. tit. 1, l. 1. (175) Tertull., *Apol.*, c. 39, p. 120. (176) " This is the last and chiefest duty of charity, the burial of strangers and the poor."—Lactant., *Div. Instit.*, VI. 12, vol. i. p. 467. (177) Julian., *Ep.* 49, p. 90. (178) ". . . ut cadaver etiam noxium sepeliet."—*De Clem.* II. 6, vol. ii. p. 40.

CHAPTER VI.

ENEMIES.

§ 1. *Personal Enemies. Criminals.*

AFTER all that we have said about love and brotherhood amongst Christians as citizens of the kingdom of God, it is almost superfluous to add anything in reference to their principles of conduct in reference to those who injured them, against whom ancient morality allowed and even commanded the exercise of the law of *talion* in its full extent. In the kingdom of God anger, premeditated offence, vengeance, ought to be unknown. How can a man who loves and respects his neighbour allow himself to feel envy and hatred towards him? In this respect, as in all others, Christianity brought a new spirit into the world, hardly dreamed of by even the wisest of the ancients. Christians were constantly exhorted to avoid the chance of irritating one another, to shun envy, presumption, and contempt, as contrary to humility and charity. If one amongst them forgot his duty and offended his brother, the offender was exhorted without delay to seek all means of being reconciled, and the injured was asked by the precepts and example of Christ to forgive and forget rather than return evil for evil. Love is perfect only when it includes enemies also, hastening to help them, and so prove that hatred is really overcome and their offence sincerely forgiven.

The Fathers desired that if any one infringed the legitimate rights of a Christian, he should rather sacrifice them than engage in a contest which always leaves bitterness behind.

For this reason the early Christians were requested to avoid lawsuits, and particularly to refrain from bringing complaints before a pagan judge, in order not to give him an excuse for doubting their love of peace.[1] They ought still more carefully to avoid personal defence in case of open attack, because it might lead to the death of the aggressor; and to kill a man, even in self-defence, is still a murder.[2] He who was guilty of such an act was excluded for seven years from the communion of the Church.[3] A reproach of excessive rigour may be brought against these principles; but this may be understood when we remember the need of making the Church a perfect contrast to the laxity of pagan morality and laws. Christians were to be distinguished from the world; their life was to be, as far as possible, a bright and continuous manifestation of boundless love, whilst surrounded by the egoism and hatred which divided ancient society. Besides, after the persecutions in the fourth century, Augustine declared that the Christian, who in defending himself against an adversary happens to kill him, must not be held guilty; the crime must be attributed to him who by his violent attack caused it to be committed.[4]

It would seem natural that the hatred of the pagans should have made the Christians look upon them as enemies with whom reconciliation was impossible. Still the chiefs and preachers in the Church taught the faithful to repress all hostile feeling. During the persecutions, in the midst of moral torture and physical suffering, they found abundant solemn opportunities of practising the supreme virtue which Christ taught them, and of which

He gave them the Divine example from the height of the cross.[5] They continued to practise it, though it drew upon them the reproach of cowardice. They knew well how much it costs to forgive persecutors who wish to force the conscience, that it is perhaps more difficult than to die for those whom we love;[6] but they knew also that it is not easy and ordinary virtues that Christ requires from His disciples. They rose with Him to that height of charity where they could pray for those who cursed them, and forgive them whilst dying beneath their blows.[7] Tertullian could rightly say, that if all men loved their friends, it was Christians alone who knew how to love their enemies;[8] and the history of all the martyrs confirms this saying.

The Fathers were convinced that this forgiving love would be more powerful to lead their adversaries to the truth than material force or logical power in controversy. Many examples showed them that charity is more triumphant than argument. They looked on their persecutors as blinded brothers, infinitely more to be pitied than themselves. They were taken before them with love in their hearts, and far from cursing them, they wished that they also might become converted and saved by Christ. The example of a gentle, humble, resigned, benevolent life seemed to them the most certain means of attaining this end.[9] Results have proved that they were not deceived in trusting to the mysterious influence of the love that Christ wakes in the heart of His disciples.

If the Christian ought personally to pardon those who attack his life or property, it is impossible that it can be overlooked by society, to which belongs the duty of protecting its members, and which has therefore the duty of punishment. Therefore the Christian wished that the influence of charity should be extended even to this department of social duty. The Fathers, with their profound respect for human life, unanimously forbid the penalty of death. They say that society has no right to take away the life of one of its members, because God alone is the Master of that life. Further, they do not believe in the justice of a punishment, which by shortening man's days, cuts off his opportunities of amendment and repentance.[10] The need felt by the judges of pronouncing the sentence of death was one of the reasons why, in early times, Christians were advised not to accept public offices.[11] The Council of Elvira, A.D. 305, excludes the magistrates, whose duties as duumvirs caused them to judge cases involving capital punishment,[12] from joining in worship during that year. When the administration of the empire became Christian, the imperial officers often hesitated to pronounce sentence of death. They told their scruples to the doctors of the Church, who agreed to grant the permission.[13] It is thus that Augustine answered Macedonius, bishop of the diocese of Africa, that it is only during this earthly life that men can improve their ways, that therefore it is not well to end this life with torture, in order that by timely correction the criminal may escape everlasting suffering.[14] In some cases this zeal was carried to excess, and gave rise to tumults, so that imperial laws were passed prohibiting violent interference with criminals led out to death.[15] Ambrose, whilst himself pleading for the condemned, desired that their pardon should be only entreated by such means as did not disturb peaceful order. Augustine himself declared that it was no sin to kill a man when it was ordered by the law, or a rightful authority.[16] In this respect the influence of the Christian spirit spread slowly: there still remained many conquests for it to make.

§ 2. *Foreigners. War.*

The kingdom of God tends to promote union amongst men by offering the same salvation to them all; therefore none can be regarded as strangers, barbarians, or natural enemies. The bad alone are excluded, and it is God who pronounces the exclusion; man, who cannot gauge the conscience, should look on all as his brothers and equals. The Christian especially ought to feel his union with all those who bear, like himself, the name of Christ. National barriers are in this respect swept away, and beyond the frontiers of his country he sees, not enemies whom he should hate and fight, but brothers to whom he must hold out his hand. "Charity," says Chrysostom, "unites Christians, notwithstanding distance; she does not inquire whence they come, but spreads her blessings to all, without distinction." From this comes the duty of hospitality offered in the name of brotherly love, which is so often commended to the Churches by the Fathers.[17]

The hospitality of the ancients was kept within narrow limits. An illustrious guest was welcomed to glorify him, and to honour the Republic; but a poor one, from whom no benefit could come, was repulsed or neglected. The house of the Christian, on the contrary, must be open, not only to distinguished people, but chiefly to poor strangers of humble rank. "The first," said Lactantius, "need nothing, the last have need of everything."[18] When the Christians wished to escape from this duty, saying that they were liable to entertain unworthy men, or that this might be done from the fund given by the Churches, they were told that it is better to entertain a bad guest than to shut out a good one, and that it is impossible for the Churches to do everything; that in any case individual charity must be exerted.[19]

This hospitality exercised by the Christian communities is a beautiful testimony to the spiritual communion of faith and love existing amongst the citizens of the kingdom of God. It is a proof of the true solidarity, founded on love, which exists between Christian society and each of its members. The Churches dedicated part of the funds from collections and oblations to the entertainment of poor strangers. We have already seen that they sent help to distant communities that were in distress. They were not less charitable to travellers destitute of resources. Clement of Rome praised the Church at Corinth for its hospitality to strangers.[20] Priests, and especially bishops, were exhorted to consider this as one of their chief duties, like Augustine and many others, whose table was simple that they might daily admit a large number of poor. They were to consider their houses as the ordinary refuge of all poor travellers. "The layman," says Jerome, "fulfils his duty in receiving as many guests as he can, but the bishop is inhuman if he does not receive them all." [21]

The monasteries were also open to travellers, who were received and often treated with a liberality which the monks refused themselves. The rigorous rules were relaxed for those who implored the hospitality of the brothers.[22] The greater number of the convents had near to them a hospice for strangers, placed under the care of the monks.[23] One of the most celebrated of these asylums was that of Mount Nitria, in Egypt. It was situated in the midst of a desert country. The stranger was allowed to remain for two or three years consecutively. During the first eight days he was left free, but if he wished to stay longer a wise rule compelled him to share the labours of the monks in the house or the fields.[24] We have before seen that such hospices were successively established near the Churches of the principal towns; they were chiefly intended for the infirm poor of the community, but they also received needy travellers. At a very early time people were found who made a trade of abusing the hospitality of the faithful and the Churches; and to remedy this abuse, which would have sacrificed the interests of the real poor in the end, the bishops gave certificates to travellers, stating their origin, and recommending them to the faithful.[25] This useful custom lasted in the Church for a long time. It became a subject of astonishment to the pagans, who tried to imitate it at a period when, to restore paganism, they adopted some of the means with which charity had inspired Christian society, but which were in reality otherwise impossible.[26]

As for the Christian there is no longer any barbarian or natural enemy, since he ought to respect the life of his equal, and never return evil for evil, it is evident that the doctors of the Church must condemn war. This question does not enter directly into the purpose of this work, which is intended to show the internal relation of civil society. We will therefore refrain from treating this subject at length, but as in this respect the principles of the Church helped to realize the new spirit brought into the world, and a civil society striving after the ideal of the kingdom of God could no longer wilfully violate the rights of people, we will give a brief summary of the opinion of the Fathers on this point.

The oldest writers of the Church, in the midst of a period of wars and troubles, tried to dissuade Christians from the profession of arms. They proved by the simplest and strongest reasoning that war is an injustice; that it is violation of the law of God, which forbids bloodshed, and of that which commands love even to the adversary.[27] Tertullian, to inspire Christians with a distaste for military glory, represents corpses as the laurels of triumph, and the tears of wives and mothers as the perfumes of victory.[28] Gibbon was wrong when he accused the Fathers of advising Christian soldiers to desert their flag.[29] Tertullian, to whom the celebrated historian particularly referred, limits himself to the demand that they shall do nothing during their time of service contrary to the Divine law, that they shall rather suffer death than consent to acts forbidden by their faith, or that they shall give up the service if that be possible for them.[30] It is true many Christians refused to carry arms, choosing degradation and death rather than a career which was condemned by their conscience. The "Acts of the Martyrs" relate several instances of this kind. Still, under the influence of circumstances, this opinion was not long in becoming modified. Even at an early time there were Christians who held a different opinion, and regarded military service as a duty towards the State. They did not shun it, provided their faith remained free. In the time of Tertullian the Roman army counted many Christians in their ranks. This ardent apologist of Christianity even glories in the fact, as showing the rapid progress of the Gospel in all classes of society.[31] Under Diocletian this progress was so great that when he decided to persecute the Church, he summoned the numerous Christian officers of his legions to choose between paganism or degradation. The greater number unhesitatingly sacrificed their rank.[32]

Although the Church allowed a man to remain a soldier when he embraced Christianity, the Christian idea as to the injustice of war never changed. The Fathers never forgot the gentle and peaceful character of the Gospel. Whilst they deplored the evils of war and begged Christian people to refrain from it, they allowed that there might be cases where it is lawful to take arms. Origen expresses himself on this subject with equal warmth and wisdom. "Jesus Christ," he said, "came to bring men peace. Beneath this Leader, filled with love, they should no more fight with one another, but should turn their swords into ploughshares and their spears into pruninghooks. They should keep their hands unsullied by bloodshed, and should fight for the emperor by prayers for his prosperity. The Republic will find their peaceful sentiments more useful than those whose hatreds stir up troubles and provoke bloody strifes."[33] Notwithstanding this, Origen admits that there are also just and necessary wars, such as those which are undertaken to repress iniquity and to defend an attacked country.[34] Chrysostom himself does not forbid the military career, but he regrets that soldiers should be more liable than other Christians to commit injustice and to be led away by passion; he begs them to keep themselves from the dangers which threaten their souls.[35]

At the time when the invasions of barbarians and the disturbances of the empire made it necessary to protect society, which was threatened on all sides, the Fathers have no longer anything but regrets for the evils which civil and foreign wars have let loose upon the world. They speak of them with deep sorrow, but how could they have plucked the arms from the hands of the combatants?[36] It was rather their duty to justify and defend, for not only was the empire threatened, but civilization and even Christian society itself. Augustine ardently desired that there should be no more war, but until that happy time when a durable peace shall be established on the basis of mutual love, he desired the Christian State to enter into no unjust war, that it should not imitate pagan

Rome, which owed its greatness to unjust conquests, but limit itself to defence against attacking foes.[37] "These defensive wars," he writes in one of his letters, "are the only just and lawful ones; it is in these alone that the soldier may be allowed to kill, when he cannot otherwise protect his city and his brethren.[38] These wars themselves can never be anything but cruel necessities, to which the good resign themselves with deep grief.[39] The glory of the Christian soldier does not consist in conquering provinces, but in repelling unjust attacks and giving the Republic peace. It may be it can only be attained through bloodshed, but he will be covered with a purer glory if he can conquer the enemy by the spiritual power of his word, and peacefully insure peace to his country." [40]

May it please God that this wish of the pious bishop shall some day be realized. At the time it was uttered the Roman empire had still some formidable struggles before it. The time was not yet come in which the sword of steel should be for ever replaced by that of the Word; but God overruled even these wars to the spread of the new spirit which must regenerate the world, and which, in a future still far away, will give it an assured peace.

Conclusion.

We shall add nothing to the picture we have just drawn of the principles and morality of the early Church. Imperfect as it is, it is still easy to recognise the difference between the spirit of antiquity and the new spirit of Jesus Christ. The natural equality of men, respect for the individual, universal and self-sacrificing love, which were all unknown to antiquity, are taught, shown in their beauty, and still better, realized in Christian society. We can repeat with Epiphanius, without fear of contradiction, that humanity and charity towards all the poor are the fruits and signs of the Church.[41] There is no longer, as in the pagan world, an egoistic state which absorbs all the powers of the citizens, and has only contempt and harshness for those who do not give it direct service; there is the kingdom of God, which is formed by the free adherence of men animated by the same sentiments, whose members are valued for their personal qualities only. One privileged class, glorying only in its strength and riches, no longer holds the rest of the world in oppressive dependence; all classes are equally honourable, for all men, both free and slave, man and woman, rich and poor, strong and weak, are equally able to tread in Christ's footsteps, and to aspire to true happiness— that of the soul.

Woman is no longer the servant of the pleasures of man or the needs of the State. Being treated with respect, she becomes the equal of man in dignity, and often surpasses him in virtue and devotion. Marriage is no longer a purely civil or political institution, it is a union of souls sanctified by religion. The child is no longer his father's chattel, of which he may dispose as he likes; he is a soul trusted to his parents that they may bring him up for the kingdom of God. The slave is no longer an inferior being, formed by nature as an instrument for his master; he is a brother, spiritually free, and intended for external freedom. The artizan is no longer a despised citizen because he is occupied with work unworthy of a freeman; the dignity of labour is vindicated, and those who give themselves to it are thought more honourable than those who lead an idle life. The poor, the infirm, the unhappy, are no longer deserted because they are useless to society, but become the objects of the most sympathetic care. The stranger, even the barbarian, is no longer a natural enemy, but a brother worthy of as much love as a fellow-countryman; and if in civil society hatred and inequality are suppressed, war between nations ought also to become impossible.

This transformation is not brought about by a sudden revolution. Christians learned to respect everything, not only true right and lawful ownership, which are the eternal groundwork of society; but they did not even rebel against injustice to which secular usage had given a legal consecration; the regeneration of the social order was only accomplished through the gentle power of charity "acting by persuasion, and with the authority of religious virtue."

When it was said in the fourth century, what none dare repeat to-day, that the doctrine of Christ is adverse to the interests of States and insufficient for the needs of society, Augustine could rightly answer, strengthening his position by an appeal to facts: "Let those who profess that the Christian religion is hostile to the Republic, give us military men, provincials, husbands, parents, sons, masters, servants, kings, judges, and administrators equal to those that Christianity has formed. Instead of resisting this doctrine, let them rather own, that if all obeyed it, it would powerfully increase the prosperity of the Republic."[42] At the same time, Ambrose, the eloquent Bishop of Milan, feeling the difference between pagan egoism and the charity of the Church, exclaims: "Let paganism show us results like those produced by the Gospel, let it count the captives ransomed with the revenues of its temples, the poor whom it has fed, the exiles whom it has helped."[43] In the East, Athanasius, carried away with holy enthusiasm, seeing in his imagination the changes that the Gospel must produce (already realized) in all the nations of the world, thus describes its condition when all are converted to Christ: "Pagan nations, filled with hatred, live in a state of permanent hostility among themselves. No one can go without danger from one country to another; men spend their whole life in arms; the sword is their only safety and defence. Jesus Christ taught us to free ourselves from these hatreds, to shun wars, to love peace and concord. The nations whose life was a perpetual conflict turn to the peaceable duties of agriculture. Hands, formerly armed, are stretched out only in prayer to God. If Christians fight still, it is only against evil passions and evil spirits with the arms of faith. Is not this a proof of the divinity of Christ, that the nations have learned from Him what they were never able to learn from the gods of paganism?" [44]

We will add that the sages themselves would not have been able to teach them the principles of the new morality, and we will close this book by repeating what we said at the beginning: God pitied men, and sent His Son to save them, by giving them a new spirit of love and faith.

(1) *Constit. Apost.*, II. 45, 46, p. 256. Athenag., *Leg.*, c. 1, 11, p. 280, 288. Cypr., *Testim. adv. Jud.*, III. 44, p. 318. (2) Cypr., *Ep.* 57, p. 95. Lactant., *Div. Instit.*, VI., 18, vol. i. p. 486. Ambr., *De Off.*, III. 4, § 27, vol. ii. p. 114. Basil., *Ep.* 199, can. 43, vol. iii. p. 296. (3) Council of Ancyra, A.D. 315, can. 22, 23; Mansi, vol. ii. p. 219. (4) *Ep.* 153, § 17, vol. ii. p. 402. (5) Tertull., *De Patientia*, c. 3, p. 141. (6) Polyc., c. 12, p. 191. Theoph., *Ad. Autol.*, III. 14, p. 389. Lactant., *Div. Instit.*, VI. 10, vol. i. p. 456. Just. Mart., *Apol.*, I. c. 57, p. 236. (7) August., *Sermo* 90, § 9, vol. v. p. 344. (8) "For we are by our doctrine commanded to love our enemies and to pray for those who persecute us, to the end that this might be our consummate virtue—peculiar to us, not shared by others. For all men love their friends, but to love their enemies is the mark of Christians alone."—*Ad Scap.*, 1, p. 69. See too Arnob., I. 31, vol. i. p. 21. (9) Just. Mart., *Apol.* 1. c. 57, p. 77. (10) Lactant., *Div. Instit.*, VI. 20, vol. i. p. 491. (11) Tertull., *De*

Idol., c. 17, p. 96. (12) Can. 56; Mansi, vol. ii. p. 14. (13) Ambr., *Ep.* 25, " ad Studium," vol. ii. p. 892. August., *Ep.* 152, " Macedonius ad Aug.," vol. ii. p. 397. (14) " There is no other opportunity beyond this life of amending the character. . . . We are therefore, by our love for the human race, constrained to interpose on behalf of criminals, lest, while they thus end this life by torture, they may, when life is ended, be unable then to end the torture."—*Ep.* 153, vol. ii. p. 398; *Ep.* 133, " ad Marcellinum," vol. ii. p. 300. (15) A.D. 392 and 395. *Cod. Theod.*, IX. tit. 40. l. 15, 16. (16) Ambr., *De Off.*, II. 21, § 102, vol. ii. p. 94. August., *Ep.* 204, vol. ii. p. 583. (17) Tertull., *De Præscript. Hæret.*, c. 20. vol. i. p. 209. Hermas II. mand. 8, p. 96. Just. Mart., *Apol.* 1, c. 67, p. 84. Clem. Alex., *Strom.*, II. 9, vol. i. p. 450. Greg. Naz., *Or.* 43, vol. i. p. 701. (18) *Div. Instit.*, VI. 12, vol. i. p. 465. (19) August., *Ep.* 38, vol. ii. p. 63. Chrysost., *Hom.* 45 *in Act.*, § 3, vol. ix. p. 341. (20) *Ep.* 1 *ad Cor.*, c. 1, p. 147. (21) Possid., *Vita August.*, c. 4, § 47, in *Act. SS. Aug.*, vol. vi. p. 435. Hieron., *Comment. in Tit.*, c. 1, vol. iii. p. 417. (22) Hieron., *Apol. in Rufinum*, III. vol. iii. p. 455. (23) Cassian., *De Instit. Cœnob.*, IV. c. 7, p. 52. (24) Pallad., *Hist. Laus.*, c. 7, p. 26. (25) Epistolæ formatæ. *Constit. Apost.*, II. 58, p. 268. Tertull., *De Præscript. Hæret.*, c. 20, p. 209, speaks of " contesseratio hospitalitatis," from which it appears that travellers were presented with tokens or tallies, called " tesseræ hospitalitatis." (26) Sozomen, *Hist. Eccl.*, V. 16, p. 618. Greg. Naz., *Or.* I. "Invect. adv. Julianum," vol. i. p. 102. (27) Tertull., *De Coronâ*, c. 11, p. 107. Lactant., *Div. Instit.*, VI. 18, vol. i. p. 491. (28) *De Cor.*, c. 12, p. 108. (29) Chap. XV. (30) *De Cor.*, c. 11, p. 107. (31) *O.c.*, c. 1, p. 100; *Apol.*, c. 37, p. 115. The traditions of the Theban and Thundering Legions likewise prove that the general opinion amongst Christians was not averse to the profession of arms. (32) Euseb., *Hist. Eccl.*, VIII. 4; X. 8, p. 295, 396. (33) *Contra Celsum*, V. 33; VIII. 73, vol. i. p. 602, 797. (34) *O.c.* IV. 82, p. 564. (35) *Hom.* 61 *in Matth.*, § 2, vol. vii. p. 613. (36) Hieron., *Ep.* 60, and 77, vol. i. p. 344, 464. (37) *Ep.* 138, § 14, vol. ii. p. 315. (38) *Ep.* 47; *Ep.* 153, § 17, vol. ii. pp. 85, 402. (39) *De Civit. Dei*, IV. 15, vol. vii. p. 78. (40) *Ep.* 229, " ad Darium comitem," A.D. 429, vol. ii. p. 634. (41) *Adv. Haer.*, III. vol. ii.; *Exposit. Fidei Cath.*, § 24, vol. i. p. 1107. (42) " Qui doctrinam Christi adversam dicunt esse Reipublicæ, dent exercitum talem qualis doctrina Christi esse milites jussit, dent tales provinciales, tales maritos, tales conjuges, tales parentes, tales judices, tales denique debitorum ipsius fisci redditores et exactores, quales esse præcipit doctrina Christiana, et audeant eam dicere adversam esse Reipublicæ, immo vero non dubitent eam confiteri magnam, si obtemperetur, salutem esse Reipublicæ."—*Ep.* 138, "ad Marcellinum," § 15, vol. ii. p. 315. (43) " Numerent quos redemerint templa captivos, quæ contulerint alimenta pauperibus, quibus exulibus vivendi subsidia ministraverint."—*Ep.* 18, "ad Valentinianum," § 16, A.D. 384, vol. ii. p. 837. (44) *De Incarnatione Verbi*, §§ 51, 52, vol. i. P 1. p. 74.

BOOK III.

TRANSFORMATION OF CIVIL SOCIETY THROUGH THE INFLUENCE OF THE CHRISTIAN SPIRIT.

CHAPTER I.

STRIFE BETWEEN THE CHRISTIAN AND PAGAN SPIRIT.

§ 1. *General Character of Christian Influence on Pagan Society.*

In our second book we tried to show how charity, in its different applications to the social conditions and relations of civil life, was taught and realized in the Church. Alongside of the Church pagan society still existed, with its own morality, laws, and vices, which may be briefly summed up in one phrase, its egoistical spirit. Christian society, which at first was small in number, increased in the midst of the surrounding paganism. Its members were forbidden to mix in the disgraceful or barbarous ceremonies of polytheism, but that did not hinder their intercourse with pagans in the daily business of life. When Christianity, which had spread throughout the empire, was finally carried to the throne of the Cæsars, pagan society, reduced in number and shorn of its strength, still lingered on in the midst of the christianised world. The two spheres touched and crossed in a thousand ways. Christians, after the triumph of the Church, became corrupted through their contact with heathen morality. Pagan society, whilst it still retained any power of government, yielded to the influence of Christian thought and morality. It is this influence that we must now trace. We own it to be the most difficult and delicate part of our work, for it is not the visible and complete influence which was directly exerted on those pagans who were converted to the gospel; but a secret one, which affected even those who remained attached to the ancient worship. It is particularly important to show the slow and progressive alteration of the spirit which regulated all civil relations.

This influence has been denied, as it has also been exaggerated. We believe it to have been very real, and more efficacious than is thought by many who do not absolutely deny it. From the earliest Christian times enlightened pagans, philosophers, emperors, jurisconsults, held ideas which were absolutely opposed to ancient egoism. They gave utterance to principles equally contrary to the harsh pride and patriotic exclusiveness of former citizens. These principles and ideas must, in our opinion, have resulted from the vivifying power of the new dogma of charity which was thrown like a fruitful seed on the furrows of the world. Doubtless this influence was restricted and difficult to define. Men, unknowingly, and in spite of themselves, submitted to it in a greater or less degree. Those who followed it showed singular contrasts in their life and thoughts; there was a struggle between the old and new morality, in which each side had in turn victory and defeat. Men persecuted Christians whilst accepting some of their doctrines; they spoke in language worthy of a disciple of the Saviour, whilst remaining themselves idolatrous or unbelieving. But though hidden and incomplete, this influence was also efficacious and unmistakable. At the time of all great changes in the history of the world, new ideas float in the atmosphere. One receives them without knowing how. They affect even those who intend to resist them, until at last they leaven and transform the whole of society.

§ 2. *Obstacles to Christian Influence.*

From the first this influence encountered powerful obstacles; it is because they were so great that some have refused to believe that the ideas of Christian charity had any influence whatever on the philosophers and lawgivers of paganism. The chief of these obstacles, the one at the root of all the others, is the natural egoism of the human heart; this was the principle of ancient morality and society, and had led to the universal corruption, whose most striking features have been traced previously. Christianity, which desired to subdue "the old man" and to replace self-love with humility and devotion, was necessarily repugnant to many pagans, as it is repugnant to-day to the man who will make no sacrifice. This repugnance shows itself under different forms, according to the condition of the men who feel it, and thus increases the obstacles to the influence of the Gospel. The religion of Christ, whilst endeavouring to substitute the justice of the kingdom of God for the iniquities of the pagan State, raised both national egoism and ancient Roman legislation in arms against it. We must look at these obstacles to measure their greatness, and so appreciate the greatness of the triumph of Christian charity which overcame them at their source. We shall see the blind hostility of the populace ally itself with philosophic prejudices and the politics of enlightened men, as also with the intolerance of the laws, to raise a barrier against the rising and resistless wave.

The people, accustomed to the superstitions of idolatry, were incapable of rising to the idea of an invisible God; they confounded religion with the observances of external worship, and looked on Christians as enemies of the gods, atheists, irreligious and impious men.[1] "They worship," they say, "only a man born of wretched parents, in a suspected union;[2] this Jesus, who had for His followers only people of low rank, and who called the ignorant and criminals to join Him, could have neither worth nor power." In Carthage a picture was exhibited representing a man with the head of an ass and a foot shaped like a wooden shoe, bearing the inscription, "*The God of the Christians.*"[3] Because of their distaste for public affairs, they were called incapable, unfit for anything.[4] Because they were compelled to meet in secrecy, they were pursued with horrible calumnies, that they were a race which fled from the light,[5] that they killed their children in order to feed on human flesh, and that they had all the women of their sect in common.[6] Public calamities, epidemics, dearths, droughts, inundations, were all laid to their charge, and appeals were addressed to the people to vindicate the outraged honour of their gods.[7] The credulous crowd, always eager for a pretext to hate those who are better than itself, passed from calumny to persecution, and sacrificed to its fanaticism Christians who never offered any resistance. Raillery was joined to violence, and they ridiculed the oppressed condition of the victims: "How can their God, who allows them to suffer, be a powerful or just God? What can be the use of a religion which exposes its followers to torture instead of saving them from evil?" Like the Jews, who expected a political Messiah, the Romans mocked at a God who did not insure fortune and glory to His followers.[8]

If we can understand these vulgar sentiments in the crowd, we still expect that enlightened men, taught in the philosophic schools, or having gained wisdom by experience, should be more accessible to a spiritual religion, which claims man for God. Their meditations on themselves or on the condition of the world should have roused needs and doubts in them which the Gospel only could satisfy. Doubtless from the earliest times there were some amongst these men who saw a Divine light in Christianity, and approached it that they might be filled with its brightness, as the consolations offered by Christ had drawn many suffering souls to Him from amongst the poor and miserable people. But the mass of enlightened men long followed the lead of the crowd, they held strange prejudices against Christians and Christianity which were so many obstacles to its influence. We do not refer only to frivolous minds who repeated the odious or absurd charges of the multitude without examination: such as the rhetorician Cornelius Fronto, the tutor of Marcus Aurelius,[9] or the Epicurean Cresceno, who was as avaricious as he was debauched,[10] and who both, to please the people,[11] reproached the Christians with impiety, with atheism, with the orgies of Thyades, and with incest. We have seen men of grave appearance in whom we have found the same absence of depth, and even the same pride. Proud of their philosophical knowledge, they despised the Christians as uncultivated people, without intelligence and hostile to letters.[12] Their religion they regarded as a pernicious superstition,[13] deserving disdain from the Romans because it had a foreign origin and barbarous doctrine.[14] The firmness with which the Christians remained unshaken in their faith in their doctrines was considered as the fanaticism of misguided minds, at which the sage might smile or feel a little pity for the victims.[15] Besides, this faith was held by so many people of low estate! Christian society was recruited from amongst the classes so unworthy of the attention of a philosopher! The poor, the simple, workmen, slaves, and women are received and welcomed! How can these people speculate on Divine things? They, who understand nothing of the business of civil life, to take upon themselves to speak of matters which should be reserved for sages! [16] Pagan pride is indignant at these pretentions, without caring to ask from whence the Christians gain their faculty of discussing these important questions, or even what these questions are. There was great astonishment for a little while when men known to be wise and virtuous embraced this mad religion, which attracted so many people of inferior rank, so many ancient sinners, so many women who were formerly frivolous; but it passed away without any one attaching special importance to these facts.[17]

The Epicurean Celsus was the chief representative of the pagan pride which rejected Christianity because it was offered to the poor, the weak, and the sinful. Celsus, and the pagans in general, understood nothing of Christian humility, which humbles itself to find true dignity of soul, nor of the love which embraces men of all nations as equally brothers in the Kingdom of God.[18] Lucian ridiculed the Christians, not only for their belief in eternal life, but especially because their lawgiver persuaded them to love one another as if they were brothers.[19] Above all, how could they love the slaves, those men of inferior nature for whom the gods had no care?[20] The equality of slaves and the duty of loving them was a mere shocking doctrine to the pagan; it reversed the order of nature, and exposed those who carried it out to great contempt.[21] The Romans, surprised and jealous at the sight of the union of these despised men in the midst of a world filled with trouble and discord, reproached them as conspirators and accused them of hating the human race.[22] The philosophers, when they could no longer refuse to recognise the virtues of Christians, asserted that these principles had been known for ages. Celsus professed that Plato had rebuked the love of riches and the desire for vengeance more emphatically than Jesus Christ.[23] The later Neoplatonists also taught that Christ learned from Plato, and that His doctrine in its purity, before it had been altered by His fanatical followers, was similar to their own.[24] At other times these feeble defenders of paganism ridiculed the too eager controversies of the Christians about dogmas, which appeared to them to be only barren speculations, unworthy of enlightened men.[25]

On the other hand, the distaste of Christians to fill public offices in the pagan State, their refusal to sacrifice before the statues of the emperors, the radical difference between their principles and Roman laws and morality, were in the eyes of political men causes of grave accusation. As a result of the narrow ancient patriotism which repelled everything which diverged from national customs, they were reproved as public enemies, rebels against the emperors, laws, and morality.[26] Much indignation was expressed at the freedom with which they spoke of the corruption and decay of the Empire.[27] Instead of seeing in polytheism and ancient egoism the true cause of the fall of Roman society, the blame was thrown upon the Christians, whose doctrines and way of life were said to be the cause of all troubles.[28] They were persecuted under this pretext, and monuments were erected to those emperors who were the most severe against these destroyers of the Republic.[29] When the ruin of ancient society was accomplished, the last defenders of national paganism still obstinately looked upon the desertion of the ancient gods and the progress of the Church as the real cause.[30] The reproach was true in this sense, that practically the

Roman world was bound to fall with polytheism, and that disappeared before the Cross.

The Emperor Julian was up to this time stronger in his reproaches and accusations than any other. Notwithstanding his Christian education, notwithstanding his cultivated mind enlightened by philosophy, notwithstanding even his evangelical reminiscences, of which we will speak afterwards, this great nephew of Constantine concentrated in himself all the prejudices and hatreds of pagan pride against Christianity, and especially against the precepts of humility and universal love. With inconceivable frivolity he made the most contradictory reproaches against Christians: he calls them impious and enemies of the gods [31] at the same time that he ridicules them for being so foolish as to consider faith to be supreme wisdom; he looks on faith as folly, as an absence of reason that he cannot at all understand.[32] He attacked the humble origin of Christianity; Jesus Christ was not an illustrious personage, and He did no great thing, for what is it to have cured some lame or blind beggars? Where is there a distinguished man who was converted to this religion in its early times, whose followers are pleased to number amongst them slaves or women?[33] Still Julian attributed the overthrow of the ancient order of things to this contemptible folly.[34] He reproached the Christians with their doctrine of the natural equality of men. In his opinion they caused deplorable confusion amongst all classes. A religion which was suitable to innkeepers, publicans, and actors, was necessarily ignoble,[35] and yet he could not be ignorant that amongst his contemporaries were orators like Basil the Great and Gregory of Nazianzus, men illustrious in the Church, by whom emperors like Constantine had begged to be received. He professed lastly, that Christianity had no power to make men better,[36] and later on we see him hold up the austere and charitable life of Christians as a model to be followed by the priests of paganism. Such are the inconsistencies of a great mind, which wore itself out in vain efforts " to kick against the pricks."

The despotism of the ancient State, which was closely allied with pagan worship, was an obstacle not less powerful than popular fanaticism and the prejudices of politicans and philosophers. At the first glance it would have appeared that the freedom with which the Romans admitted the various forms of worship of the conquered nations, would have been extended to Christianity, and that the tolerance which gave Isis and Mithras a place by the side of Jupiter, would be extended also to the God of the Christians. But the representatives of pagan society vaguely felt the profound difference between this God and the divinities of polytheism. They understood that He would not take a place by the side of Jupiter, but that He would conquer him, and the new principles taught by His disciples were not to be reconciled with the essentials of the life of antiquity.

In Greece and Rome, where the political point of view predominated over everything else, religions were national, and consequently exclusive; worship was the business of the State, and laws about religion were included in civil legislation. We know how the Greek Republics punished those who dared to deviate from official beliefs, and with what precautions the philosophers expressed their opinions on these subjects. In Rome Cicero, who in this respect expressed the mind of the people, laid down the principle that no one should be allowed to worship special, unknown, or foreign divinities, at least until they had been publicly recognised.[37] At the time when the Romans began to ridicule their gods, and incredulity spread widely in all classes of society, statesmen were alarmed at this loosening of what they called the bridle of popular passions, and were compelled to maintain and defend national worship. They admitted for themselves physical theology, which, in their opinion, was true for philosophers; they wished to banish poetic theology, which was in itself false, and at the most only fit for the theatre. They asked for political religion and civil theology for the people; that is to say, the primitive national rites.[38] They even named penal legislation amongst the means of keeping up this religion.[39]

In remembering the exclusive character of ancient polytheism, we can understand that other forms of worship must have been forbidden in Rome; this was the law of the Republic and of the early time of the Empire. New divinities were only received in virtue of decrees of the senate; but, in the general disorder, this rule was no longer observed; superstitions of every kind were introduced into Rome without the law being put in force against them. Christianity, at its origin, was one of these new religions that were not to be permitted; Christians formed an illicit faction, to whom the right of legal existence was refused.[40] They were reproached as having revolted against Judaism, which was placed in the rank of ancient national religions.[41] Their refusal to join in ceremonies, their distaste for fêtes and spectacles, their dislike to hold public office, made them suspected of conspiring against the laws; it was one more reason for accusing them of being enemies of the people.[42] Cyprian, amongst others, was condemned to death as an enemy of the laws and gods of Rome. At a later time, when Christianity had conquered the empire, it was still in the name of national religion and the worship of their fathers that several distinguished men tried to raise paganism from its fall. Ancient pride strove against Christian faith and charity to the end; it never ceased sowing difficulties in the path of the Gospel which would have stopped its progress, if it had been only the work of man. But all these obstacles together, the hatred of the people, and ridicule of philosophers, the prejudices of statesmen, the hostility of the laws, did not prevent it from influencing many, even of those who resisted it; for it was not a vain invention of man, it was the work of God.

(1) Just. Mart., *Apol.*, 1, c. 6, p. 47; also *Apol.*, 2, c. 3, p. 90. Athenag., *Leg.*, c. 4, p. 282. Arnob., III, 28, vol. i., p. 125. (2) Arnob. I., 37, vol. i. p. 24. Orig., *C. Cels.*, I, 28, p. 346. (3) " Deus Christianorum Onokoites." The God of the Christians laid in the ass's manger.—Tertull., *Apol.*, c. 16, p. 62. Min. Felix, c. 8, p. 28. There has been discovered a carved stone, representing an ass reared on its hind legs and dressed in a toga, delivering a discourse to two women, one seated and the other standing. Holstenius very plausibly conjectures that it is a representation of the Onokoites.—See *Epistolæ ad Diversos*, ed. Boissonade, Par. 1817, p. 173. (4) Tertull., *Apol.*, c. 42, p. 133. (5) Min. Felix, c. 8, p. 26. (6) Athenag., *Leg.*, c. 3, p. 282. Tertull., *Apol.*, c. 2 and 7, pp. 9, 29. Min. Felix, c. 9 & 30; pp. 27, 113. Orig., *C. Cels.*, VI, c. 40, p. 662. Euseb., *Hist. Eccl.*, V. 1, p. 156. (7) Tertull., *Apol.*, c. 40, p. 126. Cypr., *Ad Demetr.*, p. 216. Orig., *In Matth. Comment.*, § 39, vol. iii. p. 857. Arnob., I. 1, 3, vol. i., pp. 3, 5. (8) The Christians of Vienna and Lyons to the Christians in Asia; Euseb. *Hist. Eccl.*, V. 1, p. 165. Min. Felix, c. 12, p. 36. (9) Tatian, *Or. c. Græcos*, c. 25, p. 265. Min. Felix, c. 9, 31, pp. 30, 118. (10) Tatian, c. 19, p. 260. (11) Just. Mart., *Apol.*, 2, c. 3, p. 90. (12) Arnob., I. 28; II. 34; vol. i. pp. 18, 73. Libanius, *Or.* 25, vol. i. p. 591. (13) Tacit., *Ann.*, XV. 44, vol. ii. p. 241. Sueton., *Nero*, c. 16, p. 265. (14) "Βάρβαρον δόγμα."—Orig., *C. Cels.*, I. 2, p. 320. (15) Epict., *Dissert.*, IV, 7. vol. i. p. 618. M. Aur., c. 34, § 51, p. 246. Galenus, *De Differentiis Pulsuum*, II. 4; in *Opp.*, ed. Ren. Charterii, Paris, 1679, fol., vol. viii. p. 43. (16) Min. Felix, c. 5, 8, 12, pp. 12, 26, 39. (17) Tertull., *Apol.*, c. 3, p. 14. (18) Orig., *C. Cels.*, III. 59; VIII. 72, pp. 486, 795. " Humilitas quæ displicet paganis, unde nobis insultant."— August., *Enarr. in Ps.* xciii. § 15, vol. iv. p. 759. (19) *De Morte Peregrini*, vol. ii. p. 567. (20) Macrob., *Saturn.*, I. 11, vol. i. p. 244. (21) Orig., *C. Cels.*, III. 44, p. 475. (22) Tacit., *Ann.*, XV. 44, vol. ii. p. 241. Min. Felix, c. 31, p. 121. Tertull., *Apol.*, c. 39, p. 125. Orig. *C. Cels.*, I. 1; VIII. 17, pp. 320, 755. (23) Orig., *C. Cels.*, VI. 1, 16; VII. 61, pp. 629, 641, 738. (24) August., *De Civit. Dei*, XIX., 23, vol. vii. p. 428; *De Consensu Evangel.*, I. 28, § 11, vol. iii. P. II. p. 5; *De Doctr. Christ.*, II. 28, § 43, vol. iii. P. I. p. 28; *Ep.* 31, § 8, vol. ii. p. 44.

(25) Euseb., *Vita Const.* II. 61, p. 472. Greg. Naz., *Or.* 1, vol. i. p. 34.
(26) Tertull., *Apol.*, c. 2, 35, pp. 12, 108; *Ad Nationes*, I. 17, p. 51.
Lactant., *De Morte Persecut.*, c. 14, vol. ii. p. 200. (27) ". . . to whom the present age, with its excessive licence, is always hateful."— *Flav. Vop., Saturn.; in Script. Hist. Aug.*, vol. ii. p. 233. (28) Orig., *C. Cels.*, III. 15, vol. i. p. 456. (29) Inscription in honour of Diocletian : "having extirpated the name of the Christians, who had ruined the State." Quoted by Havercamp, note *f.* to chap. 2 of Tertull. *Apol.*, p. 12. (30) August., *Sermo* 81, § 9 ; 296, § 7, vol. v. pp. 306, 837; *De Civit. Dei*, II. 2, vol vii. p. 27. (31) *Ep.* 6, p. 9. (32) Greg. Naz., *Or. Invect.* 1 *in Jul.*, vol. i. p. 97. Julian., *Ep.* 7, 31, pp. 10, 52. (33) Cyr. Alex., *Contra Jul.*, VI. vol. vi. P. I. p. 191, 206. (34) "Διὰ γὰρ τὴν Γαλιλαίων μωρίαν, ὀλίγου δεῖν, ἅπαντα ἀνετράπη. . . ."—*Ep.* 7, p. 10. (35) Cyr. Alex., *Contra Jul.*, VII, l. c., p. 238. (36) L. c. (37) Cicer., *De Leg.*, II., 8, vol. xi. p. 371. (38) Varro, quoted by Tertull., *Ad Nat.*, II. c. 1 sq. p. 54; and by August., *De Civ. Dei*, VI. 5, vol. vii. p. 116. See too Plut.. *Amatorius*, c. 18, and *De Placitis Philos.*, I. 6, vol. xii. pp. 44, 365. (39) Dio Chrysost., *Or.* 12, "De Dei Cognitione," vol. i. p. 370. (40) "Factio illicita." "Non licet esse vos."— Min. Fel., c. 8, p. 26. Tertull., *Apol.*, c. 4, 38, pp. 18. 117. (41) Orig., *C. Cels.*, III. 7, p. 451. (42) Min. Felix, c. 12, p. 37.

CHAPTER II.

THE CHANNELS OF CHRISTIAN INFLUENCE.

§ 1. *Apologies and Sermons.*

BECAUSE the Gospel was Divine, Christians did not attack opposing obstacles with earthly arms; hatred was not returned by violence. They fought only with the spiritual powers of love and faith, knowing that through them they would conquer the world. In times of persecution they submitted to the established order, and extended their charity to the pagans, their persecutors.

We have seen in our second book the position of the kingdom of God with respect to earthly society, and the way in which the Church, which endeavoured to realise this kingdom, practised, in this respect, the teachings of her Founder. The Gospel taught its followers (who had been brought up in very various social positions) to submit to human authorities and the laws they laid down, because faith and love are possible in all conditions and beneath all governments. It was thus that, though called enemies of the human race, the earliest Christians remained amidst the society which despised or hated them. They proclaimed to the emperors that Jesus Christ wished them neither to employ force nor to flee from it, but so to act, with gentleness and patience, as to awaken the desire of amendment in the pagans, and thus lead them to the faith.[1] It is true that, strong in the truth of their doctrine, they did not fear to remind their adversaries of the rights of conscience, and to demand liberty in the name of natural justice and divinity itself, which can only desire willing adoration.[2] Although this liberty was long denied to them, they did not revolt and claim their natural right with arms in their hands. If they refused to submit to laws contrary to their conscience, they did not forcibly resist, but limited themselves to a public statement of their slighted principles, either by their sermons or by the noble and suitable apologies addressed to emperors or philosophers, or by the example of their life, and the firmness with which they bore death.

It will be suitable to say a few words about the apologies, as it appears to us that they exerted considerable influence, and that to them must be attributed the secret effect produced by the principles of charity upon several representatives of paganism. We do not intend to give a detailed analysis—it will be enough to characterise the spirit, choosing those aspects which refer to our special subject. We shall be struck with the unshaken confidence with which the apologists, formerly pagans, defend Christianity; they call in most frequently the effects produced by the Gospel on individuals, and on social relationships. Nothing could show more completely how pagan pride is changed, by faith in Christ, to humble and devoted love.

The principal apologies belong to the second century, notably to the time of the Antonines. Those offered to Adrian by Quadratus and Aristides are no longer in existence.[3] The earliest in date of those remaining is that of Justin, whom the Church has called Justin Martyr, on account of the death by which he honoured Christ. Justin, dissatisfied with paganism, finally found in Christianity the truth he had vainly sought in the philosophic schools.[4] He dedicated himself to it with an ardour never felt by any philosopher for his personal system. Unhappy at seeing the Christians oppressed under emperors so renowned for justice as Antoninus Pius and Marcus Aurelius, he addressed two successive apologies to them,[5] which must be mentioned amongst the finest works of ancient Christian literature. He asked the emperors not to condemn the Christians unheard, that is, not to refuse them the protection granted by law to all accused; he appealed to their equity and love of wisdom, convinced that princes who sought after piety and philosophy would do nothing contrary to reason. With the quiet and respectful courage which is given by faith, he says: "Facts ought to prove that you are what you are said to be—pious and wise, guardians of right, and friends of science; examine, then, our doctrines and life." If they persisted in their hostility notwithstanding this examination, he adds: "You may kill us, but you cannot harm us." He clears the Christians from the reproach of atheism by declaring their belief in God manifested in Christ, and in the immortality of the soul. Appealing to the vague wants and presentiments of the pagans, he showed that Christianity alone had had true prophesies, and that the idea of a Son of God has nothing which ought to be repugnant to the mind of man. It was easy for him to prove how little the divinities of Olympus deserved respect, because the most enlightened of the pagans were themselves asking that these immodest worships and immoral fables should be given up, whilst the God of the Christians had all the qualities which make Him worthy of adoration. If then the emperors permit the pagans freely to invoke these beings, of whom nothing but vice is recorded, why should they punish the Christians who worship a pure and holy God? "You, who are philosophers, if you know that idols made by the hand of man are vain, why do you condemn us for refusing them, that we may rise to the true God, who is the invisible and infinite Spirit?" Justin also represents Christianity as the fulfilment of what Socrates and Plato had foreshadowed, and as the perfection of the morality taught by the Stoics. "If then they recognised these germs of truth in the sages, why should they treat us so cruelly who possess this truth in its completeness and perfection?" It does not enter into our plan to follow the argument of Justin Martyr in this respect; but we must see how he set forth the softening influence of charity on the lives of Christians, in order to get the emperors to treat them more justly. "The Christians," he said, "do not desire an earthly throne. They do not wish for dominion, for they desire the kingdom of God. Only pure souls, who flee from sin and practise love, can enter this spiritual society, where no one is asked if he is a philosopher, but women, workmen, and the illiterate are admitted. For this reason Christians would be the best helpers of the emperors for public peace. Those who, before their conversion, sought only fleshly indulgences, now lead pure and upright lives; those who had no higher aim than the possession of riches, give their fortune to the common fund for the relief of the poor; those who hated each other, because they had neither the same country nor the same laws, are bound together in love, and instead of returning to their enemies evil for evil, they pray for them, and try, by persuasion, to lead them to the faith. Full of love and respect for man, they condemn the barbarous customs of paganism, such as the exposure of children—placing them in peril of death, prostitution, or slavery. They are patient; they bear injuries without anger, and show their willingness to help every one. They have already exerted a happy influence on many souls, through their self-devotion. The sight of their gentleness and charity has changed many violent and tyrannical men. They submit to the established government, and willingly pay the tribute. It is true they worship one God only, but they obey the emperor, and acknowledge him as their earthly head, praying to God for his preservation and power, as well as for the wisdom necessary to rule aright. However, they are ready to suffer for their faith, without fearing either death or torture." Justin adds to his first apology a sketch of the religious services of the Christians, where all was simple and pure, and where the spiritual brotherhood, symbolised in the *agapæ*, was shown by the voluntary offerings that each one brought for the poor, the sick, widows, orphans, and strangers—indeed, for all those unhappy ones who would have been neglected by pagan society.

The Apology of Athenagoras is also addressed to Marcus Aurelius. This eloquent defender of Christianity appeals, like Justin, to the justice of the emperor, whose moderation and humanity he praises. "The different nations," he says, "which compose the empire, filled with admiration for your goodness, live according to their own laws, and the whole world, through your wisdom, enjoys profound peace. We alone, although we do no evil, are persecuted, pursued, killed, only because we bear the name of Christians." Let the emperor inquire then into the faith of these men, that he may judge if they deserve such treatment. As no Christian has yet been convicted of a real crime, and there are only vague and imaginary reports about them, it is unworthy of a prince who loves justice to listen to these calumnies and to condemn the Christians unheard. Athenagoras asks nothing for them but common justice, which they deserve both for their doctrine and their life. He then sums up their beliefs and moral precepts. He recalled the teaching of the philosophers, principally Plato and the Stoics, who had some purer ideas, analogous to Christian ones. He brings forward the opinion of the pagans themselves as to the vanity and immorality of the gods and their worship. He refutes the calumnies against Christians, by contrasting their chastity with the disgraceful licentiousness of the followers of paganism, their brotherly love with the hatred which divided the world, their respect for the human soul and their charitable pity with the bloody spectacles of the gladiators and the custom of killing or exposing newborn children. Full of confidence in the justice of the "philosophic emperor," and quoting the teaching of Christ to love one's enemies and pray for one's persecutors, he exclaims in the course of his Apology, "Amongst those who resolve syllogisms and seek the origin of words, who explain homonymes and synonymes, who teach which is the subject and which the attribute, and who, in such discourse, profess to make the happiness of their hearers, where, amongst them all, are those who lead a life so pure and holy that they not only refrain from hating their enemies, but that they love and bless and pray for them? Their wisdom is only in their words, their life does not confirm it. Amongst the Christians, on the other hand, you will find the most simple people, workmen and women, who cannot put our doctrine into words and discourse about it, but who at least prove it by their conduct. They do not declaim, but they offer facts. They do not strike those that strike them. They do not follow the ravisher. They give to those who ask of them. They love their neighbour as themselves." This remarkable work closes with a prayer addressed to the emperor, to look kindly on the Christians, who pray to God to uphold the power and extent of his empire: "Grant us peaceful lives, in order that we may the more joyfully obey and serve you."

At the same time Tatian wrote his "Discourses to the Greeks." Tatian visited many countries, studied their laws and worship, sought wisdom in Athens and Rome, and found error, superstition, and immorality everywhere. He then opened the books of the Christians and recognised the truth in "this barbarous philosophy."[6] More impetuous than Justin Martyr, often obscure and diffuse in his language, he energetically blames the morality and ideas of his contemporaries. He proves without difficulty the uselessness of an immodest mythology and a contradictory philosophy, and he contrasts with these the purity, moral severity, and elevation of the Christian dogmas. He showed the difference between the gentle charity of the disciples of Christ and the pagan harshness which delighted in the sights of the arena. When professed philosophers assailed the disciples of the Gospel with odious calumnies, he referred to the scandals of their own lives and the unworthy fables in which the gods were the disgraceful actors. When they ridiculed Christian women because they were occupied with Divine things, he asked if the transactions of the sages of antiquity with the *hetæræ* were more honourable. The doctrine of these sages, lastly, could only be known by a small number of rich and unoccupied disciples, whilst no one is excluded from the kingdom of God on account of external position, because faith and love are possible to all men.

Theophilus, a contemporary of Tatian, is still more impetuous in his attacks on paganism and philosophy. He vigorously defends the Christian doctrines of monotheism and the immortality of the soul from the objections of the pagan Autolycus; like the other apologists, he insists on the immorality and deception of the divinities of polytheism. A special character is given to his work by the numerous extracts from ancient authors which are introduced to prove how uncertain and contradictory are the philosophers, how absurd and scandalous the poets, when they speak of the gods. He is not contented simply to refute the calumnious reports about Christian morality, he directly attacks pagan morality as a source of corruption. "You accuse us of having introduced community of women, but it is Plato, the greatest of your philosophers, who teaches it; whilst we condemn it, at least as severely as you. You say that we eat human flesh, but it is in the history of your gods that we must seek examples of this crime; whilst we have so great a respect for human life that we do not even frequent the combats of your gladiators, that we may not become accomplices in bloodshed. You say that we love only men of our own faith, but we have learned to love our enemies. You call us rebels, but we obey the laws. We pray for the emperors and give them the honour which is their due, but we worship God alone." Theophilus is weakest when, by arguments and calculations, he wishes to prove, to those who reproach Christianity with its novelty, that it is as ancient as the world. This part of his apology is foreign to our subject.

The authors of whom we have spoken wrote in Greek; there exists an apology in Latin, written certainly at about the same time, that is during the reign of Marcus Aurelius. It is a dialogue between the Christian Octavius and the pagan Cecilius, written by Minucius Felix.[7] It is a short but clever and well written refutation of the popular charges against Christianity. Minucius is astonished that educated and moderate men can place any faith in these reports, which are contradicted by the purity of life and belief of the Christians; he returns the reproach of atheism and immorality on the Roman world itself, whose egoistic harshness and immoral mythology he depicts with startling truth. Cecilius, conquered by the arguments of Octavius, adopts Christianity. It matters little if the two interlocutors were imaginary persons, or whether Minucius Felix attached his apology to a real fact. The most interesting thing about the dialogue is that it shows us how much and how rightly the Christians relied, for the conversion of the pagans, on the sight of the moral effects produced by faith in Christ.

We have also another apology, in the Greek language, belonging probably to the same period and marked by the purest sentiments. It bears the name of "The Epistle to Diognetus"; the author is unknown. He first shows the vanity of idol worship, and then tries to arouse Diognetus to embrace the Gospel by showing him an animated picture of Christian life. Christians are not distinguished from other men by their country, their language, or their political institutions. They do not inhabit separate cities; they do not speak another language; they lead the kind of life which is suitable for them. Some live in Greek cities, some in foreign ones. In their dress and food they follow the custom of their countrymen, and yet they show us an extraordinary and almost incredible life. They remain in their country, but only as travellers; in civil life they share everything as citizens, and bear everything as if they were not. In each far-off land they find a country, and each earthly country is to them like a foreign land. They are married like other men, but they do not expose their children.

They have a common table but not a common bed. They are in the flesh, but they do not live after the flesh; they are in the world, but their inheritance is in heaven. They observe established laws, and surpass the laws by their life. They love all men, although every one persecutes them. They are misjudged, condemned, and killed, but they rise again to life. They are poor, yet they enrich many; they have nothing, yet they abound in all. Men cover them with shame, and through the shame they attain glory. Their reputation is assailed, yet men are forced to bear witness to their justice. They are followed with maledictions and injuries, and return only respect and kind words. They do good and are punished as malefactors. They rejoice in the midst of tortures, because through them they will attain life. Jews and Greeks persecute them, yet none of their enemies can say why he hates them. To sum up, what the soul is to the body, Christians are to the world. Further on, to show the connection between love to God and love to man, the author adds, " When thou shalt begin to love God, thou wilt wish to imitate His goodness. Do not be astonished to hear that a man can imitate God; certainly, with the help of God, he can. His happiness does not consist in ruling his equals, in gaining a higher rank and having power to use violence towards the weak; this is not imitating God, for it is not in this that His greatness consists. He who imitates Him takes on himself his neighbour's burden, and if he is superior to anyone, thinks of it only as a reason to do good to his inferior. Lastly, by dividing with the poor the gifts that God has given him, he becomes in a partial way their providence. It is thus that thou wilt recognise that it is God who governs the world, thou wilt understand His mysteries; thou wilt love and admire those who are punished because they will not deny Him; thou wilt condemn error and imposture, and thou wilt no longer fear death." The author closes with this thought, which expresses the whole difference between Christianity and paganism: "True wisdom cannot exist without charity; it is the life that must bear witness to the truth of professed beliefs."

After the reign of Marcus Aurelius,[8] the defence of Christianity was resumed, under Septimus Severus, by Tertullian. The apology of this father is one of the most eloquent and vigorous pleas in favour of the new religion, which for a century and a half had striven against the errors and sins of men. Tertullian addressed it to the governors of provinces, after a persecution which was doubtless ordered by them only.[9] In language full of warmth and life, he exposes the iniquity of that way of treating Christians which condemns them only for their name, and refuses, what is otherwise granted to the most suspected, the proof of guilt. He also asks for them only common justice, ready to accept their condemnation if they are found guilty. Their faith and charity make them incapable of the crimes of which they are accused, and of which their most infuriated enemies have never been able to convict them; these accusations only prove that people know nothing about them. This ignorance makes the persecutions doubly odious; for what can be more unjust than to condemn any one without knowing why? Tertullian, like his predecessors, contrasts the pure life of the Christians, their respect for human life, their care for their family, their high idea of the holiness of marriage, with the scandal of pagan rites, human sacrifices, the bloody games of the arena, their adulteries, and the exposure and death of children. When they are reproached for holding an unlawful religion, because the

ancient laws forbid the worship of any other god than
those of Rome, he answers, not only that there is little
justice in these laws, but also that the most impartial
emperors never carried them out; also that the Romans
have no right to reprove the Christians for renouncing
their national divinities, because they themselves have
deserted them for a multitude of strange gods, and no
longer believing in the religion of their ancestors, have
lost their ancient virtues, and given themselves, both men
and women, to every vice. Tertullian enters into long
and curious details about the immorality of the pagan
myths, and about the origin and not very divine conduct
of the gods. The ancient greatness of Rome must not
be attributed to these powerless idols; they are only
demons, seeking to divide and ruin men; their worship
is utterly false, egoistic, corrupt, they are despised and
left to the contempt of the crowd even by the pagans
themselves; whilst notwithstanding the ridicule of their
adversaries, the true God and His Son are alone worthy
of worship.

Thus Tertullian returns the double charge of superstition and impiety on the Romans themselves, adding
that if they did not wish to renounce their worship, they
ought at least to give that liberty to Christians which
was accorded to the most licentious pagan religions, and
to the most contradictory and immoral systems of philosophers. To those who accused Christians of being a
faction and enemies of the emperors and of the Romans,
he answers, like Justin Martyr, that they recognise the
emperor as their earthly chief, that they pray for him
although they will not worship him, that they obey him
although he refuses them justice, that their conduct pro-
motes the peace of the empire more than that of their
persecutors. To complete his apology, he explains the

discipline, morality, and worship of the Church. He insists above all on the love of Christians for each other, because to the jealous hatred of their enemies this love itself was a subject of reproach. " See how they love one another," they say, "as if they were ready to die the one for the other." " Yes," he says, " we love one another; we are brothers, for we have a common Father, and the same Spirit has led us from darkness to light. We are also your brothers, because, although you are our persecutors, you are men like us. We support one another, we have everything in common except our wives; each one freely brings his offering to relieve the poor, the sick, orphans, widows, travellers, and prisoners. We are not incapable of the business of life, for do we not live with you, sharing your habits and necessities? We do not retire into forests; we do not flee from life, we use everything with thanksgiving; we sail with you; we mix with you in the Forum, in camps, in commerce; we offer our arts and industries to your use; we refrain only from your spectacles, sacrifices, disorders, and crimes. The extirpation of Christianity would be the greatest harm that could befall the empire, for it is only Christians whose virtues are not due to fear of man, but respect for Divine majesty." Tertullian makes some reflections on the liberty granted to philosophers, and on the credulity of the pagans who are ready to believe everything except Christianity. He then refers to the irony of their adversaries who say the Christians should not complain of persecutions which enable them to practise their much talked-of virtues of patience and pardon. "Yes," he says, in closing, " we are patient and we choose to suffer. It is true we should be sufficiently numerous to defend and revenge ourselves by force, but we have learned differently; our way of fighting is to triumph through yielding. It is as conquered that we shall overcome the world. The blood of our martyrs is the seed of the Church."[10]

We shall say nothing of the apology for Christianity with which Origen answered a book by Celsus, for this great and learned work is a defence of dogmatic truth against the objections of an unrefined philosophy: it is only in a few passages that Origen, following his adversary step by step, is led to say anything on practical questions, particularly as to the equality amongst all classes of society in the Church. The beautiful apologetic work of Lactantius, the seven books of Arnobius against the Gentiles, as well as "The City of God," by Augustine, are outside our plan, for they belong to a time when the Church, deeply rooted in Roman ground, exerted an influence too powerful to be denied. We must stop with the apologies of the second century, because then the Church was still oppressed, and in the midst of this oppression they were an efficacious means of spreading the influence of Christianity.

The first apologists were not content with the exposition of dogmas in defence of the new religion; they added eloquent pictures of Christian life as opposed to the morality of paganism. They had felt themselves that the doctrine of Christ is not only a new doctrine for the intellect, but a new principle of life. Thinking minds, who grieved over a corrupt world, when they saw virtues introduced which antiquity had hardly dreamed of when they saw simple and ignorant men surpass the disciples of sages in morality, when they saw vice resisted with an energy greater than that of Socrates or the Stoics, were necessarily struck with the contrast between Christian morality and that of mythology or philosophy.

It is impossible to doubt that the apologies of Justin

Martyr, Athenagoras, and Tertullian were read with sympathetic curiosity. It is certain that the sentiments of humanity expressed by these Fathers, and their appeals to the justice of straightforward minds, found an echo in more than one soul, which yielded to the influence of charity, even whilst still resisting faith. The same influence was also exerted by the preachers of the Church. More than one pagan, led by doubt or chance to the secret meetings of the first believers, must have been touched by the grave and simple lessons that fell from the mouth of the ministers who explained the Scriptures and spoke with emotion of the love of the Saviour and the supreme law of charity. If he was not converted to this persecuted religion, he at least reflected on the difference between the life of these oppressed ones and that of their oppressors, and he perhaps became more just and more gentle.

At a later time, when Chrysostom, Gregory, and Ambrose spoke eloquently in large churches, the pagan, who was accustomed to yield to the power of oratory, went along with the Christians to the public preaching; most frequently he only felt the esthetic pleasure inspired by art, and blended his applause with that with which the faithful drowned the voice of their orators. But we may still believe that whilst hearing of universal brotherhood, of the duty of helping the poor, of the respect due to all sorts and conditions of men, of the holiness and happiness of Christian marriage, he would retain a secret impression of the moral and social doctrines of the Gospel. The Church quickly recognised the power of this peaceful propaganda; the fourth Council of Carthage forbade the bishops to hinder the pagans from attending sermons in the churches.[11] For the same reason which excluded the apologies after the triumph of Christianity from our subject, we cannot enter into details about the influence of these great orators of the Church; it was exerted at a time when the authorities no longer opposed the propagation of Christian ideas.

§ 2. *Christian Example.*

The influence of the social doctrines of Christianity was the more powerful because the preachers and apologists in their pictures of an evangelical life were not describing an ideal state. The manners of Christian society were, especially in the earliest times, conformed to the picture which they drew. Here we may appeal to the testimony of the pagans themselves. The conduct of Christians excited the most diverse feelings in the world. Some felt a secret jealousy which added to the vigour of their hatred; others, with cold, harsh minds, incapable of understanding the spiritual emotions of the soul, made them the subject of frivolous raillery. Others again, more seriously disposed, were astonished that men with so little philosophy could attain such difficult virtues; it was this which opened their souls to the love of Christ and which turned them to Him.[12] It is not of these that we speak here; we will only bring as witnesses those who, whilst remaining pagans, recognised in the Christians a love, of which till then the world had seen no example.[13]

We have quoted already the pagan words preserved by Tertullian, "See how they love one another, they are willing to die for each other!" "The eagerness of these men," said the satiric Lucian,[14] "when one of them falls into misfortune is incredible; they spare nothing to bring him aid."[15] About the same time the celebrated physician, Galen, expresses in a writing about Plato, of which only this passage is preserved, the surprise which he felt at the life led by the disciples of Christ. "Most men," he says, "are incapable of following a logical demonstration of truth, and need to be taught by parables; it is thus that those whom we call Christians have drawn their faith from the parables of their Master. However, they sometimes act like those who follow true philosophy. We are witnesses that they despise death, and with a sentiment of modesty have a horror of carnal pleasures. There are amongst them both men and women who abstain from the conjugal union throughout their life. There are also some who in their ardent efforts to rule their souls and to live justly have reached a point where they yield in nothing to the true philosophers." [16]

The sight of pious, austere Christian women superintending the education of their sons caused the pagans to exclaim, like Libanus speaking of the mother of Chrysostom, "See what women are found amongst Christians!" [17] The Emperor Julian reproached them with using their moral purity and charity as means of propaganda. In his hatred of Christianity he looked upon it as a hypocritical deception of men; he accused the senators of Antioch and their wives, who gave large alms to the poor without distinction of worship, of spreading atheism, [18] and thus himself undeniably established the influence of Christian love. Justin had already appealed to this experience when he declared that in his time the moral character of many pagans had become changed through their intercourse with the members of the kingdom of God.[19]

The example of the death of Christians was not less powerful than that of their life; it was the supreme testimony with which they opposed their persecutors, and was

Y

consequently a great means of propagation and influence. Ready to submit to everything that was not contrary to their faith, they refused obedience only when called upon to deny Christ; but instead of violent resistance, their only protest was a quiet acceptance of death. They did not go to their tortures reviling their judges, like fanatics filled with false enthusiasm, but tranquil and resigned. In accordance with their principles of charity, they pardoned their enemies and prayed for them. We will give only one example. In the time of the Emperor Maximinus, a Christian of Palestine, named Paul, was condemned to death. Before receiving the fatal blow he prayed with a loud voice, in the presence of the judge and the people, that it might please God to give Christians a peaceful life, to bring pagans to faith and salvation, to pardon the judge who sentenced him to death, as well as the executioner who would kill him. The historian adds that all who were present burst into tears, and the dead Paul was proclaimed innocent by the crowd.[20]

It is true that many people were unable to understand this constancy of the martyrs. The Christians seemed to them to be mad. What can be more absurd, they say, than to prefer death to an act so trifling as that of throwing a little incense upon an altar.[21] Still the sight of a courage which tired the executioners, and of a love which forgave them, made a deep impression on many souls. Many pagans became Christians only after seeing the death of the martyrs. Justin said that was the chief thing that led him to Christianity.[22] Tertullian could say, "Our number increases every time that you cut us down; the blood of Christians is the seed of the Church;"[23] and Ambrose, "Our dead are the conquerors, our persecutors are the conquered."[24] The

Fathers are doubly right, for the death of the martyrs influenced even those whom it did not convert. Men not entirely hardened were compelled to ask where the Christians gained strength to give up their life, and what was even more contrary to the pagan spirit, the power to sacrifice their resentment against their persecutors. Without going the length of seeking themselves this strength in faith, they were compelled to respect those who rendered such glorious witness to it, and to submit instinctively to the force of their example.

§ 3. *The Charity of Christians towards Pagans.*

The Christians opposed pagan hatred with the charity which they practised in their view in different social relations. Their law was to love all men. In every intelligent being they saw a brother worthy of esteem and kindness. Neither religious nor national differences could be reasons for antipathy or exclusion. Their love included even their enemies, seeking reconciliation by forgiveness and kindness. Faithful to these principles, the early Christians treated the pagans with charity in whatever relationship they found themselves towards them. Those who in society filled despised and inferior positions, only found in their Christian freedom a reason for greater gentleness towards their pagan superiors. Through the mysterious but irresistible effect of this love they frequently led them to juster feelings, if not to faith.

We must mention first the influence exerted by women.[25] The Church recommended the Christian wife of a pagan husband to exercise gentleness, patience, peaceableness, that he might not be led through her to blaspheme God by slandering Christianity.[26] Often she was ill-treated, even sent away on account of her faith; a pagan husband has even himself given his wife up to judgment.[27] However, there were also cases where the humility and goodness of the wife softened the husband's feelings, strengthened the marriage tie, and brought peace to the family. Sometimes this influence was exerted by a mother on her son, by a daughter on her father. We have several examples in the highest positions of Roman society. Quintilius Marcellus, consul with Alexander Severus, and pro-consul of Africa, raised a monument to his Christian wife which bears witness to his love for herself, his respect for her virtues and faith. Though himself a pagan, he used only Christian expressions in the funeral inscription, and avoided with great delicacy any formulary that could recall paganism.[28] Julia Mamæa, the mother of the emperor of whom we have spoken, appears to have been favourable to the religion of Christ. Eusebius calls her a very pious woman. She sent for Origen to Antioch, that she might discourse with him about divine things.[29] It is therefore probable that she led Alexander Severus to his kinder treatment of the Christians.

According to Lactantius, Prisca, the wife of Diocletian, and his daughter Valeria, were Christians.[30] It is perhaps to them that must be attributed the tolerance shown by this emperor at the beginning of his reign; when many zealous Christians were to be found amongst the officers of his palace and his army.[31] After he had ordered the persecution, one of his magistrates in Thrace, Bassus, continued gentle in his dealings with the accused, because his wife shared their faith.[32] It may also be that the Christian sentiments of Constantine should be referred to the influence of his mother, Helena; as we do not know the time of the conversion of this princess, we may be allowed to believe that she was already a

Christian during Constantine's youth. Through woman, Christianity, with its gentle power, entered even the houses of the high priests of paganism. In the time of Julian there were pagan priests whose whole families, including their servants, were Christians.[33] In the early part of the fifth century, the children and grandchildren of the pontiff Albinus, at Rome, all professed Christianity. Jerome hoped that Læta, the pious and charitable daughter of this minister of a dying faith, would finally lead him also to the Gospel.[34]

From the time when Christianity had followers in the highest ranks of society, Christian sentiments were spread in the imperial palaces themselves by the officers of the court. The Emperor Constantius Chlorus surrounded himself with Christians because he reckoned more certainly on their fidelity than on that of the pagan guard.[35] In order to test them thoroughly, he ordered that the Christian officers, magistrates, and judges must choose between a return to paganism and destitution. The greater number preferred the latter, whereupon he reinstated them in their dignities, and sent away the others, saying that those who would betray their God for earthly interest are so much the more likely to betray man.[36] Amongst these faithful officers was that Lucian of whom we have before spoken. The sight of his life led several of his colleagues to Christianity and helped to make it respected by the emperor.[37]

Through Christian slaves softer feelings were awakened. Their resignation, their fidelity, their love for their pagan owners, produced a similar effect on them to that of the believing wife on the idolatrous husband. Though often the Christian slave was driven away by his master, it happened, not less often, that he yielded to the power of his servant's conduct. Christian slaves, spiritually free, bearing their pitiful state unmurmuringly, eagerly desired to gain the same salvation for other souls, and used their position to spread the teaching and virtues of the Gospel in the large houses where they followed their avocations of work or teaching. They told the women and children of Christianity and the happiness it brings, and begged them not to learn the lessons of their preceptors when they taught paganism or set the example of an immoral life. They were quiet in the presence of the masters who despised the Gospel, but secretly they spoke of the duty of a wife to be chaste, modest, and gentle, of that of the children to obey the law of God from their earliest years. By thus helping to introduce purer and gentler manners in the household, they rendered better service to their master than the slaves of his own belief.[38] This power of the Christian slave was sometimes felt even in the household of the emperor. Caracalla, the son of Septimus Severus, had a Christian nurse.[39] There were men, distinguished in the Church for their knowledge and eloquence, who were converted through slaves; we may mention Asterius, Bishop of Amasea, who was taught Christianity by a Scythian slave belonging to an inhabitant of Antioch.

The most striking contrast between pagan and Christian life is shown in the treatment of the poor and miserable by the followers of the two religions. If the pagans were astonished at Christian charity towards those of their own communion, their surprise must have been greater when they saw them extend the same love to people for whom pagan society felt only contempt, and who had frequently themselves treated Christians with fanatical hatred. When poor strangers arrived at places inhabited by Christians, they were received and treated as brothers, without inquiry as to their religion.

Pachomius, who in his youth served under Constantine against Maxentius, came one day to a town where he was astonished to see the inhabitants bring food to the troops weakened by famine. He learned that they were people of a special religion, and were called Christians. Curious to understand a doctrine which inspired them with so much humanity, he studied it, and that was the beginning of his conversion.[40] The children of poor pagans were taught without payment in the Christian schools; in that of Edessa Bishop Rabelas himself instructed them in the truths of the Gospel. When the alms of the Church were distributed, it was not Christians alone who were helped, but pagans also had a large share both of the gifts of private persons and the general alms of the Churches. We have before mentioned the Persian prisoners who were ransomed by a bishop, who sold the vases of the Church to enable him to do this.

Charity towards pagans showed itself particularly during illness, which was so much dreaded in the ancient world. Christian authors of the early ages state that many pagans were converted after they had suffered from mental maladies accompanied by physical weakness, which seem to have been very usual in this period of universal unrest. They were attributed to the influence of evil spirits. Magicians and their amulets were employed to cure them, but their formulæ and talismans were less powerful than the distress in the soul. If then the patients met with Christians who told them of the miraculous cures of Christ, the vanity of idols, the impostures of poets, and directed them to the Saviour who died for men, their troubled spirits found peace in Him. These cures of illnesses for which paganism had no remedy, surprised the pagans and were quoted by the apologists as powerful proofs in favour of Christianity.[41]

The conduct of the Christians in the great epidemics and frequent wars of the third century also glorified Christianity. When, in the plague of Carthage, 250 A.D., the pagans quitted the town and deserted their sick, the Christians tended them as carefully as those of their own communion.[42] During a famine which desolated Armenia under Maximinus the Christians helped the poor without any religious distinction; so that many pagans, seeing that the Christians alone proved their pity by their acts, "made inquiries about a religion whose disciples are capable of such disinterested devotion."[43] The Emperor Julian, the restorer of paganism, mentions the influence of Christian charity towards the pagan poor. "These impious Galileans," he says bitterly, "not only feed their own poor, but ours also; welcoming them to their *agapæ*, they attract them, as children are attracted, with cakes."[44]

Under the Christian emperors this charity towards the pagan poor seems to have cooled. Isolated voices began to proclaim it needful that the Church should, in her turn, attack her former persecutors.[45] There were popular risings against paganism, its temples and followers, who were condemned and harshly treated. But these errors were not in conformity with the precepts of the Gospel; the love of ancient times still found eloquent interpreters in the most pious and celebrated doctors of the Church. Hilary of Poictiers, addressing the Emperor Constantius, who persecuted at once both pagans and Christians, exclaims: "What have you gained by the spoliation of temples, the confiscation of goods, and the exaction of penalties you charge on God?"[46] Elsewhere the same bishop complains of the unhappiness of his time when an attempt is made to protect the Church of Christ by the help of ambition and power. "The apostles were helped only by their faith and God's power, and they have conquered the world, whilst the Church frightens men with exile, prison, and death; drives away the priests and wishes to impose faith by force."[47] Athanasius, who has been called the Father of orthodoxy, expresses the same sentiments. Those who use violence and constrain men have little true piety. The Saviour limits Himself to say, "Whoever *will* follow Me, let him follow Me." He compels no one; He knocks at the door, and only enters when it is opened. Truth is only spread by persuasion, but fear of the emperor is not persuasion; to strike terror into the adversary by punishments is not to convert him."[48] Chrysostom also asks that those who do not belong to the Church shall be treated kindly, that their errors shall be borne without anger, that they may be led to the faith through the wonderful power of charity. If harshness is persisted in, his loving soul foresees with terror that an irreconcilable war will commence in the world.[49] Without the protestations of the Fathers we might have thought that the spirit of the Church was altogether altered, but the sentiments of these true representatives of Christianity prove to us, that if there were persecutions, they must be charged on men who confounded earthly interests with heavenly ones. Charity always was, and still is, the supreme law of the kingdom of God.

§ 4. *The Part of Stoicism in the Influence of Charity.*

The diffusion of the spirit of gentleness and humanity which we have spoken of in this chapter, or in other words, the influence of charity in pagan society, found an early ally in Stoicism, which prepared the ground for the Gospel. Some have tried to attribute everything to philosophy, as others have endeavoured to refer everything to Christianity. We must guard against both extremes, and assign to each system its own share. We merely observe that a larger part must be given to Christian influence than has been allowed by many who have taken up the history of this period.

This Stoicism had been received in Rome with more favour than other philosophic systems. The Roman genius, which was more practical than speculative, had been attracted by its moral aspect. The men who had not yielded to corruption, had all followed this lofty and generous doctrine. Roman pride was perfectly suited by a system which taught it to rise superior to external accidents, boldly to face misfortunes, and to avoid all that might disturb the sage's most precious treasure— calm of the soul. But this system, like those of Plato and Aristotle, had no true moral principle. The Stoic could refrain from doing evil, but he had not learned to do well. He ruled himself sufficiently not to be guilty of violence towards his equal, but he did not know how to sacrifice himself for him. As has been said, he had only negative virtues.[50] For if it is necessary to avoid all that can disturb the soul, it is necessary also to avoid feelings of affection, pity, and sympathy; if one must never show weakness, it is not possible to pardon an offence, for in the opinion of antiquity pardon and forgetfulness of injuries were signs of pusillanimity. The maxim of the founder of the sect was, No forgiveness, no alms.[51] Stoicism thus misunderstood human nature, and by denying the rights of the emotions made its disciples indifferent to the fate of the poor, the oppressed, the unhappy, the slaves. It did nothing for such, but say to them, "Despise external accidents, rise by thought above your condition." Christianity, which speaks in a similar manner, goes one step further, a step which was impossible to Stoicism. It commands those who are less poor and unhappy to hold out to their brothers a helping hand and assist them through love. The advice given by Stoicism was a mockery; it could only be generally followed by those whose position allowed them to withdraw themselves from the miseries of life. If there were exceptions, they only confirm the rule. A society of Stoics would be impossible, for this philosophy has no bond of union for souls. Love was unknown to it, and like all the social systems of antiquity, it only produced a passing union of egoistical and unsympathetic men.

This system then could never become the regenerating principle of the world. It could not transform either society or the individual. Not teaching its disciples humanity for themselves, or love and respect for other men, it had the same moral sterility as the other ancient philosophical doctrines. Many people were Stoics in theory, but allowed themselves every vice in practice. They censured in others the debauchery and degradation to which, in secret or public, they yielded themselves. They appeared to make great efforts which ended in nothing. They resembled, as Plutarch says, those children who jump into the air only to fall back helplessly on their feet.[52] Stoicism had come to be merely a mask to hide the deep corruption of morality. Whilst Juvenal satirized these hypocritical philosophers, an author of the same time freely owned the powerlessness of the superb system they affected to hold. Convinced that the regeneration of man required more than the efforts of a proud will, he rallied the Stoics on the moral miracles they attributed to their doctrines, which, according to them would transform wild beasts into heroes and gods.[53]

However, we would not ignore the services that Stoicism, practised by earnest men, has rendered to the propagation and power of the Gospel. It awoke the human conscience and made it more sensitive to the new light. It contributed, if not to the progress of Christianity, at least to the activity of Christian ideas, by the austerity of its maxims, by its principles as to the need of rising above outward things, and meeting misfortune and misery with a calm, strong soul, by its idea of inward freedom, which it kept alive in the midst of oppression and despotism. There was a gleam of spirituality, a tendency to reinstate human personality, a foreshadowing of the individual worth of the soul, and of that justice which ought to be the basis of social relations. We do not hesitate to say that Stoicism tended to promote the reception of the charitable and humane teaching of Christianity. The ancient Christian apologists themselves recognised this. Justin Martyr especially appreciated the excellence of the moral doctrines of this philosophy.[54] This praise appears to refer to a modified form of Stoicism, rather than to the system of Zeno and his first followers, for the system did not always remain the same. All the historians notice the difference between primitive Stoicism and that of the first and second centuries after Christ. From the time of Seneca, or to refer to what interests us more, from the time when St. Paul was in Rome, this system assumed its purest and most beautiful form.[55] Men recognised in it, as we shall see circumstantially developed, sentiments unknown to ancient Stoic virtue—pity, sacrifice, almost humility.

Whence comes this progress, this amelioration of ideas and feelings? Is it a result of the natural growth of Stoicism, this benevolence and humanity, this sympathy for misery, these efforts to attain respect for the *individual*, and to apply natural justice to social questions? Are all these innovations that we see in the laws and in the systems of moralists the logical consequence of pure Stoicism? "It would be," said M. Troplong, " to do violence to all probabilities to attribute these principles, so new to the Stoical philosophy, to its elaboration or natural growth towards maturity."[56] We explain this progress by an influence to which men yielded unknowingly and in spite of themselves. We sometimes find in barren, rocky ground, charming flowers, strangers to such soil, inhabitants of a milder climate. We ask with surprise whence they come, and find that a breeze from their native land has wafted the seed from thence. It is thus that kinder feelings germinate amidst pagan harshness.

The philosophy and national pride of many educated Romans was opposed to an impartial examination of a doctrine preached and practised by unknown men belonging to the despised classes. However, Christian principles, especially moral ideas, spread insensibly; there is something in the heart of man that cannot resist a love ready for any sacrifice. The philosophers, whilst yielding to the influence of the new ideas, doubtless believed that they were only realizing the results of Stoicism; they were under the power of a mysterious impulse, without accounting to themselves whence it had come. When the germ of charity had entered their souls, it developed without their knowledge, and produced fruits unknown to antiquity. As a writer, whose words we are glad to recall says, "The harsh and corrupt pagan world was insensibly converted to humanity before it was converted to religion."[57]

We shall trace this Christian influence, first in the amelioration of ideas and feelings in the philosophers of paganism, and then in the corresponding alteration of its laws. We shall be astonished to see the despised classes looked at from another point of view than that of the ancient and true representatives of pagan civilization. We shall see a spirit unknown to the ancient State, and which must destroy its foundation, shown in the laws of civil society.

(1) Cf. Just. Mart., *Apol.* 1, c. 16, p. 53. (2) "Take heed, therefore, lest ye add this thing also to the indictment of irreligion, by withholding freedom of conscience, and forbidding to choose one's God, so that I may not worship whom I would, but am forced to worship one whom I would not. No one—not even a man—will desire to be worshipped by an unwilling subject."—Tertull., *Apologet.*, c. 24, p. 87. "It is part of man's right and innate capacity, that each one should worship what he deems proper: and no one is either harmed or advantaged by his neighbour's religion. Nor is it the part of religion to make religion compulsory, seeing that one ought to embrace it of one's own free will, and not perforce."—Id., *Ad Scapulam*, c. 2, p. 69. (3) Euseb., *Hist. Eccl.*, IV. 3, p. 116. Hieron., *Catal.*, c. 19, 20, p. 84. Quadratus' apology was yet extant at the beginning of the seventh century.—Photius, *Cod.* 162. (4) *Dial. cum Treyph.*, c. 2, p. 102. (5) The first is addressed to Antoninus Pius, A.D. 138 or 139; the second, and shorter, was written under Marcus Aurelius, between A.D. 161 and 166. As it is not here our object to make an analysis, we think we can combine in a single summary the ideas in both apologies which are connected with our subject. (6) "Βάρβαρος φιλοσοφία," c. 28, 29, 35, pp. 267, 272. (7) Since Min. Felix is mentioned after Tertullian in Jerome's *Catal. Ill. Vir.*, it has been thought that he was later in point of date; but several reasons, as, for instance, the mention of Fronto as of a man still alive, incline us to the opinion of those who put this work down to the reign of Marcus Aurelius. (8) The apologies addressed to Marcus Aurelius by Melito, Bishop of Sardis, and by Claudius Apollinaris, Bishop of Hieropolis, are lost.— Euseb., *Hist. Eccl.*, IV. 36, pp. 147, 149 sq. Hieron., *Catal. Ill. Vir.*, c. 24, 26, pp. 93, 96. The apology of Miltiades, of the same date, is likewise lost.—Euseb., *Hist. Eccl.*, V. 17, p. 183. Hieron., c. 39, p. 113. (9) Apologeticus, in the year 198 A.D. As to the date, see Mosheim, "De Ætate Apologetici Tertulliani," in his *Dissert.*, vol. i. p. 1 sq. (10) Pretty nearly the same ideas are again brought out in the two books, *Ad Nationes*, which appear to be a later revised edition of the *Apologeticus*. In the second book he refutes especially Varro, with his three sorts of religion. The apology to Scapula, Governor of Africa, likewise treats some of the same subjects; above all, that Christians ought not to be condemned without being heard, that nobody ought to be forced to embrace a religion, that Christians are obedient and faithful citizens. (11) Council of Carthage, 4, can. 84; Mansi, vol. iii. p. 958. (12) *Or. ad Græcos*, ascribed to Just. Mart., c. 1 sq., p. 1. (13) *Epist. ad Diogn.*, c. 1, p. 233. (14) *Apolog.*, c. 39, p. 121. (15) *De Morte Peregr.*, vol. ii. p. 567. (16) *De Sententiis Politiæ Platonicæ*, preserved

CHAP. II.] THE CHANNELS OF CHRISTIAN INFLUENCE. 335

by Abulfeda, *Hist. Anteiolamica*, ed Fleischer, Leip. 1831, qto, p. 109.
(17) Chrysost., *Ad Viduam Juniorem*, c. 2, vol. i. p. 340. (18) Misophognn.
in *Opp.*, p. 98. (19) *Apol.* 1, c. 16, p. 53. (20) Euseb., *De Martyr,
Palest.*, c. 8, p. 332. (21) Lactant., *Div. Instit.*, V. 19, vol. i. p. 410.
(22) *Apol.* 2, c. 12, p. 96. (23) *Apol.*, c. 50, p. 161. Lactant, *Div.
Instit.*, V. 13, vol. i. p. 394. (24) "By the death of the martyrs, our
religion has been preserved, our faith built up, our Church strengthened;
our dead are the conquerors, our persecutors are the conquered."—*De
Excessu Fratrio sui Satyri*, II. § 45, vol. ii. p. 1145. (25) Cf. Münter,
Die Christen in heidnischen Hausen, Copenhagen, 1828. (26) *Constit.
Apost.*, I. 10, p. 212. (27) Tertull., *Apolog.*, c. 3, p. 15. Cypr., *Ep.*
18, p. 27. Euseb., *Hist. Eccl.*, l. 4, c. 17, p. 137. (28) "Pescennia
Quotvultdeus | H.M.F. bonis natalibus | nata matronaliter | nupta uxcr
casta | mater pia . . . Marcellus | Procos. . . . sed et filio et |
filiabus nostris me vi | vo memoriam feci | omnibus esse perennem."
Pescennia Quotvultdeus | , daughter of , of noble rank, | born in lawful wedlock | , in marriage a chaste wife | and a dutiful mother. . . .
I, Marcellus | Proconsul . . . both for our son | and daughters,
whilst still living | have caused their memory | to endure for all ages."
This inscription was found not far from Carthage.—Morcelli, *Africa
Christiana*, Breccia, 1817, qto, vol. ii. p. 91. The name of Quotvultdeus
is a Christian name. Note, too, the absence of the formula, "Dis
manibus." (29) "Γυνὴ θεοσεβεστάτη."—Euseb., *Hist. Eccl.*, VI. 21,
p. 223. Later writers call her a Christian. Oros., VII. 18, p. 508. (30)
De Morte Persecut., c. 15, vol. ii. p. 201. According to the *Martyrol.
Rom.*, p. 345, Serena, the wife of Diocletian, was held in veneration at
Rome, but the historians make no mention of her. (31) Euseb., *Hist.
Eccl.*, VIII. 1, p. 392. (32) Ruinart, *Acta Mart.*, p. 414. (33) Sozomen., *Hist. Eccl.*, V. 16, p. 618. (34) Hieron., *Ep.* 107, ann. 403, vol.
i. p. 677. (35) Theonas, *Ep. ad Lucianum*; in the *Bibl. PP. Gallandii*,
vol. iv. p. 69. (36) Euseb., *Vita Const.*, I. 16, p. 415. (37) Theonas,
l.c. (38) Orig., *C. Cels.*, III. 55 sq., vol. i. p. 484. (39) Tertull., *Ad
Scap.*, c. 4, p. 71. (40) Ribadeneira, *Flos Sanctorum*, Col. 1700, fol.,
vol. i. p. 181. (41) Just. Mart., *Apol.* 2, c. 6, p. 93. Iren., *Contra
Hær.*, II. 32, p. 166. Tertull., *Ad Scap.*, c. 2, p. 69. Orig., *C. Cels.*,
III. 24, vol. i. p. 461; he says these states of the soul are fits of mental
distraction, "ἐκστάσεις καὶ μανίαι." (42) Pontius, *Vita Cypr.*, § 9; in
Opp., p. cxxxix. (43) Euseb., *Hist. Eccl.*, IX., c. 8, p. 357. (44)
Ep. 49, p. 90; *Fragm. Orat.*, in Opp., p. 557. (45) From Firmicus
Maternus, in his work, *De Errore Profan. Religionum*, dedicated to Constantius, between 340 and 350 A.D. He wishes the emperors to take
their models from the Old Testament, and quotes especially Deut. xiii.
6-10, to prove that paganism ought to be punished as a "facinus" or
public crime. It is known that in 353 A.D., Constantius decreed that
all those who took part in the sacrifices should suffer the punishment
of death. (46) "Auro Reipublicæ sanctum Dei oneras, et vel detracta
templis vel publicata edictis, vel exacta pœnis, Deo ingeris."—*Contra
Constantium*, c. 10, p. 1245. (47) *Contra Auxentium Mediol.*, c. 3,
4, p. 1264. Elsewhere he says: "God teaches men to know Himself,
but does not compel them."—*Ad Constantium Aug.*, I. 6, p. 1221. (48)
Hist. Arianorum ad Monachos, § 67, vol. i. P. 1, p. 303. (49) *Hom.* 29
in *Mat.*, § 3, vol. vii. p. 346: "Οὐ γὰρ δεῖ ἀναιρεῖν αἱρετικὸν ἐπεὶ πόλεμος

ἄσπονδος εἰς τὴν οἰκουμένην ἔμελλεν εἰσάγεσθαι."—*Hom.* 46 *in Mat.*, § 1, p. 482.   (50) M. Filon, "Mémoire sur l'état moral et rel. de la soc. rom." (*Mém de l'Acad. des Sciences Mor. et Rob.*, vol. i., *Savants Étrangers*, p. 814.)   (51) "Ἐλεήμονάς τε μὴ εἶναι, συγγνώμην τε ἔχειν μηδένι."—Diog. Laert., t. vii., c. i., no. 64, vol. ii. p. 785.   (52) *Adversus Stoicos, de Communibus Notionibus*, c. 23, vol. xiv. p. 32; see also the first chapters of this work, and some chapters of *De Stoicorum Repugnantiis*, vol. xiii. p. 337 sq.   (53) *Fragm. de Absurdis Stoicorum Opinionibus*, ascribed to Plutarch, c. 4, vol. xiii. p. 406.   (54) "And those of the Stoic school, when they grow into dutiful citizens by the light of their moral law through the seed of the word, inborn in every race of men."—*Apol.* 2, c. 8, p. 94.   (55) M. Troplong, *De l'Infl. du Christ. sur le droit Civil des Romains*, p. 54. M. Villemain, as above, p. 274.   (56) M. Troplong, p. 83. M. Villemain, p. 274.   (57) M. Villemain, p. 277.

CHAPTER III.

INCREASING HUMANITY IN PAGAN PHILOSOPHERS.

§ 1. *Seneca.*

THE first Roman philosopher in whom we notice elements foreign to ancient wisdom and morality, is Seneca. Few people have contested the reality of these elements, but they have attributed them to various origins. Before deciding, let us try to unite them, and to show the essential points of the humane and benevolent system of this celebrated moralist, without omitting the traits that cast a partial shadow.

Seneca, like the Stoics and ancient philosophers in general, began his meditations on man and his destiny by seeking to discover in what happiness, supreme good, consists. To live happily is to live in conformity with our reasonable nature, gifted as we are with a soul nobler than the body it inhabits.[1] This nature demands that the soul shall rise above earthly accidents, that it shall resist passion and strong feeling in order to remain unshaken in all changes of fortune. To learn how to gain this calm is virtue, to possess it is happiness, the "happy life."[2] Virtue seeks then what is good. Now nothing is good but the right.[3] And the right is what is in accordance with reason and the higher nature of man. We learn this by experience and comparison. What may be used for evil is not in itself a good. Such is wealth, rank, bodily strength. Good, then, is in the soul. We may say that virtue itself is good, for there is no difference between earnestly seeking happiness through virtue, and feeling happy.[4]

We shall see further on that this is not the negative and egoistic virtue of ancient Stoicism, but one that is active and disinterested. Before proving this, let us remark another difference between Seneca and the earlier Stoics. They taught that virtue, supreme good, happiness, the aim of life, may be completely attained, provided man follows his nature; a task which did not seem to them impossible. Seneca thought also that this aim was not in its nature above the powers of man; but he knew that no one attained it, because of the "folly" common to all.[5] He has even what may be called a feeling of sin; he knows that no one is sufficiently pure to be absolved by his own judgment; and that if he calls himself innocent, his conscience quickly reproves him.[6] It follows from this that he does not set up too high a standard for mankind; he does not ask the impossible. Man may progress towards blessedness as far as the weakness and failure of his nature permit, but no virtue can attain perfection.[7] It will perhaps be said that when he sees that his efforts to be virtuous have not succeeded, he seeks in this idea for a ready consolation. However, that proves also that his stoical pride is shaken, and that he sees in the heart of man itself an obstacle which prevents the happiness for which it hopes. We easily see how this will dispose him to leniency. He consequently feels also that to inspire a man to persevere in virtue needs another motive than praise of the power of the will; otherwise, why does he appeal so often to the law of God, to Providence, to the divine in man? It is through respect and gratitude to God, who loves good men as a father loves his children,[8] that we should seek to please Him. Seneca believes in a divine, ever active Providence, from which nothing, not even the inmost thoughts, are hidden.[9] If any *doubt* the reality of such a Providence on account of the ills which afflict both the indifferently good and the wicked, he reminds them that what happens to the good cannot be an evil in itself; that God who loves them cannot make them unhappy; that their sufferings are trials to test them, like the chastisements with which a father corrects his sons.[10]

His idea of God, it is true, is still very vague; he recognises the deplorable influence of paganism, and the falsity of the immoral and powerless gods.[11] He even acknowledges that the god of the Stoic is insufficient, "because," he says, "he has neither heart nor head";[12] that is to say, he is a cold abstraction, destitute of the intelligence and goodness that make life. He speaks oftener of God than of the gods. He feels that God is near us, in us; that He need not be sought in temples amongst the idols, that He does not desire ceremonies which lead men into superstition; that pure worship consists in belief in Him, and following His example in well doing.[13] But on the nature of God he remained tossed about between different opinions. If his hopes are still confused, if he has not the sure faith of the Christian, we are far from saying that he was an atheist.[14] The pagan Seneca had perhaps more eager and earnest feelings about God than a philosopher who, in the Christian Church, rests contented with ontological abstractions.

But however uncertain was his idea of God, it is nevertheless to God that Seneca constantly refers in his thoughts about humanity and mankind. Cicero had already spoken vaguely of a city higher than the earthly country. Seneca throws a brighter light around this thought. It rules all his morality. He sees two Republics, of which one is a great and truly general one. It includes gods and men. Its confines are measured by the whole course of the sun. The other is the Republic to which fate attached us at our birth.[15] All men have part in the first, for all are alike descended from God, and the objects of His care.[16] Seneca insists on the great principle, that because of this origin all men are equal, and therefore begins to recognise human personality, the intrinsic worth of man. He looks on social distinctions as the results of pride and violence. "What is there in reality in these words, Roman knight, slave, freedman? words invented by ambition, or injurious distinctions.[17] Riches and poverty are only external facts: the one is no glory, the other is neither a misfortune nor a disgrace.[18] All men are capable of virtue. Virtue excludes none; she opens her arms to all. She admits all, calls all, free and freedmen, slaves, kings and exiles. She has no preference for race or fortune; unclothed man is enough for her."[19] The virtuous man only is noble, and he alone is rich and free.[20] "No one is more noble than another unless he has a juster and more virtuous mind. Those who set images of their ancestors in their vestibule, and place at the entrance of their dwelling a long list of names entwined with theirs in the branches of a genealogical tree, are more known than noble. The earth is the common mother; whether we are brilliant or obscure, we shall all return to this our first origin. Never despise any man, though he may be unfavoured by fortune and surrounded with vulgar names. If your own genealogy shows only slaves, freedmen, or foreigners, bravely raise your soul, and so free yourself, at one blow, from any abjectness that could be transmitted to you; in the end you will gain supreme nobility."²¹ Man is thus "a sacred thing," whom none may despise, and whom none has the right to abuse, as the master abuses the slave, the people the gladiators, and the tyrant his subjects.²²

Seneca asks for this respect for human personality, not to exalt individual pride, but to strengthen social ties by establishing society on a surer foundation. Sprung from a common origin, and naturally equal, there is a spiritual kindred among men; they are all fellow-citizens of "the great city."²³ The individual, destined for society, member of a great body, ought to give himself for the good of all, without distinction. "Nature has made us sociable; we are born for the general good."²⁴ This is a great progress from the ancient theory that the only duty of a citizen was to the State. With Seneca, man has duties towards *men*, his equals, in whose society he lives. This society in its perfect form was not realized in the Roman State. "The laws of Rome are not the only ones; above the written law is a natural one, a standard of human right, before which all men are equal."²⁵

In this society, where each member is "holy," that is, inviolable and deserving respect, woman takes a more dignified position than in the ancient pagan world, Seneca has a deep feeling of the virtues of woman; he shows his filial reverence for his mother Helvia, in the portrait he has drawn of this noble Roman matron. He expresses with piety and delicacy ideas which we are not accustomed to find in paganism; it is a foreshadowing of the Christian wife and mother.²⁶

With the same respect for human nature, he asks that the harshness of the paternal authority shall be replaced by *clemency*.²⁷ He severely blames the excesses which fathers permit themselves, screened by the law.[28] He foresees that clemency, by bringing peace and happiness to each household, will establish the peace and happiness of the State. Concord and mutual help are the conditions of social existence;[29] men need one another, and are intended for mutual help.[30] They ought to love one another. They are disposed to this love by nature, for it comes from the consciousness of the original relationship between all men. Each should be interested in his fellow. "Let us have this maxim always in our heart and on our lips: 'I am a man, and nothing relating to man is foreign to me.'"[31]

This love is not a barren feeling; it shows itself in acts. With him who has supreme power, love is shown by clemency, and thus becomes a royal virtue, an imitation of God, the best safeguard of kings.[32] With men in all stations it shows itself in kindness towards the unhappy.

Seneca tells the poor to rise through the power of their mind above their poverty.[33] He speaks of the philosophic advantages of poverty; he thinks that the wise man should know how to want nothing, and that with contentment poverty is rather a good than an evil.[34] It would seem easy for him to say this, who owned such great riches that his enemies made them a ground of accusation against him;[35] but he justified himself by saying that the possession of riches is no wrong to philosophy, provided they are neither soiled by blood nor acquired by injustice or sordid avarice.[36] Further, he added to this justification of fortune the wisest advice as to the best way of using it. The rich man, if he would be worthy of his wealth, must give freely; with wisdom, to avoid a ruinous and useless prodigality, but without distinction. "He will give neither to people of wealth, nor to those whom he may make such."[37]

Seneca lived himself in accordance with these principles.

Juvenal, who is not liberal with his praise, has spoken highly of his willing help of unfortunate friends.[38]

This benevolence is an imitation of God, who constantly loads us with benefits. He gives them equally to the bad and good, to those who doubt His providence as to those who trust it. "He makes the sun rise for rogues, and the sea is free for pirates."[39] "As good parents who smile at the attacks of little children, the gods do not cease to load with benefits those who deny them and doubt their existence. At the suitable time they send rain on the earth; with a breath of wind they set seas in motion; by the regular courses of the stars they show the flight of time; they mitigate the intensity of winter and summer with mild, gentle, suitable winds; they tolerate the error of minds that are led away."[40] To imitate God, love to man must pass beyond the stage of feeling, it must hold out the hand to the shipwrecked, point the way to the lost traveller, divide food with the hungry.[41] It must work actively to the end of life, both for the public good and the assistance of individuals. It must do good to the unknown as well as to the friend, to the slave as to the freedman. With a tender hand it must take help even to enemies.[42] Like God who gives us benefits without waiting for service on our part—for what can we render to Him?—we should give without hesitation, without first asking if the help will be lost by misuse, and above all without asking if it will profit ourselves. Even ingratitude should not discourage us.[43]

The importance is not in that which is done for or given to the poor, it is in the intention, the wish to help, the real benevolence. An alms thrown with harshness and contempt to an unfortunate beggar, is not a true kindness.[44] Giving must be without ostentation, and without humiliation to those who are helped. "Gifts which help weakness and poverty, or which avert dishonour, should be granted silently, and be known only by those to whom they are useful. Sometimes even a slight deception is allowable towards him who is helped, so that the assistance may come without showing the hand of the giver."[45] This active, universal, disinterested benevolence may be exercised by everybody, even by those who were placed by ancient law in the power of their master, and denied the power of doing more than their duty; that is, children and slaves.[46]

There is one passage in Seneca that would almost seem to condemn mercy, pity for the suffering, as a complaint or weakness of the soul.[47] But we should wrong him if we do not go beyond this thought. As a Stoic, he wished that strong emotion and instinctive feelings, excited by false as well as true misery, should be resisted. He does not blame sympathy provided the soul remains calm and mistress of herself. What he calls mercy is what we call hollow sentimentality, easily moved by the external appearance of misfortune, pitying the melancholy fate of a condemned criminal, and doing nothing to relieve the griefs it weeps over. Here is a beautiful passage which explains Seneca's meaning in this respect. "The wise man will dry the tears of others, but he will not mix his own with them. He will give his hand to the shipwrecked, hospitality to the exile, help to the poor; it will not, however, be the humiliating alms of those who, with a great air of compassion, degrade and repel the unfortunates whom they seem afraid to approach, even whilst relieving them; but this man will give to his equal, of the common patrimony of humanity. He will give back the son to the tears of the mother, he will unloose his fetters, he will lay down his sword, he will withdraw from the arena, he will give burial even to the guilty, and he will do all these things calmly, without a change of look. Thus the wise man will not be merciful, but he will be helpful. He will render service because he is born to help his kind, to contribute to the public wealth and to procure a share for each. He will be kind even to the bad, reprimanding them and striving to correct them; but he will have the most joy in helping those who suffer from afflictions and difficulties,—he will come between them and their bad fortune. What better use can he make of his power or riches than to repair injustice of this kind? Doubtless his face would not change, his soul would not be disturbed at the sight of the beggar's rags and his failing strength, which compels him to walk slowly, leaning on a stick. But he will help all who deserve it, and like the gods will look kindly even on the unfortunates." [48] Seneca sets good above utility, but it must be the result of absolute disinterestedness, for the sole reason that good is good.

This morality is a great advance on that of Cicero; but he does not stop there, he does what none had done in the olden time. We have seen that he requires benevolence even towards his enemies, and he also acknowledges that egoism, which refers everything to its own interests, can never be the source of a "happy life." "Live for others," he says, "if you wish to live for yourselves." [49] He finds happiness even in sacrifice, "for our greatest pleasure is in acts of benevolence, even in painful ones if they relieve the pain of others; even in perilous ones, if they save others from danger; even in ruinous ones, if they diminish the needs and embarrassments of others." [50]

We are not astonished after this to find that there is still another point on which his teaching differs from the teaching inspired by the ancient spirit: that of vengeance and pardon. Society can only exist through peace. Every one ought, by his gentleness, to avoid causing anger in others. The brevity of life, the very short time during which we have the opportunity of showing kindness to others, ought to lead men to avoid the causes of hatred and trouble.[51] The interest of society still further demands it. "It is a sacrilege to destroy one's country, and consequently it is the same to destroy a citizen. He is a member of the country; when the whole is sacred, the parts are not less so. Man is therefore bound to respect man, who is a fellow-citizen with him in the great city.[52] In case of offence, antiquity requires that evil shall be returned for evil. Seneca thinks, on the contrary, that it is a greater misery to do evil than to suffer it. He thinks hatred of one's enemy is disgraceful and detestable. "The word vengeance is an inhuman word."[53] He wrote a special work to show that anger is contrary to human nature. He refutes there the excuses given by wounded self-love and egoistical philosophy to justify vengeance. He does not agree with those who, like Aristotle, think it natural because of the pleasure which accompanies it, and which makes it a stimulus to virtue; for he says, a vice can never be a stimulus to good. He is, therefore, very far from seeing in it a sign of greatness of soul.[54] He asks that before yielding to anger we shall examine whether the fault may be on our side; whether there was the intention of harming us, or if it is not ourselves, who, in being causelessly irritated, have given place to evil; whether it may not be false shame which keeps our anger alive.[55] If, after this examination, the wise man has nothing with which to reproach himself, he will nevertheless not seek to revenge himself; he will bear injuries calmly. They cannot harm him, for he is free, beyond the power of such attacks.[56] This was the principle of stoical pride. Seneca hastens to modify it by advising forgiveness. He finds the strongest motive for pardon in the consciousness of his own faults. We shall be more ready to forgive when we remember how often we ourselves need forgiveness.[57] This pardon should be sincere and thorough, otherwise it is not a proof of love, witnessing to the goodness which leads men to good. It is interesting to see Seneca's recognition of the power of love to soften men and conquer their hatred.[58] In society itself, those who err and sin should be corrected with gentleness. Hardened criminals alone must be severely punished, but still without anger, for the penalty should be a correction, not a revenge.[59] This is an essentially Christian principle, which was further developed by the Fathers of the Church at a later time.

Seneca applied specially to slaves his ideas of the relationship among men, and of universal benevolence. He developed the theory of moral servitude and liberty in a more spiritual manner than the Stoics. Every man is intended for liberty. The soul is naturally free, but she finds herself temporarily imprisoned in the body, a prison from which she may free herself by energy of thought. Man is only enslaved when he delights in his ignoble prison, obeying the passions and desires of the *flesh*, and placing therein his highest enjoyment.[60] This is a servitude unworthy of man, who was created for higher destinies.[61] Man becomes free by rising above the bonds of the body and the world, and finding the motive for action in the soul, giving the greatest energy to obey God, for "to obey God is our liberty."[62] This is the liberty to which the slave can rise, because he has the same nature as his master. He is not, as antiquity taught, of an inferior race, predestined to servitude.

The body alone is enslaved; the soul, man's best part, is emancipated, and all that comes from it is free.[63]

Seneca, having turned in the direction of respect for human personality, goes a step farther, which is another advance on his predecessors. It had been asked, Can the slave do a kindness to his master? Being his property, has he not a right to all his services? How can he go beyond his duty and do him a kindness? A kindness is a voluntary act, which may therefore be refused; is the slave free to refuse his master anything? Philosophers were not sure about it; the law denied it. The slave could do no more than his duty; the master had a right to exact all that he could do in his interest, without any need for gratitude. Seneca answers differently. We have before seen that he vindicated for the slave the power of doing more than his duty. He stated formally that he who denies that the slave may become the benefactor of the master, ignores natural right, because the important point is the disposition of the heart, not the social position of the giver.[64] The slave retains his spiritual freewill; consequently, when he does something beyond what is strictly exacted, he does a kindness to his master.[65] There have been slaves who have sacrificed themselves for their masters, bearing tortures rather than betray their secrets. Is it not so much the more a good gift "that servitude itself has not been able to interpose an obstacle"?[66] Besides, it is not the master who receives a benefit from his slave, but a man from a fellow-man.[67] Slaves should always be treated with humanity and kindness. If custom and law allow them to be subjected to the hardest work and even to ill-treatment, natural right, which is common to all men, is opposed to it.[68] The freeman should always remember that his slaves are of the same nature as himself, that he also is in a state of servitude himself on earth. He should treat them as he desires to be treated by his superiors, with kindness and esteem, so that they may rather venerate than fear him.[69]

Seneca, animated by such feelings, could only condemn energetically the gladiatorial combats, where man, "that sacred thing," as he calls him, is killed as a sign of rejoicing. Nothing seems to him more harmful to good morals "than the lazy enjoyment of a spectacle. It is then that the vices steal in most easily in the train of pleasure. Men return from the sight, not only more avaricious, ambitious, and debauched, but more cruel and inhuman." He indignantly depicts the combats of the arena and the growing barbarism of the people, who are no longer contented with comedy, but who desire bloodshed. "However, no more jests, the spectacles are only murders."[70]

If we confined ourselves to the observations we have just made as to the characteristics of Seneca, we might be accused of having taken only what served our end, and neglected contradictory facts. We distinctly declare therefore that we see this contradiction in him. He lacks internal harmony. Having only vague ideas about God, and a confused sense of the relations between man and God, he had not enough light to illumine all parts of the science of life. Ancient pride is still alive in his works, and sometimes triumphs over purer feelings. Thus whilst he requires love to man, and devotion to his service, he permits the sage to abstain from public life; though he somewhat modifies this by saying that to meditate upon God and man, and upon the principles of virtue, is to work for society. What cannot be excused is his addition that the sage may withdraw "if the Republic is too corrupt for him to be able to assist it, or if it is overweighted with bad men, because then his efforts would be useless."[71] He also says, with stoical pride, that the sage may be as happy as God, for he may be as wise as He. "He does not obey God; he freely follows Him. The life of God has nothing that the life of the sage has not also; this then may be called the Divine life."[72] There is a great difference in this respect between him and his contemporary the poet Lucan, who makes Cato say, "The victorious cause pleased the gods, but the defeated cause has pleased me." Seneca, less arrogant, exclaims "that man should think everything good that God has thought good."[73] There is also another point to notice. We know how often Seneca insisted on the thought that death, instead of being in itself an evil, frees man from all evil by taking him to a happy abode where all the secrets of nature shall be revealed to him, and where he will be in the society of souls already set free. Death, he says, in almost Christian words, "is the birthday of eternal life."[74] However, respecting this also, as respecting the idea of God, he remains vague and uncertain. He has some very materialist expressions as to the future life of the soul alongside of these spiritual ones.[75] We remark here how ancient Stoicism reappears in the approval of suicide as a means of attaining liberty if suffering from unjust oppressions.[76] Seneca himself chose this method of escape from tyranny. His life was not always free from blame. As we have said, harmony was wanting to this aspiring soul, capable of such noble flights. In the early years of Nero's reign, he tried to use his influence for the public good.[77] The Romans, in spite of increasing corruption, held him in great esteem. Rumour once spoke of a conspiracy to kill Nero and raise his former tutor to the throne on account of his illustrious virtues.[78] He showed however a forbearance towards this tyrant's vices that aroused the indignation of the people themselves. They retained amidst degradation an instinctive respect for virtue, and whilst bending under a vile despotism, they required that those better than themselves should remain faithful to their purer doctrines.[79]

Where is the source of these stricter doctrines, these purer virtues and sentiments so strange to antiquity, which in Seneca's life contrast so strongly with his remnants of paganism? Several learned men, more enthusiastic as to the form than the root, see in Seneca only a superficial eclectic, a rhetorician without conviction.[80] It is hardly necessary to refute the injustice of this opinion, disparaging to psychology, for it takes no account of the different influences which are so powerful on the mind in times of crisis. Others are not willing that Christianity shall take the honour of the purity of Seneca's moral doctrines, which they say only echo those of Plato.[81] They appear to ignore the profound difference between the moral and social principles of the two philosophers. Others refuse to believe that the preceptor of Nero was affected by unrecognised Christian influences, because he did not understand religious questions, and did not rise above the standpoint of simple humanity.[82] That was however an immense advance on paganism, and implied a new influence. It was much to have attained the human point of view of natural right in the midst of the harshness of ancient laws and customs. For ourselves, we think there is no doubt as to the origin of the new ideas in Seneca's morality, we are convinced that we have here effects produced by the influence of Christian charity. We are glad to find this opinion held also by several eminent scholars belonging to our country.[83] Without this Christian influence, Seneca is an enigma; the influence itself is not inexplicable. We know that at a very early time there were Christians in the capital of the empire whose faith was " spoken of throughout the whole world."[84] Seneca was about sixty years of age when Paul came to Rome. The Apostle preached freely during two years " in his own hired dwelling, and received all that went in unto him."[85] He gained converts even amongst the servants in Cæsar's household.[86] He had a trial in Rome, in which he defended himself.[87] He was in the care of the guard of the Prefect of the Pretorium,[88] and that was Burrhus, the friend of Seneca. It is difficult to believe that the philosopher who sought eagerly after everything, would be left in ignorance of Paul's lawsuit and the new doctrines that he preached. Seneca might even have heard of the courageous preacher before his arrival in Rome. Gallio, the Proconsul of Achaia, noted for his moderation and benevolence, had declared Paul free when the Jews of Corinth accused him before his tribunal.[89] Gallio's younger brother was a philosopher, and the intimate friend of Seneca.[90] He might have had from his brother information about the Apostle. We are in ignorance as to the relations between Seneca and Paul, or other Christians, but it seems to us impossible to doubt these relations, when we see the astonishing analogy, not only of moral principles and sentiments, but even of expressions. How can we otherwise explain the Christian sense, wholly unknown to preceding writers, in which Seneca uses certain words, such as flesh, the strife of the spirit against the flesh,[91] Holy Spirit,[92] angel,[93] eternal happiness ?[94] It may be said that the works of Seneca were written before Paul's arrival in Rome. It is true that several are of an earlier date, but the principal works, those which touch our subject most closely, are of a later time.[95]

The Fathers of the early ages were struck by the analogy between the moral ideas of Seneca and those of Christianity. The Church perhaps retained some remembrance of the relations between the philosopher and the members of the first community in Rome, already sufficiently numerous to be openly persecuted.[96] It was this opinion in early times which gave rise to the apocryphal correspondence between Seneca and Paul. No one believes now in the authenticity of these letters; but the fact of their existence is of considerable value, as testifying in favour of the tradition of an exchange of ideas between the Apostle and the philosopher.[97]

We have perhaps lingered too long with Seneca. We have done so because he is the first in whom we see traces of Christian influence, a phenomenon the more curious because it occurs at the rise of the Church, and beneath a tyrant like Nero. Seneca also gave a new direction to moral philosophy, in which he was followed by many of the most distinguished minds of pagan society.

§ 2. *Pliny and Plutarch.*

It is under Trajan, after the reign of Domitian, the Church's persecutor, that we again find traces of the slow but continuous progress of Christian influence. We see it first in Pliny the younger, the friend of Trajan. Pliny was not a theorist; he seemed to have no preference for any of the philosophical schools then in vogue; his tendencies were wholly practical. He was a man of a moral and earnest mind and benevolent heart, open to good impressions. Entrusted with the government of Bithynia, his attention was drawn to the Christians spread throughout that province; they appeared to him to be singular men, meeting on certain days for a special worship and brotherly repasts, and reciprocally engaging, not in a brotherhood of crime, but that they would *never* commit robbery or adultery, and would never break their promises. What he learned about them surprised, without irritating, him. He did not doubt their innocence; but unable to free himself from the prejudices of a Roman magistrate, he saw in them only men who disobeyed the laws, and whom, after asking the emperor's advice, he was bound to condemn as followers of an illegal religion when they publicly avowed their faith.

Is it to these dealings with the Christians of his province that we must attribute the more generous sentiments and purer ideas that we find in Pliny's writings? Or has he inhaled them in the Christian atmosphere which pervaded the capital itself, where, under Trajan, persons in the highest positions, like Hermes, the Prefect of Rome, professed Christianity? We do not know; nothing is more mysterious than the reactions which occur in the depths of the soul, often contrary to the will of him who yields to them whilst he believes he is resisting them. However it comes about, we meet in Pliny with principles which it would be difficult to believe could have originated in pagan soil. The spirituality of Seneca, though he was far from humility and Christian faith, led him to the belief that the gods prefer the prayer of a chaste and innocent soul, to carefully prepared formularies which are recited without conviction.[99] He knows that perfect purity is beyond the reach of man, and infers from this that though severity is needful with ourselves, yet others must be treated with the indulgence that we also may need. "The best man," he says, "is he who pardons others as if he himself needed pardon every day, and who refrains from sin as if he never pardoned. Implacable towards ourselves, let us forgive even those whose strictness is all for others and who shut their eyes to their own faults."[100]

To a lively sympathy with the joys and griefs of family life, Pliny added a great respect for the virtues of woman.[101] He is one of the first amongst the thinkers of paganism who, trying to free themselves from the yoke of the State, ask that parents may have more direct power over the education of their sons. He wishes to have schools in every neighbourhood, that the parents may not be compelled to send their children away, and may themselves superintend the methods of their educacation. For the same reason he desires that the masters shall not be paid by the commune alone, but that the parents, through paying fees, may be more interested in the quality and success of the teaching. He begs his fellow-citizens to found schools and engage to contribute to the cost.[102] Finally, he asks that the children in these schools, as in the home, shall not be treated with the former rigour. He wishes to put natural feeling and reciprocal affection in the place of the harshness authorized by law.[103] Seeing the melancholy fate of the children in poor families, he instituted in his native town of Como a benevolent foundation, which he largely endowed, the annual revenue being distributed amongst a certain number of poor children.[104] We shall find later other examples of this new spirit of charity unknown to antiquity.

The humanity of Pliny shows itself largely in his relations with his slaves. He found there a whole class of men, if not to re-instate,—for pagan benevolence did not attain to that,—at least to relieve in their misery. Pliny says, speaking of philosophers who, despising slaves, are not touched by the hardships of their lot,

"I do not know if they are great and wise, but one thing I do know, they are not men." [105] He was very kind to his servants, wishing to be the true father of a family to them; his house was to them almost the city of the Republic.[106] Ready to forgive their faults, he also interceded with his friends for guilty slaves.[107] When they became infirm, instead of casting them off, he treated them with still greater kindness. The fear of losing a slave who was attached to him redoubled his affection, and he sent him distant journeys to re-establish his shaken health.[108] He gave them the power to make a kind of will, which he treated as legal. He gave them freedom to dispose of the wealth which he had allowed them to acquire. They might arrange gifts and legacies amongst themselves, provided that the wealth bequeathed remained in the household.[109] In their last hour he set them free, that they might die with the consolation of liberty. It would doubtless have been a better gift to have freed them sooner, but it was a great thing for a Roman pagan to emancipate them at the hour of death. Pliny felt the injustice of slavery, and it was partly to clear his conscience that he freed them before parting with them.[110] He did not enjoy public games because of their frivolous vanity and dull uniformity;[111] but in this respect he was not always consistent. At one time he praises his friend Maximus of Verona for his intention of celebrating the anniversary of his wife's death by a combat between gladiators and African panthers; at another he applauds the noble conduct of Trebonius Rufinus, of Vienne, who, when accused before Trajan of having prohibited a combat which, in accordance with the will of a rich man, ought to have been held, defended himself vigorously, and exclaimed, "I wish that these games could be put a stop to in Rome also." [112]

The pages where Pliny expresses his more humane sentiments are worth more in our eyes than the dissertations of an ancient philosopher filled with contempt for man. If he has not elaborated his system, if his style does not show all the qualities that we admire in Cicero, it is yet not unworthy of our esteem. Has he drawn these feelings from the moral and social theories of his predecessors, or do they not rather arise from his own heart, over which has passed the mysterious and fertilizing breath of the Gospel and of charity?

Dion Chrysostom, the contemporary of Pliny, may perhaps also be said to show traces of this influence. In his moral ideas, this distinguished orator agreed with the Stoics. Virtue, according to him, consists in living in conformity with nature; pains and sorrows come only in order that one may cast them aside. It is also in the sense of the Stoics that he teaches an internal liberty and servitude, which are more real than the external conditions which are called by these names. He goes beyond abstract speculation when he holds that there is no slavery by nature, that neither violence nor written law can establish a race of slaves without infringing on the natural rights of men who are all alike created for liberty.[113] The tendency of Dion is essentially practical. He desires that wisdom shall regulate the individual life, and the welfare of the State and its members. This is the inspiring force of a discourse which he addressed to Trajan, full of admirable precepts, on the virtues and duties of a prince.[114] The practical character of his moral philosophy is a mark of progress, for ancient Stoicism was entirely subjective and egoistical. If this progress may not be attributed to Christian influence on Dion himself, it must at least be referred to the new impulse given by Seneca to stoical morality. In this sense it may be said that the doctrines of the orator, hated by Domitian and loved by Trajan, show a spirit foreign to pagan philosophy properly so called.

In Plutarch, although he did not belong to the school of Stoics, we find a like spirit, with more depth and warmth. This writer's noble and loving soul was not satisfied with the doctrines of either the Stoics or the Epicureans. He looked higher, and thought he should find more substantial nourishment in the theories of Plato and Pythagoras, to which he added some of Aristotle's principles, and perhaps even some ideas borrowed from oriental wisdom. In many parts of his works he expresses the secret needs of the heart. He is full of fears and hopes. He is one of the " men of desire," of whom St. Martin speaks. More practical than speculative, he remained electic, and did not formulate a system. He attached the greatest importance to questions relating to the life of man in his dealings with his equals, and his relations to Providence. He liked to speak with pious respect of Divine Providence. He believed that amidst the multitude of gods invoked by the crowd, only one is eternal and unchangeable,[115] and that this God is the Father and Guide of good men. There is neither anger nor hatred nor any bad thing in Him; He is goodness and clemency, and through His own nature is ready to give help and pardon.[116]

Plutarch, distressed by the immorality of his time, when pagan society, being either superstitious or atheistical, was given over to sensuality or materialism,[117] recognised the necessity of a sincere religious belief as the foundation of morality: without religion there can be neither happiness for the individual, nor safety for society. No State can exist without faith in the gods. It is the only true bond of the community, and the most solid foundation for legislation. A city may live without walls, without theatres, without riches, without science, but never without God, prayers, and sacrifices.[118] For this reason he asks that "the pious belief of the fathers" shall be re-vivified and preserved by freeing it from impure fables, which produce impiety or gross superstition.[119] Instead of going to Christ, Plutarch limits himself to the purification of mythology. "If we must take it literally," he says, "we must condemn the lips that speak it. It must be interpreted in the double sense, physical and moral, seeking only for symbols of profound ideas or of natural facts." It is true that Plutarch permitted the division then used of poetical or mythical theology, philosophic or physical theology, and political theology or national religion;[120] but he regarded the latter simply as a method of keeping order, which was not needed by enlightened men, and which they were not bound to respect. He wished to see both in the people and the philosophers a more real religion than servile fear of the gods or abstract belief in a supreme cause. He desired something of what we call, in a Christian sense, piety. He had the feeling himself, and the efforts he made to interpret the myths prove that he also strove to communicate it to others.

This piety, imperfect though it was, could not exist without love for men. Love, as Plato understood it, did not rise to the height of charity or the power of sacrifice, but it was recognised as the distinctive characteristic of humanity. "The proper end of man is to love and to be loved."[121] Plutarch wishes this love to enter into all the mutual relations of men. He wrote several treatises against the indulgence of anger, vengeance, and hatred; passions which degrade men and destroy society. He proves that it is not necessary to return injury for injury, but that enemies may be confounded by the sight of an upright and benevolent life.[122]

Above all, love ought to be introduced in the family. The movement towards a purer idea of marriage than was held by ancient civilization, of which we have seen the earliest signs in Seneca and Pliny, was more completely developed by Plutarch, in a manner more analogous to Christian principles. There is to him no more sacred union than marriage, which ought to be founded on agreement in "good and upright ways," on sincere mutual affection and reciprocal respect.[123] If there is mutual respect between husband and wife, the union will remain pure and will be a source of happiness. "In marriage," he says, "to love is a still greater good than to be loved, because it preserves husband and wife from many faults."[124] The virtues of woman are wisdom, modesty, chastity; her domain is the interior of the house; her occupation the care of the household and the education of her children.[125] Plutarch asks that she shall so submit to her husband that if he forgets her, she will not be angry;[126] but he severely blames the husband who shall make this counsel of patience to the wife an excuse for infidelity. If the woman owes submission, the husband ought not to rule her as a master over a chattel, which is his servile property, but as the spirit over the body, which feels its griefs, and is in some sort one with it.[127]

Plutarch gives wise advice as to the physical and moral education of children : that the mother shall nurse them herself, in order to attach them by one tie the more; that the father shall give serious attention to the oversight of their education.[128] At a period when the family was more and more disorganized, and when a disgraceful egoism widened the separation of parents and children,

Plutarch endeavours to re-awaken natural feelings of tenderness, that fathers and mothers may love their children and care for their future. He finds types throughout nature of the intimate tie which unites father and son. "Man alone," he says, "allows himself to be turned by his interests from the path prescribed by his instincts." [129]

The same love should be extended to slaves. A celebrated passage from the biography of Cato shows the whole difference between the ancient method of treating slaves, and the progress of ideas in those minds which were accessible to the softening influences of Christianity. After saying that Cato was accustomed to get rid of slaves who could no longer render useful service, Plutarch adds the reflections suggested to him by this method of acting. This is a re-translation from the French translation of Amyot: "It seems to me a severe step, proceeding from a harsh nature, thus to sell slaves or to drive them from the house after they have grown old in your service, treating them as if they were dumb animals, though you have received from them the help of a lifetime, in the belief that there is no great society which compels reciprocal obligations of man to man, except so long as they are of profit or use to one another. We always see that goodness reaches further than justice. Nature teaches us to treat men with equity and justice, but to extend grace and benignity to brute beasts. This proceeds from the fountain of goodness and humanity, which should never dry up in man. . . . For myself, I should never have the heart to sell the ox which had long laboured on my ground, and could no longer work on account of old age, still less could I chase a slave from his country, from the place where he has been nourished for so long, and from the way of life to which he has for so long been accustomed. I could be free from him by selling him for a small sum, but he would be as useless to the buyer as the seller." [129]

In another treatise Plutarch completes these just ideas, and relates how he was brought to treat his own servants with kindness. He began with anger when they fell into fault; then he tried the impassiveness of the Stoic, ceasing from anger, and preferring that his slaves should become bad rather than himself through yielding to passion; finally he perceived that the slaves served him better when treated with kindness and indulgence, and he acknowledged that "right" was a better commander than anger.[130] We could multiply quotations to characterise the tendencies of Plutarch, but those we have given are enough to point out the difference between the moral doctrines of antiquity and those of this benevolent philosopher, ruled by the growing power of Christian ideas.

§ 3. *Epictetus*.

This influence is still more visible in Epictetus, a contemporary of Plutarch, and former slave of one of Nero's freedmen. In this philosopher, who was banished from Rome by Domitian, we see ancient Stoicism still further transformed. This system, in the strong current of new ideas that no persecution could stop, altered increasingly from its original character, to assume a humanity and indulgence which were utterly foreign to the principles of its first representatives. Epictetus, by his deep moral sense and pious feelings, is perhaps the purest of the philosophers of paganism. It is impossible for us to understand this purity without some other influence than that of paganism, though it may be one of which

Epictetus was himself unconscious. If he had recognised it, he might perhaps have passed the last barrier that separated him from Christianity.

No other pagan has spoken of God with so much admiration and gratitude, of His sensible presence everywhere, and of the benefits with which He loads men;[131] no other has felt so keenly that the providence of God is not a general and abstract action, but a special, constant, fatherly intervention in the affairs of men and of the world.[132] Man is the child of God; he is the object of His constant protection.[133] He is created for happiness—not for a transitory happiness arising from the possession and enjoyment of external things, for these are not given to all; and if they were essential to happiness this would prove God to be unjust to those to whom they were denied. It is as impossible to separate the idea of justice from that of God as to deny that all men are destined for happiness. Happiness, then, consists in something in one's self—in peace of mind, in freedom from the desire for unattainable things, which are in themselves unimportant.[134] The great duty of man, which leads to happiness, is to obey God, to trust Him, and to conform our will to His.[135] This is a fruitful source of comfort and strength. What has he to fear who knows that he is a child of God? What can trouble him who knows that God is his Creator and Father?[136] It is in this sense that a passage in Epictetus must be explained, with which he has been reproached as marked with egoism and coldness.[137] When he asks that man shall learn to rise above everything, and give up even parents, children, friends, and country as external things, he simply means that he must not concentrate all his affections on them, otherwise he puts himself in a state of bondage, and becomes unhappy and inconsolable when he loses what he loved too much. He must turn to God for country and family. If all his desires are fixed on Him, he will never be unhappy.[138]

Every man, as a child of God, has a part in the supreme city, which includes both gods and men, and of which the earthly country is only an imperfect type.[139] The consciousness that he is a citizen of the world, an integral part of the universe, reveals to man the worth of his individuality. As with Seneca, the title of man is no longer reserved for the citizen of an earthly state, with transitory aims, but is fixed in the intelligent nature of the soul destined for a city that shall never pass away. If, then, Epictetus teaches that moral principle, "the law of life," is to live in conformity with nature,[140] he speaks of a pure life, conformed to the spiritual nature of man. Is this life possible? Ancient stoical wisdom, which exalted the moral power of man, while it judged evil less severely, never doubted it. Epictetus, on the contrary, denies it. He acknowledges that it is impossible for even the wisest man to be sinless, though each one should endeavour not to fall into faults.[141] This is no longer stoical pride. Here is some advice, in which we can even hear an echo of Christian humility: "If thou wishest to be good, begin by believing thyself to be bad." [142]

Seneca had deduced the duty of mercy and pardon from a like thought, and in this he is followed by Epictetus. "We must not judge others hastily; if any one has offended, let us think whether he may not be right in his reproaches; at any rate, let us believe that he is mistaken, and did not intend to harm us.[143] Therefore we need not bear malice against him. Instead of returning evil for evil, we should help one another, and be always gentle and ready to forgive." [144]

The law of man in his relations with his fellows is to

be useful to them. In this respect, however, the moral system of Epictetus offers the same contradictions as did that of Seneca. "The sage," he says, "is only a spectator in this world, his part is to admire and tell of the works of God." [145] However, he speaks still often of the duty of each man to remain in the place assigned to him by God; he has no right to flee, he must strive to the end. Man is a member of society; if that is a glory, it also entails an obligation. As no member of the body can isolate himself, but must serve the whole, so each man must stay at his post, regardless of praise or blame. Man is thus bound to his duty in all social relations, as father, son, husband, citizen, servant. What he does for his family he does for the whole country; he may be useful to society in the humblest position, provided that he is faithful and upright." [146]

Epictetus turned sharply on the egoism which then reigned in the world; he looked on this disposition which sacrificed everything to personal interest, as the cause of all the public misfortunes and prevalent hatreds. A pagan philosopher must have felt some new influence who was able to see the sadness and irreligion of social morality founded on egoism, and could write as follows: "Man's natural inclination is to love nothing so much as what is useful to him. Utility is his father, brother, parent, country, god. When we think that the gods oppose us in this respect, we revile them, overturn their statues and burn their sanctuaries. It was thus that Alexander, after the death of his friend, burned the temples of Esculapius. All will be safe if men will place utility in what is holy and upright, in country, parents, friends, but if they place it otherwise all will be lost, for all will be sacrificed to interest." [147]

For the salvation of society another bond than egoism

must be formed between its members. Epictetus foresaw that mutual kindness was the new tie, through which pride and anger would be subdued, and man would seek to do good to his fellow without thinking what return of usefulness he can get from him.[148] In the extreme case of a man being deserted by every one, he must assist him even if he is his enemy.[149]

This kindness must begin in the family, between husband and wife, between parents and children. In this direction, also, traces of Christian influence are to be seen in Epictetus. If it is the duty of man to keep faith in everything, he ought above all to keep it in marriage, both in regard to his own wife and to those of others. Adultery is not only a violation of the most sacred tie, it is also a crime against the Republic.[150] Epictetus bases marriage on reciprocal fidelity, on the chastity of both husband and wife. Modesty and discretion are the best ornaments of woman.[151] This philosopher's severe and sensitive conscience rouses his indignation against the corruption of the Roman ladies of his time who had forgotten these virtues, and who quoted Plato in justification of their vices, asking for the community of women. "They are rejoiced," he exclaims regretfully, "every time that they find an excuse for their sins." He also adds this warning, which is often forgotten by theorists who think they may safely play with dangerous speculations: "Guard carefully against holding out a finger, for there are always people to be found who will seize on the slightest excuses to justify their vices."[152]

He also gives good advice to a father who fled from his house unable to endure the sight of an ailing child. He reminds him of the duties of fatherly tenderness, and the supreme obligation of rendering all the services, to those whom we love, and by whom we would be beloved, which, in case of misfortune, we should like to receive from them.[153]

In respect to slavery, we find that Epictetus agrees with Seneca, Pliny, and Plutarch. Having felt the hardships of this state himself, he would naturally reflect on methods of freedom without revolt against the master. He finds in Stoicism the consolation of slaves, as well as of the poor and oppressed. Liberty and servitude are words that only affect the external condition; they are realities only when voluntarily chosen.[154] It is the same with poverty and riches, which are in themselves neither a good nor an evil.[155] Externals are indifferent. What does the state of the body signify, if the soul is free and needs nothing? It is free when evil has no dominion over it, and evil is the desire that torments and subjugates it when its object is inaccessible external wealth. Therefore to attain liberty it must learn to rule itself, to possess itself; that is, to give up the desire that is unattainable.[156] The slave set free by his master will remain a slave as long as he has not calm of soul; he can only change his servitude. It is the same with the master as with the slave, and even more with the master as long as he yields to the dominion of factitious wants, ambition and the passions. It is useless to change his state to gain freedom; he must change his feelings. The slave will be truly free by an energetic act of will, raising him to internal freedom, because he will have ceased to desire the external liberty which he cannot gain.[157] Having attained internal freedom, change of fortune produces no effect; the soul is no longer troubled about anything; the slave no more trembles before an inhuman master; the oppressed no longer fears tyrants or their satellites.[158]

There is a beauty and grandeur in these pages when Epictetus, formerly the slave of a cruel master, speaks with so much calm and nobility of the internal liberty that may be preserved in the midst of servitude. Without once speaking evil of the masters or exciting the slaves to break their bonds, he calls liberty the greatest blessing, and desires them to have in themselves a liberty purer and more real than that of their oppressors. He always felt deeply the injustice of slavery, and went so far as to express a wish for its abolition. "As a healthy man does not wish to be waited upon by the infirm, or desire that those who live with him should be invalids, the freeman should not allow himself to be waited upon by slaves, or leave those who live with him in servitude."[159] There has been held to be "a groundwork of contempt in this matter;"[160] but is it not rather a protest against the iniquity of all slavery, and in favour of the equality of all men? We see here the wish that the freeman shall so respect the natural liberty of his fellow as to make him unwilling to keep him in servitude. We even think that he desires that he may free his slaves to raise them to the dignity of freemen.

If Epictetus has not laid more stress upon this point, it is because he believes that the attained calm of the Stoic, which sufficed for him, will also suffice for his companions in slavery. But we know that this impassive calm, this absolute indifference, was difficult to practise, and impossible except to some philosophic minds; it could never be a universal remedy for all who were oppressed by pagan society. In consequence of the egoism against which Epictetus strove, but which Christian faith alone can completely subdue in the soul, he said that the remedy of the philosopher must be offered only to those who came to ask for it. The philosopher must not be like the Roman physicians, who went to seek the sick, instead of waiting to be sought by them.[161]

He has another remedy for the help of those who are not masters of themselves sufficiently to bear misfortune or servitude without a murmur, and who cannot resist the wish of bettering their state—it is the pagan remedy of suicide. In contradiction to his beautiful exhortations to the confidence that man, the child of God, should have in his Father, he says: "The door is open; imitate the children who, when their game ceases to please them, go away saying, 'I will play no more.' Quit the neighbourhood as they do, when it no longer suits you; but if you remain, utter no complaint."[162] I do not know if I am mistaken, but it seems to me that even here there is a signal progress in Epictetus. Whom does he advise to quit the neighbourhood? It is the weak, those who cannot bear trouble unmurmuringly. Suicide is therefore no longer an act of courage; it is the refuge of despair, to avoid the need of courage and resignation; it is a cowardly act. This is an advance on Seneca, who admired it as a mark of heroic pride.

Notwithstanding all this, we do not say, like some learned men of the last century, that Epictetus was a Christian.[163] Though he was, as Pascal says, "one of the philosophers of the world who have best understood the duty of man,"[164] he remained a pagan philosopher; that is to say, he never completely conquered pagan pride. He misunderstood the beliefs of the sect of the Galileans. Seeing in their contempt for death only the effect of madness or custom, he asked if reason could not give men the same strength as the Christians drew from their faith.[165] It is, however, impossible to deny that the ideas of this philosopher are coloured with a reflection of Christianity; especially his doctrines of respect for man and of charity. The reading of the books of Epictetus must have exerted a happy influence; they were a preparation for the Gospel, and helped to lead souls to Christ. Origen states that slaves and men of low and despised position were wonderfully comforted by studying the treatises of this sage.[166]

§ 4. *Marcus Aurelius.*

We place this emperor amongst the philosophers because he has told us the secrets of his soul in his book of "Thoughts." Marcus Aurelius, although the disciple of a Sophist who hated Christianity, yielded to the beneficent influence of the new spirit. He is as pious as Epictetus, and more loving. If Epictetus, formerly a slave, develops principally the theory of internal liberty and the natural equality of all men as children of God, Marcus Aurelius, who is the head of a vast empire, insists chiefly on practical benevolence, on a love imitating Providence, and of the nature of charity. He feels that there is only one God, everywhere present, whose sovereign intelligence upholds and governs the world,[167] whose wisdom and goodness are shown in his works. Nothing is the result of chance, everything happens according to a supreme plan. "God directs success and misfortune. He gives and takes away wealth and power. He sends us sorrows, as much for our personal good as for the accomplishment of His purposes for humanity; they are like a medicine for us, bitter, but useful for our spiritual health."[168]

This is a profoundly religious idea, as foreign to the philosophy as to the customs of paganism. "Man should learn to have no other thoughts than those of the Sovereign Intelligence who carries us in his bosom.[169] He should accept all that is sent to him with love and respect, without either pride or murmur. He must be resigned to His will, submitting to it with perfect confidence, walking in that way in His footsteps.[170] Here is the true calm of the soul.[171] It differs from that of the Stoics, which is an effect of pride of self; it is an acceptance of all that comes from God, a resignation which has something of the humble submission of the Christian. Thus resigned, death is no more feared than life. Sorrow and pleasure, riches and poverty, are only accidents. They are neither the real evil nor the real good, for they happen alike to the bad and to the good."[172] Temptations of the body, or as Marcus Aurelius expresses it, adopting a Christian term introduced by Seneca into the language of philosophy, the "gentle or violent desires of the *flesh*," are resisted;[173] the source of true and imperishable happiness is seen to be in the soul itself.[174] In this way we become gradually more like God. The thought that He does not wish to be flattered by rational beings, but desires them to become like Him, is a support in the conflicts of life.[175]

The duty of rising to God through submission to His will is imposed indiscriminately on all men. Marcus Aurelius recognised more clearly than his predecessors the individual worth of man, the human dignity which is independent of external conditions. "The reasonable soul," he says, "owes great respect to itself."[176] Therefore, if I thus respect myself, shall I not also respect in every man the soul which equals mine? Whatever misfortune may overtake a man, however his social position may be changed, he remains the same in the essence of his being, his moral worth is not altered.[177] All men are equal as to their rational nature. They form a society wider than any earthly country. Each individual is a citizen of the world, "that supreme city, of which other cities are like the houses."[178] " As

Antonine," he said, "I have Rome; as a man I have the world." [179]

In this universal city, each has a mission to fulfil. God, who is the Head, knows how to make use of all; He gives to each his place.[180] In the most obscure position it is possible to be "a divine man," free, modest, sociable, resigned to the will of God, and consequently happy.[181] Marcus Aurelius finds in these considerations the most powerful motives for love to men, not only to those of his own nation, but to the whole human race.[182] Men should work together for this end. No one must isolate himself in his egoism. Instead of saying, "I am only a part of human society," he must remember constantly that he is *related* to all men,[183] that he is the member of a large body which without him is incomplete; this thought must lead us to love and do good to all men.[184]

This feeling of love was so strongly impressed on Marcus Aurelius, that although he saw the hatred felt for each other by the men of his time, who seemed to have no mutual affection amongst them, he still remained convinced that they were made to love one another,[185] and that the proper aim of a reasonable soul is the respect and love of his neighbour.[186] This love must be active and helpful. It is true that he says that in order to maintain the calm of the soul, it is necessary "to mourn with no one," but that only means to avoid strong feelings that disturb the mind and produce no good results for others. For he desires that we shall help the unhappy and afflicted, and those who have lost their fortune. We are to benefit them without expecting thanks, and to continue to do so even if repaid by ingratitude. To do good is to act in conformity with our nature. This duty cannot be altered by the behaviour of others towards us;[187] we must therefore extend our benefits even to those who offend us. It is a distinctive characteristic of our nature that we can love and pardon them. The best revenge is to subdue your enemy by goodness rather than by violence, like the immortal gods, who treat sinners and good men with equal clemency.[188] The duty of the wise man, who never forgets that men are made for each other, is to teach them that they may grow better, or to assist them if he cannot improve them.[189]

These are certainly noble sentiments. It is no longer a proud greatness of soul which despises the injuries with which it refuses to be angry. It is no longer the cold indifference of self-centred Stoicism, isolated in the midst of the world. It is a benevolent sympathy, an indulgent goodness, that antiquity had neither taught nor practised before Christ. Still these sentiments had not risen to the height of Christian charity, however new they were to pagan philosophy. In Marcus Aurelius respect for human dignity had not completely destroyed the bondage of ancient prejudice; he does not seek the despised ones to raise them to his level. He speaks of gladiators with an indifference that shows that he considered them as belonging to a naturally inferior class. If he wishes to discourage combats between men and beasts, and to replace them by less cruel games, it is partly from humanity, but partly also because the taste for these spectacles is a frivolous one, a low taste, unworthy of a noble heart.[190]

Marcus Aurelius would have risen higher if his idea of God had been purer and more precise, if he had recognised in Him not only supreme intelligence, but also infinite love; if, notwithstanding his spiritual aspirations, he had not remained attached to the rites and some of the superstitions of paganism; if his ideas had been clearer about the immortality of the soul;[191] if, lastly, he had been able to offer another remedy to the man oppressed by the world or the passions, than that of suicide.[192] We find in him, as in Epictetus, Seneca, and Plutarch, striking contrasts. There are profound shadows along with rays of light. The new spirit strove against the ancient one, whilst he remained unconscious of the new powers. Naturally inclined to benevolence, he yielded to the gentle and secret influence of Christian ideas, whilst believing that he expressed only the maxims of his school and the inspirations of his own heart.

It is not "in spite of history and of facts" that we uphold this thesis. The history of the civilization and philosophy of paganism before the time of Christ proves that it is impossible to find there the source of what is new in the ideas of Marcus Aurelius and the other writers whose doctrines we have sketched. The basis of pagan morality was the natural egoism of the heart of man; therefore we never see the germ of a different kind of fruit; therefore respect and love for men could not grow out of inordinate self-love. To admit that Marcus Aurelius and his predecessors found their light and humanity in contemplation of themselves alone, seems to us less compatible with the results furnished by the study of paganism and of the human heart, than our belief as to the influence of the new ideas which tinged the intellectual atmosphere of the world.[193]

To sum up: we have traced the progress of ethical and philosophical ideas, with special reference to social relationships. The notions of an exclusive and egoistical State is gradually replaced by that of a universal city. Respect for human personality slowly replaces the opinion that only the free and rich citizen is honourable, whilst all others occupy by nature inferior positions. Marriage is to be a holier union, less easily dissolved. Children are more kindly treated by their father. The slave is recognised as man. He is taught to free himself internally, and it is acknowledged that civil emancipation is only a return to natural right. Unfortunates are less despised and looked at with attentive benevolence. The law of *talion* is more and more effaced from morality; and if before, greatness of soul was shown by vengeance, it ought now to be shown by an indulgence which is ready to forgive. What has been the cause of this progress, of this transformation of moral ideas in the philosophers of paganism? We do not hesitate to repeat, that the influence must be sought in Christian charity. The progress was not confined to the domain of philosophic ideas, it passed from theory into fact; we shall find it again throughout the pagan period, in the legislation of some of the emperors and in the decisions of the jurisconsults.

(1) *De Vita Beata*, c. 3, vol. ii. p. 81. (2) *O. c.*, c. 4, p. 82. *De Tranquill. Animi*, vol. i. p. 241. (3) *Ep.* 71, vol. iii. p. 227. (4) *Ep.* 120, vol. iv. p. 119. (5) *Ep.* 41, vol. iii. p. 121. (6) "There is no man, I say, who can clear himself from all sin ; and yet each man says he is innocent, having regard to the bystander, not to his own conscience."—*De Ira*, I. 14, vol. i. p. 18. (7) *De Benef.*, I. 1, vol. ii. p. 127; *Ep.* 57, vol. iii. p. 165. (8) *De Provid.*, c. 2, vol. i. p. 223. (9) *Ep.* 83, vol. iii. p. 302. (10) *De Provid.*, c. 1, vol. i. p. 221. (11) "Whose every action is such, that men are deservedly ashamed of their sin, if they place faith in such gods."—*De Vita Beata*, c. 26, vol. ii. p. 108. See, too, the passages from his book, *De Superstitione*, preserved in Augustine's "City of God." Some writers are of opinion that this book is not Seneca's; but the spirit and the style are both his. (12) "There is something in him of the Stoic's god, I see; he has neither heart nor head."—*Apocolokyntosis*, c. 8, ed. Pankouke, vol. ii. p. 314. (13) *Ep.* 41, 95, vol. iii. pp. 119, 424. (14) See M. J. Simon's article on Seneca in the *Liberté de Penser*, 1848, bk 12, p. 506. (15) *De Otio Sapientis*, c. 31, vol. ii. p. 116. We have used throughout the translation of M. Durozoir, Pankouke collection. (16) *Ep.* 44, vol. iii. p. 125. (17) *Ep.* 31, vol. iii. p. 101. (18) *Consol. ad Helviam*, c. 11, 13, vol. i. pp. 130, 133. (19) *De Benef.* III. 18, vol. ii. p. 187. (20)

Consol. ad Helviam, c. 12, vol. i. p. 130. (21) *De Benef.*, III. 28, vol. ii. p. 194. (22) *Ep.* 95, vol. iii. p. 419. (23) *De Ira*, II. 31, vol. i. p. 57. (24) "Hominem, sociale animal, communi bono genitum videri volumus."—*De Clem.* I. 3, vol. ii. p. 7. The "sociale animal" has a different meaning to the Σῶον πολιτικόν of Aristotle.—*Ep.* 95, vol. iii. p. 424. (25) Jus humanum."—*De Benef.*, III. 18, vol. ii. p. 187. "Æqui bonique natura."—*De Clem.*, I. 18, vol. ii. p. 25. (26) *Consol. ad Helviam*, vol. i. p. 113. (27) *De Clem.*, I. 5, vol. ii. p. 10. (28) *O. c.*, c. 14, p. 22. (29) *De Ira*, I. 5; II. 31; vol. i. pp. 9, 57. (30) *O. c.* I. 5, p. 9. (31) *Ep.* 95, vol. iii. p. 424. (32) See the whole of his fine work, *De Clementia*, addressed to Nero, vol. ii. p. 2 sq. (33) *De Provid.*, c. 6, vol. i. p. 237. (34) *Ep.* 2, vol. iii. p. 6. (35) Juvenal, X. 16, p. 112. Dio Cassius, l. 61, c. 10, vol. ii. p. 231. Tacit., *Ann.*, XIV. 52 sq., vol. ii. p. 190. (36) *De Vita Beata*, c. 23, vol. ii. p. 102. (37) Ibid., p. 103. (38) *Sat.* V. 108 sq., p. 60. (39) *De Benef.*, IV. 26, vol. ii. p. 227. Cf. Matt., V. 45. (40) *De Benef.*, IV. 31, vol. ii. p. 335. (41) *Ep.* 95, vol. iii. p.424. (42) "Etiam ignotis succurrere. . . ."—*De Ira*, I. 5, vol. i. p. 9. "Usque ad ultimum vitæ finem in actu erimus, non desinemus communi bono operam dare, adjuvare singulos, opem ferre etiam inimicis, miti manu."—c. 28, vol. ii. p. 114. "Wherever there is a man, there is an opportunity for a deed of kindness."—*De Vita Beata*, c. 24, vol. ii. p. 103. (43) *De Benef.*, VII. 31, vol. ii. p. 335. (44) "It is no kindness, unless it spring from a kind intention."—*De Benef.*, VI. 9, vol. ii. p. 279. I. 6; II. 4; pp. 134, 146. (45) *De Benef.*, II. 9, p. 150. Cf. Matt. VI. 3. (46) Ib. III. 18 sq.; 29 sq., pp. 187, 195. (47) *De Clem.* II. 5, vol. ii. p. 39. (48) *De Clem.*, II. 6, vol. ii. p. 40. (49) Nor can any one live happily who has regard to himself alone and uses everything for his own interests; thou must live for thy neighbour, if thou wouldest live for thyself."—*Ep.* 48, vol. iii. p. 136. (50) *De Benef.*, IV. 13, vol. ii. p. 216. (51) *De Ira*, III. 42, 43, vol. i. p. 104. (52) Ibid., II. 31, p. 57. (53) "Miserius est nocere quam lœdi."—*Ep.* 95, vol. iii. p. 424. " Inhumanum verbum est ultio."—*De Ira*, II. 32, vol. i. p. 57. (54) *De Ira*, I. 13, 16; II. 32; III. 3, vol. i. pp. 18, 25, 57, 67. (55) Ibid., III. 29, vol. i. p. 95. (56) *De Constantia Sapientis*, vol. i. p. 279 sq. (57) *De Ira*, I. 14; II. 34; vol. i. pp. 18, 60. (58) *De Benef.*, VII. 31, vol. ii. p. 334. (59) "Punishment, of whatever kind, I would apply in way of correction."—*De Ira*, I. 16, vol. i. p. 19. (60) *Ep.* 74, vol. iii. p. 247. (61) *Ep.* 65, vol. iii. p. 196. (62) "Deo parere, libertas est."—*De Vita Beata*, c. 15, vol. ii. p. 94. Ib., c. 5, p. 82. *De Benef.*, III. 28, vol. ii. p. 195. (63) *De Benef.*, III. 20, vol. ii. p. 189. (64) *De Benef.*, III. 18, vol. ii. p. 187. (65) Ib., c. 21, p. 190. (66) Ib., c. 19, p. 189. (67) Ib. ; c. 22, p. 190. (68) " To rule one's slaves kindly is praiseworthy, and in the case of a bondservant, instead of considering how much you may inflict with impunity, thou oughtest to consider how much is allowed by the natural law of equity and kindness, which bids thee spare even prisoners and those bought for a price. . . . For, *although it be allowed thee to treat a slave just as thou wilt*, yet there is a point beyond which the natural law common to all men forbids thee to go, because he is of the same nature as thyself."—*De Clem.*, I. 18, vol. ii. p. 25. (The words in italics do not mean, as it seems to me, that, in Seneca's opinion, any treatment of slaves was permissible, but only that no limit was imposed by law and custom, for in opposition to this conventional right he places the natural right, the "commune fas animantium.") (69) *Ep.* 47, vol. iii. pp. 131, 134, 135. (70) "Nothing is so ruinous to good morals as to sit and look at the games. . . . Now there are no more jests, they are downright human butcheries."—*Ep.* 7, vol. iii. p. 16. *De Ira*, I. 2, vol. i. p. 6. (71) *De Otio Sap.*, c. 29, 30, vol. ii. p. 115. (72) *Ep.* 73, 85, 96, vol. iii. pp. 242, 317, 430. (73) "Placeat homini, quidquid Deo placuit."—*Ep.* 74, vol. iii. p. 248. (74) "Dies natalis."—*Consol. ad Marciam*, c. 25, vol. i. p. 212. (75) From *Ep.* 102, vol. iv. p. 27. (76) "Dost thou ask which is the road to freedom? Any vein thou wilt in thy body."—*De Ira*, III. 15, vol. i. p. 81. He admires the Spartan prisoner, who, sooner than do some menial act, broke his head open, and exclaims: "How near is freedom, and yet that any one should be a slave!"—*Ep.* 77, vol. iii. p. 269. (77) Tacit., *Ann.* XIV. 52, vol. ii. p. 190. (78) "Claritudine virtutum." Ib. XV. 65, p. 260. See, too, Juvenal, *Sat.*, VIII. vv. 211 sq., p. 102. (79) Tacit., *Ann.*, XIV. 11, vol. ii. p. 158. Dio Cassius, l. 61, c. 10, vol. ii. p. 230. See, too, the *Consolatio ad Polybium*. (80) In our days this opinion is maintained more especially by German scholars: Gerlach, *Historische Studien*, vol. i. p. 277; Bernhardy, *Grundriss der Römischen Litteratur*, p. 631. M. Baehr is almost the only one who has expressed a fairer opinion of Seneca; he recognises the integrity of his moral tendencies, but he does not allow the influence of Christianity.—*Geschichte der Litteratur*, 3rd ed., vol. ii. p. 466. (81) We are sorry to find that we here disagree with so distinguished a genius as M. Jules Simon, *Lib. de Penser*, 1848, livr. 12, p. 515. (82) Möhler, *Theolog. Quartalschrift*, Tübingen, 1834, p. 93. (83) Schoell, *Hist. Abrégée de la Litt. Rom.*, vol. ii. p. 445. M. Durozoir, vol. vii. of the *Œuvres de Sen.*, Pankouke's Latin Library, p. 551. M. Troplong, *De l'Infl. du Christ.*, etc., p. 77. M. Wallon, vol. iii. p. 12. See, too, Gelpke's *Dissert.*, "De familiaritate quæ Paulo apostolo cum Seneca philosopho intercessisse videtur verissimilima." Leipzig, 1812, qto. (84) Acts xxviii. 15; Rom. i. 8. (85) Acts xxviii. 30, 31. (86) Phil. iv. 22. (87) 2 Tim. iv. 16. (88). Acts xxviii. 16. (89) Acts xviii. 10 ff. (90) It is he to whom Seneca dedicates his treatises *De Ira* and *De Vita Beata*, and he mentions him often with affection; ap. *Consol. ad Helv.*, c. 16, vol. i. p. 140. (91) "Between it (*i.e.* the soul) and this gross flesh there is a constant struggle."—*Consol. ad Marciam*, c. 24, vol. i. p. 212. Cf. Rom. vii. 18; Gal. v. 17. "We must not say that the height of human happiness lies in the flesh."—*Ep.* 74, vol. iii. p. 247. (92) "Within us there dwells the Holy Spirit, which watches and guards over our joys and our griefs." —*Ep.* 41, vol. iii. p. 119. (93) "Nec ego Epicuri angelus."—*Ep.* 20, vol. iii. p. 62; cf. 2 Cor. xii. 7. (94) "Let us inquire what it is that gives us eternal happiness."—*De Vita Beata*, c. 2, vol. ii. p. 79. (95) Seneca wrote his letters to Lucilius and two works, *De Vita Beata* and *De Beneficiis*, in the latter years of his life. (96) Tertullian calls him "Seneca noster." *De Anima*, c. 19, p. 278. See, too, August., *De Civit. Dei*, VI. c. 11, vol. vii. p. 124; ep. 153, § 14, vol. ii. p. 401. Lactant., *Div. Instit.*, I. 5, vol. i. p. 19. Hieron., *De Script. Eccl.*, c. 12, p. 66. (97) These letters are found in Fabricius, *Codex Apocryphus Novi Test.*, Hamb. 1703, p. 880 ff. (98) *Epp.* X., 97, vol. ii. p. 127. (99) *Paneg.*, c. 3, vol. ii. p. 146. (100) Lib. VIII. ep. 22, vol. ii. p. 30. (101) L. III. ep. 16;

IV. ep. 19, 11; V. ep. 16; VII. ep. 5, 19, vol. i. pp. 99, 133, 135, 170, 223, 237. (102) IV., ep. 13, vol. i. p. 125. (103) IX., ep. 12, vol. ii. p. 44. (104) I. ep. 8; VII. ep. 18, vol. i. pp. 13, 286; and the inscription found at Milan; Orelli, vol. i. p. 255, No. 1172. (105) "Qui an magni sapientesque sint, nescio; homines non sunt."—VIII. ep. 16, vol. ii. p. 22. (106) Ibid., p. 21. (107) IX., epp. 21, 24, vol. ii. pp. 55, 58. (108) V., ep. 19, vol. i. p. 173. (109) "Quasi testamenta ... dumtaxat intra domum."—VIII. ep. 16, vol. ii. p. 21. (110) "For I do not think I have lost them too soon at all, since they were free before I lost them."—Ibid. (111) IX. ep. 6, vol. ii. p. 40. (112) VI. ep. 34; vol. iv. ep. 22, vol. i. pp. 217, 136. (113) Or. 14 and 15, vol. i. p. 436 ff. (114) Vol. i. p. 43 ff. (115) De Defectis Oraculorum, c. 19, vol. ix. p. 329. (116) "... the Author of all good things and the Father of all things honourable." ... Non posse suaviter vivi sec.—Epic., c. 22, vol. xiv. p. 123. (117) Ibid., c. 21, p. 119. (118) "τοῦτο μέντοι (i.e. faith in the gods) τὸ συνεκτικὸν ἀπάσης κοινωνίας καὶ νομοθεσίας ἔρεισμα καὶ βάθρον.—Adv. Colotem, c. 31, vol. xiv. p. 192. (119) De Pyth. Orac., c. 18, vol. ix. p. 275. (120) "τὸ μυθικὸν, τὸ φυσικὸν, τὸ πολιτικὸν."—Amatorius, c. 18, vol. xii. p. 44; De Placitis Philos., I. 6, vol. ii. p. 365. (121) "... Ἄνθρωπος ὢν, ᾧ τὸ φιλεῖν ἐστι καὶ φιλεῖσθαι, καὶ τὸ χαρίζεσθαι καὶ τὸ εὐχαριστεῖν. .,. De Vitando Aëre Alieno, c. 6, vol. xii. p. 213. (122) De Cohibend" Ira, vol. ix. p. 422 ff; De Invidia et Odio, vol. xi. p. 185 ff; De Capienda ex Hostibus Utilitate, vol. vii. p. 269 ff. (123) Conjugialia Præceptau vol. vii. p. 412. (124) "Τὸ γὰρ ἐρᾶν ἐν γάμῳ τοῦ ἐρᾶσθαι μεῖζον ἀγαθόν, ἐστι. Πολλῶν γὰρ ἁμαρτημάτων ἀπαλλάττει, μᾶλλον δεπάντων, ὅσα διαφθείρει καὶ λυμαίνεται τὸν γάμον."—Amatorius, c. 23, vol. xii. p. 62. (125) Conjug. Præc., vol. vii. p. 419 ff. (126) Ib., p. 424. (127) Ib., p. 427. (128) De Liberis Educ., vol. vii. p. 1 ff. Some scholars dispute the authenticity of this work. (129) De Amore Prolis, vol. x. p. 70 ff. (130) Cato Major, c. 5, vol. ii. p. 391. Amyot's translation, ed. Paris, 1645 fol. (131) See Dissert., I. 16, vol. i. p. 90. (132) Ib., I. 14, p. 80. (133) Ib., I. 9, p. 52. (134) Ib., III. 24, vol. i. p. 484. (135) Manual, c. 31, vol. iii. p. 35. (136) Dissert., I. 9, vol. i. p. 52. (137) Richter, Geschichte der Philosophie, 2nd ed., vol. iv. p. 233. (138) Dissert., II. 17; IV. 1, vol. i. pp. 270, 551. Man., c. 15, vol. iii. p. 17. (139) Dissert., II. 5 and 10, vol. i. pp. 192, 216. (140) Dissert., I. 26, vol. i. p. 133. (141) "What then? is it possible for a man to be sinless? It cannot be, but one thing is possible, to strive without ceasing after sinlessness."—Dissert., IV. 12, § 19, vol. i. p. 667. (142) "'Εἰ βούλει ἀγαθὸς εἶναι, πρῶτον πίστευον ὅτι κακὸς εἶ."—Fragm., 3, vol. iii. p. 65. (143) Manual, c. 42, 43, vol. iii. p. 50. (144) Dissert., I. 29; II. 10, 22, vol. i. p. 163, 221, 319. (145) Ib., I. 6, vol. i. p. 35. (146) Ib., II. 5, 14; vol. i. pp. 192, 242. Man., c. 24, vol. iii. p. 25. (147) Dissert., II. 22, vol. i. p. 314. (148) Ib., I. 2, p. 67. (149) Ib., I. 18, 28, 29, vol. i. pp. 97, 144, 163. (150) Ib., II. 4, vol. i. p. 183. (151) Man., c. 40, vol. iii. p. 50. (152) "Καὶ τὸ ὅλον οἱ ἄνθρωποι χαίρουσιν, ἀπολογίας τοῖς ἑαυτῶν ἁμαρτήμασι πορίζοντες. Ἐπεῖτοι φιλοσοφία φησὶν, ὅτι οὐδὲ τὸν δάκτυλον ἐκτείνειν εἰκῇ προσήκει."—Fragm., 53, vol. iii. p. 84. (153) Dissert., I. 2, vol. i. p. 64. (154) Man., c. 8, vol. iii. p. 66. (155) Ib., c. 21 ff., vol. iii. p. 72. (156) Dissert., IV. 1, vol. i. p. 529. (157) Fragm., 44, vol. ii. p. 81; Man., c. 8, vol. ii. p. 66.

CHAP. III.] INCREASING HUMANITY OF PAGAN PHILOSOPHERS. 379

(158) *Dissert.*, I. 19, vol. i. p. 104. (159) *Fragm.*, 43, vol. ii. p. 80. (160) M. Wallon, vol. iii. p. 44. (161) *Dissert.*, III. 23, vol. i. p. 480. (162) Ib., I. 24, vol. i. p. 125. (163) Müller, *De Epicteti Christianismo*. Chemnitz, 1724, qto. Cf. Villemain, *De la Phil. Stoic.*, p. 278. (164) Pensées, vol. i. p. 150; see the whole of this fragment (M. Faugcrès edition, 1844). (165) ". . . Εἶτα ὑπὸ μανιὰς μὲν δύναταί τις οὕτω διατεθῆναι πρός ταῦτα (sc. death, etc.) καὶ ὑπὸ ἔθους ὡς οἱ γαλιλαῖοι, ὑπὸ λόγου δὲ καὶ ἀποδείξεως οὐδεὶς δύναται;"—*Dissert.*, IV. 7, vol. i. p. 618. Schweighaeuser thinks the words "ὡς οἱ γαλ." are a marginal gloss, vol. ii. p. 915. (166) Orig., *C. Cels.*, VI. 2, vol. i. p. 630. Cf. III. 54, p. 483. (167) Cap. 3, § 1, p. 16. (168) Cap. 14, § 16, p. 88. (169) Cap. 3, § 1, p. 16. (170) Passim. (171) Passim. (172) Cap. 5, § 4, p. 26. (173) ". . . ὑπὲρ λείαν ἢ τραχεῖαν κίνησιν τῆς σαρκός. . ." Cap. 27, § 27, p. 172. (174) Cap. 9, § 8, p. 54. (175) Cap. 27, § 27, p. 173. (176) Cap. 17, § 6, p. 32. (177) Cap. 14, § 2, p. 81. (178) Cap. 15, § 18, p. 25. (179) Cap. 4, § 5, p. 20; Cap. 4, § 5, p. 27. (180) Cap. 5, § 1, p. 24. (181) Cap. 31, § 7, p. 195. (182) ". . . Ψίλησον τὸ ἀνθρώπινον γένος."—Cap. 27, § 1, p. 161. (183) Cap. 8, § 3, p. 43. (184) Cap. 8, § 20, p. 48. (185) Cap. 8, § 6, p. 41. (186) Cap. 7, § 6, p. 32. (187) Cap. 29, § 5, p. 188. (188) "Ἴδιον ἀνθρώπου φιλεῖν καὶ τοὺς πταίοντας. . ."—Cap. 80, § 1, p. 190, § 4, p. 191. Cap. 29, § 1 ff., p. 184. (189) "οἱ ἄνθρωποι γεγόνασιν ἀλλήλων ἔνεκεν. δίδασκε οὖν, ἢ φέρε."—Cap. 28, § 7, p. 180. (190) "κενοσπουδία. . ." Cap. 10, § 2 p. 56. Cap. 27, § 27, p. 172. (191) Cap. 34, § 25, pp. 231, 232. (192) Cap. 27, § 27, p. 173. (193) See M. Pierrou's Introduction to his Translation of Marcus Aurelius, p. xxxviii.

CHAPTER IV.

INCREASING HUMANITY OF LEGISLATION DURING THE PAGAN PERIOD OF THE EMPIRE.

§ 1. *Influence of the Christian Spirit on the Emperors and Jurisconsults.*[1]

CHRISTIAN ideas filled the air; the Roman social body received them from all sides. Men who exerted power and authority, though not easily accessible to generous sentiments, could not resist this mysterious power. It seems to us impossible to admit that the emperors and jurisconsults who brought the element of humanity into the laws were uninfluenced by Christianity. We see, it is true, the same contrasts in their conduct as in the moral system of the philosophers. They obeyed principles unknown to ancient legislators; they showed a new spirit of benevolence and justice, but their attitude towards those from whom this spirit emanated was frequently dictated by pagan or national prejudices. However, if some instigated, or did not attempt to hinder, persecutions, others treated Christianity with tacit tolerance or with undisguised favour, which was also extended to other forms of worship. These princes, who were in turns philosophic or vaguely religious, thus rendered involuntary homage to the spirit which inspired in them, unknown to themselves, their juster sentiments. It will be interesting to recall, with reference to our subject, the measures taken in regard to the illegal sect of Christians by emperors who were renowned for their virtues. We shall see that those who did not decidedly oppose Christianity were also those who strove most vigorously to soften the ancient harshness of the civil law, or to found benevolent institutions intended to relieve the misery of the people.

Domitian attempted to reform Roman morality. After his reign, Nerva, who though weak was benevolent, recalled all who had been banished on account of religion, and forbade any new accusations under this pretext.[2] Trajan, when he gave directions to Pliny, refrained from laying down a general rule as to the conduct of governors and magistrates towards Christians. Knowing from the letters of his friend that they were inoffensive people of strict morals, he did not wish them to be sought for, and he desired that anonymous accusations, dictated by hatred, should be ignored or denied;[3] but those who publicly owned their belief must be punished as rebels against the laws. It was in virtue of these laws that Trajan brought Ignatius from Antioch to Rome to put him to death.

Under his successor, the Christians were strong enough to appeal directly to imperial justice. In 126 Aristides and Quadratus presented their apology for Christianity to Adrian. This emperor, who was taught by Plutarch, and who has been praised by the ancients for his piety, seems to have professed a religious eclecticism which did not render momentarily vivid aspirations impossible. He thought it needless to make a distinction between religions, including in the same philosophic disdain the followers of Serapis, of Jehovah, and of Christ, because in his opinion they all worshipped one idol under different names; and this unique divinity, of which they could give no account, had no existence. His god was a speculative abstraction. He rejected the myths of polytheism as completely as the possibility of a special Divine manifestation as it was fulfilled in Christ.[4] It is said that in the hour of death he showed the vagueness of his ideas by grotesque verses addressed to his soul.[5] This undecided man, whose internal conflicts we perhaps do not fully realize, sometimes supported the national worship for political reasons,[6] and sometimes wished to add Christ to the number of accepted divinities, raising to Him temples without statues.[7] It is a positive fact that he issued an edict to the pro-consul of Asia to prohibit magistrates from condemning Christians in deference to the clamour of the crowd. They were only to be punished when, after a formal accusation, they were convicted of having broken the laws.[8] It seems from this that Adrian did not wish Christians to be persecuted simply for their faith; and tacitly tolerated them, although Christianity was not yet declared a lawful religion. The Christians of the early ages themselves attest that if there were persecutions in his reign, they were carried on without his orders.[9]

Antoninus and Marcus Aurelius, to whom Justin presented this apology, also showed themselves more tolerant. The moderate language of Justin, the skill with which he linked his appeals to the equity of the emperors with philosophy, and above all, his account of the pure and benevolent life of Christians, made an impression on these princes. The tradition is preserved, that through his apology he inspired Antoninus the Pious with goodwill towards members of the Church.[10] The principle of Marcus Aurelius was to uphold the legal religion.[11] There were, even during his reign, some local and temporary persecutions;[12] he wished, however, like

Trajan, Adrian, and his father, that the Christians should not be blindly condemned, but treated with all the legal formalities, and only after a regular trial *those should* be punished who owned to practising a worship forbidden by the laws. In the following ages the Church retained a remembrance of an edict issued by one or other of the Antonines in favour of the Christians of Asia. What is preserved as the text of this edict does not appear to be authentic; but even if we admit that it is of later or doubtful origin, it proves at least that the Christians preserved the remembrance of having been treated with greater justice by these two philosophic emperors.[13] Tertullian and Lactantius express the gratitude of the Church for the "good emperors" who used no cruelty towards her.[14]

It will be perhaps astonishing to see the name of Caracalla quoted here. This prince, notwithstanding the cruelties that his foolish ambition led him to commit, was not an absolute stranger to better feelings. He had been, to quote the expression of one of the Fathers,[15] "fed on Christian milk." In his youth he showed a kind and just disposition,[16] of which some feeble traces reappear amidst the acts of violence with which his life is stained. He raised a sanctuary for Apollonius of Tyana,[17] and stopped the persecutions which his father, in the latter years of his reign, instituted against the Church.[18] We even see him influenced by a great jurisconsult to associate himself with the progress and amelioration of the laws.[19]

The need of religion, which confusedly tormented pagan society, caused singular contrasts between desires and practices. This is markedly exemplified in Alexander Severus. This emperor, with a sense of moral right and justice, professed a strange syncretism.

To end the strife of vague needs and half comprehended desires which tormented his soul, he mixed in one system the foreign superstitions prevalent in Rome, the national religion, and some doctrines belonging to Judaism or Christianity.[20] If he had no intention of renouncing pagan worship for the Gospel, he admired the holiness of Christ and the charity which He enforces on His followers; he placed a bust of Christ amongst those of the Roman gods which ornamented his household sanctuary, and he engraved on the walls of his palace, and on other public places, these words of the Saviour: "As ye would that men should do to you, do ye to them likewise." [21] The Christians in Rome enjoyed freedom during his reign, and Christianity spread into the highest families. We have before seen that Quintilius Marcellus, consul with Alexander Severus, had a Christian wife. It once happened that the tavern-keepers claimed a public site which was used by Christians for their worship. The emperor told them that it was better to worship God there in any manner whatever than to establish places of debauchery.[22]

Persecutions were revived under his successors. Christianity made little sensible progress amidst the anarchy of the empire under short-lived tyrants. In the time of Constantine it was related that the Emperor Philip intended to embrace Christianity.[23] A later historian even professed that he was the first Christian prince upon the throne of the empire.[24]

Diocletian in the early years of his reign was not unfavourable to Christianity. He respected religious liberty in his own family; his wife and daughters were Christians. We have previously said that his feelings in regard to the Church were probably influenced by this. Under his government Christians attained the highest positions in the State, and their communities prospered,[25] until, yielding to the suggestions of Galerius Cæsar, and returning to pagan superstitions, it was decided to persecute the Christians as enemies of the laws and of the State.[26]

The emperors whom we have just named were the only ones who introduced a greater spirit of kindness and justice into legislation. Tolerant towards the Church, through different motives, and in an unequal degree, they yielded to the influence of charity, and were lighted with a light whose source their eyes had not fully seen. They introduced great improvements in the laws as to the condition of persons and the relations of civil society. They were aided in this by the jurisconsults who were under the hidden influence of Christian thought, whilst believing themselves to be inspired only by Stoicism. These eminent men exerted great influence even under cruel princes, whom they induced to sign decrees of justice and equity. The name of Caracalla heads many of the best laws; this is explained chiefly by the fact that it was Ulpian who advised them. The jurisconsults acknowledged that the ancient strict and formal laws, which were absolutely enforced under the Republic, were full of injustice that ought to be remedied;[27] Trajan said that such vigour was not suitable to the age.[28] It is true that in very early times the progress of luxury, effeminacy and individual egoism produced a relaxation of the ancient Roman severity,[29] but this was quite distinct from the propagation of juster views and kinder feelings; for the latter did not spring from an egoism which tended to withdraw them from public duties, but from the new thought, expressed by the jurisconsult, Florentinus, that there exists a natural relationship between all men, which should lead them mutually to refrain from wronging each other.[30] The rights of personality began to be dimly seen. Ulpian admits that there are cases where jurisprudence ought to consider rather the individual will than the rigour of the civil law.[31] They raise a natural justice, unknown to ancient Pagan civilization, above the law. They even listen to the voice of the feelings and affections, they tend to approach equity.

Nothing is more remarkable than to see the Roman jurisconsults introduce humanity, or what they call piety, into legislation. Ulpian, the councillor of Alexander Severus, and one of the greatest reformers of the law, who has been unjustly reproached with hatred of Christianity,[32] often repeats that it is through piety and humanity that the law must be interpreted.[33] From this comes the precept to pronounce in doubtful cases for the weakest side, consulting the "rightness of natural desire."[34] This was the custom of Antoninus, who always preferred "the most humane interpretation" of the law.[35] The jurisconsult Marcellus formally declared that "to interpret things in the most favourable manner is both the justest and the safest way."[36]

Another advance appears to us equally worthy of remark. Ancient legislation recognised only *law*, which was enforced in all its rigour; the idea of *duty* appears to have been almost unknown. From the time of which we are now speaking the idea of duty gradually finds a place in the laws. For instance, in questions relating to the family, the judge has to decide not only according to law, but also in accordance with the demands of natural affection. He ought to remind of their duties those who, trusting to the established law, were disposed to neglect what the law did not compel them to do.[37] This is an advance which has not been much considered, but it seems to us a great triumph of humanity over the harshness of the olden times.

It remains for us to see the application of the new principles to the laws which prevail in civil society. In each social condition we can show a realized progress, a conquest of equity over the inflexibility of ancient law. What we shall have to say will be to a certain extent of a fragmentary character; this is an unavoidable inconvenience inherent in the nature of the thing itself. The improvement in the laws came about gradually and slowly, often caused by accidental circumstances. It is not complete, not the result of combined work, nor of a scientific revision of the whole of legislation; and therefore we often find singularly strange blanks and contradictions, which the plan of our work forbids us to enter into in detail. We must limit ourselves to observing the traces of the new spirit where we find them at this period.

§ 2. *Women and Marriage.*

Woman, though not raised to the height which she fills in Christian society, enjoyed many rights which antiquity had refused her. It was a considerable progress that the jurisconsults should themselves say that the condition of women was worse than that of men;[39] for this was an implicit acknowledgment that this unjust inferiority required redress.

During the first three centuries some steps were taken in the path of reparation, especially by the progressive transformation of ideas about marriage. Marriage, which was formerly a purely political institution, depended entirely on the father, who was the representative of the State in the family. Feelings of affection were little, if at all, considered. One of the first improvements was to introduce a freedom more in accordance with nature. Antoninus and Alexander Severus ratified a law given by Augustus, which forbade the father to refuse a dowry to his daughters, or to prohibit the marriage of his children for no other reason than his own caprice.[39] Diocletian decreed that the son should no longer be obliged to take a wife who was not to his taste, though chosen by his parents; he might make his own choice, provided he obtained the paternal consent.[40] The daughter acquired the right to refuse the husband destined for her by her father, if he was a man of worthless morals.[41]

The paternal power over married daughters, the right of reclaiming them when they had not passed *under the hand* of the husband, was next abolished. Antoninus introduced the first restriction, although in the timid form of a request. He endeavoured to persuade fathers not to use their power "harshly," [42] in order that happy marriages might not be disturbed by the exercise of paternal authority. Diocletian suppressed this power completely. He gave the husband the right to reclaim his wife, appealing, in case of need, to the magistrates, who must act according to his wishes, after they had consulted the wife also.[43] We see by this that the wish of the woman was taken into account, and that marriage began to have a higher significance. It is no longer simply a civil union in the interests of the State; it is a more intimate union in the bond of affection, and ought only to be concluded after reciprocally free choice.

Ancient legislation refused the right of property to married women. All that they brought at marriage became the property of the husband, and afterwards of the agnates. The new ideas on the character of the conjugal union slowly modified these arrangements, which were so unjust and humiliating for the woman. Return of the dowry was granted in case of the death of the husband or of divorce. Under Marcus Aurelius children are admitted to inherit after the mother in preference to the agnates. This " new succession " is a double victory of equity over ancient law; [44] it is a victory gained at the same time by both mother and children; it is an acknowledgment that the mother is the rightful owner of what she brought, and it bestows a right upon the children which was before held by the agnates. Through the same principle, other laws, claimed first by women with the intention of making themselves more independent, limited the guardianship that the agnates exercised over the wife, and allowed her the power of possessing and disposing of her fortune. The Roman ladies often abused this new liberty, amidst the corruption of Roman society; but it is still true that the principle was in accordance with that equity which was spreading in the world.

The rights of guardianship (*tutela*), in the ancient Roman sense, disappeared under Diocletian, and we meet afterwards with but few traces of it. This emperor made a step further in the legitimate emancipation of women by giving them the right of adoption, previously reserved for the father of the family alone.[45]

To strengthen still further the moral character of marriage, divorces, which had hitherto been so common and so scandalously easy, were surrounded with difficulties; and the reasons limited for which they were permitted.[46] Diocletian ordered that in a case of divorce the magistrates should have the power of deciding which parent should retain the children; they would probably leave them with the one who was not guilty of the fault which brought about the divorce.[47] Adultery was punished with redoubled severity. A law of Caracalla, doubtless suggested by Ulpian, also accuses the *husbands* if they are known to be guilty, and only permits them to reproach their wives if they are themselves without fault. This legislator considers it to be a crowning iniquity to ask from the wife alone a chastity which is not also observed with regard to her.[48] It appears, however, that the crime was only recognised when committed with free-born women, the wives of freemen; husbands were still allowed to frequent the *lupanar* or to live with slaves, which was not adultery in the eye of the law.[49] It is probably about this time that there arose an association of Roman women for the preservation of purity, the remembrance of which is preserved to us by an inscription, of unknown date, found upon a stone at Rome.[50]

Lastly, marriage was made less exclusive than in the old Roman society of the Republic and the early times of the empire. Diocletian accomplished the first reform in this respect; he allowed the master to marry the slave whom he had set free, and only senators remained subject to the former prohibitions. These restrictions, enforced afresh by Constantine, were soon afterwards finally abolished; so that no position, however dignified, prevented legitimate marriage with free women of good character.[51]

§ 3. *Children in General. Poor Children.*

The condition of children was equally improved. A series of measures, intended to restrict paternal power, testify to increased respect for the rights of nature, and tend to replace the ancient harsh and absolute authority of the father by a more affectionate tenderness; and the servile fear of the children by a more real and grateful piety. These tendencies prove that man was beginning to be valued as man, and not only for the services which he rendered as a citizen.

The first step was the suppression of the barbarous right of life or death. It disappeared early, but we do not know the precise time when it was first legally contested.[52] Already, in the time of Augustus, a father who had killed his son, was himself killed by the indignant crowd.[53] The fact that Trajan forced a father to emancipate a son whom he had ill used, "contrary to piety," seems to prove that in his time paternal power was not recognised in its ancient extent.[54] A father who killed his son for having been guilty of adultery was punished by Adrian with banishment to an island: "considering," said he, "that he acted rather after the law of brigands than after the law of a father."[55] The jurisconsult Marcian adds to this sentence an observation marked with a profoundly different spirit from that of ancient law: "The paternal power," he says, "should consist in piety, not in cruelty."[56] In the time of Alexander Severus the right of life and death was definitely suppressed. This emperor ordered that if children despised the father's authority and refused obedience to him, he might enforce his power "by sending them before the courts of justice."[57]

Legislators also endeavoured to prevent abortion and exposure. Though ancient laws and philosophers had greatly approved of these methods of disposing of weak or unwelcome children, the jurisconsult Paulus spoke of them as murders committed by people who were without mercy.[58] However, no penalty was yet imposed on parents guilty of those crimes which were so common throughout the whole duration of the Empire; the only hindrances were such as in the then existing state of morals were not of much use. Those who received and brought up exposed children had, according to the ancient laws, the right of keeping them for slaves, and those who desired their liberty must buy it with a ransom. Trajan refused this compensation to those who had brought up the exposed children; he declares them to be free by right.[59] Alexander Severus gave to the father of an exposed child the right of claiming him later, but he must defray the expenses which he had caused to the man who brought him up.[60]

Caracalla associated himself with measures intended to take away all that was exorbitant in paternal power. He declared the traffic of freeborn children to be "disgraceful and illegal." He punished the creditor who took them for payment; and although the law does not speak of the father, it is probable that there is also a punishment for him.[61] The prohibitions against selling or hiring children upon any pretext were renewed by Diocletian.[62]

Remarkable efforts were made to limit paternal power by a sense of duty, thus giving it a purer and truer character. If the father has a right to exact respect and obedience from his son, he owes him in return the cares demanded by his weakness, food, education,—briefly, "piety." Antoninus and Septimus Severus, remind parents of the obligations which the manners and laws of the times had caused them to forget. The second of these emperors declares that the duties are reciprocal: "If thou renderest to thy father that which is his due, he ought not to deny thee paternal piety." If the father refuses it, the magistrates must enforce it.[63] This paternal duty, inseparable from respect for the rights of children, enters more and more into the law. When the child attains his majority, the law, which before kept him under the power of his father, even when he was married, takes him henceforth under its protection and guarantees his natural rights.

Cicero had already found that the Voconian law, given exclusively in the interest of men, was harsh and unjust to women, and he asked, Why should not women possess wealth? Why may not a daughter inherit from her father?[64] However, a long time elapsed before the right of succession of a married daughter, who had left her father's house, was recognised. It was not until the second century that children no longer under the paternal authority were declared legitimate heirs.[65]

The right of disinheritance was also limited and submitted to more formalities, with the evident intention of discouraging its practice. If the daughter was overlooked in the father's will, the law assured her a share in the succession.[66] To remedy the severity of the law by which the unemancipated son belonged to the father, with all his possessions, Augustus, Nerva, and Trajan ordered that the wealth he might acquire in the military career should be his alone throughout the duration of his service; Marcus Aurelius added that it should belong to him also after his retirement.[67]

We have not reached the limits of reform in the law. In the ancient order of things the emancipated child had no duty towards his parent, especially he had none towards his mother. If the father became poor or infirm, only the child remaining in his power had charge of his needs; he, on his side, was not bound to do anything for the emancipated child. Ulpian, filled with the idea that the legal relations of emancipation and being in power were only factitious, and that, emancipated or not, a man remains always the child of his father, desired that these duties should be invariably the same. He goes further; he had been asked if children were bound to support their mother, and he answered that this question is decided quite simply by equity and *charity*. This opinion of the great jurisconsult was made into a law.[68] Antoninus had already declared that it is just that children should help their parents when in need.[69] Valerian and Diocletian ordered the magistrates when it was necessary to force sons to give their mothers "the reverence which is their due," and to punish severely "outraged piety."[70] All this abundantly proves that the intimate union between members of one family was more and more recognised, and that it was no longer considered as a purely political institution. The voice of natural affection made itself heard. Duty took a place by the side of law. Paternal authority existed, but was no longer an arbitrary tyranny. The servile dependence of children under the ancient laws was gradually replaced by the truer and gentler dependence of mutual love and gratitude; a great progress, due to the influence of the new spirit.

Before leaving this subject, we will mention some measures taken specially in the interest of poor children. It was not enough to place obstacles in the way of getting rid of children by exposure or murder; for many parents alleged their poverty, and the consequent impossibility of supporting a family on their fortune, as an excuse for their barbarity; and it was needful to take poor children under special protection, by providing them with a living. Here we meet for the first time with an example of public benevolence in pagan society. It was not yet a general measure prescribed by law; it was an effort, imperfect and incomplete, but at least a proof of the further progress in sentiments of humanity which the new spirit in the world inspired in some choice men.

The initiative was taken by some virtuous princes who occupied the imperial throne; it was followed by a small number of private people, perhaps also by the magistrates of some towns. Nerva was the first who extended his care to the children of poor parents, by ordering them to be supported at the public expense in all the towns of Italy.[71] Some medals bear witness to the gratitude of the people for this imperial benefit.[72] Trajan devoted considerable sums to the development of this institution, so useful in the general misery of the provinces of Rome.[73] He supported five thousand poor children in the capital;[74] in most of the Italian towns, and even in Africa, he established funds for food with the same aim. The remembrance of this is perpetuated by commemorative medals.[75] Different memorials, found in Italy a century ago, show us the way in which these institutions of help were organized. One example will suffice. We will choose that of the town of Veleia, in the ancient colony of Placentia. Trajan lent money to the inhabitants of this neighbourhood (who needed it for the cultivation of their lands), for which they mortgaged their property to him; or rather, for which they engaged to pay interest, which was intended for the support of poor children. The total interest to be paid annually was fixed at 52,000 sesterces, that is, about 9,600 francs or £400. This sum was to be used as follows: 245 boys born in wedlock were to receive 16 sesterces each a month (about 29 shillings a year); 34 girls, also legitimate, were to receive 12 sesterces each a month (about £1 a year); the smallest amount of help was given to natural children. An appendix to the act of foundation gave a revenue of 3,600 sesterces (about £27) for 18 boys and 1 girl, all legitimate.[76] We find that the largest number of these assisted children were boys. The emperor wished to provide himself with faithful servants, bound by the ties of gratitude for the care he had bestowed on their fate.[77]

The example of Trajan was followed by others. We have seen that Pliny bestowed a similar endowment on his native town of Como, to which he left annual revenues of 3,000 sesterces (£23 nearly), to be divided amongst poor children.[78] A rich lady of Terracina, Celia Macrina, founded an alimentary institution for a hundred country children.[79] These establishments had a special administration charged with the receipt and distribution of the revenues. The alimentary procurators were doubtless the same as those who presided over the distributions of wheat given to the people.[80]

By a law of Adrian, confirmed by Alexander Severus, boys received help until their eighteenth year, and girls until their fourteenth.[81] Adrian increased the funds set aside by Trajan for these works of liberality.[82] Preserved under the Antonines, they were increased by special funds intended for young girls, perhaps to save them from becoming lost through misery. Antoninus established one in honour of his wife Faustina.[83] Marcus Aurelius, on the occasion of his daughter's marriage with Lucius Verus, endowed a number of alimentary children of both sexes. The same emperor honoured the memory of his wife Faustina,[84] in spite of her frivolous conduct, by a foundation for young girls, similar to that of Adrian.[85] Numerous medals, as well as a charming bass-relief in the palace of Albano, have perpetuated the memory of the liberality of Antoninus and of his adopted son.[86] Alexander Severus followed their example by the foundation for alimentary boys and girls, in honour of his mother, Julia Mammæa.[87]

These generous and necessary institutions soon fell into decay, the public funds serving only for the luxuries or ambition of the tyrants who disputed for the throne.[88] No one thought of creating any more of these benevolent foundations. Those which already existed were destroyed in the universal disorder. The proprietors of the lands held under this condition paid no rents to the administration of aid during a series of years, so that the poor children were left in destitution. Pertinax, to whom merciful feelings were unknown, chose rather to sacrifice the whole institution than to compel the defaulters to pay their debts; he finally suppressed it.[89] Thus it was destroyed after having saved a part of the population from disgrace and misery. However, whilst still in existence, it did not hinder the frightful progress of general poverty; that needed something more than an allowance distributed monthly to poor children. The restoration of labour to the dignity of which ancient civilization had robbed it was needed for its cure. This was one of the last ideas to be received by the Romans, who made no effort to ennoble free labour, though, as we shall see further on, they made some attempts to improve the condition of slaves. Nevertheless the alimentary institutions are amongst the best titles to honour of those emperors who founded and protected them. In our opinion the feeling which led these princes to care for the poor, and especially for the neglected little ones, is a striking proof of the power exerted over them by the spirit of charity which Christianity was shedding abroad.

§ 4. *Slaves.*

Slavery was too much in accordance with the spirit and customs of paganism to fall directly before the gentle and mysterious breath of evangelical thought.

We have seen that it was retained in Christian society with a persistence which only yielded slowly to the precepts of charity. However, even in pagan society itself, charity exerted its reforming power over the condition of slaves. We have seen how it made itself felt in the conduct and theories of philosophers. It remains to show how it introduced equity and justice into the laws with regard to slaves, which had previously treated them only with contemptuous harshness. Slavery itself was continued, the right of the master to own his slave was far from being taken away, but the idea arose that the slave instead of being a machine without will, is a man like the master.

Caius still states the fact that the principal division of the law of persons rests on the distinction between freemen and serfs,[90] but the more humane philosophic emperors and jurisconsults endeavoured to soften this harshness. Trajan began this effort at improvement, which became more decided under Adrian, notwithstanding his passionate disposition. It was continued under the Antonines, and especially under Alexander Severus, who was the most benevolent of the emperors towards his slaves. He wished to be, according to the ancient custom, the father of the family, loved rather than feared.[91] His counsellor, Ulpian, was the first to embody in the law the great principle that men are born free and equal, and that slavery is not in conformity with natural law.[92] Struck with the melancholy fate of slaves, he even says that slavery is almost like death.[93] Florentinus, another jurisconsult, also acknowledges that it is contrary to nature, that it is only a "constitution of the law of man." [94]

Starting with these ideas, they began by restricting the absolute power of the masters. Antoninus, whilst still conceding that their power over their slaves ought to remain intact, seeks nevertheless to limit their harshness, because he says it is of importance to themselves that they should not refuse to assist the oppressed, who complain of cruel treatment.[95] He founds this appeal, it is true, on an egoistical motive; he appeals to the personal interest of the masters that they will be better served by their slaves if they treat them better. But in the midst of the utterly egoistical society of his time it was impossible to use higher motives. He had to speak to the pagans in a language they could understand, in order to attain his aim of improving the condition of the servile class.[96]

Adrian took more direct measures to gain this end; he deprived the masters of the power of life and death, and referred the murder of a slave to the tribunals to be punished as homicide.[97] This law was confirmed by Antoninus,[98] and finally the general principle was incorporated in the law that whoever killed a man, of whatever rank he might be, was guilty of murder.[99]

The custom of exposing old and sick slaves, which was only another kind of homicide, had already been forbidden by Claudius. This emperor ordered that exposed slaves who regained their health should be considered free.[100] Ill-treatment was forbidden. Adrian, after advising the masters to avoid it in their own interest, punished those who remained deaf to his imperial exhortations. He exiled a matron who had tormented her servants for the most frivolous reasons.[101]

Septimius Severus branded that man with infamy who was condemned for injuries to his slaves.[102] Amongst these injuries soon came to be reckoned that of giving a servant occupation which was below his talent and knowledge. Educated slaves were not allowed to be employed in work which did not demand a cultivated mind.[103]

If a man bought a slave under certain conditions, it

was contrary to the ancient idea to hold to an engagement in reference to a being without a will. Henceforward the law compelled the master to keep these engagements, and thus made a great step towards a better order of things.[104] If, notwithstanding these prohibitions, the master ill-treated his slaves, or broke his engagements with them, the law itself protected them.

So far back as the time of Seneca the custom was introduced of allowing them to seek an asylum near the statues of the gods.[105] Antoninus sanctioned this law, and ordered that the slaves who sought refuge in a consecrated place should not be sent back to their masters.[106] They were even allowed to lay their complaints of the cruelties of their masters before the magistrates. Under Nero, the prefect of the town was charged to attend to their account of the injuries they had suffered.[107] Very soon they were even permitted, through the medium of counsel, to bring a civil charge against the master; as, for instance, when he had violated a promise or contract through which they expected to gain their liberty.[108] Antoninus added an order to the magistrates which forbade them to send any slaves back to their masters who had suffered harsh and injurious treatment.[109] This measure was completed by the law of Marcus Aurelius, which compelled the masters to bring their complaints before the tribunal; that is to say, they were forbidden to administer their own justice.[110]

Legislation thus partially arrested the harshness and tyranny of the masters. It endeavoured also to increase respect for human nature by forbidding the freeman to abuse the slave for his ferocious amusements or detestable passions. The efforts yet made were timid and ineffectual; but if pagan morality resisted them so long with an obstinacy that astonishes us, so much the more must we acknowledge the humanity and moral strength of those who endeavoured to oppose them.

After the unbridled license of the times of Tiberius and Nero, some efforts were made to stop the immoral influence of the games and of the theatre. Trajan endeavoured to suppress the immodest representations of the pantomime, but his efforts were not crowned with success; the desire of the people was uncontrollable. Even the wisest and most virtuous of the emperors were unable to hinder the Romans from corrupting themselves by attending the theatres. According to the testimony of Marcus Aurelius, his father, Antoninus, did not give spectacles to gain the praises of the masses, but because he looked upon it as a *duty* of his position.[111]

Marcus Aurelius himself could go no further than to lessen the salaries of the actors.[112] It was the same with the gladiators. A law, doubtless of the time of Nero, had already forbidden masters to sell their slaves to combats with beasts, without the sentence of a judge.[113] Adrian, with the same reservation, forbade their sale to *lanists* or *lenones*.[114] Marcus Aurelius wished that none but criminal slaves should be so sold, in order that buyer and seller might be punished together.[115] Unable to abolish these games, which appeared to him as frivolous vanities, he endeavoured to moderate the passion of the people for them. He lessened the sum allowed for the support of gladiators, and endeavoured to replace bloody struggles terminating in the death of one of the combatants, by simple games of fencing, such as were practised by the athletes of ancient Greece.[116]

These efforts at reform, feeble and imperfect as they were, were restricted to the reigns of which we have spoken. For a long time the people furiously opposed the abolition of the games of the circus, and the tyrants who rapidly succeeded each other during the greater part of the third century were too much interested in pleasing the crowd to dream of disarming the troops of gladiators who were often their assistants.

There were laws inflicting a considerable fine on those who abused freemen against their will; a little later such criminals were punished with death;[117] no attempt was ever made to guard slaves from the brutal passions of their masters. The emperors dared not energetically combat a vice so common in Rome.

Domitian was almost the only one who applied the law *scantinia* to persons of the rank of knights and senators.[118] Antoninus and Marcus Aurelius had enough virtue to refrain themselves from this debauchery, but not enough courage to attack it in others.[119] Alexander Severus had for a short time the intention of suppressing public-houses inhabited by *scorta virilia*, but was withheld by the consideration of the insufficiency of this remedy.[120] When Philip, a little later, tried to put an end to this disorder, the most disgraceful of any in ancient times, he did it with a timidity which proves how strong was the power of vice, how great the perversion of public opinion; he confined himself simply to giving advice, and to recording in his biography that the evil was not extirpated.[121]

We have till now endeavoured to unite the facts which bear testimony to the efforts made by lawgivers to hinder the master, the freeman, from abusing and maltreating his slave; we have however to consider the further progress of humanity in the way in which the slave was raised, more and more, in his own eyes.

We have already stated that the right was granted to him of preferring complaints against a barbarous master before the judges; to this right others were added which gradually approximated his condition to that of a member of civil society, of a person. Until then, slaves, not being persons, were not allowed to take an oath; when called as witnesses they were tested by torture. This custom was modified by Adrian, who, in certain fixed cases, wished their testimony to be received, thus acknowledging, to a certain extent, one of the rights of freemen.[122] The ownership of the money they saved, and the power of using it to buy their liberty, was also guaranteed to them; public slaves were allowed to dispose by will of half their wealth.[123] Family rights were granted to them; the master was forbidden to separate children from their father, or the husband from his wife.[124] They might even raise monumental stones to the memory of parents who were slaves like themselves; sometimes a more than usually humane master would keep them a place amidst his own family tombs.[125]

Above all, enfranchisement was made easy.[126] Formerly slaves were so born; henceforward, in accordance with a law of Antoninus, the child conceived whilst its mother was free, though born into a state of slavery, must be considered free.[127] The enforcement of wills which freed the slaves was most carefully protected. Promises could not be eluded; in doubtful cases it was customary to decide in favour of freedom, lighting what was obscure "by the light of humanity."[128]

If in a will, or in a deed of sale to another master, a condition of liberation was found, it was always to be interpreted in a manner favourable to liberty. Alexander Severus made several protective laws on this point.[129] Liberty, once obtained, was irrevocable. A freeman could never fall back into slavery. All reserves which might be applied to his manumission were pronounced void. The full and complete enjoyment of civil rights was guaranteed to him, especially the possession of wealth, and the free power of its disposal. Alexander Severus and Diocletian lessened the number of cases in which a man could be legally reduced to slavery. Rigorous penalties were inflicted on those who stole men to sell them for slaves.[130]

Thus we have liberty better protected, enfranchisement encouraged, the condition of slaves improved, the power of the masters curtailed. This progress came about under pagan emperors through the influence of the ideas of justice and humanity, which tended to transform the laws and general disposition of civil society.

---

(1) See De Rhoer, *Dissertationes de effectu Religionis Christianæ in Jurisprudentiam Romanam*, vol. i. Gröningen, 1766 (this scholarly work, unfortunately not completed, is not so well known as it deserves). De Meysenbug, *De Christianæ Religionis vi et effectu in Jus Civile*, Göttingen, 1828, 4°. M. Troplong, *De l'Influence du Christianisme sur le droit Civil des Romains*, Paris, 1843. (2) Dio Cassius, l. 68, c. 1, vol. ii. p. 305. Cf. Lactant., *De Mort. Persecut.*, c. 3, vol. ii. p. 187. (3) Trajan's reply to Pliny, l.x, *Ep.* 98, vol. ii. p. 129. (4) See Flav. Vopisc., *Vita Saturini*, c. 8, a very obscure passage, taken from some writing of Phlegon, Adrian's freedman. *Scriptt. Hist. Aug.*, vol. ii. p. 234. (5) Æl. Spart., *Adr*,, c. 25 ; Ib., vol i. p. 27. (6) Ib., c. 22, p. 23. (7) Lamprid., *Al. Sev.*, c. 43 ; Ib., vol. i. p. 290. (8) Just. Mart., *Apol.* 1. c. 69, p. 84. The Latin original of this edict will be found ap. Rufin., *Hist. Eccl.* IV., c. 9, p. 65. (9) " . . . absque præcepto imperatoris."—Hieron., *De Viris Ill.*, c. 19, p. 85. (10) Orosius affirms that Justin, by his apology "made him lenient towards the Christians" (VII. 14, p. 491). (11) Dig., XLVIII. tit. 19, l. 30. Jul. Paul., *Sentent. Receptæ*, V. tit. 21, 92. (12) Euseb., *Hist. Eccl.*, IV. c. 23, p. 143. Cf. August., *De Civit. Dei*. XVIII. 52, vol. vii. p. 404. (13) See Appendix, Note 2. (14) "Boni principes Romani."—Tertull., *Apol.*, c. 5, p. 23 ; Lactant., *De Mort. Persecut.*, c. 3, vol. ii. p. 187. (15) Tertull., *Ad Scap.*, c. 4, p. 71. (16) Æl. Spart., *Carac.*, c. 1 ; *Scriptt. Hist. Aug.*, vol. i. p. 189. (17) Dio Cassius, l. 77, c. 18, vol. ii. p. 415. (18) There were now no more persecutions for some time except in Africa. Cf. Tertull., *Ad Scap.*, p. 69. (19) See below. In revenge Caracalla had Papinian killed. (20) See Heyne, "De Alex. Severo, Religiones Miscellaneas probante"; see his *Opuscula Acad.*, Göttingen, vol. vi. p. 169 ff. (21) Lamprid., *Al. Sev.*, c. 29, 43, 51 ; *Scriptt. Hist. Aug.*, vol. 1. pp. 278, 290, 296. (22) Ib., c. 49, p. 294. It has been thought, in consequence of this incident, that Alexander Severus was a Christian ; others again have made him a Gnostic. See Jablonski, "Dissert. de Alex. Severo, Christianorum sacris per Gnosticos mitato," in his *Opuscula*, Leyden, 1809, vol. iv. p. 38 ff. (23) Euseb.,

Hist. Eccl., VII. 34, p. 232. (24) Oros., VII. 20, p. 513. (25) Euseb., VIII. 1, p. 291. (26) Euseb., *Vita Const.*, II. 50, 51, p. 467; *Hist. Eccl.*, VIII. to X., p. 291 ff. Lactant., *De Mort. Persecut.*, c. 7 ff., vol. ii. p. 191 ff. (27) " . . . Juris iniquitates . . . "— Caius, III. § 25, p. 215. (21) " . . . Nec nostri seculi est . . . " —To Pliny, X. *Ep.* 98, vol. ii. p. 129. (29) In the reign of Tiberius, Valerius Messalinus was able to say: "Much of the harshness of the ancients had given place to better and happier principles."—Tacit., *Ann.*, III. 34, vol. i. p. 153. (30) Dig., l. I. tit. 1, l. 3. (31) E. g., in the *fidei commissum*. Ulp., tit, XXV. § 1, p. 83. (32) See Appendix, Note 3 on Ulpian. (33) "Pietatis intuitu . . . " "Humanitatis intuitu . . . "—*Dig.*, XXXIV. tit. 1, l. 14; XL. tit. 4, l. 4. (34) " . . . Desiderii naturalis ratio."—Paul. *Dig.*, L. tit. 17, l. 85. (35) " . . . humanior interpretatis."—*Dig.*, XXVIII., tit. 4, l. 3. (36) "In re dubia benigniorem interpretationem sequi, non minus justum est, quam tutius."—*Dig.*, lib. L. tit. 17, l. 192. See, too, Marcian, *Dig.*, XLVIII. tit. 9, l. 5. (37) E.g. *Dig.*, XXV. tit. 3, l. 5. (38) Papinian: "In multis juris nostri articulis deterior est conditio feminarum, quam masculorum."—*Dig.*, I. tit. 5, l. 9. (39) *Dig.*, XXIII. tit. 2, l. 19. (40) "Nor does the system of law allow that a son be forced against his will to take a wife. Wherefore thou art not hindered, so long as no precept of the law be infringed, from marrying whomsoever thou wilt; provided only that, in contracting such marriage, the father's consent be given."—*Corp. Jur.*, V. tit. 4, l. 12. (41) " . . . Si indignum moribus, vel turpem sponsum ei pater eligat."—Ulpian, *Dig.*, XXIII. tit. 1, l. 12. (42) " . . . Patri persuadetur ne acerbe patriam potestatem exerceat."—*Dig.*, XLIII. tit. 30, l. 1, § 5. (43) "If thy wife be kept at home by her parents against her will, the magistrate of the province, on thy appeal, shall bring the woman into court, and in accordance with her wish shall gratify thy desire."—*Corp. Jur.*, V. tit. 4, l. 11. (44) " . . . Nova hæreditas." —*Dig.*, XXXVIII. tit. 17, l. 1. (45) *Corp. Jur.*, VIII. tit. 48, l. 5. (46) M. Laboulaye, *Recherches sur la Condition Civile et Politique des Femmes*. Paris, 1843, p. 40. (47) *Corp. Jur.*, V. tit. 24, l. 1. (48) "Periniquum enim mihi videtur esse, ut pudicitiam vir ab uxore exigat, quam ipse non exhibet; quæ res potest et virum damnare, non ob compensationem mutui criminis, rem inter utrumque componere, vel causam facti tollere."—Ap. August., *De Conj. Adult.*, II. 8, vol. vi. p. 299; *Codex Gregorianus*, XIV. tit. 2, l. 1, ed. Haenel, Bonn, 1842, qto. p, 42. (49) Cf. Hieron., *Ep.* 77, vol. i. p. 459. (50) Sodalitas pudicitiæ servandæ.—Ap. Orelli, vol. i. p. 418, No. 2401. (51) *Corp. Jur.*, V. tit. 4, l. 15, tit. 27, l. 1. (52) Cf. M. Troplong, p. 259; M. Wallon, vol. iii. p. 471. (53) Ib., p. 54. (54) " . . . quem male contra pietatem afficiebat.—*Dig.*, XXXVII. tit. 12, l. 5. (55) "Quod latronis magis quam patris jure eum interfecit."—*Dig.*, XLVIII. tit. 9, l. 5. M. Wallon (l.c.) thinks this instances an exception which seems to prove that the right of killing one's child was still recognised, and that this father was only punished for killing, not as a father, but as a brigand. But what difference should there be between these two modes of killing? To us it would rather appear as if the legislator meant that this father was punished for behaving towards his son like a brigand instead of a father; especially may this be inferred from the comment added by Marcian. (56) "Nam patria potestas in pietate debet, non in atrocitate, consistere," l. c. (57) "Acrius remedium."—*Dig.*, XLVIII. tit. 8, l. 2. Law of Alex. Severus, 227. *Corp. Jur.*, VIII. tit. 47, l. 3. Already in the time of the jurisconsult Paulus the right of killing one's child had been done away with; he speaks of it as of a thing of the past: "quos et accidere licebat."—*Dig.*, lib. XXIII. tit. 2, l. 11. (58) "In our opinion not only is that man a murderer who suffocates his child, but he also who exposes it in some public place to attract a pity which he does not feel himself."—*Dig.*, XXV. tit. 3, l. 4. (59) Plin., X. *Epp.* 71, 72, vol. ii. pp. 114, 115. (60) 224. *Corp. Jur.*, VIII. tit. 52, l. 1. (61) *Corp. Jur.*, VII. tit. 16, l. 1. *Dig.*, XX. tit. 3, l. 5. (62) *Corp. Jur.*, IV. tit. 43, l. 1. (63) Law of Antonine, 161;—of Septimius Severus, 197: "Si patrem tuum officis debite promerueris, paternam pietatem tibi non denegabit."—*Corp., Jur.*, V. tit. 25, l. 3, 4. (64) "In mulieres plena est injuriæ . . . Cur enim pecuniam non habeat mulier?"—*De Rep.*, III. 7, ed. Lemaire, 301. (65) M. Laboulaye, *O. c.* p. 28 ff. (66) *Instit.*, II. tit. 13. M. Laboulaye, pp. 19, 29. (67) M. Troplong, p. 264. (68) "I think also that children, even though they are not in the power of their parents, ought to be supported by them, and that reciprocally the children ought to support their parents . . . And it is better that the judge should interpose on both sides, so as to assist more effectually the wants of some and the weakness of others; and, although this matter proceeds from equity and family affection, the judge ought to weigh well the desires of each party." —*Dig.*, XXV. tit. 3, l. 5. (69) "Parentum necessitatibus liberos succurrere justum est."—*Corp. Jur.*, V. tit. 25, l. 1, 2. (70) "Reverentiam debitam exhibere matri . . . Laesa pietas . . ." Valerian, 259, *Corp. Jur.*, VIII. tit. 47, l. 4, 5. (71) Aurel. Victor, *Epit.*, c. 12, p. 171. (72) A medal struck in Nerva's third consulate, A.D. 97, represents him as stretching out his right hand over a little boy and girl.—Eckhel, P. II. vol. vi. p. 408. (73) Dio Cassius, l. 68, c. 5, vol. ii. p. 307. (74) Plin., *Paneg.*, c. 28, vol. ii. p. 168. (75) A medal of the year 103 A.D., represents him stretching out his right arm towards a woman with two little children.—Eckhel, P. II. vol. vi. p. 424. There are several medals of his reign with the inscription, "Alimenta Italiæ." An inscription found at Ameria shows the gratitude to Trajan felt by the "pueri puellæque Ulpiani."—Orelli, vol. ii. p. 81, No. 3,363. (76) This is a large bronze tablet. It was found in 1747, eighteen miles from Piacenza, and published first by Muratori, "Exemplar tabulæ Trajanæ pro pueris et puellis aliment. reipubl. Velleiatium in Italia institutis." Flor. 1749 fol.; then by Wolf, "Von einer milden Stiftung Trajan's." Berl. 1808, qto.—A second bronze tablet of this description was found, in 1832, near Benevento; it is in the same style as that of Veleia; it is an acknowledgment made to Trajan by the "Liquires Bæbiani." (Published by Henzen, *Tabula alim. Bæbianorum*, Rome, 1845.) (77) Plin., *Paneg.*, c. 26, 28, vol. ii. pp. 166, 168. (78) Plin., I. *Ep.* 8; VIII. *Ep.* 18, vol. i. pp. 13, 236; and the inscription mentioned above. (79) Henzen, *O. c.* p. 7. (80) This seems to be a natural inference from an inscription in honour of L. Casurius, who is styled "Pecuniæ alimentariæ defensor et curator annonæ populo præbitæ."—

CHAP. IV.] INCREASING HUMANITY OF PAGAN LEGISLATION. 407

Orelli, vol. ii. p. 196, No. 3,908. (81) *Dig.*, XXXIV. tit. 1, l. 14.
(82) Spartianus, "Vita Hadr.," c. 7; *Scriptt. Hist. Aug.*, vol. 1. p. 9.
(83) Capitol., "Ant. Pino.," c. 8; *Scriptt. Hist. Aug.*, vol. i. p. 43.
(84) Capitol., "M. Aur.," c. 7; l. c., p. 55. (85) *O. c.*, c. 26, p. 73.
(86) Eckhel, P. II. vol. vii. pp. 22, 26, 40. The bass-relief represents the
"diva Faustina junior," and approaching her a procession of young
maidens, the empress holds in her hand a vase, from which she seems
to pour forth her favours into the lap of the foremost maiden.—Zoëga,
Li bassi-rilievi antichi di Roma, vol. i. p. 154. (87) Lamprid., "Alex.
Sev.," c. 57; in *Scriptt. Hist. Aug.*, vol i. p. 301. (88) As for example
by Commodus: "By the lavishness of his luxury he had drained the
treasury."—Lamprid., *Comm.*, c. 16; in *O. c.*, vol. i. p. 115. (89)
"Even the scanty alms-money, which Trajan first granted, and had
been owing for nine years, he refused, being dead to all sense of shame.
J. Capit., "Pertin.," c. 9; *Scriptt. Hist. Aug.*, vol. i. p. 126. (90) *Dig.*,
Z. tit. 5, l. 3. (91) Lamprid., "Al. Sev., c. 37; *O.c.*, vol. i. p. 284.
(92) "By natural law all men are born free; as far as the civil is concerned, slaves count for nothing: not so, however, according to the law of
nature, because, as far as the natural law is concerned, all men are
equal."—*Dig.*, I. tit. 1, l. 4; L. tit. 17, l. 32. (93) "Servitutem mor-
talitati fere comparamus.—*Dig.*, I. tit. 17, l. 209. (94) "Contra
naturam . . . constitutio juris gentium.—*Dig.*, I. tit. 5, l. 4. (95)
He restricts the harsher penalties of the masters, because it is most
important to themselves, "that assistance should not be refused to those
who justly claim it, against cruelty, starvation, or unsufferable wrong."
(96) Caius gives a like reason for the mitigation of the slaves' condition.
"For we ought not to use our authority wrongly, just as spendthrifts are
not allowed the control of their own possessions."—I. § 53, p. 25.
(97) Æl. Spart., "Hadr.," c. 18; in *Scriptt. Hist. Aug.*, vol. 1. p. 20.
(98) *Dig.*, I. tit. 6, l. 1, 2. (99) *Dig.*, XLVIII. tit. 8, l. 1, § 2. (100)
Sueton., *Claud.*, c. 25, p. 238. *Dig.*, XL. tit. 8, l. 2. (101) *Dig.*, I.
tit. 6, l. 2. (102) In 208 A.D., *Corp. Jur.*, II. tit. 12, l. 10. (103)
Dig., VII. tit. 1, l. 15, § 1. See M. Wallon, vol. iii. p. 62. (104) See,
for example, *Corp. Jur.*, IV., tit. 56, l. 2. (105) Seneca, *De Clem.*, I.
18, vol. ii. p. 26. (106) *Dig.*, I. tit. 6, l. 2; tit. 12, l. 1. (107)
Seneca, *De Benef.*, III. 22, vol. ii. p. 190.—Cf. *Dig.*, I. tit. 12, l. 1; and
XIII. tit. 7, l. 24, § 3. (108) See M. Wallon, vol. iii. p. 66. (109)
"Infami injuria affectos."—*Dig.*, I. tit. 6, l. 1, 2. (110) *Dig.*, XLVIII.
tit. 2, l. 5. (111) Cap. 1, § 16, p. 8. (112) Jul. Capit., "M. Aur.,"
c. 11, in *Scriptt. Hist. Aug.*, vol. i. p. 59. (113) The Petronian law,
Dig., XLVIII. tit. 8, l. 11, § 2. (114) " . . . causa non præ-
stituta.—Æl. Spart., "Hadr.," c. 18; *Scriptt. Hist. Aug.*, vol. i. p. 20.
(115) He adds, "sine judicio." It is only by a public sentence that a
criminal slave could be condemned to the circus.—*Dig.*, XVIII. tit. 1. l.
42; XLVIII. tit. 8. l. 11. (116) Jul. Capit., "M. Aur.," c. 11; *Scriptt.
Hist. Aug.*, vol. i. p. 59. Dio Cassius, l. 71, c. 29, vol. i. p. 346. (117)
See the Comment. of Godefr. on the Cod. Theod., IX. tit. 7, l. 3.
(118) Sueton., *Domit.*, c. 8, p. 381. (119) M. Aur., c. 1, § 16, p. 8.
(120) Lamprid., "Al. Sev.," c. 24; *Scriptt. Hist. Aug.*, vol. i. p. 274.
(121) Aurel. Victor, *De Cæsaribus*, c. 28, p. 124. (122) Æl. Spart.,
"Hadr.," c. 18; *Scriptt. Hist. Aug.*, vol. i. p. 20. Also Diocletian, *Dig.*,

XLVIII. tit. 18, l. 1, §§ 1, 2. ▰ (123) Ulpian, *Fragm.*, tit. 20, § 16, p.
61.   (124) M. Wallon, vol. iii. p. 57 ff.   (125) See the inscriptions
given by M. Wallon, vol. iii. p. 478 ff.   (126) M. Wallon, vol. iii. p.
67 ff.   (127) *Corp. Jur.*, IX. tit. 47, l. 4.   (128) "Humanitatis
intuitu."—*Dig.*, XL. tit. 4, l. 4.   (129) *Corp. Jur.*, IV. tit. 57.   M.
Wallon, vol. iii. p. 75 ff. ▰ (130) *Corp. Jur.*, III. tit. 15, l. 2.   M. Wallon,
vol. iii. p. 53 ff.

CHAPTER V.

PROGRESS OF IMPROVEMENT IN THE LAWS DURING THE CHRISTIAN PERIOD OF THE EMPIRE.

§ 1. *The Emperors to Theodosius.*

As we were unable to attribute the advance of the philosophers in moral truth to a progressive elaboration of the ancient systems, so we cannot see in the improvement of the laws during the pagan period a simple, natural progress of legislation itself; it is evidently the result of another cause.

The inflexible rigour of the ancient principles, which subjected everything to the State and to the citizen, and which, even for him, knew nothing higher than strict law, did not contain the germs of such a progress. The principles of harsh egoism had to be replaced by others which, working slowly and secretly, blended with the ancient laws and softened them, by introducing the motives of humanity and natural justice. That which was foreseen and taught by the philosophers who came after the establishment of Christianity, was gradually realised in facts. Custom still resisted, but legislation, in advance of custom, began to respect human personality, and to surround it with tutelary safeguards. A new spirit was found in civil society, the basis of which was being insensibly transformed.

This influence on Roman law was interrupted after the

time of Alexander Severus. Seditions, tumults, the despotism of usurpers, the general decay of the Empire, all hindered it in a thousand ways. Under these tyrants law had no longer any authority, jurisprudence was powerless. If some jurists, faithful to better traditions, decided in favour of justice and law, they incurred the hatred of the emperors, who silenced them by death or exile.[1] It is not until the end of the third century that Diocletian, having felt the power of the new feelings, undertook again the work of reform. Along with the Antonines and Alexander Severus, he prepared for the great era of the fourth century.

From this time the progress under Christian emperors was more manifest and general. Ruling principles were laid down by conscience. Obedience was no longer given to an unacknowledged, mysterious influence, but there was a real and sincere desire to bring civil laws into harmony with the principles of Christianity. It is no longer the contested though irresistible power of a persecuted or barely tolerated religion; it is the victorious Church accomplishing her work of benevolence, giving advice through her ministers, and communicating her desires and wishes to the chiefs of the empire through the bishops.

It has been thought that the changes in civil legislation, commencing with the Christian emperors, must not be attributed to the influence of charity; for they say there was in this period still too much despotism and intolerance, too much injustice and cruelty, to permit the realization of the love which Christ commanded to His disciples; that there were other causes which induced a modification of the laws, the transference of the seat of empire to Constantinople, the strengthening of imperial authority, the concentration of power in one alone.[2]

But the effects we attribute to charity cannot be referred to these last causes, which would have introduced totally different results into legislation. Further, we must not forget that charity is a principle which can only progress slowly. A free and personal sentiment can only conquer the world as it enters individual hearts. This is not done by force; this gentle quiet virtue carries off its peaceful victories through persuasion.

We must not therefore be astonished if its full results were not immediately produced, but we can no longer doubt its influence. It strove through several centuries with the pagan spirit, which was too much in accordance with the natural tendencies of man to be quickly banished from the manners of a society which had become Christian in name. To deny the intention of the Christian emperors to conform the laws to the charity and respect taught by Christ, is to shut our eyes to the evidence of facts. It is true that in certain circumstances they were liable to look on the Christian only as the citizen, as formerly the citizen only had been looked on as man; but this idea of an age when the two principles were still at strife, did not prevent the evangelic spirit from entering more and more into civil society and profoundly modifying its organic elements.

The example of him who first brought Christianity to the throne proves clearly what has just been said as to the intention of the Christian emperors to bring legislation into harmony with the new morality. Even before his conversion, Constantine showed that he had juster feelings. He was a believer in the neo-platonic syncretism of his time, which acknowledged only one God, manifested to men in different ways, and worshipped under different names.[3] These pious tendencies, though still very indefinite, led him in early life to incline towards the ideas and moral precepts of Christianity. To this may perhaps be added the influence of his mother, Helena, as well as that of Lactantius, to whom he entrusted the education of his son about 312. To put an end to persecution, in accordance with his syncretistic tendencies, he wished to establish absolute religious liberty. After 312 all Christian ministers were exempted from all municipal burdens, and enjoyed the same privileges as pagan priests.[4] In the following year he published at Milan, conjointly with Licinius, his celebrated edict which gave liberty of conscience to Christians as well as to the followers of all other forms of faith.[5] About the same time he authorized the enfranchisement of slaves in the churches.[6] In 321 he permitted the gift of legacies to religious houses,[7] sent considerable help to the African clergy,[8] and ordered the general observance of Sunday.[9]

At the same time he still continued to observe pagan rites, but the favours he granted to the Church turned the defenders of the ancient national worship into his enemies. They attached themselves to Licinius, whilst the Christians supported Constantine, so that the strife between the two competitors for the Empire became a struggle between paganism and Christianity. Licinius was overcome, and Constantine openly and definitely declared himself on the side of the Church. After his conversion political reasons compelled him still to respect the privileges of pagan priests.[10] He even retained the title of sovereign pontiff.[11] He allowed the pagans to enjoy religious liberty, but vigorously attempted to suppress their immoral rites. He destroyed the temples in Egypt and Phœnicia which were dedicated to an impure form of worship, and his soldiers dispersed the infamous priests who served there.[12]

The biographers of Constantine tell us that when he became a Christian, he endeavoured to bring the laws into greater conformity with Christianity; and we soon see proof of this.[13] His efforts related principally to personal right, he attempted to break through pagan legislation, which, although somewhat improved, still weighed heavily on certain classes. We can recognise in his measures the principles of equity, natural equality, and protection for the oppressed, which Lactantius has pointed out with so much warmth and discernment in his *Divine Institutions*.

If this emperor could not amend everything, it was because there was a vigorous spirit in pagan society which obstinately opposed him. We should be wrong to expect a new code from him. The time was not yet come to bestow a complete and fundamental revision upon the whole heritage of Roman law. A son of his age, he did as much as could be done, he prepared the way for further reforms by giving the bishops the power of protecting the weak, and of arbitrating in civil disputes. He thus placed by the side of lay jurisprudence a power which was then useful in correcting it, and further strengthening the power of Christian equity.[14]

The progress was continued under his successors, each one contributing a share to the transformation of civil law. The movement was only stopped temporarily under Julian the Apostate. This emperor was influenced by the religion he renounced. A Christian until the age of twenty, he retained the moral precepts of Christianity in his memory. Notwithstanding his hatred of the Church, he could not uproot the germs which his early education had planted in his heart. He knew that there is an original relationship between men,[15] that liberty or outward slavery is of no importance, if the state of soul does not correspond.[16] From this he deduced the duties of kindness to everybody, charity to the poor, and help for enemies, "although this is contrary to the general opinion." Even prisoners must be treated with moderation. "Justice," he says, "does not exclude humanity, it is better to treat criminals with kindness in order that unjustly condemned men may share it, rather than to be harsh to the innocent with the excuse of not being always able to discern the guilty who deserve no mercy." [17]

He saw with bitter regret that the Christians were more humane than the worshippers of the ancient gods, and that their charity and purity of life were the most powerful means of spreading their opinions. In his vain efforts to restore polytheism, he desired that the pagan priests should follow the example of "the impious Galileans." He also ordered the high priest of Galatia to establish hospitals in all villages for the use of the poor, whether they were pagans or not; "because," he said, "it is disgraceful that our poor should be supported by Christian philanthropy." He sent 30,000 measures of wheat and 6,000 of wine to be distributed to the poor. He even ordered that those who lived in the country should give their earliest fruit as an offering to them, in imitation of the oblations and collections in the churches.[18] He introduced the use of certificates for poor travellers, such as those with which Christians kept up their fraternal union and recommended one another to strangers.[19] Lastly, as if paganism could suffice for the moral regeneration of men, he ordered the priests to give exhortations to the people, as the Christian preachers did; to distinguish themselves by a sober and simple life, without cruel or licentious amusements. Julian also required that they should go neither to the theatre nor to the circus.[20] This was remarkable, as it was one of the duties of the pagan pontiffs to preside at the spectacles.

These attempts were powerless; it was impossible to endow paganism with a spirit completely foreign to its nature. The practice of charity requires more than philosophical considerations, or the jealous imitation of a detested sect; and to preach a holy and pure life a principle is needed, which is found neither in the morality of the sages nor in the fables of the gods. Julian was coldly seconded by the advisers of the pagan reaction who opposed all concession to the new spirit, and therefore he was unable to lay down any law in accordance with his beautiful maxims. Amongst the numerous constitutions which emanated from him, there is not even one which is associated with the progress of equity and the emancipation of natural justice.[21] His work perished with him. The new ideas had outrun paganism, with which they could never be reconciled; the people escaped from it more completely day by day, to be re-united round the cross of Christ.

The progress of legislation was resumed under Julian's successors. Until the close of the Western Empire the emperors continued to apply the Christian spirit to the laws and social relations, completing and extending what Constantine had begun. But placed on the confines of two civilizations, they submitted to the necessities of this difficult position. Sometimes we see them advance with wonderful hardihood, sometimes they seem to draw back and partly undo the work of Constantine and his predecessors. The struggle between the Christian and pagan spirit was full of chances and sudden changes. The one prevailed only slowly over the other, which regretfully yielded the ground over which it had reigned for centuries, and whose traces were still long visible, both in the codes and in the customs.

Valentinian III., by a constitution of 426 A.D., enforced the written laws of the jurisconsults of the third century, although the greater number of these eminent men were the first to introduce humanity into legislation and to refer strict law to natural justice. It was then an anachronism. This was therefore a retrograde step instead of an advance.[22]

The theology of the early ages had reduced neither Christian morality nor dogma to a system. We have often been astonished at the absence of a methodical work on the doctrine of the Church, although it may be explained by very natural circumstances. It is the same with jurisprudence: no one dreamt of remodelling all the laws in accordance with a social theory brightened by the light of Christianity. There was yet no Christian and philosophic science of justice. The code named after Theodosius is only a compilation of the laws and decisions of Christian emperors, often given for special cases. It is not a creation produced all at once and governed by one principle; it is an irregular collection, in which the ancient pagan law forms a singular mixture with Christian justice and charity. At this code we must stop. Its compilation only preceded the fall of the Western Empire by a few years.[23] After this epoch a new society was formed, and the great work of fusion between the Roman, Christian, and Germanic elements commenced, from which our modern civilization has arisen.

After these general considerations, it is time to note the applications of the Christian spirit to Roman legislation during the Christian period of the empire. We shall follow the same lines as for the pagan period.

§ 2. *Women. Marriage.*

The regulations of the emperors in respect to women are not numerous, but they bear the mark of justice, which proves considerable progress in this direction.

It was not the result of an illegitimate and unnatural emancipation, but was produced by a feeling of human dignity in the sex previously despised for weakness, but raised by the Gospel to the level of man.

Constantine broke down the remains of the ancient guardianship, and decided that women of cultivated mind and irreproachable conduct attained their majority at eighteen. He gave them the same right as men for the disposal of their property, except that they might not sell their lands without permission.[24] At the same time, with delicate respect for womanly modesty, he prohibited them calling one another to a court of justice, and did not wish them to be present at the deliberations of men.[25] He gave to mothers the right of succeeding, conjointly with the agnates, to the property of children who died before them; until this time the succession had belonged to the guardians alone.[26] The successors of Constantine, Valens in 369, and Valentinian III. in 426, successively added to this regulation, but without attaining perfect equity; the last step was taken by Justinian.[27]

Christian legislation only slowly acknowledged the right of a mother to the guardianship of her children and their property. The tradition of Roman law, that it was a masculine duty beyond the power of woman,[28] was long in passing away. Theodosius the Great, in 390, was the first who gave the mother a certain right of guardianship. He gave it to her in default of a legitimate guardian, on condition that she was a major and engaged not to marry again. This was a wise and just provision at that time;

the emperor did not deprive the widow of liberty to marry again, but if she did so, she must give up the guardianship of her first children, in the fear that their interests might suffer if she again became a mother.[29]

The law progressed more rapidly and energetically in the direction of securing respect for woman by restraining the excesses of passion. Even in a society converted to Christianity, the violence of this passion over-ruled morality. It hindered the suppression of the lupanars which still existed in the Christian empire.[30] The emperors were unable to suppress them, but they made generous efforts to free unhappy women from the hands of the wretches who sold them to misery and disgrace. In 343 Constantius forbade them to sell Christian slaves to any but Christian masters.[31] He hoped thus to save them from falling again into infamous hands, and hoped also that if bought by Christians they might be saved and restored through the love of Christ. In the same law he authorised priests and all Christians to ransom, even with force, all Christian women in danger of being given over to prostitution. This measure was generalized and made more effective a little later. The owners of bad houses were forbidden to impose "the necessity of sinning" on either their servants or their daughters. If these laid a complaint before the judge, they must be set free "from their misery"; and if their master detained them forcibly, he was to be severely punished.[32] No female Christian, slave or free, could be compelled to take the part of *meretrix* at the theatre; if a slave, she was, on her request, immediately enfranchised.[33] In 439 Theodosius II. completely suppressed the profession of *leno* in Constantinople; whoever attempted the prostitution of women of any condition was to be beaten with rods and driven from the city. The emperor deprived the public funds of a considerable revenue by this measure, but a generous man, Florentius, the Prefect of the Prætorium, offered to make good the loss to the treasury from his private fortune.[34] Unhappily, neither the law of Theodosius nor the charity of Florentius were successful; the profession and the tax continued to exist.

Rape was considered in pagan society rather as a theft from the father than as an injury to the girl, and was only punished if the suffering party demanded it. Henceforward the law punished the crime with death, without asking the consent of the outraged one. It is true that the laws of Constantine and of Jovian which inflict this penalty were intended for the special protection of virgins dedicated to God, and of widows, that is of the deaconesses;[35] but even in this we see a proof of respect for the dignity and liberty of woman. These virgins and widows freely devoted themselves to God. They were then no longer under the father's protective power, and would have been consequently abandoned by pagan law. Christian law, on the other hand, took them under its care and insured their tranquil enjoyment of the life which they had chosen.

Women were also protected in the conjugal relationship. The greatest changes were made in legislation in this respect, with the aim of strengthening the marriage ties and insuring their sanctity. The great principles of the doctors of the Church are incorporated in the code, which by transforming marriage and family relationships, prepares for the complete transformation of society.[36] The old law, *Pappia Poppœa*, which was the base of Roman legislation in this respect, was abolished by degrees. It deprived celibates and those who had no children of the right of inheritance. Constantine repealed this unnatural measure, "which punished as a crime what ought to be considered as a misfortune deserving compassion." He gave to marriage the liberty by which alone it can become an intimate and holy union. He recognised the right of choice in both man and woman, and definitely placed the affections and individual tastes above the despotic interest of the State. He thus carried one of the greatest victories of the new spirit over ancient egoism.[37]

On the other hand, the liberty of marriage was restricted by prohibited relationships which were multiplied by Christian law; but this was a wholesome restraint, intended to bind families more closely together, whilst purifying the love which their members had for each other. The prohibitions fixed by ancient Roman law had fallen into disuse. In the time of Constantine terrible disorder prevailed in pagan society. The license of preceding ages had disorganized the family and taken all moral meaning from marriage.[38]

In 339 Constantine revived the ancient law which forbade, under penalty of death, the marriage of uncle and niece.[39] Soon afterwards he prohibited it with a brother's widow, or with the sister of the deceased first wife.[40] Theodosius the Great even forbade the union of cousins. The children of such marriages were considered illegitimate, and the unions themselves punished as incestuous.[41] However, notwithstanding this severity of the law, a resistance was offered by prevailing customs which it was difficult to overcome.

In marriage itself the law, whilst maintaining the submission of women, introduced civil equality between husband and wife. It enforced fidelity on the husband as a sacred duty, though he had before held himself exempted. To establish equality, Theodosius II. repealed, in the year 410, the ancient rules which regulated the gifts between husband and wife by the number of their children. He wished them to be perfectly free to follow the natural impulses of their affection, which was a more certain way to bring marriage into favour than all the Julian and Poppœan law.[42] The measures taken to insure fidelity between husband and wife were numerous and severe. When we recall the dissoluteness prevalent in pagan society, the indulgence of the law for immorality, the facilities for concubinage, we see the need of an energetic interference by the Christian emperors.

Constantine began this in 320 by reminding the people that the ancient law forbade a married man to have more than one concubine.[43] A few years afterwards he ordered severe penalties against adultery, which was treated as a heavy sin, a public crime, and punished by death, without the right of appeal. Only people of the vilest profession had no right of complaint.[44] Not content with these severities against adultery, Constantine wished also to prohibit the concubinage of the unmarried man, and to stop the illegal unions which were so frequent in the later ages of Roman society. We have before seen the vigorous action of the law against public prostitution; it strove with equal energy against the relation authorized by custom under the name of *nuces injustæ*, and which were only apparently less scandalous than concubinage. Unable to stop them suddenly, Constantine tried to turn them into legal marriage. He declared those natural children legitimate whose parents consented to be married.[45] He forbade any donation or legacy to a concubine, in order that if there was any real affection marriage might be compulsory.[46] He also declared those persons infamous who lived in illegal unions, however great their office or high their dignities.[47] But these laws also were broken by the force of custom.[48]

The efforts of Constantine's successors to overcome this resistance, and to induce men of all ranks to give up a life reprobated by Christianity, were not successful. There were even emperors, who for different motives and personal reasons, relaxed the severity ordered by Constantine. Valentinian I. gave to natural children and their mothers the right of receiving what the father left to them by will. According to the pagan Libanius, this return to unchristian laxity was sanctioned by Valens.[49] Valentinian III. wished to restore the law of Constantine, but Theodosius II. would only accept it with the concession made by Valentinian I.[50] He even decided that the father should have the power of numbering his natural children amongst his rightful heirs.[51] Thus were efforts made to preserve the sanctity of the conjugal union; sometimes by sacrificing illegitimate children, whilst sometimes there was a refusal to punish them for the father's fault, and the scandal of concubinage was tolerated. The legislators are less to be blamed than the customs, which weakened the wise severity of the law.

It was almost the same with divorce. We saw in our first book how pagan society, in its decadence, abused the facility with which a legal divorce could be obtained. The high ideal of marriage in the Church should have abolished the law which permitted this rupture of the conjugal union, but the general spirit was opposed to this reform, and Christian authorities themselves were not always in agreement on this point; therefore they were contented with restrictive measures and palliatives, more or less efficacious. Constantine refused the right of divorce to women who had only drinking and gambling with which to accuse their husbands. These were doubtless very grave reasons, but Roman society had so often appealed to them when they were unfounded, that they had become only frivolous protests. The woman might only ask for separation if her husband was guilty of homicide, of witchcraft, or of violating burying places. The husband could only ask it for similar crimes—if his wife had been a poisoner, an adulteress, or if she had followed the disgraceful trade of a procuress. In these cases the husband gained the dowry and permission to re-marry; whilst if the wife proved her innocence, she took all the husband's wealth, and even the dowry of the second wife, if he re-married after the divorce.[52]

A century later divorce was permitted by Honorius on slighter grounds; he authorised the husband to keep his property, but he was compelled to return the dowry, and might not marry before two years had elapsed.[53]

Divorce for other reasons than those acknowledged by the law, was punished by loss of property and transportation to an island. It was made more difficult for husband and wife to obtain divorce, which was surrounded with formalities, though it was allowed to remain in the code. It was suppressed for a short time in the Eastern Empire at the wish of the bishops, but was re-established by Theodosius II., in 439, for reasons accepted in the laws of his predecessors.[54]

The hesitation which we have remarked in the laws as to divorce and concubinage, is not found in those relating to second marriages. Suggested by the doctors of the Church, they are imprinted with the wisdom and charity which the apostles had taught in reference to this matter. Second marriages were not forbidden—there were some restrictions for women in this respect which were more protective than irksome. The widow of less than twenty-five years of age might not re-marry without the consent of her father, or near relatives. If the latter do not agree with her choice, the judge has the power of decision, by approving him whom the woman prefers; and that the relatives may not hinder, through an egoistic hope, "an honourable marriage," the law accords the right of giving advice only to those who cannot receive the widow's inheritance, should she die unmarried.[55] To this law of Valentinian, intended to secure the widow's liberty, Theodosius the Great added another, to prevent the liberty from degenerating into an abuse. He renewed an ancient Roman law which, in the interests of public decency, branded that widow with infamy who re-married before ten months. To increase the penalty, Theodosius ruled that the woman who knew so little how to "observe the religion of mourning," should lose all the wealth bequeathed to her by her first husband.[56]

The same emperor took measures to provide for the children of the first marriage, whose interests, up to this time, had been too often neglected. By a law made in 382, and afterwards confirmed by his son Honorius, he decided that if a widow, having children, re-married, the wealth that came to her from her first husband, by whatever title she held it, should belong to the children, though she herself might use it on a secure mortgage.[57] Theodosius II. and Valentinian II. extended these regulations to the widow, with children, who resolved on a second marriage.

Thus we have seen considerable progress in the laws relating to the condition of women and marriage, due to the Christian spirit; we have also seen uncertainties caused by the persistence of pagan customs. Marriage has been made free, the wife equalised with the husband, second marriages allowed under wise restrictions, adultery punished with just severity, woman in general protected from the brutal passion of man; but neither concubinage nor the possibility of divorce was completely suppressed. Astonishing though it may be, it even seems that a marriage was admitted as legal through the simple consent of the parties concerned—without contract or dowry, without the solemnities or blessing of the Church. It was legal in the sight of the State, but only earthly and incomplete from the religious point of view.[58] We know not how to explain the preservation of this custom in the Christian ages of the empire, when the Church had so great an influence. However it happened, it was an anomaly, for though legislation about marriage had not yet reached its highest perfection, it at least admitted the moral and holy significance given by Christianity to the conjugal union. This principle was henceforward asserted by the law.

§ 3. *Children.*

Paternal authority, lessened already during the pagan period, was more and more restricted in its unnatural aspects. The exposure of children was not completely abolished. Very often, after some charitable person had taken and brought up the exposed child, the father would claim him, trying to profit at the same time by his own heartlessness and another's mercy.

Constantine deprived the fathers of any benefit from their cruelty, in order to end these disgraceful speculations, and to compel them to fulfil their natural duties. In 331 he commanded that he who claimed an exposed child, should have the right of keeping him as a son or as a slave, whichever he preferred, without the father being able to reclaim him.[59] In 374 Valentinian, in a remarkable law, added punishment to the loss of paternal rights. "Let every one," he says, "care for his children. If he exposes them, he must be punished in accordance with the law. If those who are merciful receive them, he can never reclaim them. He has no right to call those his own whose feebleness he despised." [60]

The ancient right of disposing of the liberty of children by selling them as slaves, or giving them to creditors, was already abolished by the pagan emperors, but was still often practised in these times of universal misery. Instead of maintaining the prohibition, which seemed not to have produced the expected effects, an attempt was made to turn the fathers from this inhuman exercise of power by surrounding it with difficulties, and awakening better feelings in themselves. So deeply was belief in the paternal authority rooted in the Roman world, that the law did not prohibit the crimes, but simply issued restrictive orders. Constantine decreed that if a child was sold, the buyer remained his owner; the father could only reclaim him by paying the full price, or replacing him with another slave. This law seems less just than those of Trajan and Diocletian, which we have before quoted. The one declared all exposed children to be free, whilst the other forbade their sale under any pretext whatever. But was it not through humanity that Constantine consented that the reclaimed child should be sold or kept as a slave? For without this concession, how many children would have been left to their fate of death in these unhappy times! However, in the increasing poverty of the labouring and agricultural classes, this humanity produced no results—the sale of children still went on. To stop it more completely needed a return to the natural simplicity of justice. More than half a century passed away before this return was made; it was not till the time of Theodosius the Great that those children were declared free whom the father, through poverty, had sold as slaves; the buyer who took a free child as a slave was not allowed any compensation for his price.[61]

Lastly, the ancient laws for parricides were extended to the fathers who gave their children to death. The Constitutions of Constantine and Valentinian condemn them to terrible tortures as an expiation for such a dreadful crime.[62]

On the other hand, Christian legislation still allowed the father a certain jurisdiction over his children; but it confirmed the law of Alexander Severus, which stated that "the right of domestic correction" has a limit. If the fault of the children is too great for that, they must be given to the judgment of the tribunals.[63] The right of emancipation was also maintained. It was made into a religious act, surrounded with solemnities, and accompanied with ecclesiastical sanction. According to a law of Constantine in 321, the emancipation of children and the manumission of slaves were the only legal acts that might be carried out on Sunday.[64]

In accordance with ancient law the wealth of the unemancipated son belonged entirely to the father. The pagan emperors made an exception for the possessions acquired during military service. This law was extended by Constantine and his successors, by bestowing on the son the possessions acquired by the exercise of public, ecclesiastical, or civil duties, under the title of quasi-military possessions.

Constantine also gave to the children the right of inheriting wealth left by the mother, which until now had been mixed with that of the father. They were, however, only allowed the temporary use, without the power of alienating any, of it. The later emperors applied this rule to the goods left by grandfathers; at the same time they allowed the unemancipated children the goods they had acquired by marriage, which previously reverted also to the father.[65] The ancient rights of the agnates were more and more restricted; Valentinian III. admitted the children of the daughter to a share in the succession of the maternal grandfather.[66] Through the spread of Christian ideas of justice and charity, the natural rights of children were continually more and more recognised by the law. Several blanks which remained were supplied by Justinian, who achieved the únity of this part of legislation by accomplishing its generalization.

It is hardly necessary to say that the Christian law insisted on the duties of children towards their parents, which were already written in the code by the emperors and jurisconsults of the pagan period. A legislation founded on Christianity and intended to strengthen family ties, reminded the children that emancipation itself could not free them from the duties of respect and gratitude. In 367 Valentinian commanded that the emancipated son who seriously offended his father should return under the paternal power for having made a bad use of a liberty of which he was not worthy.[67]

§ 4. *Slaves.*

We have seen how slowly and how carefully the Church prepared for the abolition of slavery, which, unjust though it was, had passed into law. It is therefore not surprising that the Christian emperors allowed its continuance, though endeavouring to advance in the path of progress already opened by pagan legislators. They found it impossible to rise at once to the height of the principles taught by the Fathers of the Church. They clung to the ancient prejudice which had different standards for the slave and the master. Law and custom only freed themselves slowly and painfully from the bondage of the former spirit.

The law still excepted the female slave from the sin of adultery. Constantine forbade free persons to marry slaves, under heavy penalties, "because," he said, "from these unions only slaves can be born."[68] He did not consider the death of a slave resulting from bodily punishment or an unhealthy dungeon as a murder. The master, he says, is only guilty of homicide if he has the intention of killing his slave or causing him to be killed.[69] The same emperor enacted very harsh laws as to the treatment of fugitive slaves.[70]

The weakness of the empire, the approach of barbarians, perhaps even half-understood ideas of Christian liberty and equality, caused many slaves to revolt. Numbers of these fugitives went through the abandoned provinces and pillaged them, or joined the attacking enemies. Society endeavoured to intimidate them by threats, and thought it needful, in self-defence, to inflict heavier penalties on them than on freemen who committed the same crimes. It would have been safer to have taken more thorough measures to fit them by a Christian education for regained freedom. However, we need not take the part of accuser. The law doubtless did all it could in this crisis, when two worlds were in their final struggle, and a third, the world of barbarism, was about to throw itself with savage energy into the conflict.

Legal freedom was also made easier. The law favoured it, though yet unable to command it without exposing society to serious peril. Constantine decreed that acts of enfranchisement performed in the churches were equally legal with those performed according to the Roman law. This gave greater solemnity to the act of emancipation, and added religious considerations to the motives of humanity which led the masters to give freedom to their slaves. The emperor gave the clergy the power of freeing their own slaves, without either witnesses or ceremonies, simply because it was their will.[71] He propounded new reasons for emancipation; the slave who denounced a man guilty of rape or of making bad money was to receive his freedom. Theodosius the Great added to these any who should point out a deserter, or one who had been circumcised by the Jews.[72] The Emperor Zeno added those who, with the consent of their masters, embraced a monastic life.[73] Other reasons for freedom were laid down by Justinian who enlarged and completed this part of legislation as to slaves, which had now become more liberal.

The Church also tended to the gradual abolition of slavery by persuading freemen to lead a plainer and simpler life, whilst Christian legislation tried to diminish the causes of servitude. Constantine inflicted the punishment of death on those who stole children to bring them up as slaves.[74]

Special efforts were made to suppress barbarous or disgraceful occupations, which kept so many unhappy ones in the servile state for the pleasures of the crowd, or the ignoble gratification of individual passions. Vigorous efforts were made to suppress spectacles of every kind, with the double aim of saving the men who were condemned to lose their soul or their life in these diversions, and of guarding the morality of the people, which was greatly lowered by the scenes of the theatre and games of the circus. The popular rejoicings called *majuma,* which were only causes of scandal, were done away with under Constantius, and again under Theodosius the Great. Arcadius wished to permit them again, on condition that decency should be observed;[75] but this was a thing impossible, and soon afterwards, seeing the same irregularities reappear, he severely forbade these "shameful spectacles." This prohibition ought not to be considered as a law purely in the interest of external public order, it was inspired by a deeper feeling of respect and love for men. The emperor was ready to allow the people to be amused in a suitable manner; but he only removed causes of corruption, by banishing the sight of what was shameful and dangerous for the soul.[76]

Theodosius, who in his youth had loved dancers and actors, tried, in deference doubtless to the rebukes of Ambrose, to restrain the depravity of which they were then both the victims and the accomplices. In 385 it was forbidden to buy or sell, to show in the theatre, or to own for personal pleasure, flute-players or any women who were skilled in music, because with the musicians this art was only a means of seduction, a pretext to conceal vice.[77] In the following year judges were forbidden to be present at spectacles after the hour of noon. It was then that the most obscene diversions and the combats in the arena were generally given. The emperor wished that these immoral representations should not have the encouragement of the presence of the magistrates, whose duty it was to make the laws respected. They had permission to attend the theatre only on the solemn anniversaries of his accession or of his birth. He forbade every kind of spectacle on Sunday.

Theodosius II. extended this restriction to all the days made by the Church into holidays.[78] Though forced by the passion of the people to tolerate the spectacles on other days, the Christian emperors tried to withdraw those unfortunates from this career who had been driven to it by misfortune and misery. They allowed the opprobrium of the law and public opinion to rest on the callings of actor and mime, in order to repel those who still retained a sentiment of human dignity. Valentinian II. called it a "shameful trade,"[79] and Theodosius qualified those who entered it as "disgraceful people." The prohibitions laid upon them were maintained. Constantine points out that, being outside the law, they are not punished for certain crimes, they are judged unworthy either to keep the law or to receive its benefits.[80] Theodosius forbade actresses the use of jewellery or robes of luxury,[81] with the intention of still further humiliating them. He even forbade Christians to enter a profession which, on account of its ignominy, should, he thought, be reserved for unbelievers only.[82]

At the same time the cases were decided in which actors of all kinds might be freed from "the bonds of natural condition" which attached them to the theatre. Valentinian I. was the author of most of these measures, dictated by pity for an unfortunate and despised class. If an actor or actress near death asked and received the sacraments of the Church, they were, in case they recovered health, free from the obligation to go on the stage.[83] If the daughter of an actress lived respectably and wished to leave the theatre, the proconsul was bound to guard her freedom from those who wished to wrest it from her.[84] The actress who became a Christian was liberated by the fact of her conversion, provided that she led a pure and respectable life.[85] Freedom ought to be refused only to those women whose conduct was unworthy of it. Those who after receiving baptism and liberty fell back into vice, were sent back to the theatre; the servitude and shame of that profession being their punishment.[86]

We are compelled to remark the contradictions in these

laws; the legislators are still far from true humanity, which is shown only in exceptional cases, leaving the greater number of actors to servile degradation, though the intention is partly to arouse their consciousness of human dignity. As long as an actor, and especially an actress, did not personally implore liberty "to break the bonds of their natural condition,"[87] which forced them to serve the amusements of the mob, they were ignored by the law, or noticed only to be branded with infamy. Valentinian II. punished the seduction of an actress by prohibiting her from assisting at anything but public immorality; he wished these poor women to suffer this shameful fate.[88] Would it not have been better to declare that the profession was not in itself degraded, but was only made so by the immorality of the pieces represented on the stage. The laws which characterized theatrical art as "a shameful trade" might prevent a few serious people from going to the theatre, but by allowing degraded people to represent disgraceful pieces, the theatre remained a source of corruption, both for actors and spectators. It would have been more rational to forbid bad plays, dances, and impure games, but that would have been impossible without suppressing the theatre altogether; no law could have triumphed over the taste of the people in this respect.

In this transition state it was impossible to emancipate dramatic art by restoring its dignity; all that could be attained therefore was to give actors the means of leaving a profession which, intended for shameful pleasures, could only be ignoble and despised.

There was quite as long a struggle against the inveterate taste of the people for gladiatorial combats. The efforts of the Christian emperors in this respect merit the more appreciation that in endeavouring to suppress these games they deprived themselves of one of the most powerful means of popularity. In 310 Constantine still allowed barbarian prisoners to be taken to the arena, for which he was greatly praised by his pagan panegyrists.[89] He made amends for this concession to the cowardly cruelty of the degenerate Romans by being the first to enter with energetic vigour the path pointed out by Christianity. In 325 he absolutely prohibited gladiatorial combats, "because these bloody spectacles could not please in a time of public peace."[90] By this law he hoped to suppress the body of professional gladiators. He also forbade condemned criminals to be sent to the combats of the arena, although ten years before he had permitted it.[91] Henceforward criminals were sent to the mines, "that they might expiate their crimes without bloodshed," a first inclination towards removing the penalty of death.

The intention of Constantine in forbidding gladiatorial exploits in all towns in the empire [92] was inspired by humanity towards the unhappy ones who were compelled to fight, and by the wish to remove this opportunity of rousing the sanguinary passions of the people whom he wished to accustom to the pleasures of peace. He had seen how these spectacles excited a taste for combats, and a thirst for blood which were irreconcilable with the era of peace that he proposed to inaugurate. But this humane law of the great emperor was never executed, it was as powerless as the eloquence of the preachers of the Church to calm the eagerness of the people. The corps of the gladiators continued to exist; criminals were still sent to the arena, and it was not long before the law of 325 relating to them was withdrawn from the code.[93] This law had been given at Berytus, in Syria, and a few years afterwards in the same province the whole population assembled at a great combat of gladiators.[94]

Several of Constantine's successors made redoubled

efforts to attain the results he attempted. They tried to diminish the frequency of the games in the arena, and to lessen the number of gladiators. Constantius forbade officers to offer money to the soldiers or slaves of the palace as an inducement to enrol in their band.[95] Valentinian I., who in his youth had shared the universal passion for combats with men and beasts, forbade celebration on the emperor's birthday, and thus suppressed one of the greatest attractions of these festivals.[96] He also forbade Christians, or officers of the palace, from being condemned to the arena, whatever might have been their crime.[97]

We can show, by many examples, the uselessness of these incomplete measures. In 385 there was a great combat with gladiators in Rome.[98] Symmachus gave these games during his consulate.[99] Theodosius himself set the German prisoners to fight one another "to amuse the people of Mars."[100] However, this emperor also made an attempt to lessen bloodshed—he forbade combats with savage bulls.[101] He was more successful, for after his reign these bloody pastimes ceased in the Eastern Empire, though ancient Roman harshness still resisted their abolition in the West. Honorius, hopeless of success, degraded the profession of gladiator still more deeply than heretofore. He refused them permission to enter the households of the wealthy as slaves. He desired them to remain in their degradation, and wished nothing to be done to lessen the shame of their "detestable name."[102] The poet Prudentius pressed him, for the sake of Christian charity, to take one more step, and forbid these barbarous struggles,[103] but he thought it still impossible.

Telemachus, an eastern monk, crossed the seas, and betook himself to Rome. He threw himself into the arena, separated the combatants, and fell a victim to the fury of the spectators. It was only after this act of martyrdom for the cause of charity that Honorius made a law, prohibiting for ever this remnant of ancient cruelty.[104] After this event we never find again traces of combats between men. Fights between wild beasts only still remained,[105] so greedy was the populace, especially of the southern provinces, of the emotions produced by the sight of bloodshed!

If Christian legislation has not completely triumphed over custom, we must at least acknowledge the perseverance with which it strove to restore these men, despised by their fellows, to their inherent dignity, to awaken in the people respect for life, and love for those around them, and to abolish these occasions of cruel contradiction of the precepts taught by the preachers of the Church. If after this time, in certain countries of the empire, men still rushed to the arena where wild beasts still fought, it was because they were Christian only in name, whilst in their hearts pagan tastes were vigorous.

A last word still to finish this article on the efforts to stop the abuse of man by man. The Christian emperors laid down very severe but just laws against the crime of παιδεραστία, still very frequent in different parts of the empire. "The law," said Constantius, "must be armed with her avenging sword, and enforce severe penalties against this infamy." [106] Theodosius and Valentinian denounced it energetically, and punished those who were guilty of it with death at the stake.[107]

§ 5. *The Poor and Afflicted.*

During the pagan period, the influence of evangelical ideas had not yet affected the condition of the poor, the infirm, the unhappy. It is true that moralists had expressed the kindest feelings on their behalf, and the individual benevolence of some emperors had attempted to save a certain number of poor children from misery, but beneficent and helpful charity had not yet passed into law. Certainly we do not think that beneficence should be commanded by law as a civil duty. We do not ask that society should undertake the support of all those who declare it to be impossible for themselves to satisfy their own needs; but in the period of which we are speaking, there was much to be done to raise the poor from the desolation to which they had been brought by the egoistical morality and aristocratic legislation of antiquity.

Religious society, the Church, for the first time practised charity on a large scale. Christian communities, like individuals, sympathised with every kind of misery. Their efforts at relief were only rivalled by the ingenuity and efficacy of their methods. The Christian emperors joined in this work of restoration and mercy. They took numerous measures on behalf of the poor, the weak, and the oppressed.

Constantine determined to improve the state of things in the impoverished districts of Italy and Africa, where, as he learned from several sources, parents, urged by the extremity of their misery, sold, pledged, and killed their children, or allowed them to die of starvation. He determined "to turn the hand of the fathers from parricide, by inspiring them with better feelings." We have seen before that he issued laws to hinder fathers from selling or killing their children. Feeling these laws to be insufficient, and of no avail against the pretext of poverty, he accompanied them with one of protective beneficence. He ordered the fiscal agents and imperial officers to provide, without delay, food and clothing for poor parents, either from the fiscal revenues, or from his own private property; "for," he said, "the help we give to children who have come into the world will not admit of delay; it is repugnant to our morality to leave some to perish with hunger, and others to turn to crime."[108] The insertion of these two laws of Constantine, in reference to the help that poor parents might claim from the public treasury, proves that they were carried out in after times.

Constantine passed, in 325, another law, not less salutary, and dictated by a profound feeling of Christian equality and respect for mankind. It concerned the right of all the inhabitants of the empire to receive justice, and the duty of judges, magistrates, and imperial officers, to exercise the strictest impartiality. He says: "Let whoever can reproach one of my functionaries with injustice, present himself to me with courage and confidence; I will listen to him; I will myself examine into the complaint, and if it is proved, I shall punish that man who had till then deceived me by a feigned integrity."[109] Constantine reiterates this injunction in his remarkable law of 331, against the venality of the judges and the vexations of the fiscal agents. Justice must be the same for the poor as for the rich. Judges and advocates who receive money are sentenced to severe penalties, as also are the fiscal agents whose exactions oppress the people. Unless their rapacious hands cease from spoiling the inhabitants, they will expiate their robberies by the tortures they deserve.[110] Constantine added to these general measures a special protection for those who, on account of their weakness and isolation, were particularly commended to Christian solicitude, as they were specially exposed to the aggressions of rich and powerful men. In 334 he decreed that if widows, orphans, the infirm, or poor, were engaged in a lawsuit, they should not be compelled to present themselves before a tribunal away from the province in which they lived. If they dreaded the influence of their adversaries, they might appeal to the emperor, who would make the parties appear before him, and would himself judge the case.[111] In 365 Valentinian I. freed widows from the plebeian capitation. Orphan boys were also exempted from this tax to the age of twenty, and orphan girls until their marriage.[112]

In the midst of the disorders which prevailed in the provinces during the fourth century, the generous efforts of Constantine to render justice equal and impartial were too frequently unsuccessful. Protection and justice were often refused to those who could not pay for them, or whose position gave them no power. To remedy this abuse, the arbitration of the bishops was made of equal force with the decision of civil judges, and the people were encouraged to take small cases to them rather than to the latter. A powerful adversary, or a usurer, might refuse to submit to the episcopal arbitrator, but the poor and feeble found their defenders in the bishops. They interceded in their behalf in the name of slighted Christian principles. They opened the convents and churches to shelter them, and supported their cause with the emperor and his functionaries. This intercession was legally recognised, the right of the oppressed to appeal to the bishop was sanctioned, and the magistrates were ordered to respect such revered intervention.[113]

Valentinian I., and Honorius, convinced that "true worship consists in helping the poor and needy," charged the bishops to superintend the execution of all laws concerning care for the poor and humanity towards the afflicted.[114] Thus the religious origin of charity is recognised, as well as the duty of ministers of the Church to superintend its exercise and to teach it by their own example. The right of asylum was confirmed, and it was forbidden to seize those who sought refuge in the churches,[115] though efforts were made to hinder the abuse of this privilege. The right of asylum was extended to the outside portico, in order that the refugees should not pass their nights or take their meals in the interior, on the steps of the altars. It was forbidden to cross the threshold with arms, and the number of cases was limited for which the right of asylum was allowed.[116] This custom had been introduced by degrees, and like the arbitration of the bishops it ought not to be needed in a society regularly organized and ruled, but it was a great benefit in this time of social decadence, when religion alone had sufficient authority to enforce justice and humanity.

A not less important benefit was the protection given by the law to the establishments founded by charity for the benefit of the sick and needy. Like the ecclesiastical possessions whose revenues were intended for the help of the poor, these establishments were frequently exposed to the robbery or unjust claims of powerful men. Honorius gave to the Churches, in accordance with their requests, special advocates who were charged to defend their causes.[117] In the Western Empire, in the fifth century, several emperors took under their special protection the houses that were opened for orphans, invalids, and poor travellers,[118] but this was after the time at which our limit is fixed. During the period with which we are engaged, we must still notice the measures taken by some princes to increase the revenues of the Churches and of their hospitals. Constantine gave lands whose produce was to be used to feed the poor.[119] A little later the property of suppressed pagan temples was given to this cause.[120] By the laws of 369 and 409 the emperors Valentinian I. and Honorius also devoted to this the product of certain fines which went previously to increase the revenues of the treasury.[121]

One of the miseries of this time was the reduction of entire populations taken captive by the barbarians to slavery. We have found previously how active was the charity of the Church and her ministers in endeavouring to bring them back. Ransomed by collections or the price of sacred vases, these unfortunates returned to the desolation of their devastated provinces. They were not overlooked by imperial solicitude. Honorius ordered that their return to the places from whence they had been carried off should be assisted, and that food and clothes should be given to them. It was made a duty for the magistrates to recommend them to the charity of the Christians inhabiting the localities through which they had to pass.[122]

Humanity entered lastly into penal legislation, though only feebly, for tortures of barbarous cruelty were still inflicted in far too many cases. The aversion of the Fathers of the Church for the punishment of death had not yet conquered custom. The isolated attempt of Constantine to suppress it found no imitators. This emperor, who recognised the image of God even in the criminal, forbade in 315 the branding of the face of those criminals who were condemned to serve in the mines or as gladiators, "because," he said, "the human face, formed after the image of celestial beauty, ought never to be disfigured." [123] He ordered also that the accused should be tried more promptly, in order that if innocent they might not be too long deprived of liberty. He saw that no accused person should be treated as guilty before conviction, and to attain this he tried to reform the discipline of prisons, which till this time had been arbitrary and in accordance with ancient barbarism. He forbade the torture of the accused, who was not to be placed in dark or unhealthy dungeons, or loaded with chains that tore the flesh, " in order that a man, who perhaps is innocent, may not be destroyed before the sentence of the judge." [124]

His successors added some further measures, marked by the same respect for human nature. Constantius ordered male and female prisoners to be kept apart to prevent the scandals which took place in the prisons.[125] Theodosius I. renewed Constantine's regulations,[126] and Honorius, who though a feeble emperor greatly ameliorated the law, charged the judges to visit the prisons every Sunday, to see that the prisoners had suitable food, and to make inquiries "whether depraved gaolers refused to treat them with humanity." [127]

We are compelled to present the result of this study of the effect of Christianity upon the law in a fragmentary manner. Legislation had not yet attained unity, but it is at least possible to trace clearly the reforming power of Christianity; we see ineffaceable traces of the spirit of love and justice which God spread in the world through Christ. At the time of the fall of the Western Empire the relations of civil society were greatly modified. The unpitying egoism and aristocratic harshness of pagan antiquity were excluded from many laws, and if the progressive conquests of charity allowed traces of ancient law still to remain, it was because the last days of a declining world were not favourable to a revision of the code. Justinian continued the transformation of the law, as far as was possible at such a period of stormy transition. He finished the work which his predecessors had

CHAP. V.] PROGRESS OF IMPROVEMENT IN THE LAWS. 443

commenced, in the collection of laws which he caused to be made. He generalized their rules and arranged them in an orderly manner. He, in his turn, abolished many remains of paganism, without being able to blot out all. In this way he fixed legislation for a series of centuries, and so it has remained; not Roman justice in the ancient sense, but Roman justice modified by Christianity. The middle ages, and later, the immortal author of the Civil Code, completed its reform.

(1) " Causidici sublati, jurisconsulti relegati aut necati."—Lactant., *De Mort. Persecut.*, c 22. vol. ii. p. 213. (2) Meysenbug, *De Christ. Relig. Vi et Effectu in Jus Civile*, p. 10. (3) Cf. Euseb., *Vita Constant.*, I. 27, p. 421. *Paneg. incerti*, c. 26, in *Opp. Plinii*, vol. ii. p. 337. Eumenius, *Paneg.*, c. 21, l.c. p. 309. (4) Euseb., *Hist. Eccl.*, X. 7, p. 394. This law was confirmed in 313 and in 319 A.D. *Cod. Theodos.*, XVI. tit. 2, l. 1, 2. (5) Ap. Euseb., *Hist. Eccl.*, X. 5, p. 388, there is only the beginning of this edict. The full text will be found ap. Lactant., *De Morte Persecut.*, c. 48, vol. ii. p. 244. (6) See above, p. 412. (7) *Cod. Theod.*, XVI. tit, 2, l. 4. (8) Euseb., *Hist. Eccl.*, X. 6, p. 393. (9) *Corp. Jur.*, III. tit. 12, l. 3. (10) *Cod. Theod.*, XII. tit. 1, l. 21 (335), and tit. 5, l. 2 (337). (11) This title, with its insignia, is still found on several medals and inscriptions. See Mionnet, *De la Rareté et du Prix des Médailles Romaines*, Paris, 1827, vol. ii. p. 226. Orelli, vol. ii. p. 231, No. 4074. (12) Euseb., *Vita Const.*, III. 55, 58; IV. 25; pp. 512, 514, 537. (13) " He revised the laws handed down by the ancients, putting them on a more equitable basis"—*O. c.*, IV. 26, p. 537. " New laws have been promulgated for controlling public morals and repressing crime."—Nazarius, " Paneg. Const.," c. 38; in *Opp. Plinii*, vol. ii. p. 361. (14) Cf. M. Troplong, p. 115 ff. It is generally admitted that it was Constantine who first gave a legal sanction to the arbitration awards pronounced by the bishops in civil matters. Cf. Euseb., *Vita Const.*, IV. 27, p. 539, and Sozomen, *Hist. Eccl.*, I. 9. At the same time no older law on this point is known than that of Honorius, 408 A.D.; *Corp. Jur.*, I. tit. 4, l. 8. Godefroy, vol. vi. p. 339, has proved the spuriousness of a pretended law of Constantine, " De episcopali judicio." This does not prevent us saying that Constantine was the first to do what afterwards became law. In 398 the privilege of arbitrating in disputes was granted to the Jewish patriarchs (*Cod. Theod.*, II. tit. 1, l. 10). It is not probable that this privilege was granted to the Jews before it had been granted to the Christians. (15) Fragm. Orat.; in *Opp.*, p. 534. (16) *Or.* 4, *ad. imperitos canes, i.e., Cynicos*; in *Opp.*, p. 866. (17) Frag. Orat.; in *Opp.*, p. 533, 557. (18) Ep. 49, p. 89. (19) Sozomen, *Hist. Eccles.*, V. 16, p. 618. Greg. Nazianz., *Or.* 1, "Invectiva adv. Jul.," vol. i. p. 102. (20) Ep. 49, l.c. (21) M. Troplong, p. 127. See too the article on Chronology ap. Godferoy, *Cod. Theod.*, vol. i.

p. lxii.   (22) *Cod. Theod.*, I. tit. 4, l. 1.   (23) It was compiled between 429 and 438 A.D.   (24) 321 A.D.   *Corp. Jur.*, II. tit. 35, l. 2, § 1. (25) 312 and 316 A.D.   *Corp. Jur.*, I. tit. 48, l. 1; II. tit. 13, l. 21.   (26) *Cod. Theod.*, V. tit. 1, l. 1; also *Corp. Jur.*, VI. tit. 58, de legitimis hæredibus.   (27) *Cod. Theod.*, V. tit. 1, l. 2 ff.   Cf. M. Troplong, p. 337. ff. (28) Law of Alex. Severus, 224 A.D.   *Corp. Jur.*, V. tit. 35.   (29) *Corp. Jur.*, V. tit. 35, l. 2.   (30) Lactant., *Div. Instit.*, VI. 23, vol. i. p. 498. (31) *Cod. Theod.*, XVI. tit. 8, l. 1.   (32) "Lenones patres et dominos, qui suis filiis vel ancillis peccandi necessitatem imponunt, nec jure dominii frui, nec tanti criminis patimur libertate gaudere . . . sed ancillis filiabusque, si velint, conductisve pro paupertate personis, quas sors damnavit humilior, . . . liceat omni miseriarum necessitate absolvi."—*Law of Theodosius* II., 428 ; *Cod. Theod.*, XV. tit. 8, l. 2 ; also *Corp. Jur.*, I. tit. 4, l. 12 ; XI. tit. 40, l. 6.   (33) *Law of Leo I*.   *Corp. Jur.*, tit. 4, l. 14.   (34) *Novell. Theod.* II., tit. 18.   (35) *Cod. Theod.*, IX. tit. 25, l. 1, 2.   (36) See De Rhœr, *De Ffectu Relig. Christ. in Jurisprud. Rom.*, p. 223 ff.   (37) 320 A.D.   *Cod. Theod.*, VIII. tit. 16, l. 1. Euseb., *Vita Const.*, IV. 26, p. 538.   (38) Cf. M. Troplong, p. 197 ff.   (39) *Cod. Theod.*, III. tit. 12, l. 1.   (40) 335 A.D. L. c., l. 2. (41) See also the laws of Arcadius, 396 A.D., and of Theodosius II., 415 A.D.   *Cod. Theod.*, III. tit. 12, l. 3, 4.   (42) *Cod. Theod.*, VIII. tit. 17, l. 2. In a law of 428 A.D., Theodosius II. says that he enacted the law of 410 "in order to give assistance to marriages," V. tit. I. l. 9.   (43) *Corp. Jur.*, V. tit. 26, l. 1.   (44) It is a "facinus atrocissimum, scelus immane."   326 A.D.   *Cod. Theod.*, IX. tit. 7, l. 1, ff.   (45) *Corp. Jur.*, V. tit. 27, l. 5.   (46) *Cod. Theod.*, IV. tit. 6, l. 1.   (47) *Corp. Jur.*, V. tit. 27, l. 5.   (48) Cf. M. Troplong, p. 248, ff.   (49) *Cod. Theod.*, IV. tit. 6, l. 1.   (50) L. c., l. 2.   (51) 443 A D.   *Corp. Jur.*, V. tit. 27, l. 3.   (52) 331 A.D.   *Cod. Theod.*, III. tit. 16, l. 1.   (53) 421 A.D. L. c., l, 2.   (54) *Novellæ Theod.* II., tit. 17.   (55) Valentinian I. 371 A.D.   *Cod. Theod.*, III. tit. 7, l. 1.   (56) 381 A.D.   *Cod. Theod.*, III. tit. 8, l. 1.   (57) Theodosius I. in 382 A.D. Honorius in 412 A.D.   *Cod. Theod.*, III. tit. 8, l. 2, 3.   (58) *Cod. Theod.*, III. tit. 8, l. 3.   (59) *Cod. Theod.*, V. tit. 7, l. 1.   (60) "Let each man rear his own offspring. But if he shall have thought fit to expose his child, he will be liable to the appointed penalty. But neither to master nor to patron do we allow any opportunity of recovering such children, if some compassionate person of kindly affection have taken in the child whom he had exposed, for all he knew, to death ; nor will he be able to claim as his own the life which he despised when helpless and perishing."—*Corp. Jur.*, VIII. tit. 52, l. 2. See, too, the law of Honorius, 412 A.D. *Cod. Theod.*, V. tit. 7, l. 2.   (61) 391 A.D.   *Cod. Theod.*, III. tit. 3, l. 1.   (62) 318 and 374 A.D. *Cod. Theod.*, IX. tit. 15, l. 1 ; tit. 14, l. 1.   (63) Valentinian I. 365 A.D. *Corp. Jur.*, IX. tit. 15, l. 1; also *Cod. Theod.*, IX. tit. 13, l. 1.   (64) *Cod. Theod.*, II. tit. 8, l. 1.   (65) M. Troplong, p. 264 ff.   (66) 389 A.D.   *Cod. Theod.*, V. tit. 1. l. 4 ; completed by Justinian.   (67) "For unruly sons, who have offended their fathers either by the bitterness of their railings or the pain of some flagrant injustice, the law decrees that their emancipation be repealed, and that they be punished by the loss of a freedom they do not deserve."—*Cod. Theod.*, VIII. tit. 14, l. 1.   (68) 319 A.D.   *Corp. Jur.*, V. tit. 5, l. 3.   *Cod. Theod.*, IV. tit. 9 ; IX. tit. 9, l. 1.   (69) 319 and 326 A.D.   *Corp. Jur.*, IX. tit. 14, l. 1.   *Cod.*

CHAP. V.] PROGRESS OF IMPROVEMENT IN THE LAWS. 445

Theod., IX. tit. 12, l. 1, 2.   (70) *Corp. Jur.,* VI. tit. 1, l. 3.   (71) According to Sozomen, *Hist. Eccl.,* I. 9, p. 414, Constantine promulgated three edicts on this subject. The first is lost; the second was in 316 A.D., the third in 321 A.D. *Corp. Jur.,* I. tit. 13, l. 1, 2.   (72) *Corp. Jur.,* VII. tit. 13, l. 2–4; I. tit. 10, l. 1.   (73) *Corp. Jur.,* I. tit. 3, l. 38. (74) This law was made 315 A.D. Those guilty are condemned to the circus; if they survive the fight with beasts, they are to fight as gladiators, but in such a way as to be killed before they can do anything in self-defence.—*Cod. Theod.,* IX. tit. 18, l. 1.   (75) 396 A.D. *Cod. Theod.,* XV. tit. 6, l. 1.   (76) The emperor does not wish "to produce melancholy by the excessive restriction of these (*i.e.,* the theatrical) arts;" but he wishes to suppress "the foul and indecent spectacle." 399 A.D. l. c., l. 2. See Godefroy's Comment.   (77) *Cod. Theod.,* XV. tit. 7. l. 10. (78) 386 A.D. *Cod. Theod.,* l. c., l. 2; 425 A.D., ib., l. 5.   (79) "Munus turpe," 380 A.D.   *Cod. Theod.,* l. c., l. 4.   "Personæ inhonestæ," 394 A.D., ib., l. 12.   (80) "Quas vilitas vitæ dignas legum observatione non credidit." Constantine, 327 A.D.; *Cod. Theod.,* XXV. tit. 7, l. 1. (81) 393 A.D. *Cod. Theod.,* l. c., l. 11.   (82) 394 A.D. L. c., l. 12. (83) 371 A.D. L. c., l. 1.   (84) 371 A.D. L. c., l. 2.   Valentinian II. also grants them liberty, if they claim it at the hands of the emperor himself; 380 and 381 A.D., l. 4 and 9. This right was repealed by Honorius 413 A.D.; l. c., l. 13.   (85) 380 A.D. L.c. l. 4; 381 A.D., l. 8. These two laws were made at Milan; law 9, 381 A.D., to the same purport, is from Carthage.   (86) See the laws of 371 and 380 A.D., l. 2, 4. (87) Vinculum naturalis conditionis. Law 380, l. c., l. 4.   (88) " . . . ita ut voluptatibus publicis non serveat." Law 380, l. c., l. 5.   (89) Eumenius, *Paneg.,* c. 12; in *Opp. Plinii,* vol. ii. p. 303. Cf. *Paneg. Incerti,* c. 23, ibid. p. 335.   (90) "Cruenta spectacula in otio civili et domestica quiete non placent; quapropter omnino gladiatores esse prohibemus."— *Cod. Theod.,* XV. tit. 12, l. 1.   (91) 315 A.D.: "si quis in ludum fuerit damnatus."—*Cod. Theod.,* IX. tit. 18, l. 1; tit. 40, l. 2.   (92) Not in Syria only, as has been mistakenly asserted, on the ground that this law was made at Berytus. The law has altogether a general scope; Eusebius (*Vita Const.,* IV. 25, p. 537) says expressly that Constantine commanded " μὴ μονομάχων μιαιφονίαις μολύνειν τὰς πόλεις "—"Not to pollute the cities with the butcheries of the gladiators." "Then, *for the first time,* was the spectacle of gladiatorial combats prohibited amongst the Romans."— Sozomen, *Hist. Eccl.,* I. 8, p. 411.   (93) It is not found in the text given in Justinian's Code, *Corp. Jur.,* XI. tit. 43, l. 1.   (94) Libanius, *De Vita Sua,* vol. ii. p. 3.   (95) 357 A.D. *Cod. Theod.,* XV. tit. 12, l. 2. (96) Ambros., *De Obitu Valentiniani,* § 15, vol. ii. p. 1178.   (97) 365 and 367 A.D. *Cod. Theod.,* IX. tit. 40, l. 8, 11.   (98) August., *Confess.,* VI. 8, vol. i. p. 90.   (99) 391 A.D. II., ep. 46, and VII. ep. 4, pp. 50, 167.   (100) Symmach., X. ep. 61, p. 295.   (101) Prudent., *In Symmachum,* II. v. 1123, p. 490.   (102) 397 A.D.   "Nomen detestandum." *Cod. Theod.,* XV. tit. 12, l. 2, 3.   (103) "Forbid these hecatombs of wretched human souls, Nor let the mob in penal torture thus exult."— *In Symmach.,* II. v. 1124 ff., p. 490.   (104) Theodoret, *Hist. Eccl.,* V. 26, p. 234.   (105) Prudentius does not dare to demand the suppression of these wild beast fights: "Nunc solis contenta feris infamis arena, Nulla cruentatis homicidia ludat in armis."—*Adv. Symmachum,* II. v. 1126 ff., p. 490. Even so late as 462 A.D. there were to be seen in the

East "ferarum lacrimosa spectacula."—Law of Leo I.; *Corp. Jur.*, III. tit. 12, l. 11. (106) About 357 A.D. *Cod. Theod.*, IX. tit. 7, l. 3. (107) 390 A.D. L. c., law 6. See, too, Godefroy's Commentary on this law. (108) See the two laws "De alimentis quæ inopes parentes de publico petere debeant." XI. tit. 27, l. 12. It has been thought that this was merely a continuation of the alimentary foundations of Trajan and the Antonines (Pauly, *Real Encycl. der Classischen Alterthums-wissenschaft*, vol. iv. p. 1556); but it seems perfectly clear to ourselves that it is a new institution; the alimentary foundations have long since fallen into decay and been forgotten. (109) *Cod. Theod.*, IX. tit. 1, l. 4. (110) *Cod. Theod.*, I. tit. 7, l. 1. (111) *Corp. Jur.*, III. tit. 14, l. 1. (112) *Cod. Theod.*, XIII. tit. 10, l. 4. (113) *Corp. Jur.*, I. tit. 4, l. 12; XI. tit. 40, l. 6. (114) Valentinian I. in 364 A.D., and Honorius in 409 A.D. *Corp. Jur.*, I. tit. 4, l. 1, 9. In 364 Valentinian charges the bishops to watch that the merchants do not extort exorbitant prices, seeing that for Christians "verus cultus est adjuvare pauperes et positos in necessitate."— *Corp. Jur.*, I. tit. 4, l. 1. (115) Honorius, 414 A.D. *Corp. Jur.*, I. tit. 12, l. 2. (116) Theodosius deprives bankrupts of the right of asylum in churches, 392 A D.—*Cod. Theod.*, IX. tit. 45, l. 1-3. (117) 407 A.D. *Cod. Theod.*, XVI. tit. 2, l. 38. (118) Leo and Anthemius. *Corp. Jur.*, I. tit. 3, l. 32, 35. (119) Euseb., *Vita Const.*, IV. 28, p. 539. (120) Ambros., *Ep.* 18 *ad Valentinianum*, ann. 384, § 16, vol. ii. p. 837. (121) *Corp. Jur.*, I. tit. 4, l. 2, 9. (122) *Cod. Theod.*, V. tit. 5, l. 2. (123) "Si quis in ludum fuerit, vel in metallum damnatus, minime in ejus facie scribatur . . . quo facies, quæ ad similitudinem pulchritudinis cœlestis est figurata, minime maculetur."—*Cod. Theod.*, IX. tit. 40, l. 2 (124) 320 A.D. *Corp. Jur.*, IX. tit. 4, l. 1; *Cod. Theod.*, IX. tit. 3, l. 1 (125) 340 A.D. *Cod. Theod.*, IX. tit. 2, l. 3. (126) 380 A.D. *Cod. Theod.*, IX. tit. 3, l. 6. (127) " . . . ne his humanitas clausis per corruptos carcerum custodes negetur."—*Cod. Theod.*, IX. tit. 3, l. 7, *Corp. Jur.*, I. tit. 4, l. 9.

CHAPTER VI.

REACTION OF THE PAGAN SPIRIT ON THE CUSTOMS OF CHRISTIAN SOCIETY.

Conclusion.

WE have seen how slowly and quietly Christian ideas established the foundations of a new social order, how their influence, at first unrecognised, gradually became open and avowed. During a period of four centuries these principles transformed civil society without appealing to any other force than that of persuasion; yet in such a manner as to show a complete difference from what it was when ruled by pagan religion and philosophy.

If we rapidly sum up the fundamental difference between the ancient State and Christian society, we find on the one side, egoism, pride, vengeance, *talion*; on the other, charity, humility, forgiveness, kindness. In the one, the rights of personality are despised, and subordinated to the despotic interest of a State which is founded on the inequality of men; in the other, men are respected and loved for their inherent qualities, and are equal in a free and brotherly community. In the one, woman is lightly esteemed, marriage reduced to a civil institution, the family servilely submissive to the father's authority; in the other, woman is honoured, marriage sanctified, the family united by reciprocal ties and duties. In the one, work is despised and left to the lower classes, especially to a race said to be destined by nature to servitude; in the other, work and workers are respected, and slavery is gradually abolished. In the one, the poor and weak are abused by the powerful and strong; in the other, charity draws all classes to help one another. Lastly, in the one, men are honoured in proportion to their wealth, the poor being despised and kept down; in the other, the poor and afflicted are cared for with tender solicitude, as being as much children of God as the happy and rich.

It seems to us that we must be singularly blinded not to see the cause of these contrasts in that of the different faiths. How could a society given over to immoral superstition, or to incredulity still more immoral, pass through a normal development of its principles to a civilization founded on radically different doctrines? Yet even to-day there are men who say that this progress is not the work of Christianity, that humanity was developed from its own powers without Christ, that the Saviour's coming even arrested its progress. To say this is to be blind to the history of all nations, and to the history of the human heart. Both proclaim loudly that charity cannot be the product of egoism, nor humility of pride; that without the intervention of God no new spirit could have regenerated individuals and the world.

We must admit that in the ages we have portrayed, Christian society is far from presenting a perfect representation of the Kingdom of God. The ideal was most nearly approached in the early ages of the growing Church. She swerved from it again even during the period when, in the laws and moral systems, she brought out more fully the influence of charity. Whoever has felt the constantly recurring difficulties with which egoism opposes the sentiments that faith in the Saviour inspires in mankind, will not be astonished at this. The history of the struggles of the human heart is the history of the struggles of humanity. The Gospel reigns in society only in the proportion in which it reigns in individual hearts. To make our picture faithful we must add some dark touches; but even these shadows will only show more clearly the heavenly beauty of the principles that the Son of God has revealed to the world.

Alongside of the action of Christianity on pagan society, there was a reaction of paganism in the life of Christians. This reaction began early, but showed itself more markedly than before after the external and political triumph of the Church. It is worthy of remark, that whilst Christianity exerted a profound and salutary influence on the laws and institutions, the pagan reaction was not strong enough to affect them. Its power was exerted on the morality of individuals. It may have hindered more rapid progress, but never completely arrested it. If, therefore, we find shadows, we find them rather in the personal life of a larger or smaller number of Christians than in the general effects of the new spirit communicated to humanity.

It is not difficult to find the causes of this pagan reaction. The chief was the resistance of the human heart, which manifests itself differently according to circumstances. There was also the position of the Church in the world, and the changes in this position during the early ages. Christian society, living and growing in the midst of pagan society, necessarily felt its influences, even whilst exerting its own power over those who did not belong to it. As long as its members were persecuted, they were saved from contact with pagan morality, they had a vivid sense of the need of distinguishing themselves from the world, their bonds with one another were strengthened, and in the midst of trials their faith became more ardent and their life more pure. But in the intervals of repose from persecutions, this life was relaxed. The tacit tolerance enjoyed by the Christians under some emperors lowered their primitive piety and cooled their first love. The Fathers, grieved with these relapses, frequently reminded the Church that it was for her chastisement that God permitted new persecutions.[1]

When Christianity was acknowledged as a religion by the emperors, this laxity increased. The Church was invaded by worldly and ambitious men, who entered her service not to satisfy their spiritual desires, but to seek means of power, or to strengthen their position.[2] Indifferent to paganism, which no longer inspired them with faith, they quitted it when it ceased to be upheld by the authority of their prince. When Julian wished to re-establish the altars of the ancient gods, many of these men, as faithless to the Gospel as they had been to the religion of their fathers, hastened to desert the Church and resume their idolatrous practices.[3] Later, and chiefly in the time of Theodosius, when paganism was officially suppressed and the empire enjoyed some years of peace, most of the rich and powerful families accepted Christianity, but they brought into the Church pagan dispositions and customs which were more difficult to give up than ceremonies and fables.

In the Church itself, the tranquil possession of power and fortune, repose and security, cooled the zeal of many members who, stimulated by persecution, would probably have shown more fidelity. They imitated the manners of the new converts, and fell back into tastes contrary to the spirit of the Gospel. Chrysostom appeals to the testimony of the pagans themselves, that in times of trial the Christians, though less numerous, had purer virtues.[4]

The complaints of the Fathers are unanimous in this respect; and even admitting that in their holy austerity they exaggerated the evil, we are still compelled to admit that it was real and great, and that the political victory of the Church, instead of being a definite triumph of Christian principles in men's lives, had rather brought a return of the vices that Christianity came to uproot.

A great love of riches and luxury was one of the first to reappear. It was gratified, in many respects, by the legal proscription of paganism. Many powerful lords were enriched with the spoils of the temples,[5] whilst they continued to levy a tax on the sanctuaries which they allowed the cultivators of their lands to use clandestinely.[6] Bishop Zeno, of Verona, a preacher of the fourth century, exclaims sorrowfully "that avarice has so entered into all hearts, that it has almost ceased to be called a vice."[7] Amongst women, whom Christianity had raised so high, were some whose lives formed a distressing contrast to those of Paula, Fabiola, Melania. In Carthage as in Constantinople, in Antioch as in Rome, they soon rivalled the pagan ladies in luxury of clothing and richness of ornaments. Forgetting the noble simplicity which the orators and poets of the Church had counselled, they felt ashamed to appear with fewer ornaments than women brought up in paganism, or to decline the pleasures in which these found their delight.[8] We are obliged to say that the clergy themselves did not always escape this worldly spirit. Prelates and clerks, who loved riches and eagerly sought worldly honours, were soon to be found alongside of men who, in the highest and humblest ranks of the priesthood, gave eternally sublime examples of abnegation and simplicity.[9]

The natural effect of the revival of a love of riches, was a coolness in the love of Christians amongst themselves.

Cupidity and charity cannot exist together; it is impossible to serve "Mammon and God" at the same time. Loving the world, Christians became detached from heaven and forgot the precepts of Jesus Christ. The tie which should unite them as a family of brothers was loosened for many of them. Jealousies, rivalries, and hatreds reappeared.[10] More than a hundred years after Eusebius had mentioned this relapse, Salvian mourned it anew, sorrowfully comparing the life of Christians with those of the barbarians who invaded the empire.[11]

The decline of Christian love is shown in all the social relations which Christianity had strengthened and sanctified, through charity. As many members of the Church, both men and women, sought pleasure and luxury before everything, marriage was for them no longer a holy union, a school of virtue and reciprocal fidelity. In Greece, Africa, and Gaul rich men had often mistresses as well as wives. These mixed not unfrequently with the slaves who were exposed to their master's passions.[12] The pagan principle was constantly upheld that infidelities may be allowed in the husband that would not be permissible for the wife. It was considered no sin to have a concubine, provided that no husband's rights were infringed, and the public places were not resorted to.[13] Women, thinking that the examples of their husbands, released them from fidelity, hastened to follow their example. "The towns," said Salvian, "are full of bad houses frequented by women of quality. They regard this libertinism as one of the privileges of their birth, and are as proud of surpassing other women in impurity as in noble birth."[14]

The principles of conduct toward slaves, which led the masters to love men called to the same spiritual liberty and salvation as themselves, were no more observed by many Christians than the sanctity of marriage and respect for woman. Not only were there still many households crowded with useless and idle slaves, who ministered to ridiculous requirements, or who swelled the train with which the master or mistress appeared in the streets,[15] but they were treated with the same contempt, the same lack of charity, as in pagan society. Instead of being raised by affectionate treatment, they were left in their degradation and its accompanying vices. They had a pretext for corruption in the examples before their eyes, and, by being loaded with heavy work and cruel punishments, they were tempted to falsehood, plunder, flight, and open revolt.[16] The doctors of the Church answered those masters who complained of the vices of their slaves, that they must seek the cause in themselves;[17] they suffered for their contempt of the slaves by yielding also to the influence of the bad life which they led just in their sight.[18]

The preachers of the Church remonstrated frequently and energetically against the abuse of Christians by their brothers when they used them for amusements or passions condemned by the spirit of the Gospel. The taste for all kinds of spectacles, for the theatre, the dance, and combats in the arena, hardly extinguished in many pagan converts, survived the suppression of paganism in its ancient strength. In the fourth century, according to the testimony of Augustine, the Christians attended the games in greater numbers than the Jews and pagans;[19] they sought relaxation and found only lessons in corruption, luxury, and cruelty. Some, who thought themselves stronger, felt their ancient passions re-awaken at the sight of the blood reddening the arena, and fell into saddening relapses.[20] They filled the amphitheatres on the most solemn festivals of the Church, even during the hours of worship on Easter day. The Fathers lamented this scandal with bitter grief,[21] and contrasted it with the rude austerity of the barbarians, who knew nothing of such spectacles.[22] The pagans themselves were astonished at the contrast between the principles of Christians and their life.[23]

Public dangers, the dissolution of the empire, the approach of the Germanic nations, were unable to restrain this infatuation. After the taking of Rome by the barbarians, the Romans who took refuge in Carthage, instead of lamenting over the loss of their *eternal* city, mixed eagerly with the frivolous crowd who attended the theatres, and when Carthage itself fell into the hands of the Vandals, the cries of the combatants in the street were mixed with the applause of the populace who were amusing themselves in the amphitheatre.[24] The same madness prevailed in other parts of the empire. Some nobles at Trèves who survived the sack of their city, asked the emperor, as a remedy for all their ills, to send them some gladiators.[25] The Roman people in the capital and in the provinces were a prey to this folly, whilst rushing to their destruction. "They die and they laugh," said Salvian, the indignant spectator of this great misery. The Romans no longer thought of anything but enjoying their remaining moments. They were careless as to the fate of their country, careless as to the fate of the unfortunates who filled the towns and and villages, careless even as to their own fate. With many of them faith was asleep and charity dead, neither the voice of their preachers nor the louder call of circumstances being strong enough to re-awaken them.

Could there have been any time in which charity, brotherly, sacrificing love, was more required than in this period of misfortune, poverty, and suffering, of all kinds!

REACTION OF THE PAGAN SPIRIT.

There were doubtless some who still guarded the Divine treasure and spread it around their path. In the midst of the egoism of some and the distress of others, they testified to the power of Christian faith, and the life of love that this faith kindles in the soul.[26] But the majority of men had forgotten these sentiments, without which the name of Christian is only a melancholy mockery. It was in vain that the preachers of the Church repeated continually that the gold ought to be given to the help of the poor which was bestowed upon clothes, furniture, slaves, and horses.[27] It was in vain that they represented to the rich, who were occupied with their pleasures, the suffering of the poor, the widow, the forsaken orphans.[28] It was in vain that they stigmatized as unworthy of Christians that disgraceful prodigality which threw to actors, dancers, and fallen women, what ought to have been given to the afflicted members of the body of Christ.[29] The faithful, who no longer deserved their name, in their foolish infatuation listened no more to exhortation or to blame. They continued insensible to the misery which contrasted so terribly with the riches and luxury of the last great proprietors of the Roman world.

This misery resulted from despotism, ancient slavery, the disturbances of the empire, the general aversion for work, even more than from the ravages of the barbarians. It was a melancholy heritage, bequeathed by paganism to the society which was converted to Christianity. It was supreme everywhere, in the East and in the West, in the towns and in the country; it weakened natural feelings of affection, and the respect due by man to himself. The poor people exposed or killed their children to leave themselves free, or they sold them as slaves, or hired them to usurers; a terrible example of the persistence of pagan customs in populations calling themselves

Christian.[30] The parents of these condemned little ones, unwilling to work for a respectable livelihood, flocked to the towns, where they encumbered the streets and squares soliciting alms, either by showing real or sham infirmities, or by threatening those who did not wish to relieve them.[31] These beggars were so numerous that, in 382, the Emperor Valentinian passed a restrictive law; the aged or sick poor were alone allowed to implore help in the streets, while those who could work were sent back to labour in the fields.[32]

The churches, the bishops, and the benevolent laity made many sacrifices to alleviate this evil; but there were too many Christians whose hearts were untouched by compassion, and who continued, with ancient pagan harshness, to make all they could out of populations and individuals.

Notwithstanding the law of Diocletian, which branded usurers with infamy, and notwithstanding the earnest exhortations of the Fathers, their trade flourished to a frightful extent. If the poor man could not pay his debts, the creditor took possession of his children to sell them in the public market.[33] Even the collectors of the public revenue were guilty of this barbarity, which, though authorized by pagan law, was not in accordance with a law and society ruled by the Gospel; they seized the sons of a father who could not pay his taxes.[34]

In the country, the great proprietors ruined their labourers by unjust tributes; to this they added their own special taxes, which they compelled the despairing unfortunates to pay.[35] In the towns the iniquity of the magistrates was added to this oppression; instead of defending the interests of the inhabitants, they only robbed the defenceless and enriched themselves. In the midst of general disorder, with no one keeping watch over them, they brought the heaviest accusations against poor men, who through their obscurity fell an easy prey to their exactions. "There is no town," said Salvian, "not a municipality nor a borough, where there are not as many tyrants as there are curials."[36] Thus it came about that the small proprietors grew fewer and fewer, the free agricultural and industrial population decreased rapidly. To escape spoliation, the greater number of small proprietors preferred the hard condition of labourers to that of freemen, which had become unendurable; they exchanged their independence for the oppressive protection of the great. Others sought among the barbarians a refuge which the empire could no longer give them.[37]

Besides the avaricious men who throve on the misery of the people, there were others who sought a short-lived glory by great almsgiving, similar to the largess of the pagan ages. Sometimes men and women, preceded by slaves, took their way to the space in front of the churches, and there gave money to numbers of the poor, that they might be praised for their charity;[38] sometimes their liberality was bestowed upon unworthy favourites, successors of those parasites who had filled the vestibules of the Romans of the decadence.[39]

The doctors of the Church, notwithstanding the great need of alms, ceaselessly opposed this pagan tendency to adulterate charity with ambitious ostentation. It was not splendid gifts nor external alms that they claimed from the faithful; they desired, before everything, a real love, capable of self-sacrifice and full of respect for others. This love is inseparable from humility. They were grieved to see this most glorious mark of the Church fading away, and they saw with alarm that Roman society would be destroyed and dragged down by an irresistible current.[40] Some even thought that the end of the world was at hand.[41] When the Christians were aroused from their carelessness by the voice of a crumbling empire, and anxiously asked why God had deserted them, the Fathers answered that their sufferings were merited by their vices, that they should remember their vileness and crimes, and should reflect whether they were worthy of the protection of God.[42]

Salvian, the author who expresses himself in this way, looks further; he sees that a new element is required to revivify this worn-out society, and he foresees that the invasion of the barbarians will be the means employed by the wisdom of God to recruit the failing strength of the Roman world.[43] Paganism had dragged humanity into an abyss of corruption. Spirit was weakened, courage enervated, character shattered. Christianity was alive only in individual souls. Though it had transformed social relations, it did not reign supreme; the customs of the masses had not yielded to its power. To save what was durable and great in ancient civilization, a younger race must be blended with the one which had lost its power; and for Christian faith and charity to produce their full fruits of justice, love, and peace, it required the hand of God to feed anew the expiring flame of the civilization of the world.

It is with regret that we have pointed out these signs of the cooling of Christian love in the customs of the later period of the Roman empire, but it is only possible to be an accurate historian through the strictest fidelity. We must not deserve the blame of showing only one side of the great picture that we have sketched.

Shall we be accused, on the other hand, of depreciating the power of Christianity because we speak of the need of a new power to complete the regeneration of the world? This objection is powerless. We have already shown that the Gospel of Jesus Christ is alone sufficiently powerful to soften and save individuals, and to establish society on its true foundations; but it must have ground in which its seeds can germinate. It had fulfilled its part on Roman soil as it had been left by ancient morality; it had opened a new era in the history of the Roman race. Paganism, and the society formed in its own image, were overthrown. To realize the new civilization brought about by the influence of Christianity on Roman society, needed an admixture of fresh and vigorous generations who knew nothing of the ideas and practices of the classic world. The pagan reaction had not altered the Christian spirit, which remained in its heavenly purity, eternally superior to all attacks. Pious men continued to set an example of all the virtues that this spirit inspires, in the midst of the crowd who fell into degradation. Above custom rose the institutions of the Church and the improved civil laws. Above a dying world rose the Gospel, with its principle of Divine life, removing the disorders of society, as beforetime the Spirit of God had worked on the chaos of the elements. Therefore the ancient forms might disappear, the corrupt Roman world might perish, the barbarians might cover the soil with its immense ruins—for in the midst of these ruins two things remained intact: the Gospel, the source of salvation for souls and peace for society; and the code which guaranteed individual rights and regulated social relations. What was durable in Roman civilization, transformed and completed by Christian influence, could not be carried away by the storm; the germs were planted in the furrows traced by the revolutions which tried mankind, and will certainly reappear, to blossom and bear fruit anew.

These germs were preserved because true justice is as immortal as true charity, because the cross of the Saviour rose on the world as a symbol of love and peace, as a luminous beacon whose light no tempest can extinguish. Confessedly the work of charity is not yet perfectly accomplished. Customs are still, in many respects, tinged with paganism. Egoism still rules in the world because it still rules in the soul. Many great vices may yet be seen along with great miseries. Men sought a remedy on all hands. Many thought to find it only in a return to the order of things where the individual is absorbed by society, giving up his freedom of thought, his voluntary activity, all that constitutes his personality; where the miserable and poor are expected to find a better fate in the exclusive satisfaction of terrestrial wants, where they are to be happy without being either relieved or respected. To-day, as beforetime, man impatiently seeks for happiness, and too often accuses society if all do not possess it in equal proportion. He confounds it with the temporary welfare of the body, or with the stormy pleasures of the senses, instead of placing it in the calm and eternal region of the soul. He thinks to bring it to all men by changing the forms of government, or reconstituting society, and regards this amendment as possible without the moral regeneration of individuals. This would be no progress, it would be only a renewal of the experience of the pagan world, followed quickly by universal retrogression. We need not fear this danger, as in the fifth century, in the decline of the Roman empire. The Cross is still visible, and we have faith in the promises of Christ and the progress that they insure.

If the Gospel has been too often abased to the service of the world, and has not yet completely triumphed, if the kingdom of God is not yet realized upon earth in all its perfection, if the spirit of error and sin still resists the Holy Spirit, yet the charity given by the Saviour to the faithful of His Church will keep them still unwearied; their efforts for the relief of all who suffer will be redoubled, and by the regenerative softening and freeing of individual souls a better future will be prepared for society. They alone can do it, for charity, ready for the greatest sacrifices, and stronger than death, draws back from no obstacle that opposes the true happiness of men. Consequently it is charity alone that can establish true justice in the world; the man who loves alone knows how to be perfectly just, for heal one knows how to respect the rights of his brother. "Ubi caritas non est, non potest esse justitia." ("Where charity is not, justice cannot be.") This saying of the Bishop of Hippo sums up the whole of our work, for it marks, with admirable precision, the difference between Christian society and all those which rest on another foundation.

(1) Cypr., *De Lapsis*, p. 182 ff. Euseb., *Hist. Eccl.*, VIII. 1, p. 292. Orig., *Hom.* 25 *in Num.*, § 4, vol. ii. p. 367; *Hom. in Jos.*, § 1, p. 447. (2) Orig., *Hom.* 4 *in Jos.*, § 3, vol. iii. p. 144. (3) Asterius, *Hom. adv. Avaritiam*, p. 43. (4) *Hom.* 24 *in Act.*, § 3, vol. ix. p. 197; *Hom.* 26 *in* 2 *Cor.*, § 4, vol. x. p. 623; *Hom.* 29 *in Act.*, § 3, vol. ix. p. 229. (5) Amm. Marcell., XXII. 4, vol. i. p. 290. (6) Zeno Veron., I. tract. 15, p. 130. (7) L. I. tract. 9, *De Avar.*, p. 122. (8) To combat these earthly tastes Tertullian wrote his essay, "*De Cultu Feminarum*," p. 149 ff., and Cyprian his "*De Habitu Virginum*," p. 173 ff. See also Tertull., *De Velandis Virg.*, c. 3, p. 174. Commodianus, *Instruct.*, v. 919 ff., p. 643. Basil., *Hom. in Divites*, § 2, vol. ii. p. 53. Chrysost., *Interpret. in Jes.*, c. 3, § 9, vol. vi. p. 45; *Hom.* 17 *in Matt.*, § 3, vol. vii. p. 225; *Hom.* 27 *in Joh.*, § 3, and *Hom.* 61 *in Joh.*, § 4, vol. vii. pp. 157, 367. Paulin. Nol., *Poema* 22, p. 126. For a general idea of the luxury of the age of Theodosius, see Müller, *De Genio, Moribus et Luxu ævi Theodosiani*, Copenh. 1798, 8vo. (9) Cyprian complains of this, *De Lapsis*, p. 183. Salvian, *Adv. Avaritiam*, I. 1, p. 218. Cf. Fleury, *Mœurs des Chrétiens* (Panth. Littér., Par. 1837), p. 259. (10) Euseb., *Hist. Eccl.*, VIII. 1, p. 292. (11) *De Gubernat. Dei*, V. 4, p. 102. (12) Chrysost., *Hom.* 69 *in Joh.*, § 4, vol. viii. p. 470. "As though it were a sort of chastity to be content with a few wives."—Salvian., *De Gubern. Dei*, IV. 5, p. 71; VII. 5, p. 153. (13) August., *Sermo* 9, §§ 4

and 11 ; *Sermo* 224, § 3, vol. vi. pp. 36, 40, 674. (14) *De Gubern. Dei*, VII. 5 ff. p. 153 ff. (15) Hieron., *Epp.* 54, 89, vol. i. pp. 290, 505. Chrysost., *Hom.* 27 *in Joh.*, § 3, vol. viii. p. 157. *Hom.* 40 *in Cor.*, § 5, vol. x. p. 385. Greg. Nazianz., *Orat.* 16, vol. i. p. 249. (16) Chrysost., *Hom.* 4 *in Tit.*, § 3, vol. xi. p. 753. Salvian., *De Gubern. Dei*, IV. 3, p. 67 ff. (17) "How great must be the corruption of the slaves, where the corruption of the masters is so bad."—Salvian., *De Gubern. Dei*, VII. 4, p. 155. Cf. Hieron., *Epp.* 54, 117 (August. ad Hieron.), vol. i. pp. 284, 788. (18) Chrysost., *Hom.* 15 *in Eph.*, § 3, vol. xi. pp. 113, 114. (19) *Sermo* 88, § 17, vol. v. p. 333. (20) For example, Alypius, Augustine's friend, who was a spectator of a gladiatorial combat at Rome, 385 A.D. August., *Confess.*, VI. 8, vol. i. p. 90. See too Chrysost., *Hom.* 37 *in Matth.*, §§ 6, 7, vol. vii. p. 422 ; *Hom. Contra Ludos et Theatra*, vol. vi. p. 272. *Hom.* 68 *in Matth.*, §§ 3, 4, vol. vii. p. 673. (21) Chrysost., *Hom. Contra Ludos et Theatra*, §§ 1, 2, vol. vi. p. 272 ; *Hom.* 58 *in Joh.*, § 4, vol. viii. p. 342. August., *Enarr. in Ps.* cxlvii., § 7, vol. iv. p. 1233 ; *Sermo* 361, § 4, vol. v. p. 982. (22) Chrysost., *Hom.* 37 *in Matt.*, § 7, vol. vii. p. 982. (23) Amm. Marcell., XIV. 6, vol. i. p. 20. (24) Salvian., *De Gubern. Dei*, VI. c. 12, p. 139. (25) *O.c.*, VI. 15, p. 143. (26) See the instances cited in the course of Book II. Salvian, speaking of the Gallic provinces, says, "They have been ravaged indeed, but not by all, and therefore they still, in some few corners, breathe a lingering life ; they have been maintained by the occasional though rare uprightness of a governor, though they have been plundered by the rapacity of most."—IV. 4, p. 70. (27) Chrysost., *Hom.* 27 *in Joh.*, § 3, vol. viii. p. 157. (28) Asterius, *Hom. de Divite et Lazaro*, p. 3. (29) "It is a very small thing to bear the name of Christians. How much do ye give to actors ? How much to wild beast trainers ? How much to the votaries of shame ? Ye give to those who kill you."—August., *Sermo* 9, § 21, vol. v. p. 44 ; *Sermo* 51, § 1, vol. v. p. 197. Asterius, *Hom. in Festum Kalend.*, p. 58. (30) Lactant., *Div. Instit.*, VI. 20, vol. ii. p. 491. Constantine's Laws, *Cod. Theod.*, XI. tit. 27, l. 1, 2. *Cod. Theod.*, III. tit. 3, l. 1, and V. tit. 8, l. 1. (31) Ambros., *De Off.*, II. 16, vol. ii. p. 88. Asterius, *Hom. in Festum Kal.*, pp. 55, 56. (32) *Cod. Theod.*, XIV. tit. 18, l. 1 ; with Godefroy's Commentary. (33) Ambros., *De Tobia*, c. 8, § 29, vol. i. p. 600. Basil., *Hom. in partem Ps.* xiv., § 4, vol. i. p. 112. (34) Hieron., *Vita Paphnutii, in Vitis SS.*, Col. 1547, fol. (35) August., *Ep.* 247, vol. ii. p. 663. Chrysost., *Hom.* 60 *in Matt.*, § 3, vol. vii. p. 614. Salvian, *De Gubern. Dei*, IV. 6, p. 73. (36) *O.c.*, V. 4, p. 103 ; V. 7, 8, p. 107 ff. (37) *O.c.*, V. 8, 9, p. 111. (38) "Hoc ipso cupiunt placere, quod placere contemnunt."—Hieron., *Ep.* 22, vol. i. pp. 110, 117. (39) "Most of the matrons are accustomed to bestow gifts on their flatterers, but, while lavish on these few favourites, even to excess, refuse all help to others."—Hieron., *Ep.* 108, vol. i. p. 707. (40) "Oh woe, woe ! the kingdoms of the world are perishing in ruins, but in us our sins perish not."—Hieron., *Ep.* 128, vol. i. p. 965. (41) "The end of the world is at hand."—Petr. Chrysol., *Sermo* 47, p. 200. (42) Salvian, *De Gubern. Dei*, IV. 12, p. 82. (43) "And do we wonder if the land of the Aquitani, or even all our lands are given by God into the hands of the barbarians, when the barbarians are now purifying with chastity what the Romans had polluted with fornication." —*De Gubernat. Dei*, VI. 6, p. 157.

NOTES.

Note 1.

SOME few years ago there appeared in Germany a work on the Christian Spirit in the writings of Tacitus: *Prophetische Stimmen aus Rom, oder das Christliche im Tacitus, und der typisch-prophetische Charakter seiner Werke,* by Bötticher; 2 vol., Hamburg, 1840. It is a remarkable work, displaying great scholastic enthusiasm combined with dogmatical, almost bigoted, prepossessions, and savouring strongly of Teutonic pride. The author's design is to bring what he calls a deeper and more spiritual interpretation to bear on the writings of Tacitus; accordingly he discovers analogies, sometimes specious, but more frequently forced, and in no instance such as to indicate any Christian elements in Tacitus. Bötticher talks sometimes of the deep faith of Tacitus, and of the keen sensitiveness of his religious conscience; sometimes he says that this faith, said to be so keen, was full of hesitancy and perplexity; he maintains that in Tacitus the Spirit of God testifies to the need and longing for a Saviour, but he adds that the author himself is unconscious of this. The work is full of these inconsistencies; it was hard to escape them, when once the writer had determined to uphold a system at variance with the truth.

In the midst of the general degeneracy and decay under the tyrannical sway of the emperors, Tacitus is the type of an old Roman under the severest republican regime; there is the old virtue, the old patriotism, an unmistakable moral force, but devoid of vigour or enterprise, and weighed down by the necessity of the times; there is a resignation to fate devoid of aspiration to a higher state, devoid of hope, and, above all, devoid of charity. It is the fact that freedom is banished and Rome's glory tarnished that makes Tacitus sad and rouses his anger; nothing else moves him. It is only with great caution that he ventures to pray that he may see the return of better days; he forbears to express fully the bitterness of his doubts as to the justice of the gods (e.g. *Ann.*, xvi. 33, vol. ii. p. 298; *Hist.*, i. 3, vol. iii. p. 5). Why then force him to say what he has not said? why seek for types and prophecies where nobody would suspect them? In this matter, Bötticher gets lost in the most extraordinary subtilties; he draws from Tacitus, for example, types for the destinies of the house of Hohenzollern and the providential mission of Prussia. Lastly, Bötticher is wrong when he says that true Romanism (Römerthum) is very near to Christianity; there are not two terms more removed from each other; the civilisation of republican Rome was no nearer to Christianity than the civilisation of Rome corrupted and enslaved under the empire.

Note 2.

The fact that Antonine issued a rescript in favour of tolerance is confirmed by a fragment of Melito's apology, preserved by Eusebius, *Hist. Eccl.*, iv. 26, p. 148. But it is very questionable whether this rescript is the same as we have under the name of "Edictum ad Commune Asiæ." It is possible that this passage of Melito furnished the occasion for ascribing to Antonine, or Marcus Aurelius, a text subsequently drawn up after the pattern of Adrian's edict, and afterwards appended to Justin Martyr's first *Apology*, c. 70, p. 85. A slightly different text is found in Eusebius, *Hist. Eccl.*, iv. 13, p. 126. Its authenticity has been upheld principally by Hegelmaier, *Comment. in Edictum Imp. Antonini Pii pro Christianis*, Tübingen, 1767, qto; and, secondarily, by Gullander, *De Epistola Antonini Pii ad Commune Asiæ*, Lund, Sweden, 1839, qto. The arguments to prove its spuriousness are much more conclusive; they are stated by Scaliger, *Animadv. ad Chron. Eusebii*, p. 203; by Thirlby, ed. Justin, London, 1722, p. 2; by Haffner, *De Edicto Antonini Pii pro Christianis ad Commune Asiæ*, Strasb., 1781, qto.

Note 3.

In the seventh book of his work, *De Officio Proconsulis*, Ulpian collected the edicts of the emperors against the Christians (Lactant., *Div. Instit.*, v. 11, vol. i. p. 390). There is also a passage in the *Martyr. Rom.*, March 2nd, p. 99, which says that, under Alexander Severus, while Ulpian was Prefect of Rome, several Christians were crucified in that city. From this fact it has been inferred that the great jurisconsult was inspired with hatred towards Christianity. Mr. Troplong himself says, p. 79: "Ulpian, who ordered the Christians to be crucified, himself used their language in several of his philosophical maxims, while he seemed to himself to be using the language of Stoicism." But neither the evidence of the martyrology, nor the object of Ulpian's work, are sufficient to prove his aversion. In his work he collected all the constitutions bearing on what was then considered to be a crime or an offence; and so he was obliged to include in it the edicts against those who did not conform to the recognised religions. As to the fact recorded in the martyrology, it scarcely agrees with the positive testimony of the historians, who say that under Alexander Severus the Christians were free at Rome. See e.g., Lamprid., *Alex. Sev.*, c. 22: "Christianos esse passus est" (in *Scriptt. Hist. Aug.*, vol. i. p. 272). But, even though it were admitted, it would not be sufficient to prove that Ulpian was the implacable enemy of the Gospel; if the Christians suffered martyrdom while he was prefect, it must be attributed to the edicts against prohibited religions. M. Baehr the scholarly historian of Roman Literature, says in his *Geschichte der Römischen Literatur*, 3rd ed., vol. ii. p. 654, "The charge made against Ulpian of aversion to the Christians is not proved." See, too, De Toullieu, *Oratio de Ulpiano an Christiano infenso*, Göttingen 1724, qto; and Pothier's preface to the Pandects, Lyons 1782, fol., vol. i. series "Jurisconsultorum," § 79, p. xxxix.

LIST OF AUTHORS QUOTED.

ANCIENT AUTHORS.

Ælianus, Variæ Historiæ, ed. Perizonius, 2 vol., Leyde, 1701, 8vo.
Ammianus Marcellinus, Historiæ, 2 vol., Leyde, 1701, 8vo.
Aristophanes, ed. Invernizzi., 2 vol, Leipz., 1794, 8vo.
Aristoteles, Ἠθικὰ Νικομαχεῖα, ed. A. Koraï, Paris, 1821, 8vo.
„ Πολιτικῶν τὰ σωζόμενα, ed. id., Paris, 1822, 8vo.
Athenæi Deipnosophistæ, ed. Joh. Schweigh., 14 vol., Strasb., 1801, sq. 8vo.
Aulus Gellius, Noctes Atticæ, 2 vol., Bip., 1781, 8vo.
Ciceronis Opera, 12 vol., Bip., 1781, 8vo.
Dio Cassius, ed. Imm. Bekker, 2 vol., Leipz., 1849, 8vo.
Dio Chrysost., Orationes, ed. Reicke, 2 vol., Leipz., 1784, 8vo.
Diogenes Laertius, De vitis, etc., philosophorum, ed. Longolius, 2 vol., 1739, 8vo.
Dionysius Halicarn., Antiquitates Romanæ, 2 vol., Oxf., 1704, fol.
Epicteti Opera, ed. J. Schweigh, 3 vol., Leipz., 1799, 8vo.
Euripidis Dramata, ed. Bothe, 2 vol., Leipz., 1825, 8vo.
Gnomici poetæ Græci, ed. Brunck, Str., 1784, 4to.
Herodiani Historiæ, ed. Pareus., Frankf., 1630, 8vo.
Horatii Opera, ed. Oberlin, Str., 1788, 4to.
Josephi Opera, ed. Sigeb. Havercamp, 2 vol., Amst., 1726, fol.
Juliani Opera, Par., 1630, 4to.
„ Epistolæ, ed. Heyler.
Juvenalis et Persii Satiræ, Bip., 1785, fol.
Libanii Opera, ed. Morelli, 2 vol., Paris, 1627, fol.
Luciani Opera, 2 vol., Amst., 1687, 8vo.
Lucretius, De rerum natura, Bip., 1782, 8vo.
Macrobii Opera, 2 vol., Bip., 1788, 8vo.
Marci Aurelii Pugillaria, ed. Joly, Paris, 1774, 12mo.
Martialis Epigrammata, 2 vol., Bip., 1784, 8vo.
Menandri et Philemonis Reliquiæ, ed. H. Grotius and Clericus, Amst., 1709, 8vo.
Mulierum Græcarum quæ oratione prosa usæ sunt fragmenta, ed. J. Chr. Wolf, London, 1739. 4to.
Oratores Attici, ed. Imm. Bekker, 5 vol., Berlin, 1824, 8vo.
Ovidii Opera, 4 vol., Bip., 1783, 8vo.
Pausanias, Descriptio Græciæ, ed. Schubart and Walz, 3 vol., Leipz., 1839, 8vo.
Petronii Satyricon, ed. Burmann, Utr. 1709, 4to.

Platonis Opera, ed. Fr. Ast, 11 vol., Leipz., 1822, 8vo.
    Symposium, vol. iii.
    De Republica, vol. iv.
    De Legibus, vol. vi. and vii.
Plauti Comœdiæ, 2 vol., Bip., 1779, 8vo.
Plinii Epistolæ et Panegyricus, 2 vol., Bip., 1789, 8vo.
Plutarchi Opera, ed. Hutten, 14 vol., Tüb., 1791, 8vo.
Quintiliani Opera, 4 vol., Bip., 1784, 8vo.
Sallustii Opera, ed. Planche, 2 vol., Par., 1825, 8vo.
Scriptores Historiæ Augustæ, 2 vol., Bip., 1787, 8vo.
   „   „   Romanæ minores, Bip., 1789, 8vo.
   „   rei Rusticæ, 4 vol., Bip., 1787, 8vo.
Senecæ Opera, 4 vol., Bip., 1782, 8vo.
Stobæi Florilegium, ed. H. Grotius, Par., 1623, 4to.
Suetonius, Bip., 1783, 8vo.
Symmachi Epistolæ, Par., 1604, 4to.
Taciti Opera, 4 vol., Bip., 1779, 8vo.
Terentii Comœdiæ, 2 vol., Bip., 1779, 8vo.
Themistii Orationes, ed. Dindorf, Leipz., 1832, 8vo.
Valerius Maximus, Bip., 1783, 8vo.
Xenophontis Opera, ed. Schneider, 6 vol., Leipz., 1816, 8vo.
Zosimus, ed. Imm. Bekker, Bonn, 1837, 8vo.

INSCRIPTIONS.

Reinesius, Syntagma Inscriptt. antiq., Leipz., 1682, fol.
Gruterus, Inscriptiones antiquæ, Amst., 1707, fol.
Muratori, Novus thesaurus Inscriptt., Milan, 1742, fol., vol. iv.
Orelli, Inscriptionum latin. selectarum amplissima complectio, 2 vol., Zür. 1828, 8vo.
Boeckh, Corpus Inscriptt. Græcarum, Berl., 1828, fol., vol. i.

LAWS.

Corpus Juris, ed. Kriegel, 2 vol., Leipz., 1836, ff., 8vo.
Codex Theodosianus, cum comment, Gothofredi, ed. Ritter, 6 vol., Leipz., 1737, fol.
Gaii Institutionum commentarii, ed. Goeschen, Berlin, 1842, 8vo.
Ulpiani Fragmenta, in Jus civile antejustinianeum, ed. Hugo, vol. i., Berl., 1815, 8vo.

FATHERS OF THE CHURCH, Etc.

Acta sanctorum, cura Bollandi, etc., 53 vol., Antwerp, 1643, sq., fol.
Ambrosii Opera, ed. Bened., 2 vol., Paris, 1686, fol.
Arnobii Disputat. adv. gentes, ed. Orelli, 2 vol., Leipz., 1816, 8vo.
Asterii Homiliæ, ed. Phil. Rubenius, Antwerp, 1615, 4to.
Athanasii Opera, ed. Bened., 4 vol., Padua, 1777, fol.
Athenagoras, Legatio ad Græcos, in Just. M. Opp.

LIST OF AUTHORS QUOTED.

Augustini Opera, ed. Bened., 11 tom., Antwerp, 1700, fol.
Barnabas, Epistolæ, in tom. I., PP. Apost.
Basilii Magni Opera, ed. Garnier, 3 vol., Paris, 1721, fol.
Bibliotheca Patrum, ed. Gallandius, Venice, 1769 fol., vol. i. ii. iv. and v.
Cassiani Opera, Leipz., 1733, fol.
Chrysostomi Opera, ed. Montfaucon, 13 vol., Par., 1718 fol.
Clementis Alex. Opera, ed. Potter, 2 vol., Venice, 1757, fol.
,, *Romani* Epistolæ, in vol. I. PP. Apost.
Commodianus, Instructiones adversus gentium Deos pro Christiana disciplina, in vol. iii. of the Bibl. PP. Gallandii.
Conciliorum collectio amplissima, ed. Mansi, Flor., 1759, fol., first 6 vols.
Constitutiones Apostolicæ, in vol. I. PP. Apost.
Cypriani Opera, ed. Baluzius, Par., 1726, fol.
Cyrilli Alex. Opera, ed. Aubert, 6 vol., Paris, 1638, fol.
,, *Hieros.* Opera, ed. Touttée, Par., 1720, fol.
Epiphanii Opera, ed. Den. Petau, 2 vol., Col., 1682, fol.
Eusebii Hist. eccl. et Vita Const., ed. Valesius, Mayence, 1672, fol.
Fabricius, Bibliotheca ecclesiast., Hamb., 1718, fol.
Firmicus Maternus, De errore profanarum religionum, in vol. v. of the Bibl. PP. Gallandii.
Gennadius, De viris illustribus, in Fabric., Bibl. eccl.
Gregorii Nazianzeni Opera, ed. Prunaeus, 2 vol., Leipz., 1690, fol.
,, *Nysseni* Opera, 2 vol., Par., 1638, fol.
Hermas, Pastor, in vol. I. PP. Apost.
Hieronymi Opera, ed. Martianay, 5 vol., Par., 1704, fol.
,, Epistolæ, vol. I. of Vallaroi's edition of his works, Venice, 1766, 4to.
,, Catalogus virorum illustr., in Fabr. Bibl. eccl.
Hilarii Pictaviensis Opera, ed. Bened., Paris, 1693, fol.
Ignatii Epistolæ, in vol. II. PP. Apost.
Irenæus, Contra hæreses, ed. Massuet, Par., 1710, fol.
Isidorus Pelusiota, Epistolæ de interpretatione divinæ Scripturæ, ed. Rittershusius, S. C., 1605, fol.
Justini Martyris Opera, ed. Bened., The Hague, 1742, fol.
Lactantii Opera, ed. Lebrun and Lenglet Dufresnoy, 2 vol., Par:, 1748, 4to.
Macarii Homiliæ et opuscula, ed. Pritius, Leipz., 1714, 8vo.
Martyrum primorum Acta, ed. Ruinart, Amst., 1713, fol.
Martyrologium Romanum, ed. Baronius, Antwerp, 1613, fol.
Minucii Felicis Octavius, ed. Cellarius, Halle, 1699, fol.
Nili Abbatis Opuscula, ed. Suaresius, Rome, 1673, fol.
Origenis Opera, ed. Delarue, 4 vol., Par., 1733, fol., vol. i., Contra Celsum.
Orosius, Adversus paganos historiæ, ed. Havercamp, Leyde, 1767, 4to.
Palladius, Historia Lausiaca, Par., 1555, 4to.
Patrum qui temporibus apostolicis floruerunt Opera, ed. Cotelerius, 2nd ed., Joh. Clerici, 2 vol., Amst., 1724, fol.
Paulini Nolani Opera, 2 vol., Par., 1685, 4to.
Petrus Chrysologus, Sermones, Mayence, 1607, 8vo.
Polycarpi Epistola, in vol. II. PP. Apost.
Prosper Pomerius, De vita contemplativa, Col., 1536, 8vo.
Prudentii Opera, ed. Cellarius, Halle, 1703, 8vo.
Rufinus, Historia eccles. Eusebii, Basle, 1542, fol.

Salviani Opera, ed. Baluzius, Par. 1684, 8vo.
Socratis et Sozomeni Hist. eccles., ed. Valesius, Mayence, 1677, fol.
Tatianus, Oratio adv. Græcos, in Opp. Justini Mart.
Tertulliani Opera, ed. Rigaltii, Venice, 1744, fol.
   ,,   Apologeticus, ed. Sig. Havercamp, *ib.*
Theodoreti Opera, ed. Schulze and Noesselt, 5 vol., Halle, 1769, 8vo.
   ,,   et *Evagrii* Hist. eccles., ed. Valesius, Mayence, 1677, fol.
Theophilus, Ad Autolycum, in Opp. Justini Mart.
Victor Vitensis, Hist. persecutionis Vandalicæ, ed. Ruinart, Par., 1694, 8vo.
Zeno Veronensis, Tractatus, in vol. V. Bibl. PP. Gall.

INDEX.

A.

ABORTION, considered by the Fathers a kind of homicide, 203; condemned by later pagan teachers, 391.

ACTORS, usually slaves, 88; despised, 90; an hereditary class, 91; often banished, 91; their treatment by the Church, 232; efforts of Theodosius to reform, 431, 432.

ADRIAN, his treatment of Christians, 382; his measures for supporting poor children, 396; deprives masters of power of life and death over slaves, 399.

ADULTERY, considered by pagans not a sin but an infringement of a husband's rights, 45; vengeance for, allowed, 45; husband had impunity to commit, 45; how treated by the Church, 200, 201, 202; by Epictetus, 366; Caracalla's law respecting, 390; Constantine's laws respecting, 421; amongst degenerate Christians, 452.

AFRA, St., 203.

AGAPÉ, the, 179, 180.

AGRICULTURISTS, their miserable state, 261; oppression of, under later empire, 456.

ALEXANDER SEVERUS, his treatment of Christians, 384; his measures for support of poor children, 396; his benevolent laws for slaves, 398, 403.

ALMSGIVING, taught by Christ, 143; ostentatious practice of, among degenerate Christians, 457.

AMBROSE, on charity, 254; on widows, 258; forbids Theodosius to approach the altar with bloodstained hands, 262.

ANCIENTS, the, their principle of morality an egoistic principle, 5.

ANTONINUS, his treatment of Christians, 383; restricts paternal power, 388; his support of poor children, 396; limits power of masters, 398, 400.

APOLLONIUS of Tyana, his religious ideas, 129.

APOLOGIES, the, 306, 309.

APOSTLES, the, poor, 153; preached to all classes, 153; follow and apply Christ's words, 154–159.

APOSTOLIC CONSTITUTIONS, on charity, 248; on widows and orphans, 257.

ARISTIPPUS on the aim of life, 5.

ARISTOTLE places happiness in activity, 7; on the State and the individual, 10; on the position of the labourer, 17; on the moral capacity of woman, 28; on the exposure of children, 52, 112; on work as degrading, 64; on slaves, 78–85; on marriage, 112; on art, 123.

ART unable alone to raise mankind, 122; grew obscene in Pagan times, 124.
ARTISANS, low in ancient social scale, 64; effect of this on them, 66.
ASCETICISM, 178, 192.
ASTERIUS, his picture of a Christian lady, 195.
ASYLUM in churches, right of, 259, 440; in temples, granted to slaves, 400.
ATHANASIUS on effect of Christianity on political life, 287.
ATHENAGORAS, apology of, 300.
ATHENS, treatment of slaves at, 82.
AUGUSTINE, his City of God, 181; on the cares of married life, 192; on slavery, 222; on the political effects of Christianity, 287.

B.

BARBARIANS, Greek and Roman ideas of, 108; virtues of, despised by Greeks and Romans, 15; Christian ideas of, 282; invasion by, necessary to regenerate society, 458.
BEGGING, increase of, under later empire, 456.
BENEVOLENCE in Rome neglected, 69; Socrates on, 114; Seneca on, 343.
BISHOP, the, chief guardian of the poor and the poor fund, 251; powers of arbitration conferred on, by Constantine, 413, 439.
BROTHERHOOD of Christians, 179.
BURIAL, Christian, 270.

C.

CAPITAL punishment, 279.
CARACALLA, treatment of Christians by, 383; his laws to restrict paternal power, 392.
CATO, selling his aged slaves, 84.
CELIBACY, penalties against, in Greece, 37; Christian, 193; laws against, repealed by Constantine, 419.
CICERO, on the moral standard, 8; on religion and patriotism, 15; on working for money, 66; less egoistic in his ideas of friendship than his predecessors, 20; on slaves, 81, 85; on gladiators, 99; on Roman justice, 108; on degeneracy of the Greeks, 109; on charity, 115; on belief in the gods, 126; on tolerance, 301.
CHARITY, pagan, considered unprofitable by Plato, 69; narrow, 72; largesses, 72, 73; by State, to secure order, 73; in Athens, 73; in Rome, 73; results of, 74; principles of, in Plutarch, 359; in Epictetus, 364, 366; in Marcus Aurelius, 372; in Ulpian, 394.
CHARITY, taught by Christ, 143; Christian, 165, 170; an object of exhortation, 245, 254; of bishops in Apostolic Constitutions, 248; Christian, contrasted with pagan, 249; given to distant Churches, 253; in monasteries, 254; instances of, among Christians, 255, 256; in sickness and epidemics, 264, 265; springs from love to God, 314; Tertullian on, 317; towards pagans, 327; influence of, on laws, gradual, 411; growing coolness of, in later empire, 451; essential to justice, 461.
CHILDREN, property of father, 33, 52, 53; exposure of, 53; belong to kingdom of God, 205; sale of, endeavours to stop, 426; rights of inheritance and possession of, under Christian emperors, 427; duty of, to parents, enforced by law, 393, 428.

CHILDREN, poor, institutions for, by pagans, 394-396; decay of these institutions, 397.
CHRIST, condition of world at birth of, 137, 138; His circumstances, 138; His teaching, 139; the kingdom of, 139, 140; on poor, 140; on woman, 140; His kingdom unexclusive, 141; commands to love, 142; on divorce, 145; perfect character of, 146; His conduct condemns egoism, 148; His death the cause of salvation, 149; Divine, 151; sinless, 151; unites men, 152; regenerates society by giving fundamental principles, 160; did not appeal to force, 160; pagan mockery at, 296.
CHRISTIANITY not communistic, 169, 240, 241; honours all men, 177; takes the sting from slavery, 218; how it regards the poor, 257; despised by philosophers, 297; no tolerance extended to, for a long time, 301; INFLUENCE of, on pagan society, 293; by sermons, 319; obstacles to, 295; on Stoicism, 333; on philosophers, 337-375; on emperors and jurisconsults, 380-387; on position of women and laws of marriage, 387-390; on treatment of children, 390-394; on institutions for poor children among pagans, 394-397; on condition of slaves, 397-404; on treatment of criminals, 441, 442; denied by some, 448.
CHRISTIANS as leaven in society, 162; union among, 178, 179; slanderous charges against, 296; ridiculed, 296; obtained the confidence of Roman emperors, 184; persecuted as rebels, 299; relieved under Constantine, 412; example of, a most powerful means of spreading Christianity, 414; inconsistencies of, under later emperors, 454.
CHRISTIAN society, 176-187; not opposed to civil society, 145, 182; in relation to actors, 232; contrasted with pagan, 447; imperfections of, 448; growing corruption of, under Christian emperors, 450.
CHRYSOSTOM on asceticism, 178; on marriage, 193; on religious education, 206, 207; on idleness, 214; on slavery, 218, 224, 226; on charity, 246; on usury, 247; on revolt and disturbance, 261; founding hospitals, 268.
CITY of God, 181.
CLEMENCY, mixed motives to, among pagans, 23, 24; Christian, 278.
COMMERCIAL classes excluded from office by Greeks and Romans, 64, 65.
COMMODUS acting as gladiator, 98.
COMMUNISM among pagans, 10; Christian, explained, 169, 240, 241; in Plato's idea of the State, 11; and of women, 30.
CONCUBINAGE in Rome, 42; how treated by the Church, 200.
CONSANGUINITY, how treated by the Church, 197.
CONSTANTINE the emperor, his attitude towards the slaves, 100; his Christianity traceable to his mother's influence, 324; his tendency to Christianity, 411; his measures for relief of Christians, 412; his conversion, 412; his endeavours to suppress pagan immoral rites, 412; laws of, respecting women, 417; repeals laws against celibacy, 419; his laws on marriage, 420; on adultery, 421; on exposure of children, 425; on slaves, 429, 430; on kidnapping, 430; prohibits gladiatorial shows, 434; his efforts to relieve poverty, 437; his laws against venality, 438; his alleviation of penal laws, 440.
CONSTANTIUS endeavours to repress gladiatorial shows, 435.
CONSTANTIUS CHLORUS, his test of Christians, 325; his laws for protection of women, 418; his suppression of games, 430.

CONTRADICTIONS, moral, in the finer minds of antiquity, 114.
COSMOPOLITANISM, Socrates on, 114; Seneca on, 340; Epictetus on, 364 Marcus Aurelius on, 371.
CRYPTEIA, the, 82.
CYPRIAN on charity, 245; his example, 255; put to death as an enemy to the laws, 302.

D.

DAUGHTERS, married, allowed by laws to inherit, 393.
DEACONESSES, 252; protection of, under Christian emperors, 419.
DEATH, expiatory, of Christ the cause of salvation, 149.
DECLINE of ancient society, 109; of religious belief, 123, 125, 126; a cause of decline in morals, 128.
DEIFICATION of emperors, 128.
DEMOCRITUS on the aim of life, 5.
DION CHRYSOSTOM, traces of Christianity in, 357.
DIOCLETIAN, tolerance of, due to Prisca, 324; laws of, on marriage, 388, 390; gives right of adoption to women, 389.
DIOGNETUS, epistle to, 313.
DISINHERITING, rights of, limited by law, 393.
DIVORCE, introduced after the decline of morals, 48; practised by Mæcenas, 46; limited by Augustus, 49; claimed by women, 49; teaching of Christ on, 145; St. Paul on, 163; easy, condemned by the Fathers, 200; granted against husband, 200; restrictions placed upon, by emperors, 390; and by Christian emperors, 422, 423.
DUTY, principle of, recognised by lawyers, 386.

E.

EDUCATION, ancient, 55; by the State, 55; in Sparta, 56; chiefly physical and intellectual, 57; of girls, 57; in later days of Roman empire, 58; Pliny on, 355.
EGOISM of ancient morality, Plato, Aristotle, the Stoics, and Cicero, 7, 8, 107, 110; dominant in later Roman empire, 21; bridled by regard to civic virtues, 109; condemned by Christ, 143; an obstacle to Christian influence, 295; rebuked by Epictetus, 365, and by Marcus Aurelius, 372.
EMANCIPATION of slaves, 86; Christian mode of, 168; by Christian masters, 226: an ecclesiastical act, 227; Constantine's laws on, 429.
EMPEROR-WORSHIP, 128; the statues, 261.
ENEMIES, personal, how treated, 276, 277.
EPICTETUS and the influence of Christian ideas, 362, 369; his thoughts on God and happiness, 363; cosmopolitanism of, 364; on man's imperfection, 364; on forgiveness, 364; on egoism, 365; on love the bond of society, 366; on marriage, 366; on slaves, 367; on suicide, 369.
EPICUREANISM promoted selfishness, 110.
EPIDEMICS, conduct of Christians in, 264, 265, 328.
EPIPHANIUS on charity, 286.
EQUALITY of men proclaimed by Christianity, 176; Seneca on, 340.
EUCHARIST a token of common love, 179.

EXAMPLE, the, of Christ, 146, 147.
EXPOSURE of children, 51, 52, 112; forbidden by Christianity, 204; milder ideas concerning, 391; endeavours of Constantine to suppress, 425.

F.

FAMILY, the, 26 seq., 188–211; considered by pagans simply a political institution, 50, 107; Plutarch on, 360; Epictetus on, 366.
FATHER'S power over child, 33, 52, 53; restricted, 388, 392; power over child's life abolished, 391; over children under Christian emperors, 427.
FATHERS of the Church, on slavery, 217, 223; on riches and poverty, 238, 239; on simplicity of life, 228; on usury, 247–261; on virginity, 193; on hospitality, 281; on the deaths of the martyrs, 322; protests of, against persecution of pagans, 329; protests of, against degeneracy of Christians, 453, 455; against ostentatious almsgiving, 457.
FILIAL piety, but few examples of, among pagans, 113.
FOREIGNERS, contempt for, 16; Seneca on, 347.
FRIENDSHIP considered possible to equals only, 19; for reasons of utility, 20; not considered a union of congeniality, 20; numerous instances of disinterested friendship, 20; condemned by some writers, 21; Christian, 180.

G.

GALEN on Christians, 321.
GIRLS, education of, 58.
GLADIATORS, 92; from prisoners of war, 95, 99; left as legacy by rich men, 95; at banquets, 95; ambitions of, 96; hire of, 97; tombs of, 97; owned by the State, 98; revolts of, 98; Christians condemned to be, 98; refused baptism by the Church, 230.
GLADIATORIAL shows, origin of, 92; popularity of, 92; patronised by great men, 93; women present at, 93; a form of largess, 93; spread into Greece, 96; at Rome, 100; results of, upon morality, 101; condemned by Fathers, 229, 230; by Seneca, 349; by Pliny, 356: Marcus Aurelius on efforts to reform, 373, 401, and to suppress, 430; prohibited by Constantine, 434; endeavours to suppress, 434, 435; final suppression of, 436; passion for, among Christians, 453.
GODS, foreign, introduced, 129.
GOLDEN rule, 143; and Alexander Severus, 384.
GOSPEL of Christ alone sufficient to regenerate the world, 459.
GREECE, civilization on same fundamental principle as that of Rome, 3; celibacy in, 37; second marriages in, 36; degeneracy of, 109.
GROWTH of Christian influence, 184. *See* CHRISTIANITY, INFLUENCE OF.

H.

HAPPINESS, the aim of ancient social morality, 5; sought by pagans in external things, 5; said by Socrates to lie in wisdom, 6; by Aristotle to lie in activity, 7; Epictetus on, 363; Marcus Aurelius on, 371 consists not in wellbeing of the body, 461.
HELOTS of Sparta, 83.

HETÆRÆ, courted but despised, 41; in Corinth, 41; followed by the nobles, 41, 42.
HILARY of Poictiers protests against persecution, 328.
HONORIUS endeavours to suppress gladiatorial shows, 435.
HOSPITALITY, ancient, analysed, 16; Christian, 281; abused, 282.
HOSPITALS, 70, 267, 268; fostered by emperors, 440.
HUMAN nature, its inherent capacities tested by paganism, 130, 131.
HUMAN sacrifices, 124, 125.
HUMILITY, a ground of contempt, 18; taught by Paul, 158.
HUSBAND, master of wife, 28, 34, 35; could be proceeded against for adultery under Christian laws, 200; not under paganism, 43.

I.

IDLENESS condemned by Christianity, 215.
IMMORTALITY of the soul, denied by Cæsar and Cato, 126, 127; Seneca on, 350.
INDIVIDUAL, the, overshadowed by the State, 11, 12, 13, 14, 17, 107; not free, 17; regeneration of, the true way of regenerating society, 152, 161.
INSTITUTIONS, alimentary, 394-397; charitable, protected under Christian emperors, 440.
INTEREST not to be charged on poorer brethren, 247.

J.

JULIA MAMMÆA, 324.
JULIAN, his hatred of Christianity, 300; his testimony to charity of the early Christians, 321, 328; influenced by Christianity, 413, 414; encouraged pagans to follow Christian example, 414, 415.
JURISCONSULTS, growing humanity of, 385.
JUSTICE among the Romans, 108.
JUSTINIAN, code of, 442.
JUSTIN MARTYR, 306; his apologies, 307-309.
JUVENAL, indignation of, at corrupt state of society, 115.

K.

KIDNAPPING, punished by death under Constantine, 430.
KINGDOM of Christ, 139, 140; spiritual, 145; not antagonistic to earthly kingdoms, 146, 182.

L.

LABOUR, made a duty by the Church, 212; considered noble, 213.
LABOURING classes, 63, 212, 213-236; honoured by Paul's words and example, 165, 166.
LACTANTIUS on exposure of children, 204; on shows, 230.
LEPERS, 265.
LIBERTY confined to full citizens in ancient times, 27; of Christians, 167.
LOVE in ancient times chiefly sensual, 39; Plutarch on, 359; the bond of society, Epictetus and Marcus Aurelius, 366, 372.

LOVE, highest, absent from pagan morals, 131; Christ commanded it, 142; made universally a duty, 143; in service, the Christian ideal, 144; the foundation of Christian society, 146, 150; to Christ, the Christian motive, 150.
LOVE, concentrated as well as diffused, 145.
LUCIAN, his dialogues of the gods, 125; ridicule of Christians, 293; testimony of, to Christian brotherly-kindness, 320.
LUCRETIUS on religion, 127.
LUXURY in Rome, 67; of Christian ladies under Christian emperors, 451.

M.

MAGIC, practised in Rome, 129.
MAGNANIMITY, virtually pride, 18.
MANILIUS against the shows, 101.
MANKIND, equal, 176; deserving of respect, 177, 340, 371; imperfections of, Seneca on, 338; Epictetus on, 364.
MARCUS AURELIUS on God and His providence, 370; on the influence of Christianity, 374; on resignation, 371; on human dignity, 371; cosmopolitanism of, 371; noble sentiments of, 372, 373; on the shows, 373; his treatment of the Christians, 382, 383; his measures for the support of poor children, 396.
MARRIAGE, a political institution for perpetuation of the State among the ancients, 29; low idea of, produced licentiousness, 30; primitive Roman customs of, 33; kinds of, 33; tie of, became loose, 36; second marriage among the Greeks, 36; encouraged by Augustus, 38; teaching of Christ on, 145; Christian idea of, 163, 191, 198; solemnized by the Church, 192; considered by some a hindrance to holiness, 192; by others a help, 193; rendered voluntary for woman, 193; best between believers, 196; forbidden with pagans, 196; second, forbidden by many Fathers, 198; a more lenient view of second, 199; legislation of Christian emperors respecting second, 424; Plutarch on, 360; Epictetus on, 366; later legislation on, 388; made less exclusive in respect of social rank, 390; laws of Christian emperors respecting, 420–425; degradation in Christian society of, produced by pagan reaction, 452.
MARRIED daughters allowed by laws to inherit, 393.
MARTYRS, blood of, the seed of the Church, 321; constancy of, regarded as fanaticism, 297, 370.
MASSES, the, despised, 65.
MASTERS, their duties enjoined, 225; persuaded to emancipate, 225; duties of, Plutarch on, 361; powers of, limits imposed on, 398–400.
MATERIALISTIC philosophy encouraged and excused selfishness, 110.
METHODS of Christianity and of Christian progress, 160, 161.
MILITARY service, Christian attitude towards, 283.
MINUCIUS FELIX, his apology, 312.
MONASTERIES, Christian, 180; entrance to, not compulsory, 181; trades taught in, 214; mere contemplation rebuked, 215; hospitality in, 281.
MORALITY, Christian, its fundamental principles, 137–175; adduced as evidence by the apologists, 308; pagan, attacked by Theophilus, 312.
MORALS of early Christians perplexed the pagans, 172; contrasted by apologists with pagan morals, 308–315.

MOTHERS to educate their children, a Christian principle, 207.
MOTIVE of Christians, love to Christ the chief, 150.
MYTHS, immorality of, 316 ; regarded by Plutarch as symbolic, 359.

N.

NATIONS, barriers between, broken down by Christ, 143, 280.
NATURAL morality, 116, 117.
NERO compelled ladies and Christians to act as gladiators, 98.
NERVA, tolerance of, 381 ; orders poor children to be supported at the public expense, 395.
NEO-PLATONISTS, 129-299.
NITRIA MOUNT, asylum on, 281.

O.

OBEDIENCE to the laws enjoined by the apostles, 162.
ORIGEN on the poor, 238 ; apology of, 318.
ORPHANS, protected by the archons in Athens, 54 ; in Rome cared for if wealthy, 54.
OVID, against shows, 101.

P.

PACHOMIUS, conversion of, 327.
PAGANISM, not wholly evil and dark, 119 ; sacrifices of, a true idea, 119 ; lacking in moral power, 119 ; its want of unity, 120 ; chained man to nature, 120 ; bad character of the divinities, 121, 123 ; its worship linked with vice, 121 ; lack of love and humility in, 131 ; reaction of, on Christian society, 449.
PAGAN society, Christian influence on, 293.
PARENTS, permitted to destroy unserviceable children, 50-52 ; limitation of the prerogatives of, 51 ; power of, in Christian times, 52 ; authority of, over children, 53 ; power of disinheriting, 53 ; allowed to sell children, 54 ; taught by Paul to recognise responsibilities, 164 ; taught by the Fathers to treat children mildly, 205, 206 ; duty of, according to Plutarch, 360 ; according to Epictetus, 366 ; Septimus Severus on, 392.
PAUL, St., on pagan society, 156 ; on nature, 157 ; missionary work of, 157 ; on humility, 158 ; on divorce, 163 ; on parents and children, 164.
PEACEFUL character of Christians, 284-288.
PENAL legislation, alleviation of, under Christian emperors, 441.
PERSECUTIONS, Christian charity in, 259 ; under Diocletian, 385.
PITY for the unfortunates, not common in Rome, 71.
PLAGUE at Athens, the occasion of selfishness, 71.
PLATO, on the supreme good, 6, 7 ; his doctrine practically egoistic, 7 ; his idea of the State communistic, 11 ; on privileges of citizenship as depending on wealth and leisure, 17 ; on women, 30, 112 ; on exposure of children, 51 ; on the State in education, 55 ; on the relative dignity of occupations, 64 ; on helping the sick poor, 69 ; on slaves, 77-85 ; on the poets, 123.
PLATONIC love, its true character, 40.

PLATONISTS, New, 129.
PLINY the Younger, his treatment of Christians, 351; his moral ideas, 354; on schools, 355; his benevolence, 355-396; his clemency to slaves, 356; on games, 356.
PLUTARCH, philosophy of, 358; on religion, 358; his interpretation of myths, 359; on love, 359; his pure ideas on marriage, 360; on education and duty of parents, 360; on slaves, 361; his gentle treatment of slaves, 362.
POLITICS (with war), only occupation thought fit for freemen among the ancients, 63.
POLYCARP, on the duty of obedience and its limits, 183.
POOR, the, care of, taught by Christ, 140, 237, 238; comforted by Christ, 140; offerings for, 250; their patrimony, 251; helped by monks, 254; Christian treatment of, 326; Julian's care for, 414; condition of, under Christian emperors, 436-443; oppression of, by magistrates, 456.
POOR children, institutions for, amongst pagans, 394-397.
POVERTY, despised, 67, 68; of apostles, 153; Christian view of, 164, 237; not a help to salvation, 243; Seneca on, 342; Epictetus on, 367; Marcus Aurelius on, 371.
PRIDE, under name of " magnanimity," 18.
PRIEST-ACTORS, under the later empire, 90.
PRISONERS of war, 263; ransomed by the Church, 441.
PRISONS, improvement of, by Christian emperors, 442.
PROPERTY, rights of, not violated by Christianity, 170, 241, 242; God the source of, 242; not to be taken by force, 244.
PROSTITUTES, their treatment by the Church, 203; laws of Christian emperors respecting, 418.
PROSTITUTION in Rome, considered infamous when public, 43; taxed, 44; a mode of punishing Christian girls, 44.
PUNISHMENT, capital, some Christian bishops against, 279.
PURITY, some idea of, found in ancient writers, 111.

R.

RAPE in Rome, 45; punishment of, under Christian emperors, 419.
RELIGION, the only true bond of society, 358.
RELIGIOUS belief, decline of, 125, 126; attempts to arrest decline of, 129.
RETALIATION, a law of conduct among the ancients, 22, 23; Christianity abolished it, 142; rebuked by Plutarch, Epictetus, and Marcus Aurelius, 359, 364, 366, 373.
REVOLUTION, not the way to regenerate society, 161, 183, 216.
RICH MAN, the, the only good citizen according to ancient philosophers, 17.
RICHES, Christian view of, 237, 239, 243; love of, in the Church, 451.
ROMAN LADIES, cruelty of, towards slaves, 84.
ROME, civilization of, rested upon same principle as that of Greece, 3; luxury in, 67; concubinage in, 42; do. legalized in, 43; harshness of parents in, 54; State charity in, 74; decay of, 74; slaves at, 83; gladiatorial shows, 92-96; civilization of, its influence on modern history, 459.

S.

SACRIFICES, human, 124.
SALVIAN on libertinism, 452; on the games, 454; on oppression of the poor, 457; on the invasion by barbarians, 458.
SAVIOUR, a, Jewish and pagan ideas of, 138.
SCHOOLS, Christian, 208.
SELFISHNESS. *See* EGOISM.
SENECA, on the supreme good, 337; conscious of man's imperfection, 338; his belief in a Divine providence, 339; his idea of God, 339; recognises equality of men, 340; and intrinsic worth of man, 340; his idea of society, 341; his respect for woman, 341; on clemency, 341; on poverty, 342; on benevolence, 343; on self-sacrifice, 345; on vengeance and forgiveness, 346; on slaves, 347, 348; on gladiatorial shows, 349; on public life, 349; on immortality, 350; on suicide, 350; influenced by Christianity, 352.
SICKNESS, 264; epidemic, 266, 328.
SIMPLICITY of life, the Fathers on, 228.
SLAVERY, thought indispensable by ancients, 77–81; better opinion of ancients on, 113; Christian attitude towards, 166, 167, 215, 219, 220; later Fathers preach against it, 216, 218; though without clear ideas, 217.
SLAVES, not citizens, 76; often virtuous, 77; treatment of, 84; considered mere chattels, 79, 80; mild treatment of, at Athens, 82; harsh treatment of, in Sparta, 82; at Rome in early times, 83; later, 84; punishments of, 83; torture of, 83; cruelty of Roman ladies towards, 84; often deserted in age, 84; master's interest, the only protection of, 86; emancipation of, 86; moral character of, 87; occupations of, 87, 88; learning of, 88; actors, 88; Seneca on, 347, 348; Pliny's kind treatment of, 356; Plutarch on, 361; Epictetus on, 367; their condition improved by law, 398–404; condition of, under Christian emperors, 428–436.
SLAVES, Christian, influence of, on their masters, 325.
SOCIAL character of Christianity, 152, 168; early history of Christianity explained to be social not communistic, 169, 240.
SOCRATES on wisdom as the condition of happiness, 6; on friendship, 20; on woman, 112; on slavery, 113; on cosmopolitanism, 114.
SOPHISTS, the, on aim of life, 5.
SOUL, worth of, taught by Christ, 140.
SPARTA, education in, 56; treatment of slaves in, 82.
SPARTACUS, revolt of, 98.
STATE, the, supreme in ancient life, rationally anterior to individual, according to Aristotle, 10; composed of freemen only, 11; forbad celibacy, 37; Christians obeyed the laws of, except in cases of idol-worship, 183; offices in, declined by Christians, 184; despotism of, an obstacle to Christianity, 301.
STOICISM, egoistic, 7.
STOICS, their paradox on slavery, 78, 80, 368.
SUICIDE, recommended by philosophers, 350, 369, 374.
SUNDAY, observance of, ordered by Constantine, 412, 427; by Theodosius, 431.
SYMMACHUS, on the shows, 100.

T.

TACITUS, on love of country, 14; lament of, over corruption of society, 115.
TATIAN, discourses of, to the Greeks, 311.
TAX-GATHERERS, cruelty of, under later empire, 456.
TELEMACHUS, devotion of, 435.
TERTULLIAN, on human brotherhood, 177; on second marriages, 198; his apology, 315.
THEATRE, the, degenerated from days of Sophocles, 89; a place of obscenity, 89; plays and worship, 89; attitude of Christians towards it, 230; endeavours to reform and to suppress, 401, 430, 433; passion for, survived among Christians, 454.
THEODOSIUS the Great, code of, 416; gives to mothers the right of guardianship, 417; his laws on marriage, 420; on second marriage, 424; his suppression of games, 430.
THEODOSIUS II. suppresses prostitution, 418; laws on marriage, 421.
THEOPHILUS, his defence of Christianity, 311.
TORTURE of slaves, 83.
TRAJAN, treatment of Christians by, 381; measures for support of poor children, 395; endeavours to suppress pantomime, 401.

U.

ULPIAN, on equity and the interpretation of the law, 386; and the Christians, note 3 p. 464.
UNNATURAL vice, 106 (note, 172), 229.
USURERS, rapacity of, under later empire, 456.
USURY, denounced by Fathers, 247-261.
UTILITY, considered the standard of conduct by Aristotle, 7.

V.

VALENTINIAN I., retrograde legislation of, 422; punishes exposure of children, 425; laws on duty of children, 416; measures for benefit of actors and actresses, 432.
VALENTINIAN II., his law to restrict begging, 456.
VALENTINIAN III., retrograde legislation of, 416.
VENALITY, laws of Constantine against, 438.
VIRGINITY, commended as a higher state than marriage by some of the Fathers, 193.

W.

WAR and politics, regarded as the only fit occupations for freemen, 63; Fathers on, 282; sometimes necessary and just, 284.
WIDOWS, marriage of, 36; laws of Christian emperors on marriage of, 423; helped by the Church, 171; often made deaconesses, 252; laws of Constantine and Valentinian I., for benefit of, 439.
WISDOM and virtue, considered one by Socrates, 6.
WIVES, sold, 34; allowed right of property, 388; Plutarch on duties of, 360.

WOMAN, despised as physically weak, 27; not so low as the slave, 28; the property of husband or of father, 28; could inherit in absence of male heirs, 28; encouraged in vice through being despised, 28, 46, 47; isolated, 32; degradation of, in later empire, 48; licentiousness of, in higher classes, 47; higher ideas of, 112; present at shows, 93; recognised as spiritually equal with man by Christianity, 162–189; taught virtues, 162; the mother of Jesus, 189; result on woman of the higher opinion of her, 190; eminent Christian women, 191, 207; the sphere of, 194, 195; free to marry, 197; ought to educate her child, 207; Seneca on, 341; Pliny's respect for, 355; Plutarch on, 360; condition of, improved by legislation, 387–390; laws of Christian emperors respecting, 417–425.

WOMEN, Christian, examples of, 321; influence of, 323.

WORK, considered servile, 63; enjoined for sake of charity, 214.

WORKERS, virtually excluded from civic privileges, 17; raised by Christianity, 212, 213, 215.

X.

XENOPHON, his eulogy of a wife, 112.

Z.

ZENO of Verona, on avarice, 451.

www.ingramcontent.com/pod-product-compliance
Lightning Source LLC
Chambersburg PA
CBHW051159300426
44116CB00006B/373